LINDA RAINALDI

OUTSIDER ART OF CANADA

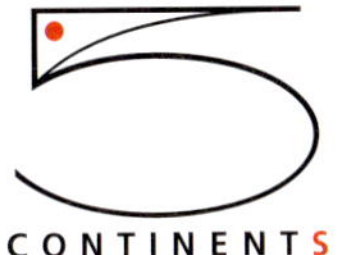

INTRODUCTION

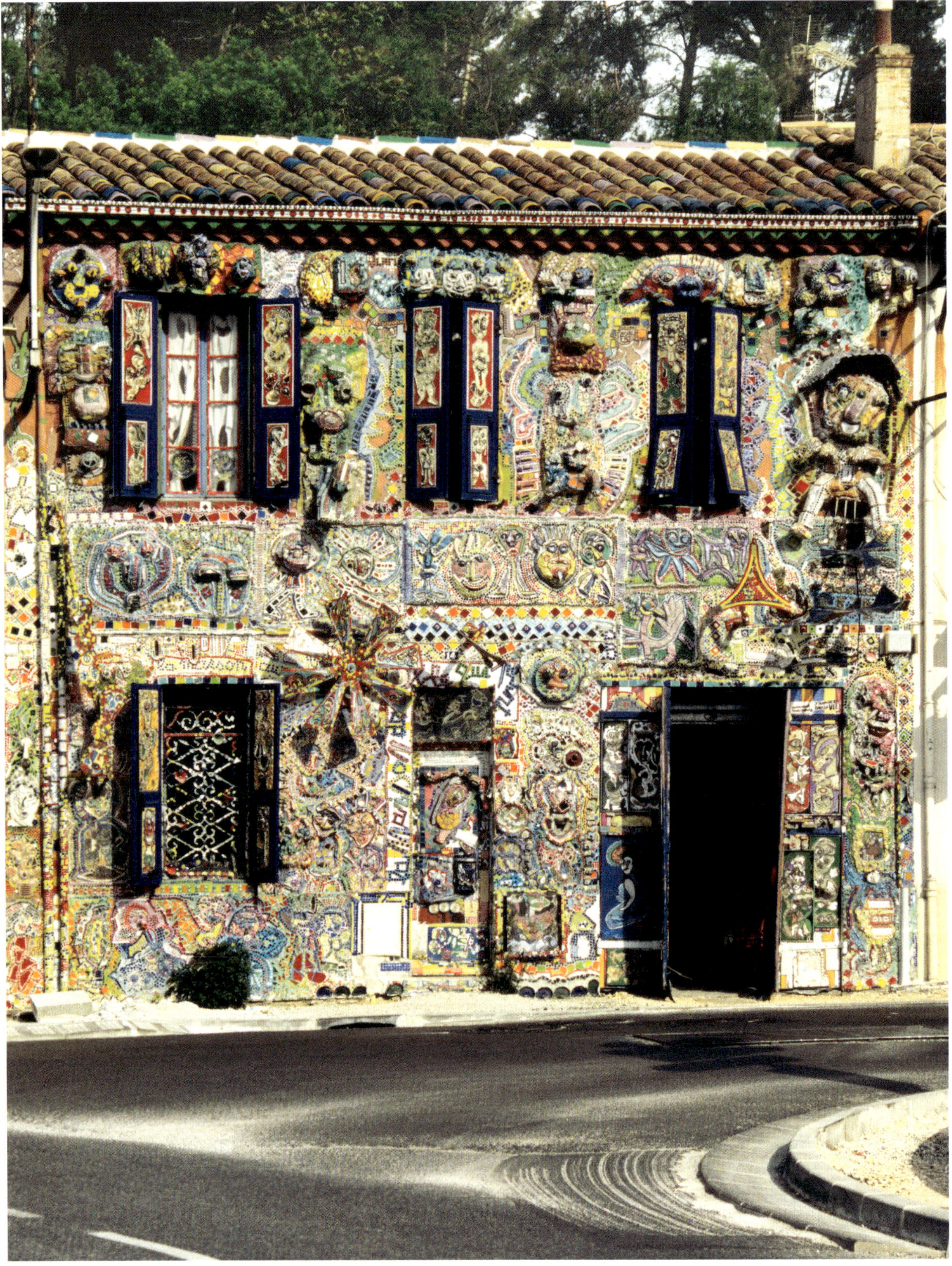

Exterior of Danielle Jacqui's
house, Roquevaire, France

toward image-making and consumption. Its curator called for art to come down from its pedestal and function as a tool for interpreting our visual culture. There was a mixed reaction to the inclusion of outsider artists at the Biennale. Naysayers felt it was a curatorial cop-out because it ignored new talents who would become the defining voices of their generation. Those in favour echoed the sentiments of French artist Jean Dubuffet (1901–1985)—who gave a name to the genre in the 1940s—declaring outsider art to be a counterbalance to the turbocharged world of contemporary art. They appreciated "a view of the human imagination as an untameable beast, dominated by dark desires and impulses, now finally unleashed and allowed to roam free."[2]

A confluence of ideas and postmodern attitudes have brought outsider art to the forefront in recent years, but not without some resistance from high-brow cultural institutions whose *raison d'etre* is to showcase movements in art history. As its name suggests, outsider art is outside the continuum of art history, outside the boundaries of art recognized by established art institutions, and outside the collective discourse of the mainstream art world. This might suggest that outsider art is a catch-all category of "everything else," that is, art that is not recognized by the art establishment. But it is not so simple. While outsider art is a distinct genre, its definition remains fluid and somewhat elusive, leading to rounds of term warfare among its advocates.[3] Even its proper name is disputed. Its historical name, coined by Dubuffet, is *art brut* (raw or uncooked art), a term that is still used in Europe, where its original definition remains relatively unchanged. However, in the United States, the definition of outsider art has expanded to include some contemporary American folk art. While the general term "self-taught art" has been the preferred label over the past decade, that, too, is falling out of favour, as it does not accurately describe some specific genres, such as Black contemporary artists living in the Southern United States.[4] Another point of contention is the politicization of outsider art in the United States and Canada, where some advocate to include artists who have been marginalized by any number of factors, including poverty and mental health. To complicate matters, there is little agreement about the parameters of outsider art itself, the characteristics of its makers, and whether it should be recognized as a distinct genre or absorbed into the world of contemporary art. Perhaps because of its inherent ambiguity, seasoned collectors defend their opinions with this incontestable statement: "I know it when I see it."

My first encounter of the outsider kind took place, quite by accident, two decades ago in Roquevaire, France. Driving along a quiet rural route, I happened upon a magical house completely covered in a mosaic of ceramic chips. It belonged to Danielle Jacqui (born 1934, and known locally as *celle qui peint* or "she who paints"), and nothing could have prepared me for the magnitude of her creation; every surface—inside and out—was covered in mosaics, yet she continued to find improbable spaces to set her gems. Even the kitchen table and chairs sparkled with colour. It was a strange and dazzling sensation, like standing inside a life-size jewellery box. It was impossible to distinguish between Jacqui's life and her art, for they were the same. I wondered if she would ever complete this impossible project, like the fairy-tale princess tasked with counting every grain of sand before daybreak. No one directed her to undertake this work, and no one collaborated in her vision. I met with Jacqui several times and learned more about her life as an artist, but never considered that a label might be attached to her endeavours; nor did I know her well enough to ask *why* she was engaged in this undertaking. The following year I was thumbing through a book about fantasy environments and discovered an article about Jacqui. I learned she belonged to the world of outsider artists. Further research revealed it was a large world indeed.

Curiosity led me to libraries and international outsider art exhibits, but the absence of Canadian outsider artists was puzzling. I did not find their artwork written about, publicly exhibited, or included in public art collections. I think of outsider art as having no fixed address; by that I mean it is not linked to one place in the world, nor to a group of artists who share a common outlook. It exists because individuals who are not schooled in art techniques are driven to bring forth images from their own imaginations. So, even though they had not been identified, I knew that outsider artists must live and work in this vast country. But how to find them? Launching an inquiry into this relatively unexplored area of art was not easy, for there is no compendium of Canadian outsider art. Establishing an online presence was crucial to making connections within this art world, and there I met other Canadians who shared my interest in outsider art, as well as an international audience who was curious to learn about art in my own country. My research methodology, if you will, was talking to people who had some connection with outsider art and following up on their leads. Patience and persistence eventually connected me to a network of art-loving Canadians who told me about people they called outsider artists. Although I was engaged in a dialogue about outsider art, I was confronted with a plethora of different opinions and a bewildering list of questions. If there was no clear definition of outsider art, how would I identify it in Canada, and how could I justify my criteria to others? I was back to square one.

There are many definitions of outsider art, but a string of words does not always capture the essence of its subject. The true meaning of outsider art lies in the interpretation not of the artwork itself, but in how the genre has been rationalized in various settings. I came to understand the social climate seven decades ago that triggered Dubuffet's rally against the tyranny of art institutions and his search for the source of pure creativity. He believed he found it in institutionalized psychiatric patients and other isolated outcasts who were "ignorant of any order but their own obsession with image-making."[5] While it is true that many of Dubuffet's collection of artists had little formal education, he argued that this had no bearing upon their intelligence or creativity. To dismiss their abilities, he said, was merely another example of cultural prejudice that "only educated people can create good art."[6] Dubuffet's artists were simply obsessed with creating images and, lacking artmaking skills, achieved their goals in unconventional ways. Their spontaneous creations sprang from a need to express themselves through their own invented visual language. Art brut began as a collection of art that focused entirely on the biography of the artists—alienated individuals who suffered from some form of psychiatric disorder or extreme cultural isolation. I questioned the classification rationale for outsider art, especially as I observed its definition expanding in the United States, where artists with disabilities were sometimes included. Even more peculiar was the trend to include artists defined by their marginalized status in society due to addictions, mental health issues, or economic circumstances. I wasn't sure how to begin my search for outsider artists in my own country. Should I adhere to Dubuffet's treatise or reinterpret his definition as a Canadian living in the twenty-first century?

The first hurdle was to clarify what we mean when we talk about outsider art. Are we chasing down Dubuffet's vision of pure creativity or are we exploring the work of artists marginalized by any number of factors? Perhaps it is somewhere in between. There is no simple answer, but I came to understand that varying perspectives about the nature of outsider art are just that—points of view and opinions that individuals and institutions use to interpret the genre. In turn, these interpretations spring from deeply rooted personal beliefs and social expectations about who can call themselves an artist. This seemingly inconsequential conclusion is important because it challenges our preconceived notions of what art *should* be like and makes room for discussion about social issues around artmaking and how specific art forms become part of a nation's cultural narrative.

Canada is new to the conversation about outsider art, and that is an enviable place to be, for it allows us to observe the landscape with fresh eyes. We also bring a distinctly Canadian perspective: one that echoes our unique national identity, free from the entrenched views of others. Not surprisingly, because we share historical roots with Europe and a border with the United States, our interpretation of outsider art borrows from both perspectives. Appreciation for traditional and contemporary folk art across Canada informs our opinion of art that is crafted outside the mainstream art world. I also explored the unique perspective of our country's Indigenous artists who instructed me on the nuances of their artwork. To craft a distinctly Canadian definition of outsider art is an ambitious undertaking. It requires each of us to examine our personal opinions about art and those who make it. It calls for us to relinquish myths and stereotypes about the source of creativity and to consider the work of self-taught creators who are compelled to express themselves in unique ways. It also demands that we acknowledge, and perhaps confront, not only our decision to apply the outsider art label to certain artwork, but the role of art institutions in shaping our opinion of so-called great art. Most importantly, it insists that we consider one weighty question posed by Roger Cardinal in 1972: What else could art be like?[7]

I have met many engaging artists on this journey, and that has been an immeasurably rich experience. All have been generous in sharing their thoughts with me, explaining when and why artmaking became the focus of their lives and what it has meant to them. While, of course, every artist has his or her own personal story to tell, I have noted some common themes in their narratives. I have never met an outsider artist who planned to be an artist in any traditional sense of the word; in fact, they are often reluctant to call themselves artists, as they have taught themselves how to bring their visions to life and the "artist" label has been given to them by others, including myself. It is not that they scorn art institutions but, rather, do not know of them or care that they exist. Outsider artists are compelled to create art. It is not a profession or a hobby, but an activity vital to their existence. They do not seek the recognition or approval of an audience, nor do they wish to engage with them. Their artwork is a solitary practice, and their discourse is with themselves—a soliloquy of sorts.

Much has been written about outsider artists and their creations, but the artists themselves have been conspicuously absent from the conversation. This is due, in part, to the very nature of outsider artists, who tend to shy away from public discourse. Without the artists' input, it is tempting to attribute meaning and intention to their work, but that, I believe, is only an act of conjecture which leads to myths and falsehoods about outsider art and its makers. I am troubled by the failure to seek the views of living outsider artists, as they have much to teach us about the passion to create, unapologetically and without regard to public opinion. I began my journey across Canada with the goal of meeting artists who create outside the mainstream world of art. The artists featured in this book are merely a selection of the many remarkable Canadians I met on my travels; given the vastness of this topic, I limited my inquiry to painting, drawing, and sculpture. I offer you a first-hand account from those who were willing to share their stories with me.[8]

The next chapter of this book, "From Art Brut to Outsider Art," outlines the origin of the genre as described by Jean Dubuffet. It ends with an introduction of the term "outsider art" by Roger Cardinal, a pivotal point in the history of this genre. The third chapter—"Outside of What?"—examines the evolution and expansion of outsider art over the past forty years. It describes what outsider art *is* and, equally importantly, what it *is not*. Outsider art has long been associated with artists who struggle with mental health issues, but that does not define the genre. The link between madness and the pursuit of genuine creativity is examined in the fourth chapter—"Madness Sells: The Search for Creative Authenticity." The final chapter, "Hic Sunt Leones," introduces Canadian artists and their work.

[1] Massimiliano Gioni (ed.), *Il palazzo enciclopedico* [The Encyclopedic Palace] (Venice: Marsilio, 2013), 23.

[2] Alastair Sooke, "Venice Biennale 2013: The Encyclopedic Palace, Central Pavilion and Arsenale, review," *The Telegraph*, May 30, 2013.

[3] Gary Alan Fine, *Everyday Genius* (Chicago: University of Chicago Press, 2004), 26. See also Charles G. Zug III, "Folk Art and Outsider Art: A Folklorist's Perspective," in M. Hall & E. Metcalf, Jr. (eds.), *The Artist Outsider: Creativity and the Boundaries of Culture* (Washington, DC: Smithsonian Institution Press, 1994), 145–60.

[4] See "On Language" by Souls Grown Deep Foundation website, https://www.soulsgrowndeep.org/foundation/language#.

[5] Thomas Messer, *Jean Dubuffet & Art Brut* (Milan: Mondadori, 1986), 32.

[6] Roger Cardinal, *Outsider Art* (New York: Praeger, 1972), 30.

[7] Cardinal, *Outsider Art*, 12.

[8] The length and depth of the artist statements vary. They reflect information the artists shared with me, not my preference for any particular artist.

FROM
ART BRUT
TO
OUTSIDER
ART

What is outsider art? That is a question I have been asked many times. I usually respond with my own question: How do *you* define art? It is difficult to begin this conversation without at least trying to address this complex question. Everyone seems to hold a firm opinion about what is *good* art. The documentary accuracy of images has long been preferred in Western culture, and many people are still fixated on this quality in paintings.[1] For others, the image must be beautiful or evoke a mood. Some seek out artwork that matches their furniture, thinking of art as decoration rather than the creative expression of a particular individual. Most insist that the artist demonstrate sophisticated technical skills. When those skills are not readily apparent, or the artist utilizes ready-made or found materials, the result is declared to be *bad* art—something the viewer declares he could have created himself.*

But to engage with art, especially outsider art, does not necessarily begin or end with aesthetic considerations; it demands that each of us examine our own beliefs about the relationship between personal expression and whatever it is that we call art. Most importantly, it asks that we let go of preconceived notions of what art *should* be.[2]

When I studied art history in Canada decades ago, I learned about the evolution of art movements, the biographies of famous artists, and the aesthetic features of masterpieces housed in distant museums. Art brut was mentioned as a peculiar blip in the annals of art history—a curiosity describing Jean Dubuffet's rant against the art establishment. Art brut was not described as a genre, but merely a catalyst for certain avant-garde art trends that followed. Strangely, I never heard of it again. That is to say, I never heard it mentioned in the hallowed halls of the university or saw it displayed in art museums that I visited. I assumed that art brut was dead, buried in the pages of art history books, with Dubuffet's cheeky challenge to art institutions entombed along with it. My chance encounter with a peculiar mosaic artist some thirty years later revealed that art brut was very much alive and well, living under the name "outsider art." That meeting started my personal exploration of artistic endeavours outside the narrative of art history.

So what are we talking about when we talk about outsider art? A conversation about outsider art always includes a discussion of what it is *not* because, as its name suggests, it is outside the boundaries of mainstream art—that is, art that is typically found in a commercial art gallery or an art museum. Outsider art does not conform to any particular style because the work is idiosyncratic, bearing the unique imagery and style of each individual artist. It is not an art trend or an "ism," endorsed by artists who share a common vision, for the artists work in isolation, oblivious to each other's work. In fact, outsider art is nothing new; it has always existed, and has been recognized by many names in various social contexts, most significantly when Dubuffet described it as art brut. The chronicle of art brut and outsider art begins in a psychiatric institution and touches on a range of topics including madness, creativity, modernism, primitivism, Surrealism, and postmodernism. It even references Canadian Indigenous art.

The story begins in the early twentieth century with a growing interest in psychopathological art—that is, art created by individuals with a mental illness.[3] Most early collections were assembled by psychiatrists interested in their patients' art as a diagnostic tool.[4] But it wasn't all about clinical analysis; it was recognized that patients were striving to express themselves

* But didn't.

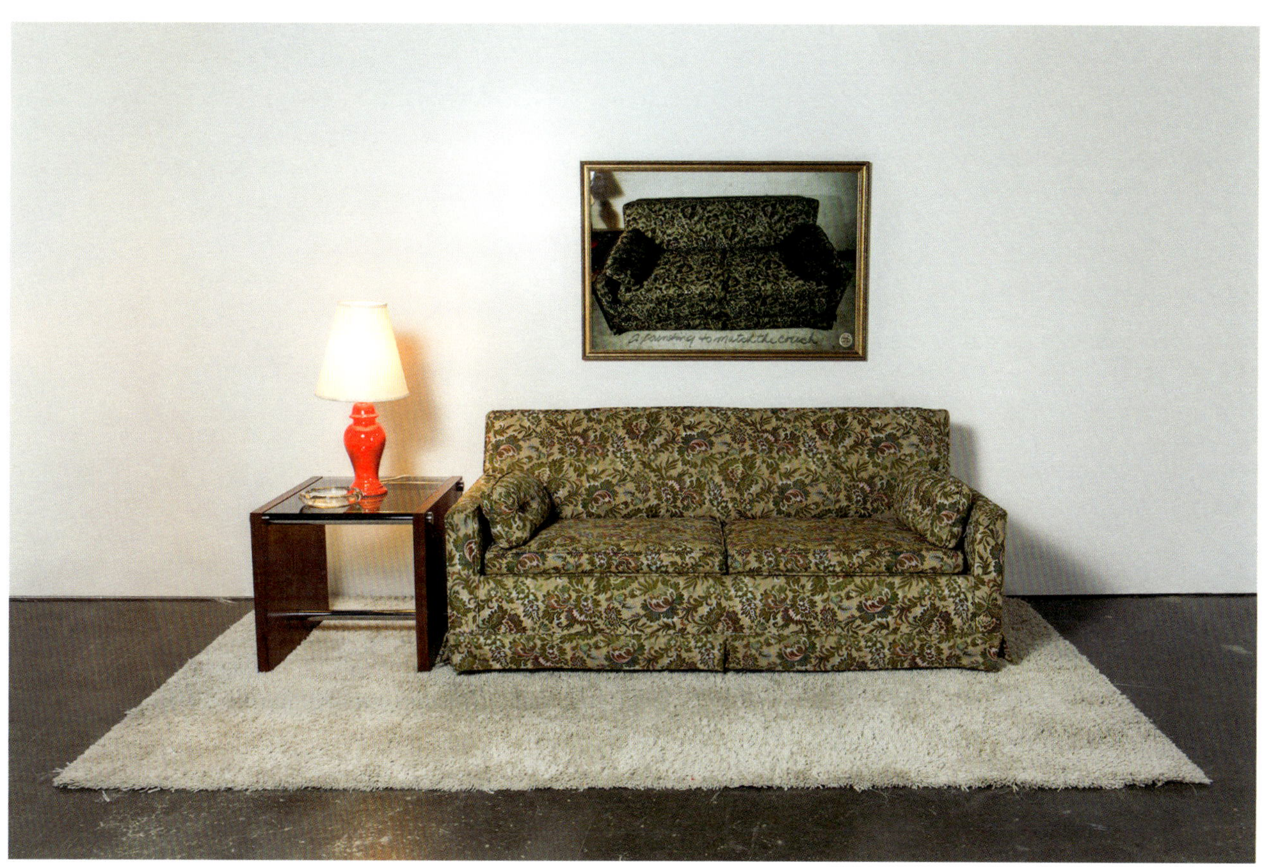

N. E. Thing Co., *A Painting to Match the Couch*, 1974–75
Installation with chesterfield sofa, color photograph, etc.
183 × 295 × 180.5 cm

It can be difficult to understand the world of outsider art because so many different terms are used to describe it. For the sake of clarity and conformity, I have used the following terms in this book: ● **Art brut** is a term invented by Jean Dubuffet in the 1940s, and I use it only to describe work in his original collection. ● **Outsider art** is a term coined by Roger Cardinal in 1972 as the English equivalent of art brut. Although the term is controversial, it is commonly used in the international art world; I use it as a generic term to describe all forms of artwork including paintings, assemblages, carvings, and sculptures. In broad terms, the category of outsider art recognizes idiosyncratic self-taught artists who create without reference to the traditional fine art system. Although outsider art is often called art brut in Europe, I have chosen to use the English term for the sake of consistency. ● **Self-taught art** is the preferred term in the United States. It has come to replace the term outsider art, which is considered a pejorative tag that signifies the artist's position in society. The very term "self-taught art" suggests that a broader base of art is considered in this category. I have chosen to use the term outsider art in this book to avoid confusion with a specific category called "self-taught art." ● **Mainstream art**, admittedly a vague and awkward term, describes all other art discussed in this book unless a specific genre is named. It refers to art that is exchanged in a commercial setting. Although it does not perfectly describe art that is "not outsider art," it is a term commonly used in the literature. Mainstream artists may or may not be professionally trained but they all aspire to be recognized and sell their work to the public. The category is very broad and includes the full spectrum of creators, from self-taught hobbyists to those who have studied in art school. ● **Contemporary art** is a specific genre of mainstream art. It refers, generally, to art created after the mid-twentieth century, and more specifically to art made today. But it is more than that: it describes the institutionalized network through which art presents itself. It is an expanding subculture with its own principles and language. Most contemporary artists have professional training (and art degrees) and create art intended to stimulate a dialogue about contemporary culture, society, personal identity, and critical world issues. It is globally influenced and culturally diverse. It lacks a uniform principle or ideology.

and had invented a personal language to do so.[5] In 1907, Dr. Paul Meunier introduced psychiatric art in a book called *L'art chez les Fous*, which suggested that pure expression lived in art that shed the trappings of conventional form.[6] Psychiatric art moved beyond the walls of the institution for the first time when a few pieces were exhibited in England and France, creating a stir in artistic circles.[7] Hans Prinzhorn[8] is usually credited with introducing the artwork of psychiatric patients to the public. Prinzhorn, an art historian and psychiatrist who worked at the Heidelberg Psychiatric Hospital, was tasked with expanding the collection of its patients' artwork. Aside from their use in diagnosis, Prinzhorn argued that these works should be studied and appreciated for their own merits. In his view, psychiatric patients did not have the freedom, self-awareness, or skill of trained artists, but they did exhibit an uninhibited drive to create and an ability to present unique and unimagined worlds. Prinzhorn published a book of his patients' artwork in 1922, titled *Bildnerei der Geisteskranken* (Artistry of the Mentally Ill). He used the term *bildnerei* (image making) as opposed to *kunst* (art) to distinguish the patients' creative output from the work of professional artists. Although Prinzhorn wasn't the first to take an interest in such artwork, his book connected with the right audience.

The medical community dismissed the artistic merits of Prinzhorn's collection, declaring the images to be nothing more than signs of the artists' debilitating mental illnesses.[9] However, when artist Max Ernst (1891–1976), who had long been interested in so-called asylum art, took Prinzhorn's book to the art community in Paris, it was enthusiastically received.[10] In the devastating aftermath of World War I, Western Europe was receptive to new ideas or, perhaps more accurately, was ready to reject accepted values and societal norms. Traditional, bourgeois attitudes were replaced with more liberal ideals rooted in the Romantic period when truth was no longer restricted to external, physical reality; introspective practices that led to subjective, relative realities were held to be equally valid ways to understand and experience the world. Thus began the trend to glorify art that was both idiosyncratic and expressive.[11] The French art community was struck by the liberating work of Prinzhorn's psychiatric patients who, they believed, took voyages of discovery to the unconscious. It gave them permission to imagine, improvise, and experiment with their own art practices, and that led to new perspectives in art. Most importantly, it started a discussion about conventional ideas of beauty and realistic representational imagery in the external world.

It is fair to say that art brut was a symptom of specific moments in modernism;[12] that is, it was an ideological phenomenon that exemplified the decentering and fragmentation of twentieth-century aesthetics, society, and institutions.[13] So, while highly idiosyncratic artwork had undoubtedly been made by individuals in previous centuries, it would have been received without an underlying theory to give it context and likely dismissed as the peculiar expressions of madmen. Modernist thinkers focused on the self and the psyche, a radical shift away from the rubric of logic and reason, the dominant thinking of the previous century. The provocative theories of Sigmund Freud were widely discussed and, while many of his propositions subsequently proved to be fantastically misguided, he introduced the concept of the subconscious mind and its effect on human behaviour. Later, Carl Jung proposed the existence of a collective unconscious, with its archive of archetypal images and symbols, suggesting to artists that they were inextricably bound to each other by their use of universal icons.[14] These interests coincided with, or possibly triggered, an interest in so-called primitive art,[15] where myth, ritual, and the tasks of daily life were interwoven.[16]

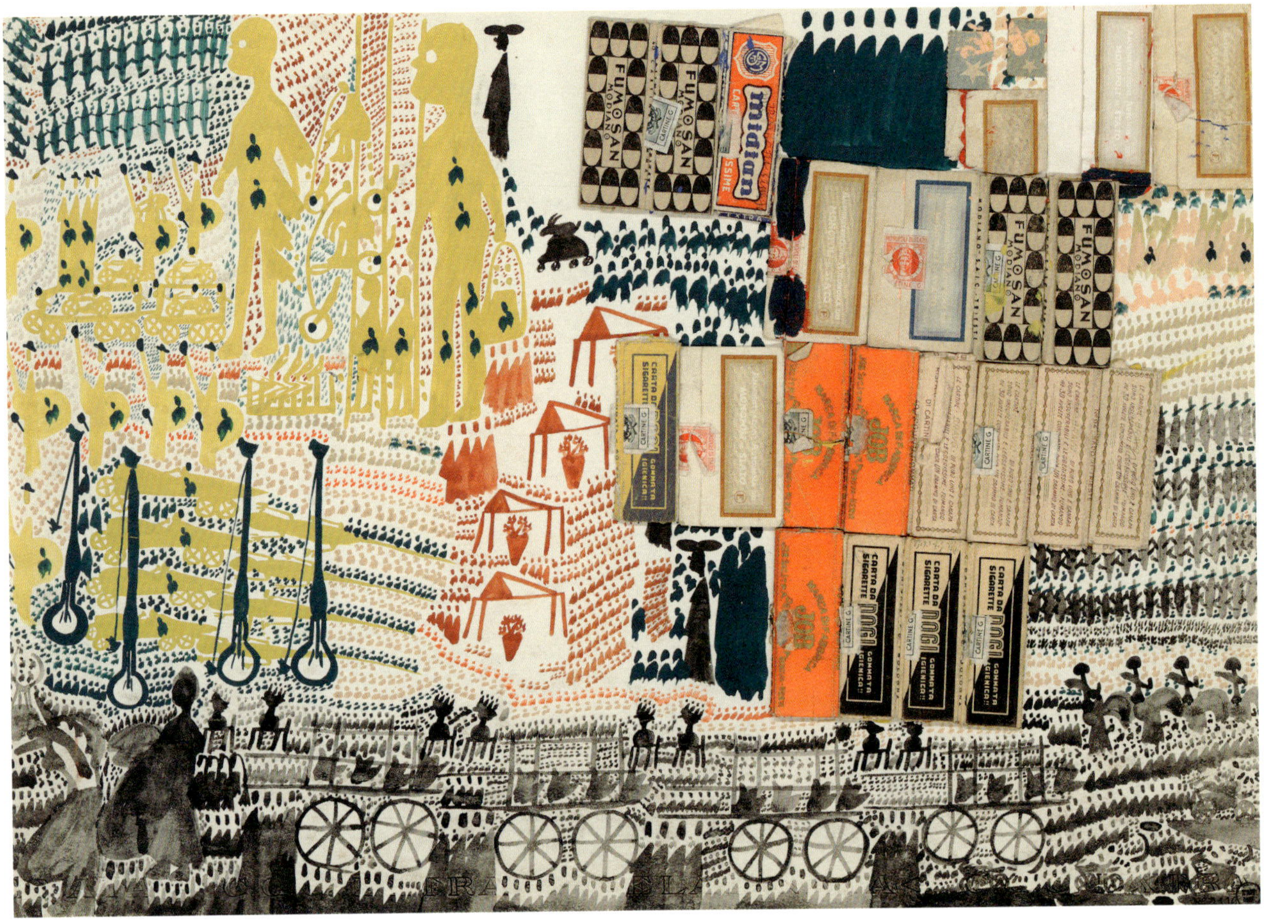

Carlo Zinelli, *Untitled*, 1962
Painting and collage
35 × 50 cm

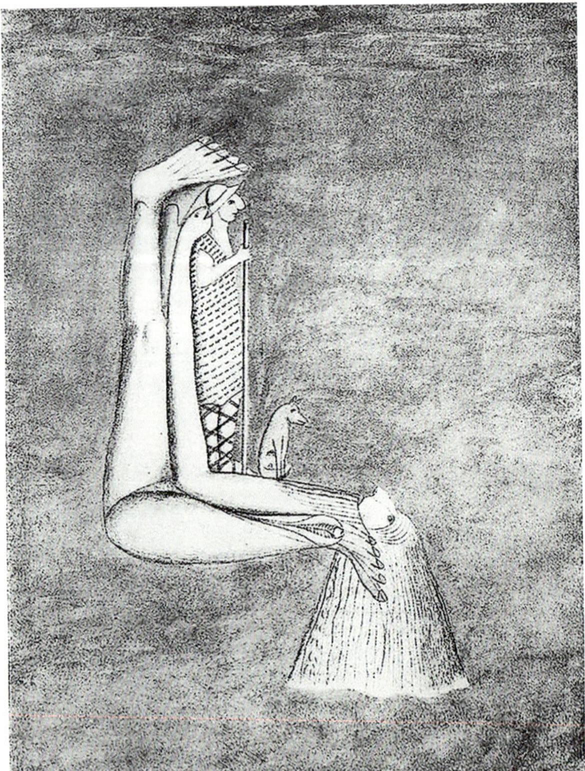

August Natterer,
Wunder-Hirthe, c. 1911–17
Pencil on paper
24.5 × 19.5 cm

Of course, in hindsight, it was a Eurocentric and biased appreciation of non-Western art and artifacts, but, in addition to the dissolution of traditional ways of interpreting the world, it indicated that the distinctions between Western and non-Western, utilitarian and ritual, and found and made artifacts were beginning to blur.

Primitive cultures intrigued those in André Breton's (1896–1966) Surrealist artistic and literary circle. The ultimate goal of Surrealism was to break free of rationalist thought, to create an absolute or super reality from the seemingly incongruous states of dream and reality. One way to achieve that was to explore the role of dreams in the lives of primitive peoples, as well as their apparently harmonious relationship with the universe.[17] The Surrealists began to collect and exhibit artifacts from North American Indigenous groups, travelling as far as Alaska and the west coast of Canada in search of a "kind of absolute reality."[18] Breton himself was interested in psychoanalytical writings and believed that the unconscious mind, which produced dreams, was the source of artistic creativity. The Surrealists set out to explore the realms of the unconscious and the liberating state of madness. In an attempt to mimic psychosis, they studied dreams and practised automatic writing, activities they believed approximated madness because there was no governing logic, reason, or structure in these altered states of mind. In a sense, insanity was a metaphor for total artistic freedom. Creativity, they concluded, is rooted in the subconscious, and it is far more powerful and authentic than anything the conscious mind could produce. The Surrealists created their own cult of insanity.[19] Undoubtedly, recognition of both psychiatric expression and primitive art were significant to the development of modern art.[20]

Artists aligned with Breton's group, including Jean Dubuffet, were absorbed in a debate about creative authenticity and the source of the artistic impulse. Dubuffet valued savagery in art, by which he meant instinct, mood, passion, violence, and madness.[21] In fact, it has been suggested that art brut was Dubuffet's way back to primitivism,[22] a state of mind that allowed the artist to express real life and real moods. Although Dubuffet was an academically trained artist, he argued against the traditions of art history, claiming that art had become a parlour game wherein participants must understand a secret language to appreciate the artwork.[23] According to the rules of the game, if the public does not understand the artist directly, an art critic will step in to interpret the work and persuade them to embrace it.[24] Dubuffet idealized the innocence of Prinzhorn's patients who were so far removed from the cultural conventions of the art community that they did not consider themselves to be artists. In his view, the patients created art the way it should be—spontaneous, direct, uninhibited, original, and unique. This is how he explained art brut:

> By this [art brut] we mean pieces of work executed by people untouched by artistic culture, in which therefore mimicry, contrary to what happens in intellectuals, plays little or no part, so that their authors draw everything (subjects, choice of materials employed, means of transposition, rhythms, ways of writing, etc.) from their own depths and not from clichés of classical art or art that is fashionable. Here we are witnessing an artistic operation that is completely pure, raw, reinvented in all its phases by its author, based solely on his own impulses. Art, therefore, in which is manifested the sole function of invention, and not those, constantly seen in cultural art, of the chameleon and the monkey.[25]

Dubuffet's anti-cultural manifesto was intended to subvert and expose the emptiness of conventional modern art and explode the holy trinity of artist, critic, and public. Art standards, he said, are simply the result of cultural conditioning and stereotyped opinions whereby no one dares question the value of an artwork. We have been taught to fetishize the "great masterpiece" and to believe that only art that hangs in a museum is worthy of consideration.[26] It begs the question: Does it hang in a museum because is it a masterpiece, or is it a masterpiece because it hangs in a museum?[27] He urged the public to not blindly accept the status quo but, rather, to embrace other kinds of art. Art that is unadulterated by culture, he said, is visual creation at its purest because each artist is forced to invent his or her own language and means of expression.[28] What began as an interest in the uninhibited expressions of psychiatric patients spread to an interest in the art of "cultural illiterates," that is, the art of untrained artists.

Dubuffet assembled a collection of artworks in 1945, which is now housed in the Collection de L'Art Brut in Lausanne, Switzerland. His artists were isolated outcasts who were obsessed with image making and, lacking artmaking skills, achieved their goals in unconventional ways: patients in psychiatric institutions; mediums and clairvoyants; prisoners; and those without access to cultural convention, such as isolated provincials and those without formal education.[29] These artists did not ask to be understood; in fact, there was no attempt to communicate with others at all, as they were solely preoccupied with imagery from their own imaginations.[30] In essence, Dubuffet's "un-artists" were the "uncultured" of the art world; that is, creators who were unaware of being artists.[31] It is now generally accepted that it is—and always was—impossible to be totally acultural.[32] Dubuffet later conceded that idea to a utopian vision,[33] and revised his narrative from the acultural outsider to the asocial outsider[34]—artists who did not comply with social norms. In other words, it is more likely that a person would be ignorant of cultural conventions or isolated from society either by choice or personal circumstance. Dubuffet was not promoting a certain aesthetic style, but rather an environment where artists did not kowtow to the dictates of the art establishment. Art brut artists were his case in point, for they were oblivious of the opinions of others. It is important to distinguish a nonartist from one who thumbs his nose at the art establishment—the latter being rebels who are engaged in an intimate dialogue with others about the very nature of art.

Dubuffet was deliberate in his categorization of art brut art and artists. In assembling his collection, he specifically excluded categories of art with some aesthetic similarities, like naïve art, children's art, and art made by psychiatric patients at the request of doctors to aid diagnosis and treatment. He also excluded primitive art and folk art because they have their own traditions and cultural stereotypes.[35] It would be convenient if Dubuffet's definition of art brut remained static, but the ground began to shift at a few critical junctures: first, when Dubuffet reconsidered his own inclusion criteria; then when he introduced art brut to North America; and, finally, when the term outsider art was coined in 1972.

As Dubuffet's art brut collection grew, it became clear that some artwork did not fit neatly into his narrow, restrictive definition of art brut.[36] Although the work was powerful and inventive, the artists' connection with society and awareness of their own work precluded their classification as art brut.[37] For example, Dubuffet admired the artwork of Gaston Chaissac (1910–1964) for its simple, direct style. He was from the French rural working class and taught himself to paint—both biographical prerequisites for inclusion in Dubuffet's collection. However, Chaissac sought input and instruction from prominent painters, and this troubled Dubuffet. Did their instruction taint Chaissac's artistic innocence, he wondered? Another artist, Louis Soutter (1871–1942), was a professionally trained painter before his mental health became compromised.[38] Dubuffet admired the unconventional artwork that Soutter produced in his later years, but concluded that his early art training disqualified him as a pure art brut artist. Artworks like these were moved into the Annex Collection in 1982, and re-named *neuve invention*. These problematic pieces did not meet Dubuffet's exact standards for art brut (that is, free from all cultural influences), but were nevertheless far enough removed from the fine-art system to challenge cultural institutions.

Like Soutter, Canadian artist FRANK TRAVIS did not meet the stringent definition of an art brut artist, but his altered concept of reality suggested that his artistic expressions were as uninhibited and eccentric as those of psychiatric patients who had no prior exposure to art.[39] Travis was born in Toronto, Ontario, in 1914. When his father left the family in 1924, his mother placed Travis and his sister in separate Catholic orphanages. Travis pursued his interest in technical drawing in high school[40] but did not complete the program and left to work at various temporary jobs. He joined the Royal Canadian Air Force in 1941. The war had a profound effect on Travis and he became increasingly withdrawn. After the war, he returned to his art studies at the Ontario College of Art where he came close to completing a four-year diploma program in fine art. Unfortunately, Travis's mental health deteriorated, and at age thirty-five he was diagnosed with schizophrenia and committed to a psychiatric hospital where he lived the rest of his life.

Travis became preoccupied with anatomy, physics, chemistry, and crystallography. In a series of pencil and chalk drawings on brown wrapping paper,[41] Travis created "body machines"—stiff, robotic figures, fitted out with peculiar devices. Notes jotted on the drawings reference his artistic vision: "square heads, round heads, plastic ears, plastic valves for plastic noses, plastic lips, plastic fingers, plastic arms, plastic hands, mechanical auricles and ventricles in plastics, plastic boxes and cedar chests, etc."[42] The drawings became increasingly robotic as "anatomical fragments were slowly replaced by mechanomorphic forms: ball bearings and joints, valves, severed tubing, and die-cast components; blue-prints for a reconstituted self."[43] Travis, it was said, was "presiding over his own complex and systematic destruction."[44]

Dubuffet struggled with the parameters of his art brut collection. Not only had some artists been trained, like Soutter and Travis, some exhibited their work in order to make a living.[45] In deciding what should be included in the art brut collection, Dubuffet created a paradox he hoped to avoid and, without intending to do so, he created a new orthodoxy of inclusion. In hindsight, establishing the neuve invention collection marked the beginning of taxonomy problems that continue to plague the genre.

When Dubuffet announced his thesis to the French art community, it was a novel and provocative statement about the biases of art institutions. His idea subsequently took root in other countries in the context of their own cultures, particularly when it travelled from France to the United States. In 1951, Dubuffet delivered a lecture in Chicago—"Anticultural Positions"—reiterating his subversive, anti-art-establishment message to America.[46] It resonated with the American art community, which was exploring its own ideas of consciousness

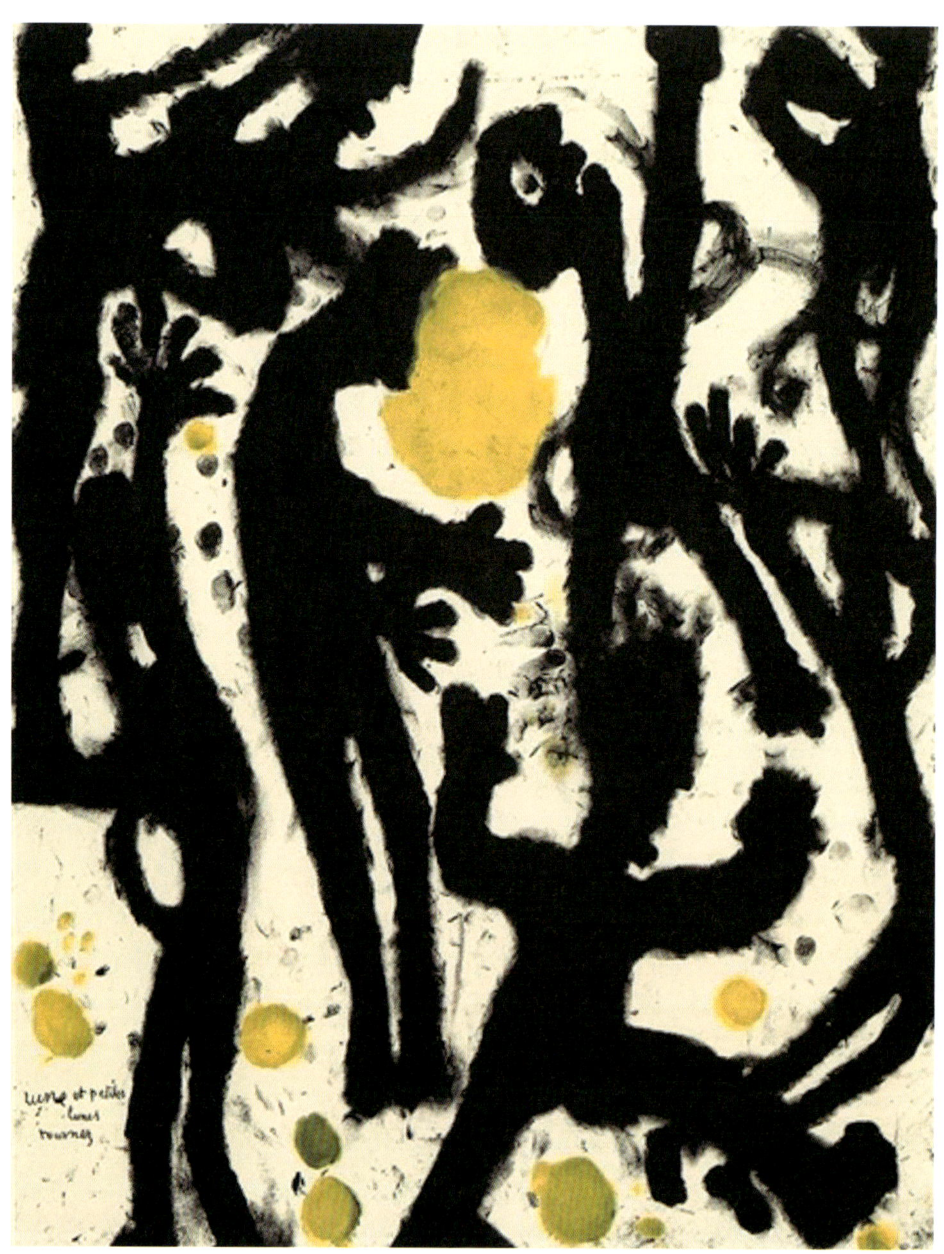

Louis Soutter, *Lunes et petites lunes-tournez*, before 1947
Finger paint on paper
50 × 38 cm

and beauty.[47] It was, however, interpreted in the context of America's own social history, where admiration for the common man, and later, the goals of the civil rights movement, became defining principles.[48] In the end, reverence for folk art in the United States has added another dimension to the conversation about outsider art. While folk art is not synonymous with outsider art, the distinction between the two is less clearly articulated in that country. So, while there is a clear demarcation between folk art and outsider art in Europe, the relationship between the genres in the United States and Canada is more nuanced. Both fall under the umbrella of what Americans often call self-taught art, a term that is not used in Europe. Until recently, the terms "naïve" or "folk" were commonly used in Canada to describe both traditional folk and self-taught artists.

Outsider art and folk art, especially contemporary folk art, are often confused, and it is easy to understand why. Both genres are outside the narrative of art history and both have an unsophisticated and homemade appearance. Neither category is shaped by traditional art institutions nor are the artists part of the mainstream art community, even if their work is admired by those who are. The two genres are, however, distinct. Traditional folk art refers to handiwork, typically from rural communities. It reflects the customs of a particular ethnicity, culture, or region, with skills handed down from one generation to the next. The work is regional and is tied to familial, ethnic, religious, or cultural traditions.[49] Inspiration for folk art usually comes from external sources, such as daily life and religious beliefs, and folk artists enjoy having an audience that appreciates their work.

There are some aesthetic similarities between folk art and outsider art, but folk art has never been given the intellectual rationale that Dubuffet gave to art brut, and there are important differences between the two.[50] American folk art echoes its homestead past and is said to reflect the honest and direct American spirit. It stirs nostalgia for simpler times. In Canada, folk art has been described as people's art—the unpretentious and humble personal expressions of untrained artists for the enjoyment of ordinary folk. "It is a reflection, direct and unhampered, of life as it is seen and felt by people immersed in a variety of work and leisure."[51] The work provides a record of settler society and key relationships therein: Maritimers to pictures of the sea, les Québécois to reflections of their faith, Westerners to images of wheat fields.[52]

Outsider art, on the other hand, springs from the artist's imagination and hints at other ways of experiencing the world. It venerates artists who are outside society's influences and suggests an alternative way of being.[53] It is an intensely personal practice that is not motivated by public recognition. While Dubuffet excluded folk art from his original collection (and it remains a distinct genre in Europe), the United States is more inclined to embrace it as its own homegrown version of art brut.[54] To a lesser extent, the same may be true in Canada, although such a direct comparison has never been made.

Oddly, it was a literary event, not an artistic one, that changed the face of art brut. British scholar Roger Cardinal set out to write about art brut in 1972 and, looking for a catchier title that would appeal to the English-speaking world, he called it "outsider art." Although the term "outsider art" was not used in the text of the book, Cardinal intended it to be synonymous with art brut and, from the outset, inclusive of the categories of both art brut and neuve invention.[55] Echoing Dubuffet's philosophy, Cardinal defined outsider art as the

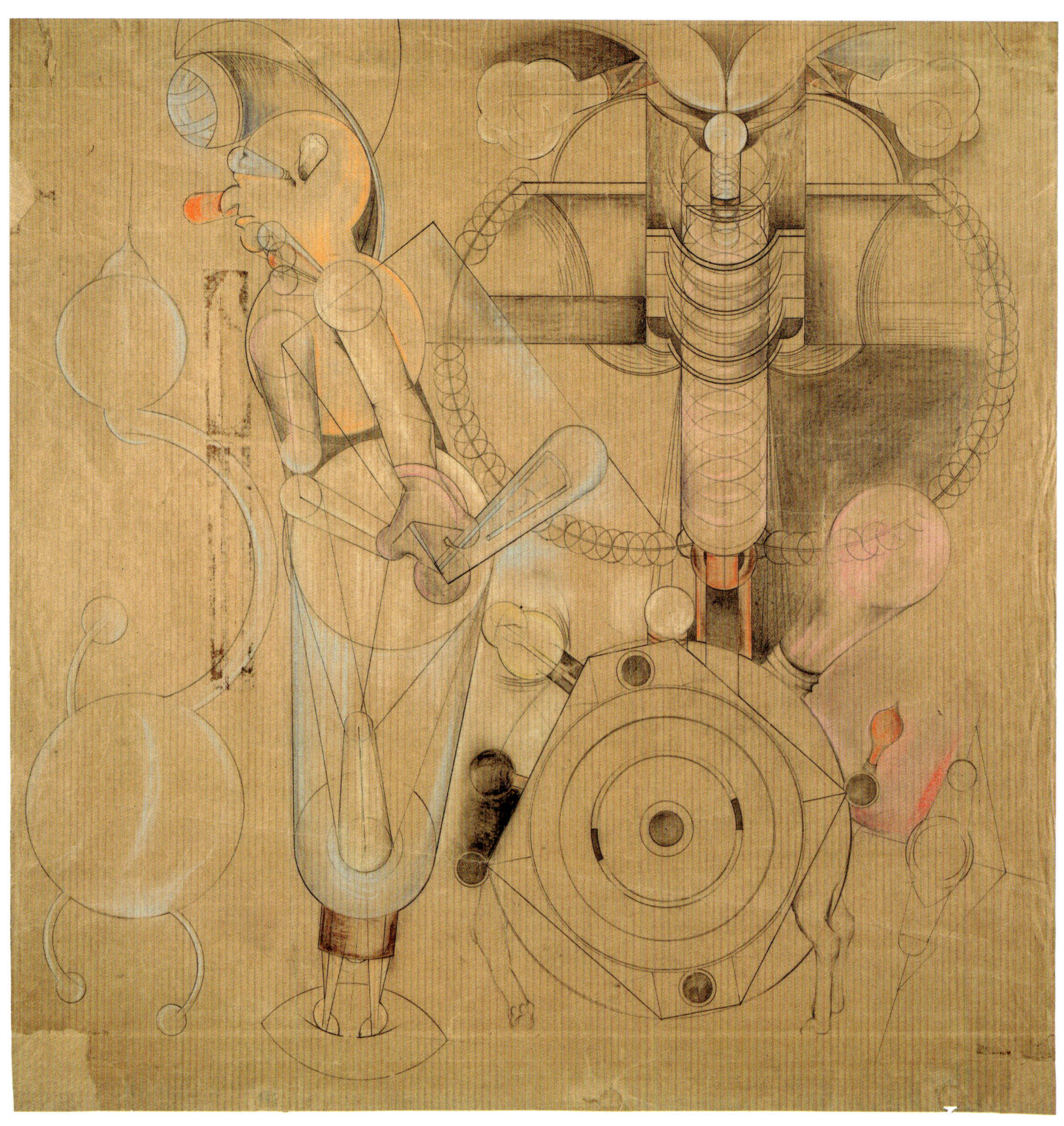

Frank Travis, *Untitled*, c. 1953
Graphite and coloured pencil
on wrapping paper
61.6 × 59.7 cm

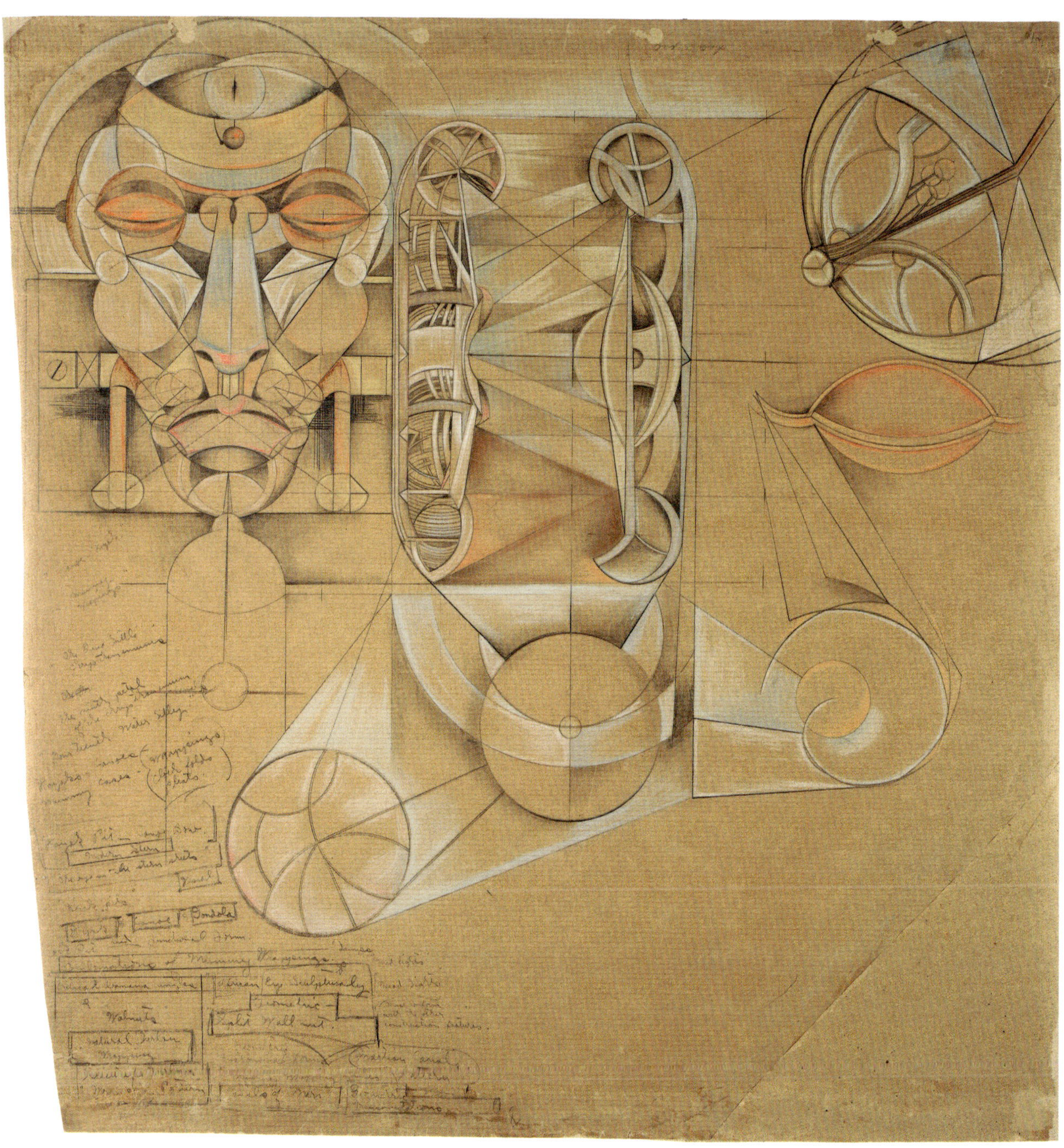

Frank Travis, *Untitled*, between 1940 and 1960
Graphite and coloured pencil on wrapping paper
91.3 × 89 cm

inward-looking work of untutored artists who have an intense inner life and are not connected to the traditional art world.

It was not Cardinal's intention, but the world of art brut was turned upside down. Since then, the term "outsider" has been taken literally, triggering a debate about the meaning of that word as well as the type of art it describes. Some argue that it simply underscores the artist's marginalized social status and call for abolishing the pejorative label.[56] Others interpret the term as outside and independent of the mainstream art world, that is, without reference to it.[57] Many curators, however, recall Dubuffet's interest in artmakers secluded from society and continue to focus on the artist's biography as the defining characteristic of outsider art. My own definition references the artist's personal narrative and honours other ways of navigating life.

1 Roger Cardinal, "Outsider Art and the Autistic Creator," *Philosophical Transactions of the Royal Society of London. Series B, Biological Sciences* 364, no. 1522 (2009): 1459–66, https://doi:10.1098/rstb.2008.0325.

2 Although outsider art is unconventional and sometimes strange, Dubuffet believed that art is intended to address itself to the mind, not the eyes. Dubuffet, "Anticultural Positions," 1951, accessed January 5, 2020, http://www.logosjournal.com/issue_5.2/dubuffet.htm.

3 John MacGregor, *The Discovery of the Art of the Insane* (Princeton, NJ: Princeton University Press, 1989), 161.

4 MacGregor, *The Discovery*, 188.

5 MacGregor, 171.

6 Marcel Réja, *L'art chez les Fous* (Paris: Société du mercure de France, 1907). It was later revealed that Marcel Réja was Dr. Paul Gaston Meunier.

7 MacGregor, 172.

8 In 1919, Prinzhorn (1886–1933) became assistant to Dr. Karl Wilmanns at the psychiatric hospital. His task was to expand a collection of spontaneous art (i.e., not made under a doctor's direction).

9 Colin Rhodes, *Outsider Art: Spontaneous Alternatives* (London: Thames & Hudson, 2000), 87.

10 Thomas Roeske, "Max Ernst's Encounter with *Artistry of the Mentally Ill*," accessed January 7, 2020, https://archiv.ub.uni-heidelberg.de/artdok/3955/1/Roeske_Max_Ernsts_encounter_with_Artistry_of_the_Mentally_Ill_2009.pdf.

11 Joanne Cubbs, "Rebels, Mystics, and Outcasts," in Michael D. Hall and Eugene W. Metcalf, Jr. (eds.), *The Artist Outsider: Creativity and the Boundaries of Culture* (Washington, DC: Smithsonian Institution Press, 1994), 79.

12 James Elkins, "Naïfs, faux-naïfs, faux-faux naïfs, would-be faux-naïfs: There is no such thing as outsider art," in J. Thompson (ed.), *Inner Worlds Outside* [exhibition catalogue], (Dublin: Irish Museum of Modern Art, 2006), 71–79.

13 Lucienne Peiry, *Art Brut: The Origins of Outsider Art* (Paris: Flammarion, 2001).

14 Marie Mauzé, "Surrealists and the New York Avant-Garde, 1920–60," in C. Townsend-Gault, J. Kramer, and Ki-ke-In (eds.), *Native Art of the Northwest Coast: A History of Changing Ideas* (Vancouver: UBC Press, 2013), 274.

15 An unfortunate and outdated ethnocentric concept referring to non-Western cultural artifacts.

16 Mauzé, "Surrealists," 270.

17 Mauzé, 270.

18 Mauzé, 274. Kurt Seligmann (in 1938) and Wolfgang Paalen (in 1939) travelled to the Pacific West Coast to collect artifacts. Seligmann bought ceremonial pieces, including a totem, from the Gitksan. Paalen was said to put together a remarkable collection of old and authentic objects. Adopting Paalen's views of Northwest Coast art, artists of the New York School (including Jackson Pollock, Mark Rothko, and Barnett Newman) proclaimed their brotherhood with the primitive artists and their goal to create a universal art.

19 Allan Beveridge, "A disquieting feeling of strangeness?: The art of the mentally ill," *Journal of the Royal Society of Medicine* 94, no. 11 (2001): 595–99, http://www.ncbi.nlm.nih.gov/pmc/articles/PMC1282252/.

20 MacGregor, 162.

21 Dubuffet, "Anticultural Positions," 1951, http://www.logosjournal.com/issue_5.2/dubuffet.htm.

22 Rhodes, *Outsider Art*. Is outsider art another example of Western culture's quest for the primitive? Consider, for example, an exhibition of Basquiat's paintings with Kongo carvings: "Resonance Jean-Michel Basquiat et l'Univers Kongo," Paris, 2022.

23 Mildred Glimcher, *Jean Dubuffet: Towards an Alternative Reality* (New York: Pace Publications, 1987), 55.

24 Thomas Messer, *Jean Dubuffet & Art Brut* (Milan: Mondadori, 1986), 27.

25 Excerpted from *Jean Dubuffet L'art brut préféré aux arts culturels* (Paris: Galerie René Drouin, 1949).

26 Cardinal, *Outsider Art*, 9.

27 Cardinal, 9.

28 Glimcher, *Jean Dubuffet: Towards an Alternative Reality*, 55.

29 Glimcher.

30 Messer, Jean Dubuffet & Art Brut.

31 Messer.

32 Glimcher.

33 Berst, C., "Art brut: Definitions," accessed January 8, 2020, http://www.christianberst.com/en/art-brut-definitions.html.

34 Jean Dubuffet, *Asphyxiating Culture* (New York: Four Walls, Eight Windows, 1988).

35 Naïve art was said to emulate cultural traditions. Children's art was excluded because children do not have the psychic depth necessary for true creation and are easily influenced by their audience. European folk art generally refers to household crafts, that is, decorative or functional pieces made by a person not professionally trained in making those items. It is not to say that folk art did not have an effect on mainstream art in Europe, but rather that they remained quite separate entities.

36 Rhodes, *Outsider Art: Spontaneous Alternatives*, 47.

37 Rhodes.

38 Rhodes.

39 Images of Frank Travis's work can be found in the Collection de l'Art Brut in Lausanne,

OUTSIDE
OF WHAT?

> Jean Dubuffet, *Woman*, 1956
Lithograph from original on paper
31.75 × 24.1 cm

When Dubuffet began collecting the artwork of psychiatric patients and isolated provincials, it was more than a protest about the tyranny of art institutions: it was a powerful illustration of his belief that authentic art exists only outside museums. Since then, the art community—or at least one part of it—has been considering his proposition. As I began exploring outsider art in Canada and seeking dialogue on the subject, my conversations with others often met a dead end. Most people admitted they had never heard of outsider art; some assumed it was public art displayed outdoors; a few insisted that graffiti was a good example because it was subversive *and* outside; and one perceptive artist could offer only that it is art talked about by the folks who talk about outsider art.[1] So, there's that.

My own attempts to explain outsider art were clumsy, and I had to acknowledge that there were unresolved, contentious issues about the genre. People pressed for visual markers of the art, hoping to identify its common features. Dubuffet himself proposed a set of stylistic indicators observed in his collection, and others have added to that list.[2] But, although the work of some outsider artists may look similar, there are few, if any, connections between makers. An outsider artist's access to resources is often limited, and so the use of unconventional materials may give a false impression of a common style. In other words, every outsider artist may have his or her own visual vocabulary or recognizable style, but likenesses between bodies of work are only coincidental, as the artists themselves are unaware of or indifferent to each other's work.

Appearances can be deceiving, particularly when outsider aesthetics are mimicked by others. It is especially surprising to see celebrities claim status as outsider artists when they not only exude cultural norms but also define them.[3] I have observed interested parties reconfigure the work of untrained artists so as to make it more appealing and convincing. In other cases, professional artists spurn their formal art training, making it difficult to distinguish them from outsider artists. Dubuffet, for example, was a renegade and painted in a brutalist style, but he was not an outsider artist because he originally adhered to, and subsequently rejected, the rules articulated by the dominant art institution of his time. That is to say, he knew the rules and set out to break them. Thus, mavericks and other nonconformers have the language to engage in a dialogue with the art establishment if only to deride and dismiss it. They orient themselves to the world of conventional art because their work is created in defiance of the rules they reject. Ironically, their work might not be acknowledged until other artists join the rebellion and it becomes a movement.[4] And, while there may be aesthetic similarities between an outsider creation and a work of mainstream art, the likeness ends there. There is no greater illusion in art than the view that similarity of object entails similarity of vision.[5] Unconventional materials may be utilized for vastly different reasons.[6]

One of the most significant events in the history of outsider art was the publication of Roger Cardinal's book *Outsider Art* in 1972. The introduction of the term "outsider art" to the English-speaking world led to more than a change of terminology; the genre underwent a major shift in thinking. Although there is still little agreement about what "outsider" means, the introduction of the term prompted various ways of interpreting it.

Some frame the genre as a social justice issue, while others focus on the artist's biography: their mental or cognitive disabilities, lack of formal art training, or unconventional lifestyle.

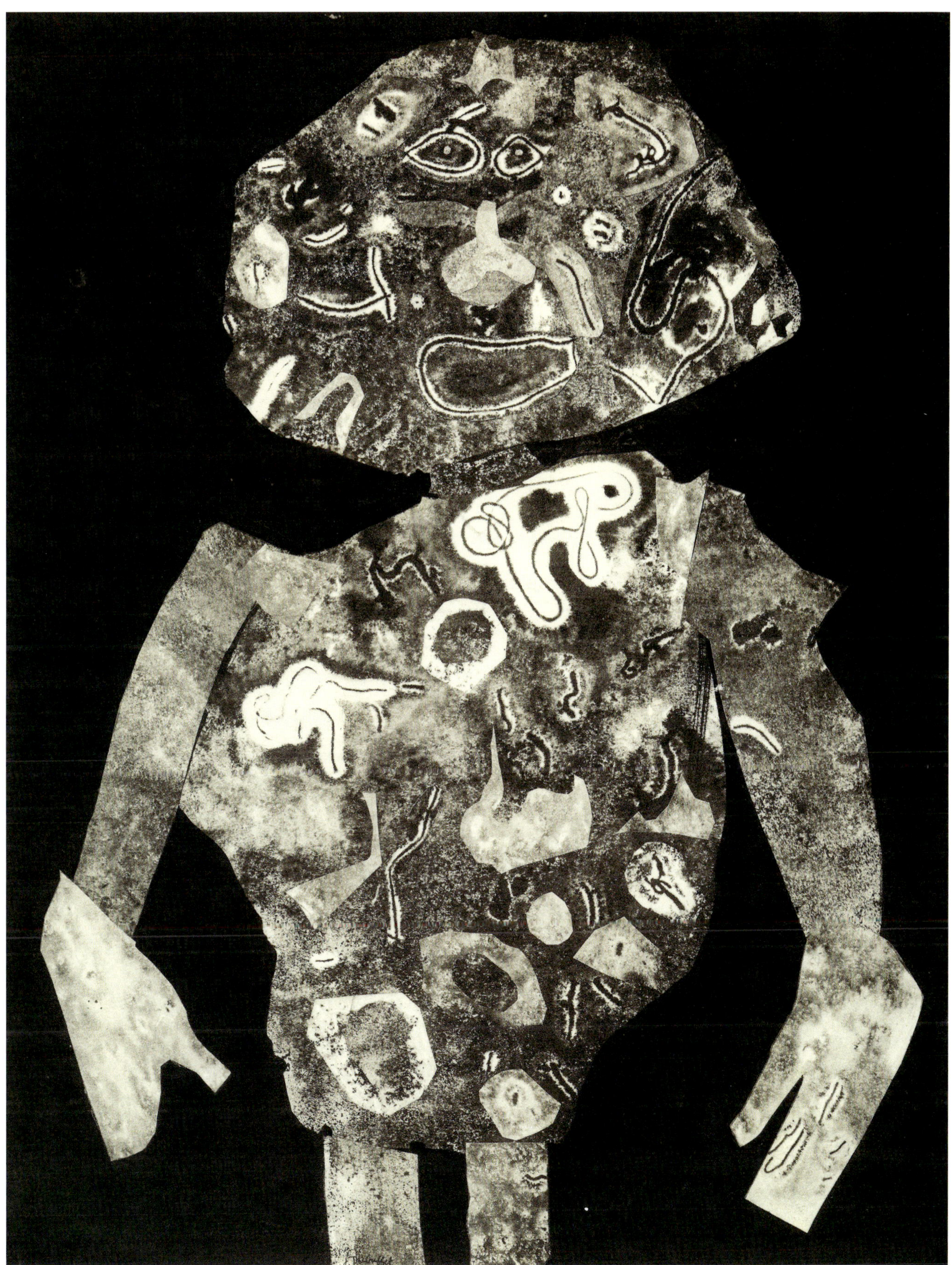

For those who characterize the outsider label as a social justice issue, outsider art is said to exist only in binary terms; that is, inside and outside define each other's boundaries. Like primitive art, the outsider category exists only because of cultural elitism and class differences, such that the margins are defined by the centre.[7] Art critic Lucy Lippard, for instance, asks: Outside of what? Outside of society, she says, according to a situation that has arisen from systemic class discrimination. Thus, the artist is dismissed twice: first, by those who hold the power (by status, wealth, education, or privilege); and second, by the mainstream art world. If defining art reflects society's ethics, morals, and spiritual state, then outsider art is a negative concept that promotes a dehumanizing concept of art.[8]

To characterize outsider art as a social justice issue echoes Dubuffet's protest that art is the monopoly of academics, art institutions, privileged intellectuals, and professional artists. However, it strays from Dubuffet's original proposition in a significant way: he did not define the issue in political terms. His artists were not excluded from the mainstream art world because, in fact, they never knew of its existence nor sought to be part of it. Dubuffet himself took aim at the controlling views of the art establishment and demanded that it stop dictating what art *should* be. To now declare that all marginalized artists are outsider artists is to rewrite history and give Dubuffet's artists a sense of purpose they never had. So, while an artist's personal circumstances may have resulted in social marginalization, that reality cannot be the only factor that identifies an outsider artist. The concept of outsider art describes the artist's state of mind when creating art, not his or her personal circumstances.

It is a mistake to recast Dubuffet's artists as neglected heroes of the art world. The genre would collapse under its own weight if marginalization were its sole determining factor; the category would become so inclusive as to be meaningless. Moreover, it begs this question: Why should the artwork of some marginalized populations invite the outsider label while others do not? For instance, some contend the outsider label applies to the artwork of Canada's Indigenous population, who endured years of systemic discrimination.[9] That is an untenable proposition. Not only does traditional Indigenous art reflect deeply rooted cultural narratives, it overlooks the experience of other groups that are routinely ostracized and repressed.

While outsider art in North America is sometimes framed as a social justice issue, there is little mention that *all* artists, professional or otherwise, struggle to achieve recognition and obtain gallery representation. An artist's acceptance into the commercial realm of mainstream art is dependent on a multitude of factors, from marketing and competition to the aesthetic characteristics of the work. And, of course, it is critical that someone champion their work. Art is not a free, autonomous activity of an individual influenced by social forces, but rather is part of a pre-existing social structure made up of institutions like art academies and museums, support systems of influential patrons and critics, and prevailing stereotypes about artists and artmaking.[10] In the end, it may be a business decision for those who promote art in the commercial sector: Is the artwork marketable or not? Feeling excluded from the art market is not unique to marginalized individuals who create art. It is the unfortunate reality of being an artist.

Decades after the publication of Cardinal's book, it remains difficult to talk about outsider art without wading into the definition debate. Its proper name is in flux: some call it "self-taught art," a few prefer the term "vernacular," and others dismiss the need for any type of label. Among Francophones in Canada, it is sometimes called marginal art or *art singulier*. "Autodidactic art" is bandied about, in my view, only to befuddle an uninitiated audience. Recently, I have observed the word "outlier" gaining popularity, although it is simply a variation on outsider. Dubuffet himself was drawn into the debate and proposed art *hors les normes* (outside the normal) as a way to end the intellectual squabbles surrounding art brut.[11] Today it seems that a new term pops up with every exhibition. While novel and creative naming schemes may be an attempt to sidestep the tangled mess of old terminology, they serve only to complicate matters. The most troubling question is whether the outsider label can explain the work of such disparate groups as psychiatric patients in European hospitals and twentieth-century Black self-taught artists from the Southern United States. Can they—and should they—be squeezed into one category?[12] We have travelled a very long way from Dubuffet's treatise on the biases of art institutions.

Clearly the word "outsider" is fraught with problems, but it has become entrenched in our vocabulary. At best, it is associated with originality; at worst it hints at stigma, rejection, and exclusion. For this reason, the phrase "self-taught art" is the preferred term in the United States. That would appear to be a simple solution, but, although the name is alluringly simple, it can be misleading and it is far too broad to be meaningful. Some mainstream artists are self-taught,[13] and many self-taught artists are highly skilled in other occupations. It describes art hobbyists, yet, unlike outsider artists, many hobbyists strive to emulate a particular style and are proud to receive recognition for their efforts. Black artists living in the Southern United States are affronted by the descriptor because it is never used to define successful, self-taught white artists.[14] The American Folk Art Museum in New York, however, now embraces the work of all historic and contemporary folk artists, as well as outsider artists, under the umbrella term "self-taught"—that is, creators who have honed their skills though practice rather than formal art training. Inspiration for these artists comes from "unsuspected paths and unconventional places, giving voice to individuals who may be situated outside the social mainstream."[15] It is a well-crafted description of artists working outside the continuum of art history and judiciously omits reference to the artist's biography, specifically his or her mental status, a prerequisite that is common in the European classification system.

While artists with mental health issues have historically been described as outsider artists, artists with disabilities are sometimes included in the genre, particularly in North America. With the emergence of new social ideals in the 1970s, the idea of disability as a culture took root, along with the establishment of art centres meant to foster the creative potential of those with disabilities.[16] While very few individuals are completely removed from modern-day culture, as Dubuffet once declared, the parameters of outsider art are elastic enough to include those who at times dwell in their own private art worlds.[17] Although some define the word "autistic" in a medical context, others might use the word in a nonmedical sense to address an artist's apparent secrecy about their work and reluctance or inability to communicate in a direct way.[18] The work may seem impenetrable to the viewer simply because it has been created without regard for a potential audience. It is the artist's drive to articulate an inner reality that makes the work so compelling.[19]

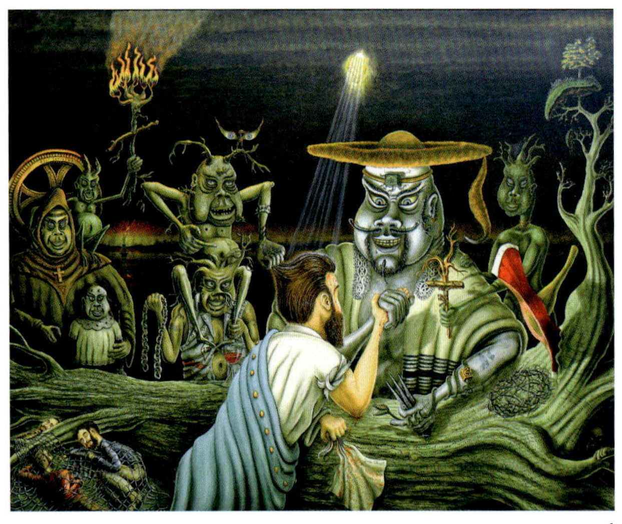
1

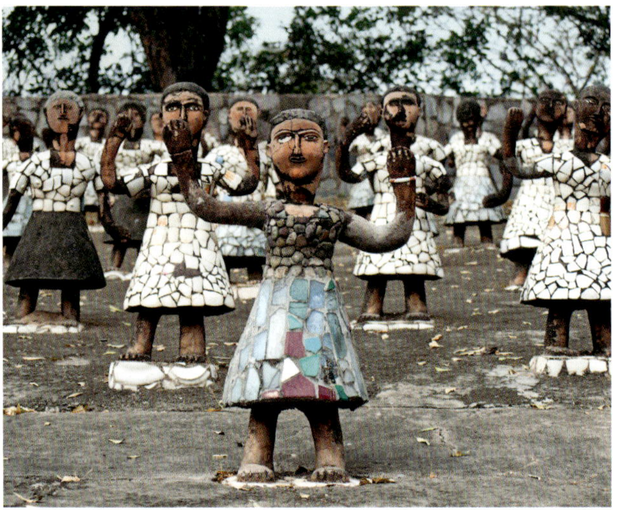
2

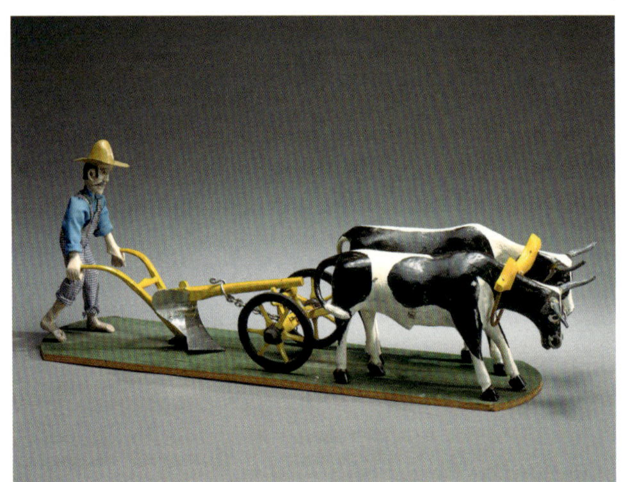
3

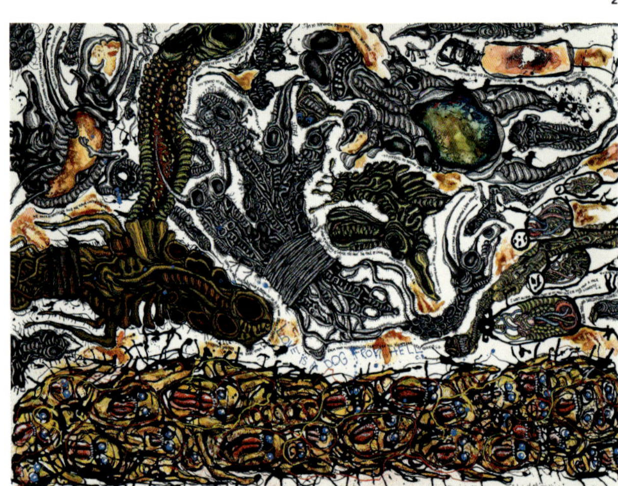
4

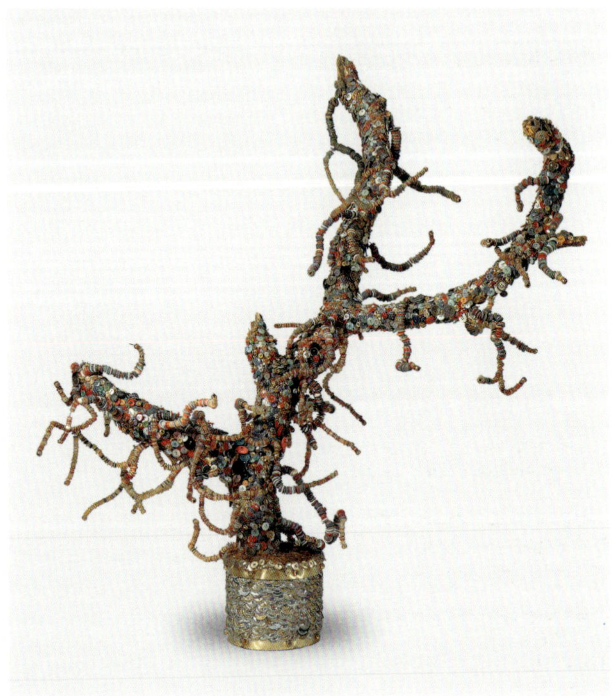
5

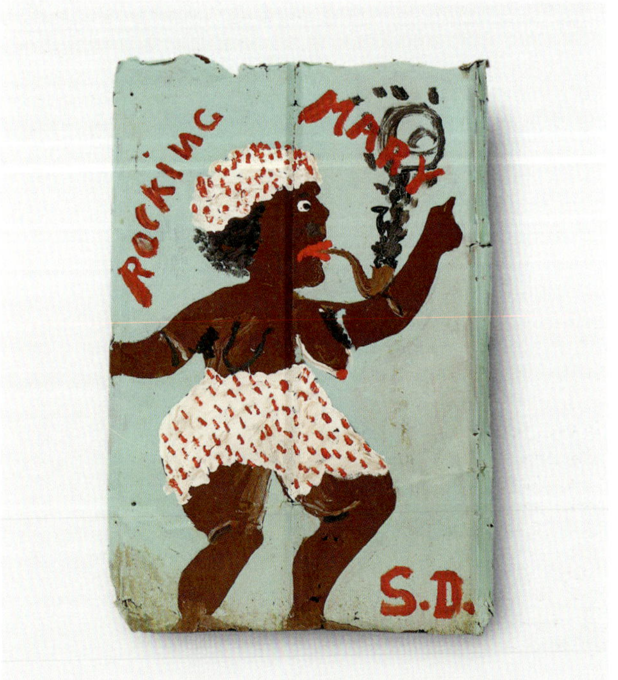

6

Outsider art today is an inexact umbrella term that includes many subcategories, including these: ● **1. Visionary** or **intuitive art** describes an artist's expression of religious or spiritual experiences. It also describes artists who create imaginary, utopian worlds. ● **2. Visionary environments** (fantasy worlds) are vast, imaginative installations built from unconventional materials. ● **3. Folk art** generally describes homemade crafts and the traditional decorative skills of rural communities in Europe and North America. Folk art painting and naïve art typically refer to untrained artists who produce illustrative work, such as landscapes, animals, and people going about their daily activities. ● **4. Marginal art or art singulier** are terms commonly used in Québec and Europe to describe self-taught artists who inhabit the grey area between Dubuffet's art brut and mainstream art, much like the category he called neuve invention. ● **5. Contemporary folk art** references a multitude of art forms that are often categorized as outsider art, from bottle-cap-covered figures to sculptures assembled from pieces of scrap wood. ● **6. Black artists** living in the Southern United States prefer that no label be attached to their work, arguing that the term "self-taught" derives from market-driven biases against artists of colour. Is all of this outsider art? And what does it mean in a Canadian context?

1. Norbert Kox, *Agony in Gethsemane: The Tribulation of Yesu Christ*, 1989
Acrylic glaze and oil on canvas
122 × 152.4 cm

2. Nek Chand, *Rock Garden of Chandigarh*, 1957–76
Rocks, found materials
160,000 sq.m

3. William Stefanchuck, *Tilling the Soil*, c. 1940–1950
Wood, plaster, textile, metal
21 × 82 × 30 cm

4. Sylvain Martel, *Terrain miné* (Minefield), 2010
Watercolour, acrylic, and ink
40.6 × 30.5 cm

5. Gregory Warmack (Mr. Imagination), *Button Tree*, 1990–92
Wood, cement, buttons, bottle caps, and nails
142 × 86 × 152.5 cm

6. Sam Doyle, *Rocking Mary*, late 1970s
Paint on tin
91.4 × 61 cm

When all is said and done, would we even be having this discussion if the term "outsider art" had not replaced "art brut" some forty years ago?

There are calls to abolish the binary concept because it does more harm than good.[20] Abolition of the outsider label would make all art and artists equal. In other words, it is all *art*. The call to drop any descriptive terminology for art, like the term "outsider," is not limited to those who advocate for social equity. Every outsider artist I have met is puzzled (and often offended) by the term. A few declare that genuine outsider art died a natural death when psychotropic drugs were introduced to psychiatric patients in the 1950s, stifling their creativity along with other significant parts of their identity.[21] Others blame the mass media and promotion of the genre in the art market for its loss of purity.[22] No longer strange, outsider art is said to be suffocating under the interest it has generated.[23] Others note the difficulty of labelling contemporary folk and outsider art when their makers seek grants, participate in exhibits, and actively promote their work.[24] Some note the futility of keeping a separate category, calling instead for the same level of artistry that we demand for any kind of art.[25] A growing number in the art community take the same position. Art is art, they say, and a label declaring its subordinate position and the artists as "other" prevents those artists from moving into a globalized art market and contemporary art galleries.[26] While Dubuffet's art brut may once have served to challenge the elevated status of high art that modernism set out to destroy, the distinct category of outsider art has perhaps outlived its usefulness in this postmodern era when categories are collapsing into each other, the periphery has become the centre, and the distinct identities of the key players (artists, collectors, curators, gallery owners) and institutions (commercial, not-for-profit, public, private, established, independent) are in flux.[27]

The challenge is to rearticulate outsider art in a postmodern (or post-postmodern) era. Perhaps we should call it post-art brut. It is a good time to reconsider and reframe our views on outsider art. Diversity and democracy govern the mainstream art world today; previously excluded points of view challenge traditional, ingrained ways of thinking. Not only are other perspectives sought out, multiple points of view are validated. The days of controlling culture from the top down are over. In a sense, the current mood echoes Dubuffet's anti-cultural manifesto.

Plus ça change, plus c'est la même chose.

If we were to drop all descriptive art terms like "outsider," there would be one less thing to debate about the legitimacy and parameters of outsider art. But not everyone is ready to make that conceptual leap.[28] Among art historians and curators, outsider art and mainstream art are two different species: mainstream art (particularly contemporary art) engages in a complex social dialogue while outsider art is made by artists who are socially disconnected and idiosyncratic in style. They say the genres must be kept separate in order to preserve the integrity of both genres, particularly outsider art, asserting that the mainstream art world is one of prostitution, where recognition comes at the price of social exploitation and commercial appropriation. And, as one proponent of outsider art declares, to be admitted into contemporary art museums "is tantamount to boasting of the Mafia's approval."[29] Art historians contend there are significant factors that make outsider art a separate and distinct genre from mainstream art. Outsider art is ahistorical and purely personal. Professional artists break art-historical traditions but outsider artists do not. In fact, outsider artists never knew such traditions existed. Moreover, they contend, elevating the common man to the status of an artist threatens the continuity of art history and its sustaining infrastructure. Even if we wanted to, how could we incorporate outsider art into the mainstream art world in the face of this incongruity?[30] It is an ongoing debate that is not easily resolved. Art historians have valid reasons for not embracing "art for art's sake"[31] and accepting the idiosyncratic work of eccentric individuals into the narrative of art history. Outsider art is *not* part of art history, nor does it run parallel to art history. Aside from reciting when certain events occurred in the world of outsider art, such as where and when certain terms were coined, there have been no identifiable outsider art movements, trends, or ideologies. Outsider art is entirely dependent on the vision of its maker, not the shared discourse of the artists themselves or the broader art community. It remains in the public eye due to the activities of outsider art enthusiasts. What has changed over time is our acceptance of outsider art as a creative endeavour worthy of consideration.

In any event, to reconceptualize outsider art as *art* (without a qualifier) at this point in time would unquestionably disrupt the chronicles of both art history and outsider art. Maybe that is a good thing, or at least an inevitable outcome. It may take some time for art historians to measure and reconsider the significance of outsider art in the context of art-historical trends. It certainly had an impact on Dubuffet and his colleagues, and, in Canada, I came to understand that artists learn from and are influenced by each other regardless of their status in the art world. It is, perhaps, only art institutions that insist there is but one story line. Still, even questioning the status of outsider art in the context of art history, as we are doing here, disrupts its narrative. It is a delightful paradox, for the mere idea of outsider art in a post-modern world forces us to re-examine the very definition of art. As one of Douglas Coupland's *Slogans for the Twenty-First Century* proclaims: ART IS UP FOR GRABS AGAIN.

Clearly, there are many ways to define outsider art and many persuasive arguments for preserving its status. What distinguishes a contemporary artist from a present-day outsider artist is the former's level of training and their desire to engage in a dialogue with the public and art institutions about critical social issues, including what art is and ought to be. Outsider artists are not part of the mainstream art world; they have come to their art with only their imaginations, without the benefit or hindrance of training or critique. To be an outsider artist is to be *external* to those conversations. Outsider art is best understood, then, not in terms of the artist's personal circumstances or the characteristics of the artwork itself, but in the absence of a relationship with any established art world.[32] As one art critic describes it, to be an artist means to have internalized the prevailing discourse of the art world. To be a [*fill in the blank, e.g., outsider*] artist is to be external to those discourses.[33] What constitutes *art* in any given art world is an ongoing debate, and that can make the categories appear arbitrary, particularly as work that was once rejected may be assimilated later. Think of the French Impressionists, for example, who were originally barred from the French art academy because they violated the established rules of painting at the time.[34] Although their work is easily recognizable today, the movement was once a radical departure from accepted art norms. Impressionism is now so firmly rooted in art history that, a century later, it would be hard to imagine an art museum that did not include such work. It serves as a reminder of the ever-shifting ground upon which our belief systems are founded.

Mainstream art is the product of a complex system of artists, art academies, patrons, and the prevailing mythologies and traditions of any given culture. This closed system supports its members by providing feedback and facilitating dialogue within that discipline. In other words, there is an inscribed subtext and protocol for accepting a work of art into any existing order. The criteria for acceptance into the contemporary art world, for instance, may seem rigid, rule-bound, contrived, and exclusive, yet the criteria are in place to meet objectives established within that specific discipline. Those constraints, of course, were exactly what Dubuffet targeted in his anti-cultural manifesto. Some artists participate in an established art world while others do not. Participants engage in a dialogue with others in that world, like curators, critics, and other artists. They produce work that is recognizable (and recognized) by others within that system and to the public. There are rules that govern it. For this reason, what makes artwork acceptable lies not in the work itself but in the willingness of an art world to accept it and its creator from among the millions of artworks presented to it. Not only is outsider art *outside* the continuum of art history, it is *outside* the parameters recognized by established art institutions, and *outside* the collective discourse of the mainstream art world.

There is a world of outsider art in that there is a community of those who advocate for it, but there is no outsider art world per se, for that would suggest that the artists within that world are engaged in critical dialogue with each other and with supporters such as collectors, gallerists, and academics. In reality, outsider artists are not connected to any art-related world; their work is personal, singular, and highly individualistic. If their work looks radical or avant-garde, that is just an illusion, for they are not challenging established conventions. And, if their eccentricity suggests "madness," such features may merely reflect their inability or unwillingness to articulate a narrative the viewer recognizes. Cardinal offers the powerful analogy of an archipelago of outsider art, with each artist inhabiting their own private domain. There is no way to compare the work of individual artists other than by their singular features, as the artists are free from the constraints of technical, aesthetic, and art-historical rules.[35] Their works "just are."[36]

While the history of outsider art is well documented, it remains difficult to offer an authoritative definition of the genre, particularly in Canada where its parameters have not been closely examined. Cardinal unintentionally opened the door to new interpretations of art brut, and today the labels are sometimes more controversial than the art itself. That may not be a bad thing; Dubuffet asked that we consider art in all its forms, and we have responded to that proposition with not one but many opinions. But these varying perspectives are just that—viewpoints that interpret and give meaning to the world of outsider art. Those who advocate for a particular definition are, often unwittingly, promoting their own agenda to advance a pet social cause or support their own art preferences. It is always important to ask who is formulating the questions about outsider art (or any art) and what purpose they serve.

The more fundamental question, perhaps, is not what outsider art *is*, but why it exists in the first place. It arose from Dubuffet's tirade against the stultifying strictures of art institutions. But, in some ways, the essence of Dubuffet's anti-cultural manifesto has been distorted. He challenged artists to resist the dictates of the art establishment but imposed his rebellious, nonconformist views about art onto individuals who had no voice and, in most cases, did not consider whether they were creating art. In that respect, he gave those particular artists a sense of agency and purpose they did not have; it would be wrong to assume that all artists working outside the norm are mavericks driven by a rebellious spirit. Outsider artists are not anti-heroes of the art world. They don't intentionally challenge art institutions. They simply don't fit into a historical discussion of art.*

It may be that there are many definitions of outsider art because a single definition does not suffice to cover the wide and varied styles inherent in the genre. In fact, this ambiguity could be fundamental to its definition. In the end, all characterizations of outsider art are merely interpretations made by ordinary people who hold diverse views about the world in general and the art world in particular. This is further complicated by the fact that the debate spans many countries, each adding their own aesthetic preferences, cultural mores, and social histories into the mix. The definitions spring from the intangibles of conjecture, ideology, and belief. Outsider art may defy definition because it is a construct that cannot be reduced to a single summary description about the nature of the art or the characteristics of the artists. It is an idea, a model for reflecting on the nature and spirit of art. To promote one overarching definition of outsider art that everyone agrees upon may be untenable. Even if we could reach a consensus, that definition will be reconsidered and reframed, as it should, by every subsequent generation.

* Yet.

1 Artist Caril Chasens, who lives up a bush road north of Hazelton, British Columbia.

2 Read together they provide a catalogue of common features found in outsider artworks: representation of inner psychic and mental states rather than the visual world; compulsive repetition; chance; automatism; microscopic or macroscopic views; rejection of perspective, scale, proportion, or naturalistic colouration; combining images and writing; bricolage (using found or unorthodox material); dense ornamentation; dense and hermetic; compulsively repeated patterns; metamorphic accumulations; appearance of instinct through wayward symmetry; configurations that occupy an equivocal ground between the figurative and the decorative; other configurations that hesitate between representation and enigmatic calligraphy or seek the perfect blending of image and word; and certain favourite subjects (e.g., self-portraits).

3 Miley Cyrus's artwork, for example, was described as "southern outsider art." *Artnet News*, December 3, 2014, https://news.artnet.com/art-world/jeffrey-deitch-compares-remarkable-miley-cyrus-to-mike-kelley-188274.

4 Dada, Pop art, and Surrealism are but a few examples of art movements that were radical statements against traditional art standards but have been accepted into modern culture and art history.

5 Arthur Danto, "The Artworld and Its Outsiders," in *Self-Taught Artists of the 20th Century* (San Francisco: Chronicle Books, 1998), 23.

6 Consider the work of two artists who used highly unconventional materials: contemporary British artist Chris Ofili, and one of Prinzhorn's psychiatric patients, Karl Brendel. Brendel created sculptures with pieces of chewed bread; they come with no introduction. Locked in a psychiatric institution, he simply had no access to traditional art materials to fuel his compulsion to create. He improvised. (See Tomas Roeske, in *Network Aging Research*, May 12, 2009, accessed January 11, 2020, https://www.nar.uni-heidelberg.de/en/service/int_roeske.html. Ofili's mixed-media painting *The Holy Virgin Mary* (1996) depicts a black Madonna with a ball of dried elephant dung in place of her bare breast. The painting is also supported on two balls of dung. The work is described as a hybrid of high and low, the sacred and the profane, calling into question the power of images and their ability to address fundamental questions of representation. To stand before his work is to engage in an exchange with the artist about the power of images in contemporary culture. Both Brendel and Ofili employ unconventional materials, but Brendel chose his medium by necessity, and Ofili chose his medium for its shock value.

7 Eugene W. Metcalf Jr., "From Domination to Desire," in Michael D. Hall and Eugene W. Metcalf Jr. (eds.), *The Artist Outsider: Creativity and the Boundaries of Culture* (Washington: Smithsonian Institution Press, 1994), 214.

8 Lucy Lippard, "Crossing into Uncommon Grounds," in Hall and Metcalf Jr., *The Artist Outsider*, 3–18.

9 This topic is explored in chapter "Hic Sunt Leones." See also Leah Sandals, "When Is First Nations Art Also Outsider Art?" *Canadian Art*, January 22, 2016, accessed January 5, 2020, https://canadianart.ca/features/when-is-first-nations-art-also-outsider-art/.

10 Linda Nochlin, *Women, Art and Power and Other Essays* (New York: Harper & Row, 1988), 158. Nochlin argues that artworks are not the creation of isolated individuals but result from cooperation between different artists, suppliers of materials, art distributors, critics, and audiences, who together make up the art world. See also Howard Becker, *Art Worlds* (Berkeley: University of California Press, 1982). He suggests that all works of art are collective actions.

11 John Maizels, *Raw Creation: Outsider Art and Beyond* (London: Phaidon Press, 1996), 63.

12 Maurice Berger, "Critical Fictions: Race, 'Outsiders' and the Construction of Art History," in *Self-Taught Artists of the 20th Century*, 28–37.

13 Consider, for example, self-taught Canadian painter Matthew Wong. At a young age, Wong was diagnosed with depression, Tourette's syndrome, and autism. Although he obtained an MFA in photography, Wong taught himself to paint and was described as "one of the most talented painters of his generation." Roberta Smith, "A Final Rhapsody in Blue from Matthew Wong," *New York Times*, December 24, 2019. What distinguishes him from other compulsive, self-taught artists was his earnest study of the modern masters and his fierce desire to be recognized in the contemporary art world.

14 See "On Language," Souls Grown Deep Foundation website, https://www.soulsgrowndeep.org/foundation/language#, which offers the example of Andrew Wyeth, who received only informal art training from his father, a professional illustrator.

15 It is interesting to observe how the American Folk Art Museum has framed its collection over time, particularly after incorporating outsider art. In 2011, self-taught artists were typically described as common folk whose authenticity portrayed culture in individual ways. See Charles Russell, *Groundwaters: A Century of Art by Self-Taught and Outsider Artists* (Munich: Prestel Verlag, 2011). In 2014, the Museum described the self-taught movement as one that is entrenched in a culture of self-actualization, a positive attribute that contributed to the growth of a new country. It reflects the personal vision of its maker and is synonymous with American thought, spirit, and achievements. See Stacy Hollander, "Breaking the Rules of Art: Genius and the Emergence of the Self-Taught Artist," in Stacy Hollander and Valérie Rousseau (eds.), *Self-Taught Genius: Treasures from the American Folk Art Museum* (New York: American Folk Art Museum, 2014), 17.

16 Art centres in both Canada and abroad foster inclusion by providing space and art materials

to mentally and learning challenged individuals. While academics acknowledge that the outsider art label may be appropriate for artists working in studios without guidance or instruction, some organizations do not apply the label. In Canada, some artists with disabilities distance themselves from the paternalistic label and exploitative practices of outsider art. Other artists adopt the outsider art label to promote a justice-oriented approach to art. See Eliza Chandler et al, "Insiders/Outsiders of Canadian Disability Arts," *Journal of Epidemiology and Psychiatric Sciences* 32 (2023): e47, https://doi.org/10.1017/S2045796023000598.
For further analysis of this issue, see Tom di Maria, "Shifting Focus, a Brief History of Disability Art in Global Contexts," in Lisa Slominski, *Non Conformers: A New History of Self-Taught Artists* (New Haven: Yale University Press, 2022), 251–83. See also Sue Steward's overview "Art & Disability," in *Raw Vision*, Autumn/Fall 2011, 20–27. And see Daniel Wojcik, *Outsider Art: Visionary Worlds and Trauma* (Jackson, MS: University Press of Mississippi, 2016), 262–63.

17 Roger Cardinal, "Outsider Art and the Autistic Creator," *Philosophical Transactions of the Royal Society of London. Series B, Biological Sciences* 364, no. 1522 (2009): 1459–66.

18 Cardinal, "Outsider Art and the Autistic Creator," 1459–66.

19 Cardinal.

20 Kenneth Ames, "Outside Outsider Art," in Hall and Metcalf Jr., *The Artist Outsider*, 253–72.

21 Michel Thevoz, "An Anti-Museum: The Collection de l'Art Brut in Lausanne," in Hall and Metcalf Jr., *The Artist Outsider*, 63–74.

22 Lucienne Peiry, *Art Brut: The Origins of Outsider Art* (Paris: Flammarion, 2001), 255.

23 Peiry, *Art Brut: The Origins*, 263.

24 John Fleming and Michael Rowan, *Canadian Folk Art to 1950* (Edmonton: University of Alberta Press, 2012).

25 James Elkins, "Naïfs, Faux-Naïfs, Faux-Faux Naïfs, Would-Be Faux-Naïfs: There Is No Such Thing as Outsider Art," in Felix Andrada, Eimear Martin, and Anthony Spira (eds.), *Inner Worlds Outside* (London: Whitechapel, 2006), 78; see also Roberta Smith, "Outside In," *New York Times*, January 26, 2007.

26 Tom di Maria, "Shifting Focus," 254.

27 Nicola Trezzi, "Are the Art World's 'Peripheries' Becoming the New Centers?" *Artnet News*, June 29, 2016, accessed November 27, 2019, https://news.artnet.com/art-world/how-museums-look-to-peripheries-527435.
I reference postmodernism in its broadest terms because its philosophical principles were evident in Dubuffet's era and it links this discussion back to his original thesis. The postmodernist perspective stems from a reaction to, and rejection of, hierarchical systems and ways of thinking, like the ranking of high and low art or, in this case, the status placed on mainstream art over the work of idiosyncratic creators. It denies all-encompassing theories that underlie the cultural narrative of knowledge and experience (such as the grand narratives of the Enlightenment, democracy, and Marxism), dismisses inflexible genre distinctions, and challenges the concepts of authenticity and originality. It prefers fragmentation, discontinuity, ambiguity, spontaneity, and a propensity to observe oneself observing. In other words, we should no longer assume that things are how they appear to be, particularly if we have been told that they are so. Hence, while the aesthetic and stylistic features of contemporary artists may be radically different from each other, they bring a common attitude and outlook to their work.

28 Thevoz, "An Anti-Museum," 63–74. See also Colin Rhodes, *Outsider Art: Spontaneous Alternatives* (London: Thames & Hudson, 2000).

29 Peiry, *Art Brut: The Origins*, 255.

30 Valerie Rousseau, "The Oblique Angle: When the Self-Taught Artist Shapes the World," in Hollander and Rousseau, *Self-Taught Genius*, 43–65.

31 Art for art's sake is a philosophy expressed in the late nineteenth century: art has its own value and should be judged separately from themes it puts forward, such as morality, religion, or politics. Visual and sensual qualities of art and design were prized over moral or narrative matters. See Tate Museum, "Aesthetic Movement," accessed February 10, 2020, https://www.tate.org.uk/art/art-terms/a/aesthetic-movement.

32 Becker, *Art Worlds*. And see Arthur Danto, "The Artworld and Its Outsiders," 18–27. Danto gave the notion of the "art world" a philosophical definition: the art world provides the theories of art which all members of the artworld tacitly assume in order for there to be objects considered as art.

33 Danto, "The Artworld and Its Outsiders," 27.

34 That is, rules referencing subject, technique, and style. The early Impressionists exhibited at their own "Salon des Refusés" when their work was rejected by the Paris Salon.

35 Roger Cardinal, *Outsider Art* (New York: -Praeger Publishers, 1972), 52.

36 Becker, *Art Worlds*, 260. Note, however, that their works become art when the viewer takes note of them.

SELLING MADNESS: THE SEARCH FOR CREATIVE AUTHENTICITY

An artist I know exhibited at an international outsider art fair. I asked if he'd had an opportunity to meet any other artists there, but he was quick to advise that he had not because "all outsider artists are either crazy or dead." I resisted the temptation to point out that since *he* wasn't dead, he was, ipso facto, crazy. It's true that outsider art was first considered in the context of psychiatric patients, but is it fair to say that all outsider artists suffer from a mental disorder?

The biography of the artist is central to the popular definition of outsider art. It's not just the artist's mental status and lack of training that's important; it's his disinterest in and ignorance of the academic side of art—that is, the trends, movements, and scholarly discourse of art history. Beyond that, there is an (impossible) expectation that the artist be untainted by popular culture. The stereotypical outsider artist, then, is one who struggles with mental health issues, has no art training, is removed from society by choice or circumstance, and is private about his or her obsessive art practice. These conditions stem from Dubuffet's search for the source of authentic creativity and, even though few outsider artists meet these stringent requirements, they remain core principles of the genre. But there is no "universal" outsider artist profile because they are simply people who create art according to their own invented rules. It's not a counter-culture movement except to those like Dubuffet who used the work of these artists to support his anti-art establishment agenda. Some artists are gregarious and engaging while others are introspective and reclusive. Many are familiar with the icons of Western art while others are disinterested in any art but their own. All are puzzled that a label would be attached to them or their artwork: insider, outsider, marginal, outlier—all are meaningless concepts to these prolific creators.

Creating art is an intense and all-consuming practice for outsider artists. While every artist is driven to create, it is an *imperative* for an outsider artist, who might create art all day, every day. Because the compulsion to create does not depend on having conventional materials at hand, the outsider artist never runs out of supplies: boards, scraps of paper, boxes, and walls will suffice. I have visited homes so filled with artwork that it is difficult to find a place to stand or sit down. When I ask these artists what motivates them to create, they describe it as something they *must* do. One artist compares it to having Tourette's syndrome, which can make it impossible to hold back a tic.[1] Cardinal calls it an "expressive impulse,"[2] the need to get on with something—a surrender of sorts. The creative urge sometimes arrives suddenly, much to the surprise of the artist. In some cases the artist responds to an inner imperative. In others, the artist answers to a higher power or a command from God,[3] or allows a spirit to guide them.[4]

It is often said that outsider artists are secretive about their work. Indeed, some bodies of work, like that of Chicago artist Henry Darger, are discovered only after the artist's death. While I've met extroverted artists who are keen to engage with an audience, most are private individuals who prefer to be left alone to create art. I met one Ontario artist, the **DODO BIRD**, who avoids publicity and declined to be interviewed for this book. I have been introduced to individuals whom others described as artists but who would not allow me to see their work. They might refer to their artwork as "just something I do" and of no interest to anyone else. When asked if they consider themselves to be artists, a long pause inevitably follows. The question is unexpected because they have never thought of themselves in that way. Professional artists are eager for recognition and success, which may take the form of representation by a well-respected gallery, regular exhibitions, positive reviews, frequent sales, and, in general, an ability to make a living as an artist. Outsider artists define success in different terms: having access to unlimited art supplies and infinite time to create. Their goal is not public recognition or the money that might flow from that status. I have explored this topic with many outsider artists and have consistently heard the same response: financial reward is irrelevant.

Although the power of divine madness has been bestowed on artists since classical times, it wasn't until the Romantic era that madness was equated with creativity. Thus, the myth of the mad genius was born. Insanity brought its own form of genius and granted permission to oppose both artistic and social norms.[5] Dubuffet's mission to illustrate his theory of pure, untainted creativity began with the work of patients in psychiatric institutions, where madness opened the door to special insight and creative genius. While such work formed the basis of Dubuffet's original collection, he argued against what he called the art of the insane. There was no such thing, he said, as "the art of the mad any more than there is an art of people with sick knees."[6] The artist's mental state was not a *defining* characteristic of art brut but, in Dubuffet's view, it was unquestionably linked to authenticity of expression. Dubuffet's ideology reflected the principles of modernism, wherein the desire to access true creativity and art for art's sake were fundamental principles of his anti-cultural manifesto.[7] Seventy years on, we are still searching for authentic experience, perhaps in an effort to resist the homogenizing effect of globalization. In fact, the quest for authenticity continues to be one of the fundamental principles of postmodernism: the insistence on authenticity in everything from travel experiences to fashion blogging. It is even suggested that outsider art itself is a metaphor for the modern touristic adventure in that it allows viewers to journey to the furthest reaches of human experience.[8] It is no surprise that interest in outsider art has surfaced as an antidote to the "self-propagating MFA-ocracy"[9] of the contemporary art world and the bewildering introduction of non-fungible tokens (NFTs) into the art market.

It would be convenient if outsider art were defined as the work of artists with recognized disorders and disabilities; in that case there would be nothing left to discuss beyond a medical diagnosis. But not all art created by such artists is outsider art, and not all outsider art is created by people with compromised mental health. It's not that simple. At times it seems that mental illness and outsider art are linked in order to support personal or political platforms. Nevertheless, the outsider art community is enamoured with the idea of the mad artistic genius, often defining the genre as art created by those with psychiatric disorders. It is a cliché to say that there is no genius without a touch of madness, and I question the soundness of that statement. I much prefer Québec artist Claude Bolduc's declaration that genius comes from the extravagance of God. Whether one accepts the veracity of the myth, it is widely accepted in the outsider art community.[10] The foundation of many collections is based on the work of artists with mental health challenges. Some private collectors seek only the work of schizophrenic artists.[11] It is also a topic of discussion at outsider art gatherings.[12] Madness sells.

It is a common belief that the outsider artist's impulse to create is precipitated by a traumatic event or life crisis, but I have not found that to be so. Conflating ideas about trauma, despair, and creativity may be used to advance stereotypes about suffering artists and their supposed pathologies.[13] There is no direct link between madness (mental illness) and creative genius. It is a stubborn myth, despite a dearth of scientific evidence that such a connection exists. While some research purports to confirm the connection,[14] other studies dismiss any significant relationship. One vocal critic describes the dramatic presentation of mad geniuses in the media as the insanity hoax, presenting information as fact, not theory.[15] She challenges the research as unscientific: anecdotal at best, and self-serving at worst.[16] Others have concluded that there is no specific personality type that correlates with outstanding creativity. Contrary to popular opinion, creative individuals do not necessarily exhibit erratic, childish, egotistic, eccentric, or rebellious behaviour. What is present in all creative people is the motivation to create.[17] In short, "creativity is not interwoven with suffering; tragedy and emotional pain are not prerequisites for artistic activity."[18]

In the end, the mad genius myth is far too alluring to give up; it is old and glamorous and shimmers with a pseudoscientific patina. The artist meme is that of a tragic figure: a misunderstood visionary who struggles to be recognized. Our empathy endures for the underdog and the anti-hero, particularly those alienated and uncommunicative figures of the art world. Perhaps such sentiments account for our interest in the outsider artist's pedigree as much as his artwork. Nevertheless, outsider art and madness are now so intertwined that an artist's mental state can override all other considerations. The ailing artist who regains his mental health is sometimes cast out of the outsider nest to fend for himself in the big wide world of mainstream art.[19] And, while it is generally accepted that outsider artists are self-taught, a mainstream artist who succumbs to a mental illness can sometimes claim status as an outsider artist.[20] Does this mean the artist forgets or abandons all his professional skills upon becoming unwell? Does he acquire special insights by reason only of that illness? It seems unlikely. It is more probable that the artist loses normal modes of organizing reality.[21]

It would be unfortunate if the artist's mental status were the defining characteristic of outsider art. There is no universal definition of madness *or* genius. Even if there were, how would we measure them? Mental illness is, to many, merely a social and cultural construct; I have encountered diverse perspectives in my own work and travel. The medical model of mental illness that prevails in the Western world is only one way to explain unconventional behaviour. An eccentric person with unusual ideas may be defined in different ways in different parts of the world. An artist living in a small village in Europe might be described as an "odd neighbour," yet on London's Harley Street would be called "plumb crazy."[22] Simply put, our personal mythologies can lead us to different conclusions about the source of eccentric beliefs. What one believes is a vision sent by God, another may interpret as a symptom of psychosis. Is it madness or transcendence? Trying to divide madness from reason may itself be a form of madness.[23] Madness means different things at different times and is always clouded by the moral assumptions of the viewer. When all is said and done, madness and genius can only be provisional definitions that will be subject to skeptical review by our successors.[24]

The persistence of the mad genius myth troubles me, and it certainly offends the outsider artists I know. It calls into question their artistic abilities, restricting the genre of outsider art to works by lunatics and prophets. It shifts attention from the art to the artist and demotes their art to a curiosity. First, to view the artist through a warped, generic lens reduces his creative output to a product of mental illness. Second, the myth becomes a truism. If it is so alluring, we may fail to question whether it is based in science or wishful thinking.[25] It implies that a life of psychological torture is the price one must pay for this rare gift. Sadly, it also

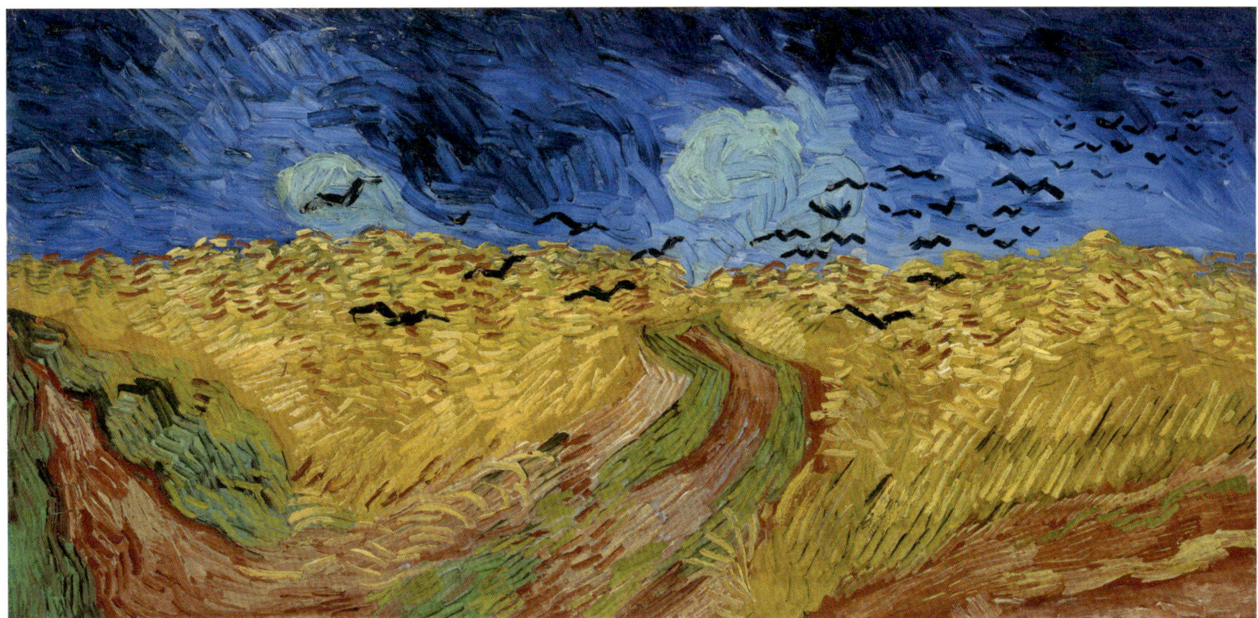

Vincent Van Gogh, *Wheatfield with Crows*, 1890
Oil on canvas
50.5 cm × 103 cm

trivializes the devastating consequences of deteriorating mental health and glamorizes the profound truths it claims to reveal. Consider Van Gogh, the poster boy for mad genius.[26] He is remembered as the prolific artist who produced eccentric paintings, cut off his own ear, and ultimately committed suicide. What we fail to acknowledge are his poverty, epilepsy, loneliness, artistic failure, absinthe poisoning, and suspected diagnosis of tertiary syphilis with symptoms that mimic those of bipolar disorder. His life circumstances alone would surely lead to despair. Third (and equally concerning), it may be tempting to praise whatever the artist produces, for surely it is the work of a genius. The uncomfortable truth is that very little work produced by psychiatric patients is memorable.[27] The work is meaningful to the artist, of course, but it does not always reveal a great artistic talent.[28] Finally, what we believe to be true predicts our reading of a situation; knowing that an artist struggles with mental health issues can greatly influence our response to a work of art.

Consider the image of Van Gogh's *Wheatfield with Crows* (1890). If the painting is presented without supporting text, we observe crows flying over a wheat field, divided by a path. The sky is turbulent; a storm is brewing. Perhaps the crows are heading to shelter in their roost. But what if it is subsequently presented with this descriptive caption: "This is the last picture that Van Gogh painted before he killed himself."[29] The work is seen in a different light: the artist as a profoundly disturbed man contemplating suicide. It portends tragedy.

So what to make of Dubuffet's belief in the freedom that madness brings? Freedom suggests that the artist is relieved of the burden of respecting aesthetic standards, but, since the artist never knew those rules in the first place, it is more likely that his artwork is the projection of an experience that can't be expressed any other way. Language breaks down; words lose their meaning. Nova Scotia artist JOHN DEVLIN describes his first experience with mental illness as a frightening and baffling experience: the world "becomes a puzzling body of signs, bewildering signs without a code or key."[30] Language could not be used to communicate what he wanted to say, so he was forced to describe his inner state with drawings and diagrams.[31] In many cases, creating art is the only way for a patient to articulate

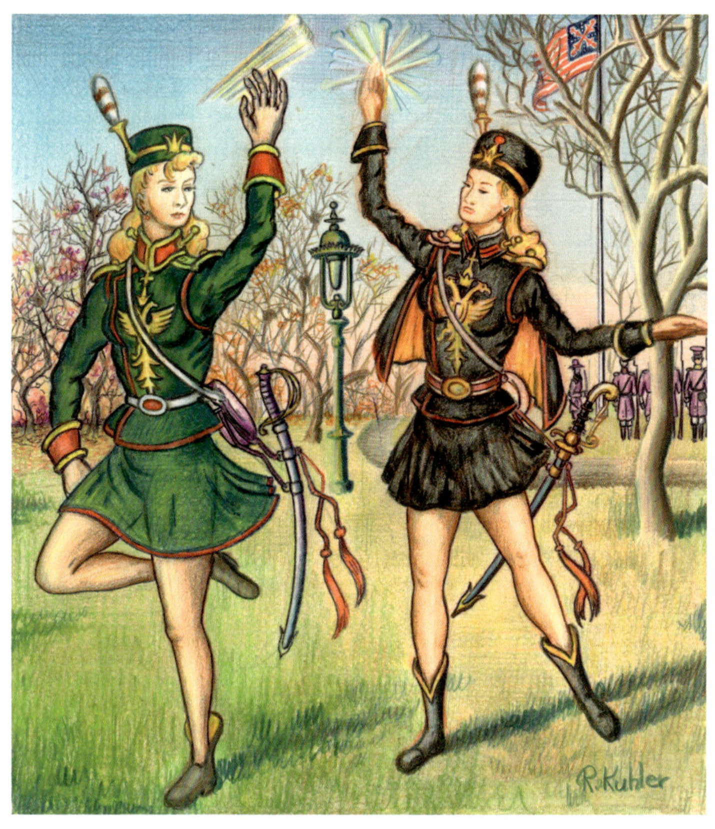

Renaldo Kuhler, *Parade Welcoming Home the Grand Army of the Confederacíon*, 1960
Coloured pencil on sketch paper
27.3 × 24 cm

what he needs to express of his private world. The viewer's challenge is to understand psychosis as a human experience with its own language.[32] It is not easy to decipher a cryptic message from a mute messenger. This enigma, for many, is the lure of outsider art. It is not only the aesthetic qualities of the work that are engaging—it is the intensity of the artist's practice and the embedded, obscure messages within.

Some critics suggest that the unique iconographies of outsider artists are a strategy to conceal meaning.[33] That view, however, suggests that the artist formed an intention to mislead prospective viewers. Yet many artists never intend for their work to be seen. It is equally likely that their choice of metaphor is simply one that we do not understand. Attributing meaning to these artists' creations is only an act of conjecture. If the artist is not able or inclined to speak about her work, members of the broader art community may offer interpretation. This undoubtedly adds to the mystery (and falsehoods) surrounding outsider art. Unlike other art genres, outsider art does not necessarily invite interpretation, and viewers are left to ponder the meaning of another's interior reality.

An outsider artist's entire life's work can be the creation of a private, fantasy world. The work may provide a means of narrating their own story or a way to understand, reinterpret, or reinvent it. It is an intensely personal practice. I think of American artist Renaldo Kuhler (1931–2013), whom I met some years ago. A scientific illustrator at the North Carolina Museum of Natural History, Kuhler worked secretly most of his adult life to create the imaginary world of Rocaterrania. He described this fantasy nation through meticulous texts and paintings that detailed the lives of emperors, czars, presidents, dictators, and civilians. He eventually disclosed this remarkable work to a trusted friend.[34] In talking with Kuhler, I learned that I misinterpreted his opus as a fantastic tale. Rather, Kuhler explained that it was his way of coming to terms with his troubled life. It was not a utopia, a fairyland, or a dream world, but the story of his life.[35] Always a misfit, he felt ostracized and misunderstood. He was a failure in the eyes of his father. His complex fantasy world had elements that were easily understood: people who did not treat him well in real life were cast as citizens of Rocaterrania who suffered abominable misfortunes; those who had been kind to him in life were rewarded in his private dominion. It was, undoubtedly, a cathartic exercise. When I asked Kuhler if he was a featured character in Rocaterrania, he provided a telling response. He said, "I *am* Rocaterrania." I then understood the magnitude and depth of his art practice—it was not done for entertainment but was, in a sense, his entire identity. I recall how Nova Scotia artist John Devlin described his hypothetical utopian city to me: "Each of us is a whole universe, each different. I am a radical solipsist: masturbation creates the art which brings Nova Cantabrigiensis and its inhabitants into being. Like God creating the world."[36]

I've spoken often to Devlin about his vision for a new university, his experience with mental illness, and his forty-year quest to discover the source of his acute aesthetic response to King's Chapel in Cambridge. In explaining his experience, he referred to Clive Bell, an art critic associated with the Bloomsbury Group, who argued there is a particular kind of aesthetic emotion provoked by some visual art. He called it significant form. The combination of shapes, forms, and colours stirs an emotion more profound and sublime than could ever be described with words. Standing before something important and meaningful carries the viewer "out of life into ecstasy."[37] With less inspiring art, a viewer may remember only the subject matter portrayed. It does not take him to a new world of aesthetic experience; rather, he turns a sharp corner and comes straight home to the world of human interests. Old material is stirred; nothing new is added to the viewer's life.[38] While significant form may be a purely subjective hypothesis, Devlin believes it to be an objective truth. One day he will uncover its mystery.

Devlin didn't set out to be an artist; he studied architecture and finance in Nova Scotia before heading to the University of Cambridge to read theology. An incident there in 1979 changed his life forever. He had an epiphany at King's Chapel that he is still trying to comprehend; the magnificent courtyard, unique architecture, and voices of the choir engulfed him in a singular moment of rapture. Unfortunately, that revelation coincided with a mental breakdown and he was forced to return home to Nova Scotia. Devlin recalls being

John Devlin, *Cambridge*, 1988
Mixed media on paper
21.6 × 28 cm

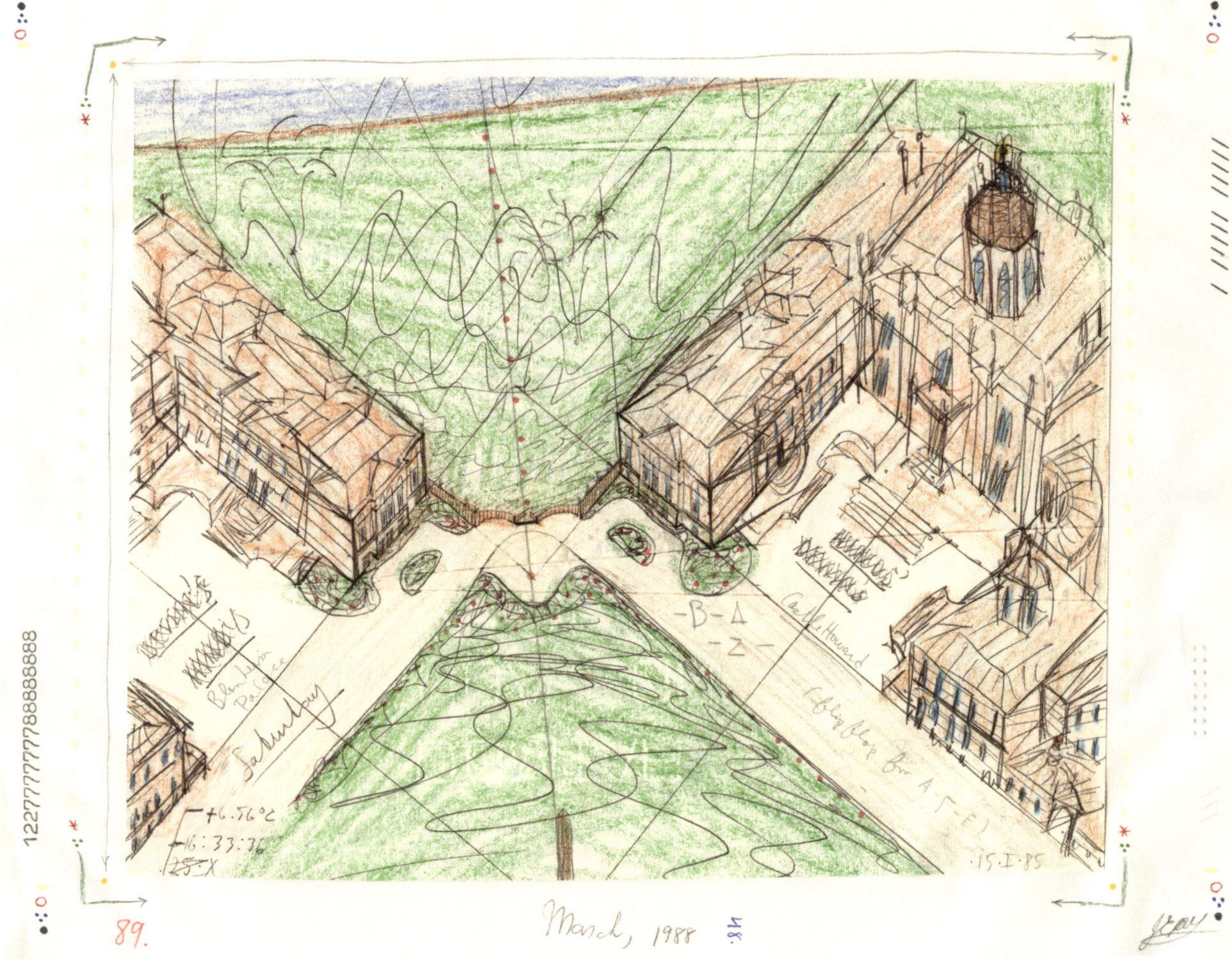

overwhelmed by bossy voices, paranoia, and hallucinations in the early stages of his illness. He was prescribed Tegretol two harrowing years later, which he credits for both his recovery and his outpouring of creativity. It's a knife's edge, he says, between being unwell (when he produced nothing of interest) and being overmedicated (when he produced nothing at all). Artists like Nick Blinko (1961–) risk "total psychological exposure" in order to make art.[39] Although Blinko's frenetic drawings of miniscule, interconnected forms bring no relief from tormented delusions, his compulsion to make pictures is stronger than his need for the mental stability brought by creativity-quashing therapeutic drugs. In Devlin's case, he found his true vocation as an artist when he took up his younger sister's collection of coloured pencils and crayons and started on his Nova Cantabrigiensis project. He drew continuously for four years,[40] hoping to make sense of his intense experience at King's Chapel.

Devlin's university is modelled on Cambridge but situated in the Minas Basin of Nova Scotia where he lived. Nova Cantabrigiensis was a utopia of sorts, an idyllic campus without the stress of academics or the expectations of old-school ethos. In this visionary world of his own construction, he could wander the campus at will, dog at his side, friends just around the corner. Devlin set out to discover the enigma of King's Chapel. The key, he believed, lay in the mathematical ratios employed in the building's design. There is a certain truth in that reasoning; the beauty of mathematics *is* expressed in special ratios. Phi (the golden ratio), for instance, describes nature's building blocks and universal patterns. Nature relies on this innate ratio to maintain balance, and the art world has implemented the principle of divine proportion for centuries. As Einstein said, "Pure mathematics is, in its way, the poetry of logical ideas."[41]

Devlin theorized there is a constant ratio for ideal design:

> I was on a Faustian quest for arcane knowledge that would explain the magical ambience of Cambridge. I thought that if I could capture that ambiance as a mathematical formula, then I wouldn't have to go to England. I thought I could think my way out of mental illness, back to the happy times in Cambridge before things began to fall apart on me.[42]

The logic and rationality of numbers could, perhaps, impose order on a chaotic mental landscape and restore balance to his life. He was trapped in a psychotic universe where normal laws did not apply:

> It was like going through a looking glass, or down a rabbit hole. Kepler, Newton, Darwin, et al. were abandoned there. Other laws governed the psychotic world, and it was terrifying. Like those who expose themselves to LSD, my life was changed forever. I was given a twisted sort of illumination, but the price of wisdom was damnation. Like Adam and Eve, or Jonathan in the Old Testament who ate the forbidden honey, I saw with new eyes: enlightened, frightened.
>
> I have ever since been trying to fathom the laws which govern and explain the psychotic universe which cut me off so completely from my former life. I had wisdom, but I spoke in riddles. People were mysteries to me, and I found language no longer communicated what I wished. Thus thwarted, I was forced to find other ways of communication, and turned to sketches and diagrams to describe my inner state.[43]

Nova Cantabrigiensis was about structure and the search for beauty through numbers, ratios, and proportions. Devlin used shorthand notations to record his impressions for details like the measurements of a building, the number of windows, and so on. The drawings are composed of layers of paper, glued together on the edges. He wrote numbers on the back page and inserted slips of paper with numeric sequences between the layers of his drawings, hoping to "aesthetify" each piece with the *right* numbers, which had magical powers. Every picture contained a secret, like a private message set adrift in the universe. The message might be symbols in the ratio of the interior of King's Chapel measured in feet (40:80:289), the dimensions of the chapel that Henry VI stipulated in this will in the fifteenth century (40:90:288), the ratio of vowels to consonants in the name Jesus Christ (3:8), or some other formula that he latched onto in his desire to find something unshakable to believe in.

0000000000000000000000000000000000000000000000000000000000555555555555555555555555
5555555555555555555555555555555555555555555555555555555222222222222222222222222
22222222222222222222222222222222222222222222222222222222222222222222222222222222
22222222222222222222233333333333333333333333333333333333333333333333333333333333
33333333333333333333333333333333333333333333333333333333333333333333333333333333
33333333333333333333333333333333333333333333333333333333333333333333333333333333
33333333333333333333333333333333333333333333333333333333333333333333333333333333
33333333333333333333333333333333333333333333333333333333333333333333333333333333
3333333333333333333333333
77777777777777777777777777777777777777777777777777777777777777777777777777777777
77777777777777777777777999999999999999999999999999999999999999999999999999999999
999999999999999999999999999999999999999999999999999999999999

Devlin's quest to quantify the magic of Cambridge in order to express a universal truth was, he admits, a risky and dangerous business. He held onto his Catholic faith during this phase to keep him grounded in the event his search came to naught and he was left with nothing but a vacuum, a hoax, a falsehood. He is no longer working on the Nova Cantabrigiensis project and, in hindsight, realizes it was a fiction—something of himself that he projected onto the idealized campus. I imagine his room reverberates with the thousands of numbers he recited and recorded on the backs of his drawings. He still thinks of the enduring, numinous force of King's Chapel and continues to explore the power of ratios in his new work.

Inspired by the splendor of Klimt's *Portrait of Adele Bloch-Bauer I* (1907), which he saw in 2014, Devlin is now working with gold and silver leaf, patiently laying down square upon square on paper. He describes a life of quiet solitude. I picture him toiling at his grandmother's desk, illuminating his world like a medieval monk bent over a manuscript. I know I am interrupting a deep meditation when I call—disrupting the continuity of his thoughts and taking him away from the pursuit of that singular aesthetic truth. More recently, he has been exploring collage, combining homoerotic images and drawings with silver and gold leaf. Some find the images offensive and others are dismissive of his efforts. What they don't understand, he says, is that the subject matter has changed, but his search for significant ratios continues. It permeates all his work, like *Limen Eternum*, pictured here. The verso of the work shows Devlin's calculations of the ratios he gleaned

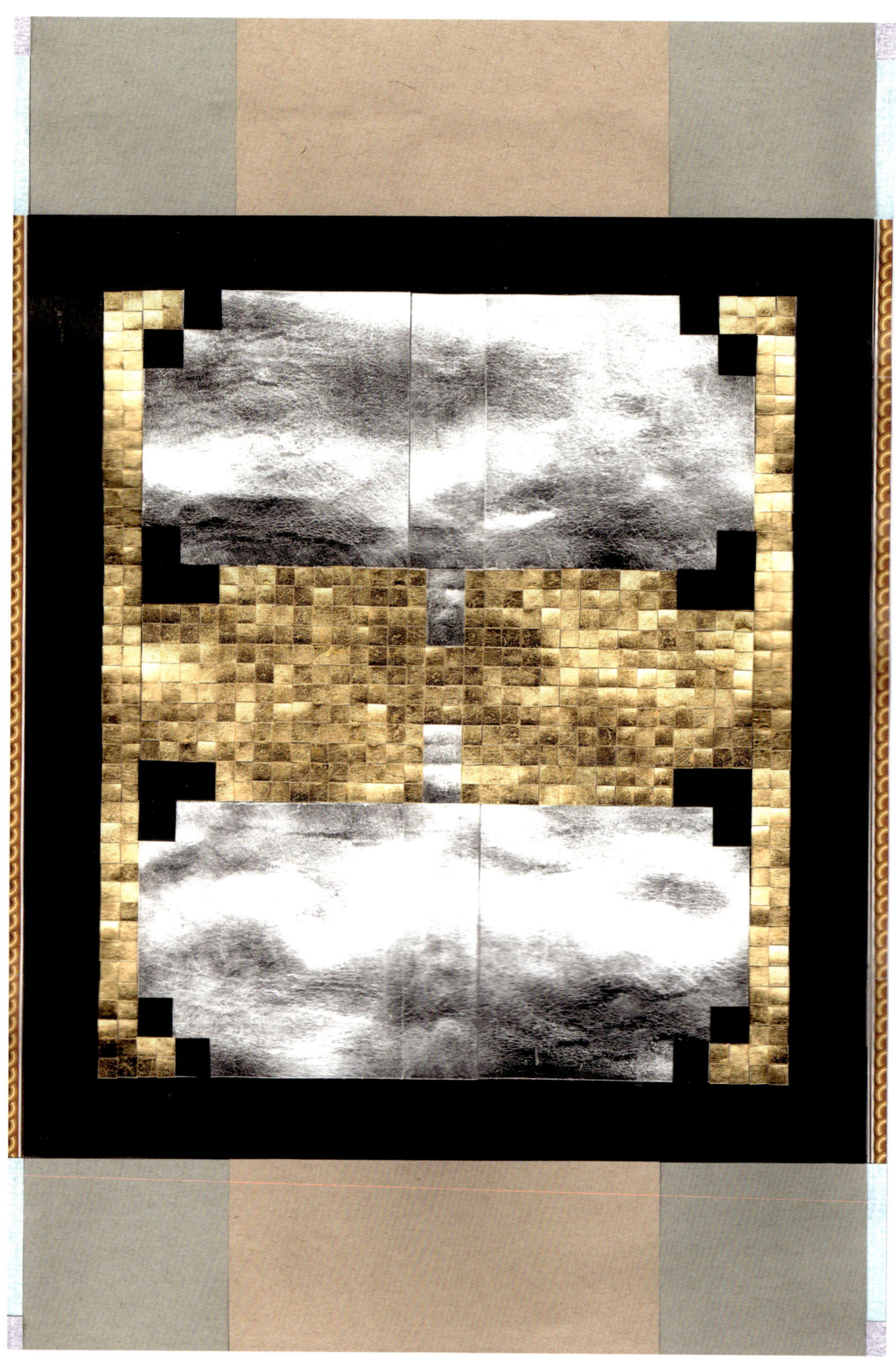

John Devlin, *Limen Eternum* (*recto*), 2020
Collage with gold leaf
and silver leaf on paper
43.18 × 29.21 cm

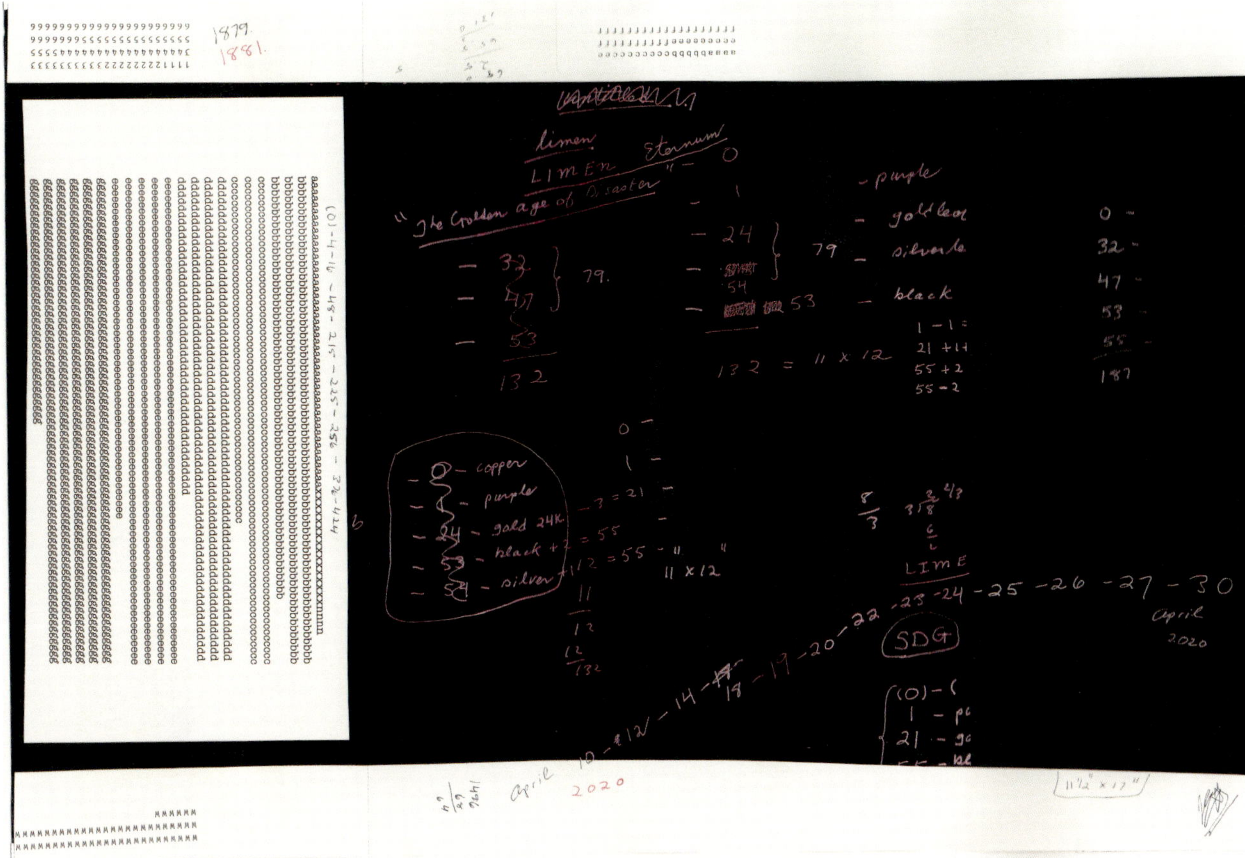

John Devlin, *Limen Eternum (verso)*, 2020
Collage with gold leaf and silver leaf on paper
29.21 × 43.18 cm

from its assembly. One day he hopes those numbers will explain the mystery of King's Chapel and illuminate the exquisite harmony of Nova Cantabrigiensis.

Devlin first heard of outsider art when his drawings were exhibited at the Technical University of Nova Scotia School of Architecture in 1988. He would prefer that his art not be considered in the academic realm and doesn't really understand the label that has been applied to it. He admits that his new work doesn't attract the attention of his opus, Nova Cantabrigiensis. He is philosophical about the situation and believes there is a natural delay between the time he creates art and its acceptance into the art world. Someday, he says, the work will garner its due respect.

I ponder the irony of the situation. Devlin discovered that his true calling was not as an architect, a financier, or a priest, but as an artist. His Nova Cantabrigiensis project defined his status as an outsider artist and he enjoyed the notoriety that followed. He now sees himself developing as an artist—exploring fresh ideas, experimenting with new techniques, and learning new skills. But by regaining his mental equilibrium he seems to have lost his status as an outsider artist. His obsessive calculations have diminished, along with the backstory that made him a novelty in the world of outsider art. His psyche has been plundered and the world isn't keen on his newfound confidence, it seems, nor on the direction he is heading. His fall from grace is rather an affront to Devlin's spirit, surviving years of mental hell only to be lauded as a mad artist. It is disappointing but doesn't much matter to him; his labour brings him great joy. Nevertheless, it raises a disturbing issue in the context of

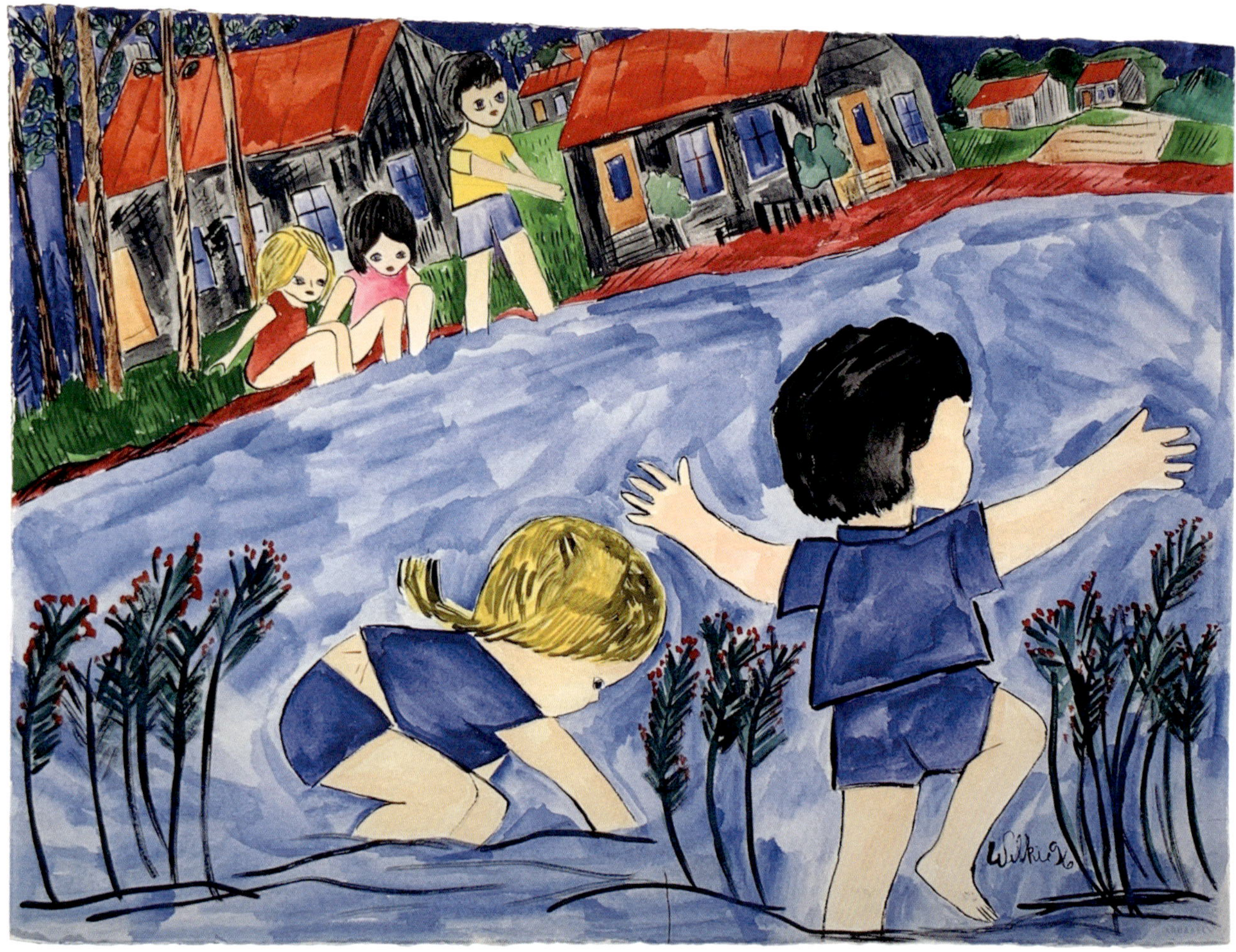

Roland Wilkie,
The River War, 1996
Watercolour and India ink
on Arches paper
57 × 76 cm

outsider art—that is, the peculiarity of an artist's thought process as a measure of his acceptance. Devlin is still preoccupied with the magic of numbers and ratios, but he keeps those thoughts to himself.

The lure of a private universe is testament to the artist's need to narrate his own story or, perhaps, to understand, control, reinterpret, or reinvent it.* Kuhler created Rocaterrania to reconcile events in his life. Devlin invented Nova Cantabrigiensis to bring his utopian university back to Canada where he was forced to retreat—a phenomenological approach to art, as it were. It affords an opportunity for the artist to examine and reframe life events. I call it "artobiography."

ROLAND WILKIE spent a significant part of his life as a patient at a psychiatric hospital in Québec City. He was diagnosed with schizophrenia but refused medication, choosing to deal with the illness on his own terms. Wilkie's fantasy world took form when he was encouraged to draw whatever preoccupied him, triggering a prolific outpouring of drawings and paintings of his complex world of children and imaginary beings. There Wilkie engaged in war with his personal demons: the *Gochaï*, star-shaped extraterrestrial beings who could take human form; and Êl., a vengeful Persian female entity who appeared to him as a flame. While doctors believed Wilkie hospitalized himself in the 1990s to protect children from harm, Wilkie claimed he was there to understand and protect himself as well as children.[44]

*Isn't that also the intent of those who participate in online virtual worlds?

He described his life prior to being hospitalized: "My life was filled with violence. It is still this way, but less so. My life is a perpetual war."[45] Êl. was a ruthless foe: she accused Wilkie of killing his younger sister with sounds he emitted from his head. (In fact, his sister died of complications from the mumps.) Êl. would inflict pain on his fingers if he crossed her. It must have been a hellish existence for Wilkie.

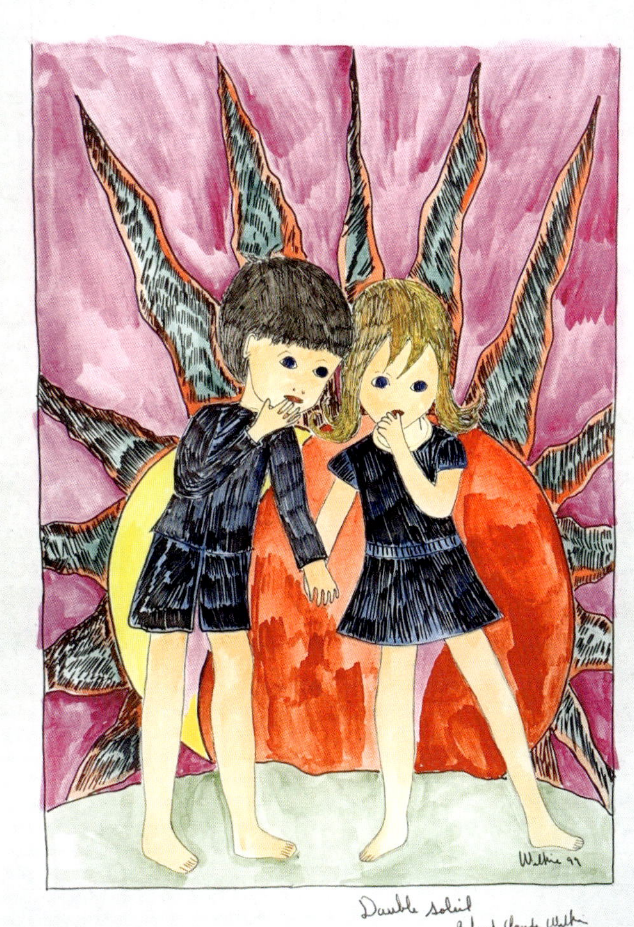

Roland Wilkie, *Twin Sun*, 1999
Watercolour and India ink on paper
53 × 38 cm

Wilkie's paintings are compelling and disturbing. His choice of bright watercolours and India ink belies the troubling details that close examination reveal. I was struck by their resemblance to the work of Chicago artist Henry Darger. Both artists feature children in their paintings, created by tracing figures in books and magazines. While Wilkie's children bear the physical scars of an unspeakable prior existence, Darger recounts stories of the Vivian Girls, a family of sexually ambiguous, prepubescent girls. These seven sisters, who live in the Christian land of Abbieannia, revolt against evil beings who enslave children and, in doing so, suffer unimaginable abuse—strangulation, torture, hanging. Learning about Darger's own childhood sheds light on the horrors inflicted on the Vivian girls and the enslaved children. He grew up in one of the most sordid neighbourhoods of Chicago, where he was exposed to dysfunctional behaviour, prostitution, and sexual abuse. His family lived in wretched poverty. When he was four years old, Darger's mother died giving birth to his sister. His ailing father was unable to care for him, and young Darger was sent to a Catholic boys' home, then to orphanages, including the Illinois Asylum for Feeble-Minded Children (which also housed "incorrigible" adults).[46] Darger ran away from there when he was seventeen, walked two hundred miles back to Chicago, and found work in a hospital where he worked as a janitor for the rest of his life.

Aspects of Wilkie's biography echo Darger's, particularly Wilkie's preoccupation with the death of his younger sister. He claimed to have had little contact with his younger sister, as he spent the first three years of his life in a hospital, strapped to a pediatric harness.[47] He grew up in foster homes in Montréal and described a childhood of physical and sexual abuse, violence, prostitution, and drugs—which led to various encounters with the law. He claimed he didn't attend school, but other evidence suggests his schooling ended at sixth grade due to illness. He later had six children of his own, three of whom were adopted out. Although Wilkie was born into a Catholic family, he was intrigued with Judaism, and wove the two ideologies together to create his own complex mythology. His preferred attire was a skullcap and sidelocks, along with clothing he designed himself—a military-style uniform bearing a menorah crest and Hebrew characters.

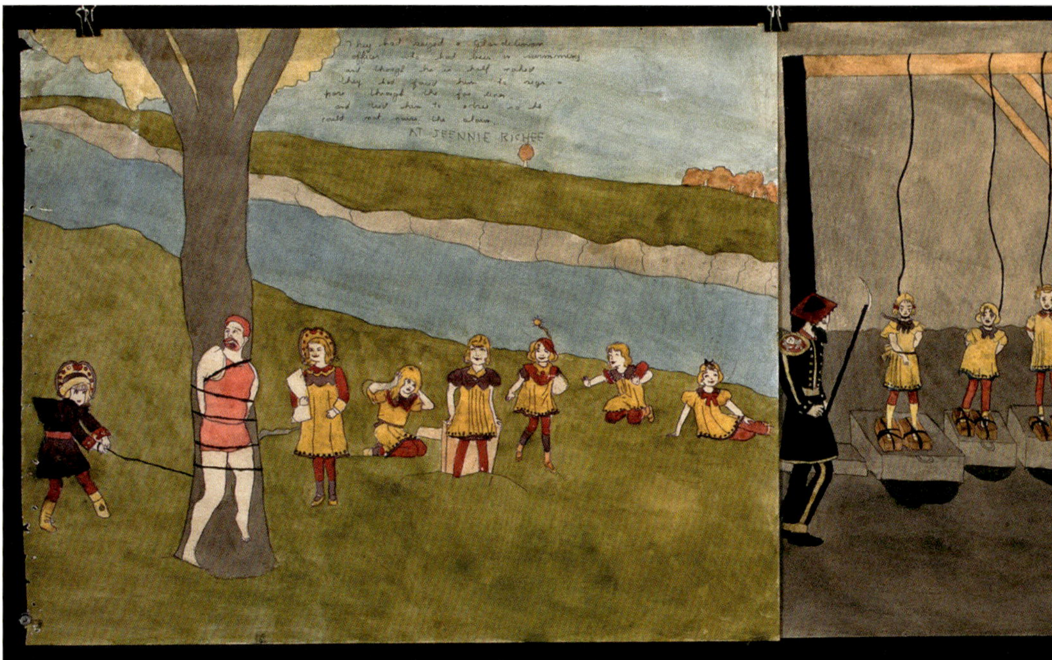

Henry Darger, *1-Seize Glandelinian Officer; 2-Glandelinians Were About To Hang; 3-They Attempt To Hide In Fiddle Case*, n.d.
Watercolour and pencil on paper
48.3 × 178 cm

Wilkie said he tried, but failed, to control his thoughts about sexuality in his drawings. And, like Darger, he presents as both protector and assailant of children. In one painting, for example, Wilkie sits beside a young girl, wearing a cape. His presence posed no danger, he explained, because she wears a "median belt" that protects her from harm. In another, Wilkie, wearing full military gear, guards two nude girls. He is poised to protect them with his rifle. His painting *The River War* is a masterpiece. A river divides groups of children—those in blue uniforms are abused youngsters from "the institute," where they have been placed under the benevolent care of Miss Ratched[48] for their own protection. The scars on the young girl's back are evidence of the life she escaped. The children on the opposite side of the river are from the "normal" world, where children wear brightly colored clothes and live in charming houses. It's not just a river that separates the children; they are worlds apart, divided by past experiences and the sad reality of their present situation. The painting is a testament to Wilkie's own lived experience: a childhood of abuse and a life stigmatized by mental illness. He is forever in exile, ostracized on the other side of the river.

In *Twin Sun*, twin children hold hands in front of a double sun. Joined for security, they study what lies before them. They don't know what to expect. Childhood, for Wilkie, was uncertain and unpredictable.

In some of Wilkie's paintings the children are crying, but there are few details to explain their sorrow. They are simply there, forlorn and motherless. One work, titled *I'm Crying*, is a portrait of a weeping child, tears streaming from his eyes. A fence bars his entry to a house in the background, with beautiful flowers growing along a path to the front door. In another, a crying child kneels before a wolf at a pond. Its title, *The Story of My Youth*, is likely a reference to the artist's own feral childhood, isolated from the warmth and security of human contact. Wilkie explained that these paintings alluded to the abuse he suffered as a child. "Trust [lack of] and hatred have been the cornerstones of my life. At

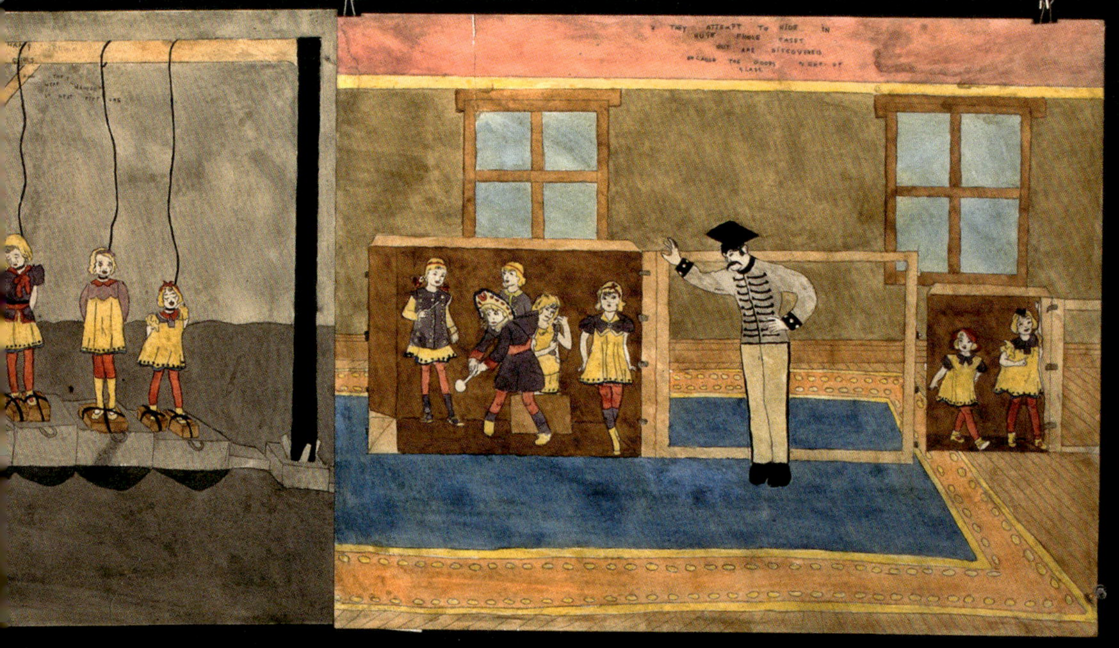

the age of eight, I knew as much about sex as a fifty-year-old. Some people believe that I'm antisocial because of what I experienced as a child. I don't buy that."[49]

It is important to put art into context; by that I mean the environment in which the work of art was created. This, of course, includes the artist's biography. Particularly with outsider art, where the artist's intention may not be readily apparent, his or her biography can bring meaning to the work.[50]

Wilkie's mental illness prevented him from articulating the literal and metaphorical meaning of his paintings, and Darger, whose work was revealed posthumously, never had the opportunity to do so. When an outsider artist is not willing or able to discuss the images they create, it is crucial to remember that their work springs from a complicated and unknowable place. One of Darger's biographers, offended by speculative accusations that Darger's images proved him to be a pedophile, sadist, or serial killer, examined the cultural environment and personal circumstances of Darger's life, including his novels, autobiography, and journals. He concluded that Darger was probably gay, and that his art was an outlet for expressing his complex personal situation.[51] The author also reviewed an extensive report from a government investigation into child abuse at the institution where Darger was incarcerated as a child. The report detailed the caregivers' acts of physical abuse against disobedient children, including beating and choking. The author concluded there was nothing to support the suggestion that Darger was a degenerate pedophile. What he believed was, in fact, the opposite. Young Darger was the victim of predators. His stories were not his own fantasies of torturing and murdering children, but more likely a confession of what happened to him and other children at the institution.[52] That is to say, his artwork may have been a testament to his own trauma and his manner of coming to terms with an abusive childhood. As one curator observed, it is "natural for contemporary audiences to regard and interpret art like this through the political or other critical lenses of today, but we're trying to shed light on the cultural and social contexts

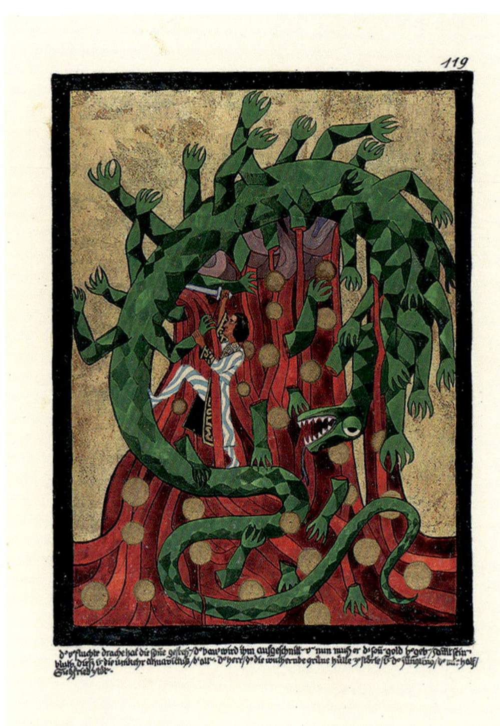

Carl Jung, *The Red Book*,
c. 1914–30
Ink and paint on paper
22 × 29 cm

in which Darger lived and made his art."[53] There may be, at some level, sexualization of his subjects, but he is a storyteller. "It's the stuff of fairy tales."[54] If we "let Darger be Darger, inquisitively and not so judgmentally,"[55] it may open the door to understanding this enigmatic artist's work. In the same vein, if we "allow Wilkie to be Wilkie" and approach his work from a neutral place, what do his paintings reveal? His life was one long and painful war. Darger's trauma was, perhaps, expressed through the trials of the Vivian girls, while Wilkie's was through his fantastic and delusional world of forsaken children. It is the same story with different narratives.

While I know only a few outsider artists who explore their life in fictional worlds, every artist I've met, whether or not they reference mental health issues, describes their work as a therapeutic exercise—a personal, non-directed, and reflective activity. It is the *creation* of the artwork that provides the therapy, not its interpretation, as in art therapy. Artists have described to me how creative periods can alleviate symptoms of anxiety or curb the need for medication. A professional artist I know says it keeps her grounded and centred, like meditation. The creative ventures of *all* artists, it seems, leads to the euphoria of being "in the zone"—a feeling of great fulfillment and satisfaction.[56] It is the process of creation, as opposed to the outcome, that provides the meaningful experience.[57] Perhaps it is simply a method for self-discovery.[58]

Carl Jung had much to say about art as therapy. In an illuminated folio manuscript called *Liber Novus: The Red Book*, Jung documented his private imaginative experiences over a period of fifteen years.[59] Every day he would deliberately evoke a fantasy, then enter into it as a drama to discover what took place when he turned off his conscious mind. It was, in essence, dramatized thinking in pictorial form.[60] Jung described this liminal place of self-induced visions as one of creative abundance and potential ruin, the same places travelled by lunatics and great artists. He called them "cryptograms of the self."[61] He described his pursuit of inner images as the most important time of his life, from which everything else derived. He acknowledged that to the uninformed observer, the result would look like madness. *The Red Book* was sometimes present in Jung's office, but only a few trusted friends were permitted to read it. Upon his death, in 1961, Jung's heirs secured it in a vault to protect his privacy and refused access to it by scholars and others.[62] It was significant, then, that *The Red Book* was displayed in the Central Pavilion at the 2013 Venice Biennale. The catalogue describes it not as a work of art, but as a collection of primordial images capable of combining a personal destiny with a collective one. By posing a question remarkably similar to Dubuffet's search for pure, unadulterated art, viewers were prompted to consider how to rediscover the intensity of those images today.[63] They were invited to draw a parallel between the two; that is, the manner in which both Jung and outsider artists have given form to—or perhaps illustrated—their inner worlds. I am always struck by the similarity between Jung's images and those of outsider artists. In both cases, the artwork is created for self-consideration, not public consumption. They are soliloquies: monologues of unspoken reflections. The creations are not *about* art or *about* the human condition. They are *about* the artist's personal experience.[64]

The fundamental difference between outsider art and mainstream art is captured in this concept. Mainstream artists hope to draw me into a dialogue; outsider artists do not. Rather, I feel that I am witness to a private and personal event.[65]

Ontario artist KARL GOERTZEN painted his way through a difficult life. He was candid about his mental health issues and his use of art as a form of self-directed therapy. His widow, Jennifer, advised that he would have wanted me to shout his story from the rooftops.

I know Goertzen only through others, for he died at an early age. He suffered from delusions and crippling suicidal thoughts from the age of sixteen, and was eventually diagnosed with schizo-affective disorder, which meant he lived with symptoms of psychosis and extreme depression. Jennifer described him as a quiet, unconditionally kind man with bright eyes. They knew each other in high school in Ottawa, and reconnected later in life when she attended his art exhibition in 2008. It was only when Goertzen had to leave work after experiencing a mental breakdown that he took one art class and began painting in earnest. She described her shock at seeing his huge canvases on display; at first glance they appeared "normal," but something just wasn't right. Her reaction echoed the words of Prinzhorn, who said the work of his patients embodied a *Fremdheitsgefühl* (a sense of strangeness).[66] An inexplicable *X* in the corner of one painting, a man with horns growing from his head in another, and figures with blank eyes all made the work seem a bit peculiar. Jennifer found it to be an overwhelming but moving experience. She learned that Goertzen had become socially isolated, spending his days painting in his apartment. "My art is an outlet for my illness—the daily journal I couldn't keep no matter how many psychiatrists told me to. My paintings are my therapy. My real journal. My world. This time my thoughts spelled out on the canvas, literally."[67] Jennifer bought the red painting, pictured here, and married the artist.

Many of Goertzen's symptoms were well-controlled, but obsessive suicidal thoughts remained a constant throughout his life. He wrote openly and eloquently about his illness and his work:

> People rely on diagnostic proof of disease. If you have cancer it can be pointed out on a scan or shown in laboratory results. Unfortunately you can't take a scan of my brain and point out the disease. But I can tell you about being in mania, in psychosis, not being able to sleep, up for days on end. Getting up at 4:00 a.m. to run for three hours in order to burn off some of the excess energy brought on by heightened states. I can tell you about being hospitalized and what it's like at the psych wards of the General and the Queensway Carleton. I can tell you about electroconvulsive therapy and the schizophrenic ward at the Royal Ottawa. I can tell you about being terrified of myself. I can tell you about attempting suicide.
>
> [. . .]
>
> My paintings provide the viewer a window to the landscape of my mental illness, moving between the sometimes hopeful to the absolutely terrifying and intensely crushing ideas of suicide. My works are vivid in colour to express the powerful strength of the delusions and suicidal ideation. Painting is also the one outlet where I feel in control of

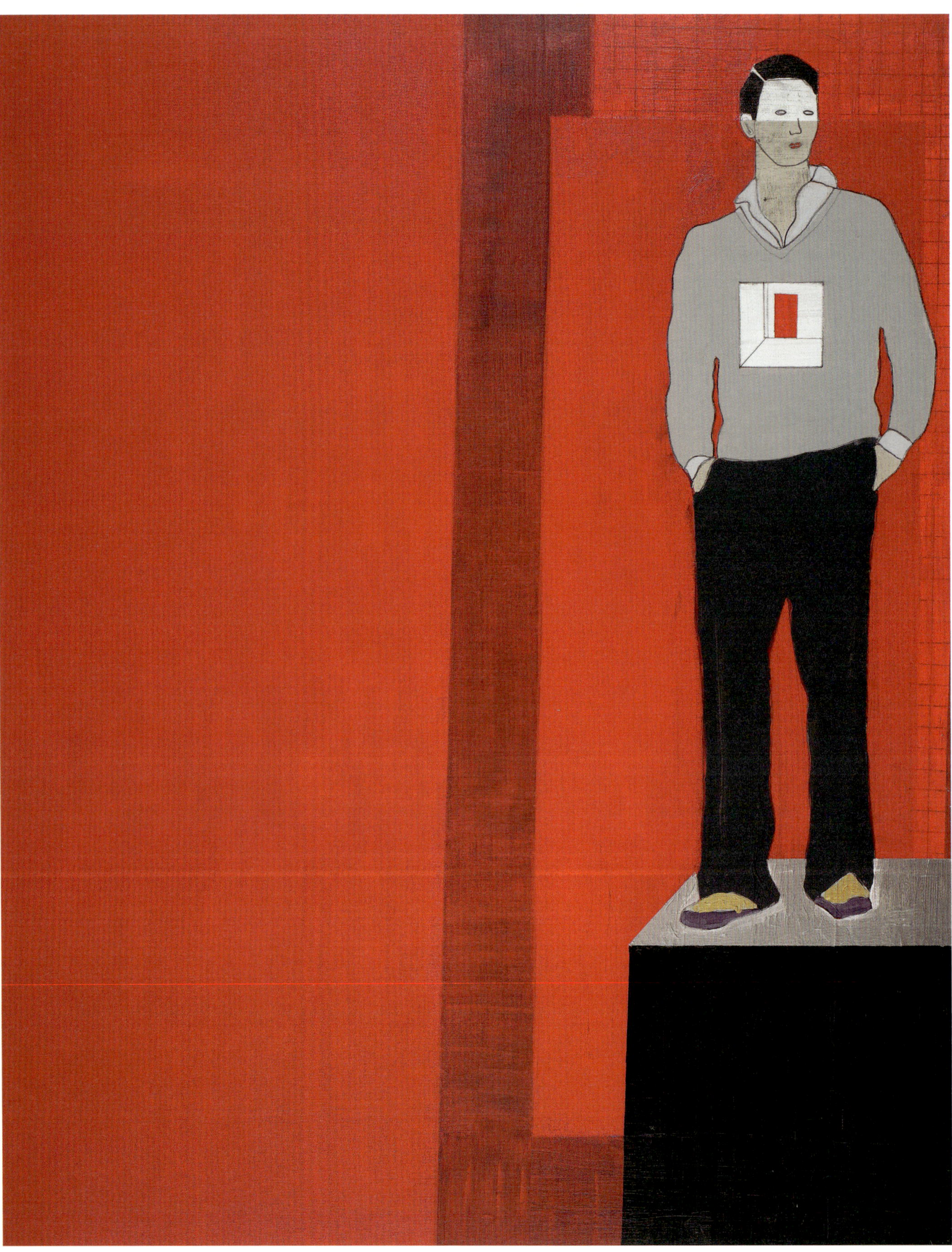

< Karl Goertzen, *I Walked into a Red Room and Found Fear Was Waiting to Dance*, 2008
Acrylic and mixed media on canvas
152.4 × 122 cm

> my thoughts. I am attempting to break down the walls of my disorder and the stigma that is still so often attached to people suffering from disorders like my own. I hope that by exposing my work to a much larger audience that others suffering from mental illness will take comfort in, or feel their own spark of inspiration from, my paintings.[68]

Goertzen's art practice was both therapeutic and cathartic. His style, Jennifer said, varied according to his mental state. When he was feeling manic, his paintings were busy. When he was feeling depressed, his paintings had a calmer appearance. The red painting is one of his quiet pieces—minimalistic, structured, with solid blocks of colour. He was enrolled in architectural studies for one year in college, and his love of grids, solid forms, and straight, clean lines shows through the surface of the paint. Jennifer explained that Karl did not intend it to be a self-portrait, but it does reveal his internal state. He was not comfortable talking about his feelings and, indeed, the eyes of the figure are blank, unreadable. The red door on his chest appears in many of his paintings. I wondered if it was a door to his heart, his mind, or another dimension. In fact, it is a reference to the red door of his childhood home. He dreamt about it often. It was always closed, and he did not know what lay behind it. It might be good, but it might be bad. He just never knew.

Goertzen was diagnosed with cancer in 2010. Although it was shocking news, he admitted that "after years of tortuous thoughts, it was in fact somewhat of a relief to my tormented mind." He painted a series of canvasses expressing his response to the diagnosis. One read, "I'm so happy I have cancer!" Another stated, "I will make you a believer in suicide." Not surprisingly, the paintings enraged viewers who were unaware of his life-long struggle with suicidal ideation. It was a relief for the artist, in a curious way, to know that his cause of death would not be by his own hand.

Despite Goertzen's often-debilitating mental health issues, he truly loved life:

> Sometimes at work people are concerned for you because you are acting totally crazy but they are not sure what to do or how to help. Sometimes you get diagnosed with mental illness. Sometimes you have to leave a job you love because you are way too messed up to perform it. Sometimes you want to commit suicide. Sometimes you hear voices. You go into mania. You go into psychosis. Sometimes you are so high you become dangerous. Sometimes you want to stop taking your medication because it makes you feel thick and dull and dead inside. Then you find the girl. Sometimes they tell you you've got cancer and probably about two months to live. But then, sometimes you find the right psychiatrist; the right combination of medication. Sometimes you find an amazing gallery owner who believes in your work. Sometimes you finally get on a plane after thinking you will never be able to fly again. Sometimes you survive cancer for two years and counting. Then you marry the girl and it is freakin' amazing. Sometimes . . . [69]

Karl Goertzen is only one of many artists who describe their practice in therapeutic terms. And, in some cases, therapy becomes art.[70] It is a profoundly personal experience, and one that is not intended for scrutiny and analysis by others. It is art *as* therapy. An astute observer proposed this idea: What if your therapy became art?[71] Yes, what if?

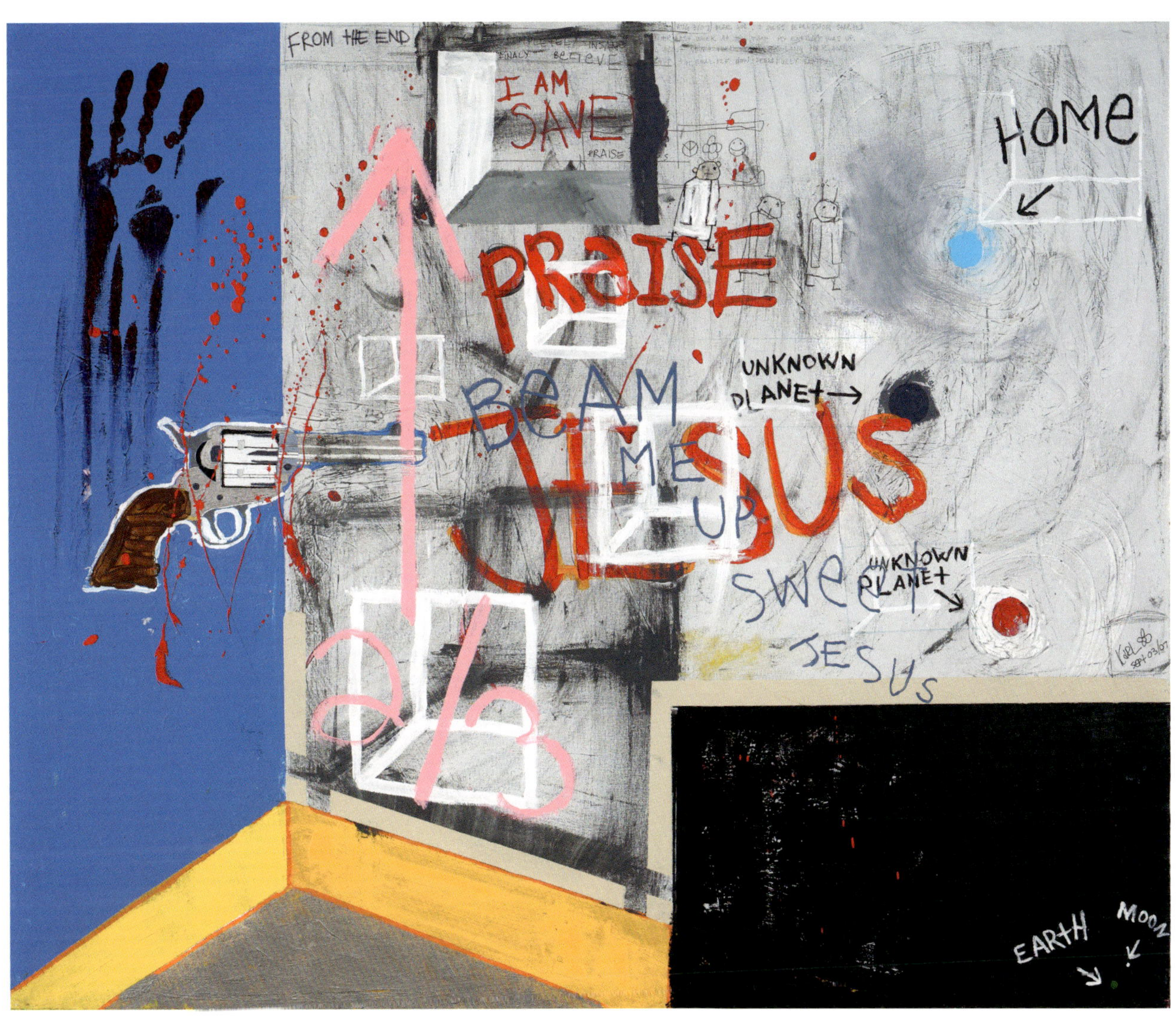

Karl Goertzen,
Top Secret Map, 2007
Acrylic on canvas
122 × 122 cm

1 Pandora, interview with the author, Vancouver, British Columbia, October 24, 2019.

2 Roger Cardinal, "Toward an Outsider Aesthetic," in Michael D. Hall and Eugene W. Metcalf Jr. (eds.), *The Artist Outsider: Creativity and the Boundaries of Culture* (Washington, DC: Smithsonian Institution Press, 1994), 30.

3 See, for example, Sister Gertrude, Howard Finster, Norbert Kox, Bill Anhang, and Arthur Villeneuve.

4 See, for example, Madge Gill, Guo Fengyi, and Alma Rumball.

5 Joanne Cubbs, "Rebels, Mystics, and Outcasts," in Hall and Metcalf Jr., *The Artist Outsider*, 78.

6 Thomas Messer (ed.), *Jean Dubuffet & Art Brut* (Milan: Mondadori, 1986), 33.

7 See page 47, note 31.

8 Eugene W. Metcalf Jr., "From Domination to Desire," in Hall and Metcalf Jr., *The Artist Outsider*, 217.

9 Douglas Coupland, "What is the Future of Art?" *Artsy*, March 1, 2016, https://www.artsy.net/article/artsy-editorial-the-future-of-art-according-to-douglas-coupland.

10 Michel Thevoz, "An Anti-Museum: The Collection de l'Art Brut in Lausanne," in Hall and Metcalf Jr., *The Artist Outsider*, 63–74.

11 Gary Alan Fine, *Everyday Genius: Self-Taught Art and the Culture of Authenticity* (Chicago: University of Chicago Press, 2004).

12 During discussions about artists' mental health issues at a conference of the European Outsider Art Association in 2013, questions were raised about whether an artist's psychiatric diagnosis should be noted on the exhibition label beside the artwork and how the artwork of patients could be obtained from psychiatric hospitals. Some gallery collections promise a glimpse of madness, declaring that the artist lives in a place where madness and genius intermingle. Also of note was a presentation on art and paranoid psychosis scheduled for the Outsider Art Fair, New York, 2014. The Creative Growth organization in California offered a presentation in October 2015 on the intersection of psychoanalysis and outsider art.

13 Daniel Wojcik, *Outsider Art: Visionary Worlds and Trauma* (Jackson, MS: University Press of Mississippi, 2016), 195.

14 An oft-cited study is K. R. Jamison's "Mood Disorders and Patterns of Creativity in British Writers and Artists," *Psychiatry* 52, no. 2 (1989): 125–134.

15 Judith Schlesinger, "Creative Mythconceptions: A Closer Look at the Evidence for the 'Mad Genius' hypothesis," *Psychology of Aesthetics, Creativity, and the Arts* 3, no. 2, (2009): 62–72. At worst, the opponents say the oft-cited study provides only self-serving proof that one researcher's bipolar disorder elevates her to the status of genius.

16 There was no obvious control group.

17 Albert Rothenberg, *Creativity and Madness: New Findings and Old Stereotypes* (Baltimore: Johns Hopkins University Press, 2009).

18 Rothenberg, *Creativity and Madness*. See also Wojcik, *Outsider Art*, 195.

19 As for Nova Scotia artist John Devlin.

20 For example, artists Louis Soutter (1871–1942) and Frank Travis (1914–1976) discussed in the chapter titled "From Art Brut to Outsider Art."

21 As Stanley Grof suggests of patients involved in therapeutic psychedelic drug research: *Realms of the Human Unconscious* (London: Souvenir Press, 1996), 498.

22 Carl Jung, *Collected Works of C. G. Jung, Volume 18* (Princeton, NJ: Princeton University Press, 1976), 35.

23 Michel Foucault, *Madness and Civilization: A History of Insanity in the Age of Reason* (New York: Random House, 2002).

24 James Hollis "Review: 'History of Madness' by Michel Foucault," *The Jung Page*, October 27, 2013, accessed January 11, 2020, http://jungpage.org/learn/articles/book-reviews/871.

25 Schlesinger, "Creative Mythconceptions."

26 Schlesinger.

27 Christian Beetz, *Between Madness and Art: The Prinzhorn Collection* (Brooklyn: Icarus Films, 2007), 75 min. See also John M. MacGregor, "Marginal Outsiders: On the Edge of the Edge," in Simon Carr et al., *Portraits from the Outside: Figurative Expression in Outsider Art* (New York: Parsons School of Design, 1990).

28 John M. MacGregor, *The Discovery of the Art of the Insane* (Princeton, NJ: Princeton University Press, 1989), 198.

29 John Berger, *Ways of Seeing* (London: Penguin Books, 1977), 28. Recent research suggests that Van Gogh's last painting was *Tree Roots*.

30 Annie Rogers, *Incandescent Alphabets: Psychosis and the Enigma of Language* (New York: Routledge, 2016), 46.

31 John Devlin, "Strength in a Delusion: Personal Views of Psychosis & Art," July 19, 2016, https://artgalleryofnovascotia.ca/blog/john-devlin-his-personal-views-psychosis-art.

32 Devlin, "Strength in a Delusion."

33 Valerie Rousseau, "The Oblique Angle: When the Self-Taught Artist Shapes the World," in *Self-Taught Genius: Treasures from the American Folk Art Museum* (New York: American Folk Art Museum, 2014), 43–65.

34 Writer and director Brett Ingram, in Greensboro, North Carolina.

35 Brett Ingram, *The Secret World of Renaldo Kuhler* (New York: Blast Books, 2017), 23.

36 John Devlin in discussion with the author, March 24, 2020.

[37] Clive Bell, *Art* (New York: Frederick A. Stokes Company, 1914), Project Gutenberg eBook, accessed January 3, 2020, https://www.gutenberg.org/cache/epub/16917/pg16917-images.html.

[38] Bell, *Art.*

[39] Colin Rhodes, *Outsider Art: Spontaneous Alternatives* (London: Thames & Hudson, 2000), 120.

[40] 1984–88.

[41] Albert Einstein, "Obituary for Emmy Noether," *New York Times*, May 5, 1935.

[42] Tony Thorne, "John Devlin: Heavenly City," *Raw Vision* 77 (Winter 2012/13): 42–45, 43.

[43] Devlin, "Strength in a Delusion."

[44] Christian Shriqui, "Innocence Lost," *Raw Vision* 25 (Winter 1998/99): 58.

[45] Christian Shriqui and Nicole Desjardins, *L'oeil dévoilé: Oeuvres de Roland Claude Wilkie & Jacques Dion* (Charlevoix, Québec: Musée de Charlevoix, 1997), 27.

[46] Jim Elledge, *Henry Darger, Throwaway Boy: The Tragic Life of an Outsider Artist* (New York: Harry N. Abrams, 2013), 114. Darger was institutionalized because his heart "was not in the right place." In other words, Darger masturbated in an era that equated self-abuse with insanity, impurity, and homosexuality.

[47] Shriqui, "Innocence Lost," 57.

[48] She is the opposite of cruel Nurse Ratched, the fictional character in Ken Kesey's novel *One Flew Over the Cuckoo's Nest.*

[49] Shriqui and Desjardins, *L'oeil dévoilé*, 25.

[50] Eric Donald Hirsch, *Validity in Interpretation* (New Haven: Yale University Press, 1967).

[51] Elledge, *Henry Darger.*

[52] Elledge.

[53] Curator Leisa Rundquist quoted in Edward Gomez, "The Sexual Ambiguity of Henry Darger's Vivian Girls," *Hyperallergic*, June 24, 2017, accessed January 12, 2020, https://hyperallergic.com/387178/the-sexual-ambiguity-of-henry-dargers-vivian-girls/.

[54] Gomez, "The Sexual Ambiguity of Henry Darger."

[55] Gomez.

[56] Scott Barry Kaufman, "Creativity in the Brain," *Scientific American Blog*, November 27, 2013, accessed December 7, 2019, https://blogs.scientificamerican.com/beautiful-minds/creativity-in-the-brain/.

[57] Charles G. Zug III, "Folk Art and Outsider Art: A Folklorist's Perspective," in Hall & Metcalf Jr., *The Artist Outsider*, 145–160.

[58] Roger Cardinal, *Outsider Art* (New York: Praeger, 1972), 44.

[59] Circa 1915–30.

[60] C. G. Jung, *The Red Book: Liber Novus*, edited by S. Shamdasani (New York: W. W. Norton, 2009), 221.

[61] Quoted in Massimiliano Gioni, *Il palazzo enciclopedico* [The Encyclopedic Palace] (Venice: Marsilio, 2013), 24.

[62] Sara Corbett, "The Holy Grail of the Unconscious," New York Times, September 20, 2009, accessed January 11, 2020, http://www.nytimes.com/2009/09/20/magazine/20jung-t.html. The book was released in 2000.

[63] Massimiliano Gioni, *Il palazzo enciclopedico*, 25.

[64] Messer, *Jean Dubuffet & Art Brut.*

[65] This raises the issue of how the artwork has been collected and exhibited. The artist must consent to others viewing and taking his or her work. It is not only an ethical issue but a legal one. If the artist is unable to give his or her informed consent (due to mental health issues or death), someone must consider the request on the artist's behalf.

[66] Roger Cardinal, "Outsider Art and the Autistic Creator," *Philosophical Transactions of the Royal Society of London. Series B, Biological Sciences* 364, no. 1522 (2009): 1459–66. It also reflects the impression of Allan Beveridge in "A Disquieting Feeling of Strangeness?: The Art of the Mentally Ill," *Journal of the Royal Society of Medicine* 94, no. 11 (2001): 595–99.

[67] Artist statement provided by Jennifer Goertzen, Ottawa.

[68] Ibid.

[69] Artist Statement provided by Guy Bérubé, Ottawa.

[70] It is not traditional art therapy, an interactive, therapeutic process in which thoughts and feelings that are difficult to articulate can be expressed in a supportive environment.

[71] See, for example, Mark Hogancamp's story of recovery as documented in Jeff Malmberg's *Marwencol* (New York: Cinema Guild, 2010), 1 hour 23 min.

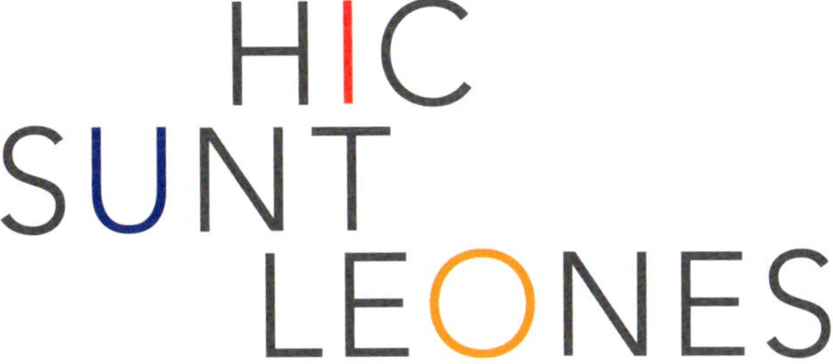
HIC
SUNT
LEONES

Ancient cartographers inscribed HIC SUNT LEONES ("Here are lions") to indicate that unexplored lands lay beyond the edges of the map. Travellers beware! Mystical and dangerous creatures might inhabit those uncharted territories. It seems an appropriate caveat for this section of the book, which charts my voyage into the world of outsider art in Canada. I was an outsider in all provinces except my own and did not know what lay beyond the edges of my territory. I set off for unknown lands, so to speak, my only compass being my views on outsider art.

I have an incomplete knowledge of Canadian art history.* I suspect I am not alone in confessing that. Other than the usual suspects, like Emily Carr and the Group of Seven, many of us would be hard-pressed to name artists or art movements that are distinctly Canadian. Why is that? We are not a nation of self-promoting braggarts, so perhaps that is part of the problem; inadequate art education in schools is another. To open a dialogue about outsider art in Canada is a daunting task, as so little has been discussed to date. That may be a good thing, as it affords a rare opportunity for a fresh start. I asked the same question of everyone I met, from friends and acquaintances to staff at art institutions: "Why don't we talk about outsider art in Canada?" The answers ranged from "I don't know" to an insouciant shrug in Québec. I wasn't sure of the answer myself. Some thoughts were offered along with a few lectures on the lack of support for *all* arts in this country. Many felt that art is seen as an elitist pursuit, acquired as an investment only by those who can afford it, and questioned, as others have,[1] whether a hefty price tag on an artwork truly reflects its aesthetic value. One gallerist suggested that Canadian tastes remain traditional and conservative. Another pointed out that the emphasis in Canada's education system is not the liberal arts, but science. I persisted in spite of the uncertain terrain. I asked questions and probed for answers. I learned a great deal from people who had not considered outsider art before, but had much to tell me about self-taught artists in their communities, what those individuals taught them about creating art, and why their work was important. I became a student of local art historians who were knowledgeable about artists working outside the fine-art system. Every discussion raised issues that forced me to examine my own definition of and assumptions about outsider art. While Canadians may not be engaged collectively in a discussion about art on the margins, many individuals offered thoughtful observations on the subject.

Because of the highly idiosyncratic nature of outsider art, there is obviously nothing uniquely Canadian about it. But, given the vastness of this nation, it is not surprising that the concept of outsider art holds different meanings across the country, reflecting local histories, regional social issues, and particular cultural trends. On the west coast, the idea of outsider art is intertwined with issues of social justice. Canada's central region venerates the art of its early twentieth-century European settlers, and their understanding of outsider art begins with a discussion of folk art. Québec, too, is proud to lay claim to generations of *les patenteux* as well as recent collections of *l'art singulier*. And, to many, the Atlantic Provinces are synonymous with folk art, a notion that underscores conversations about contemporary self-taught creators. Canada's Indigenous population inhabits a unique art world of its own.

I set out to explore outsider art and found myself being introduced to diverse collections of art that challenged my impulse to apply labels to art in the first place. I was left with unanswered questions about the significance of folk art in Canada and its relationship to outsider art. I returned home with hundreds of pages of notes and reference material that required an extra suitcase, a sort of mobile repository of information and opinions on

* Sorry.

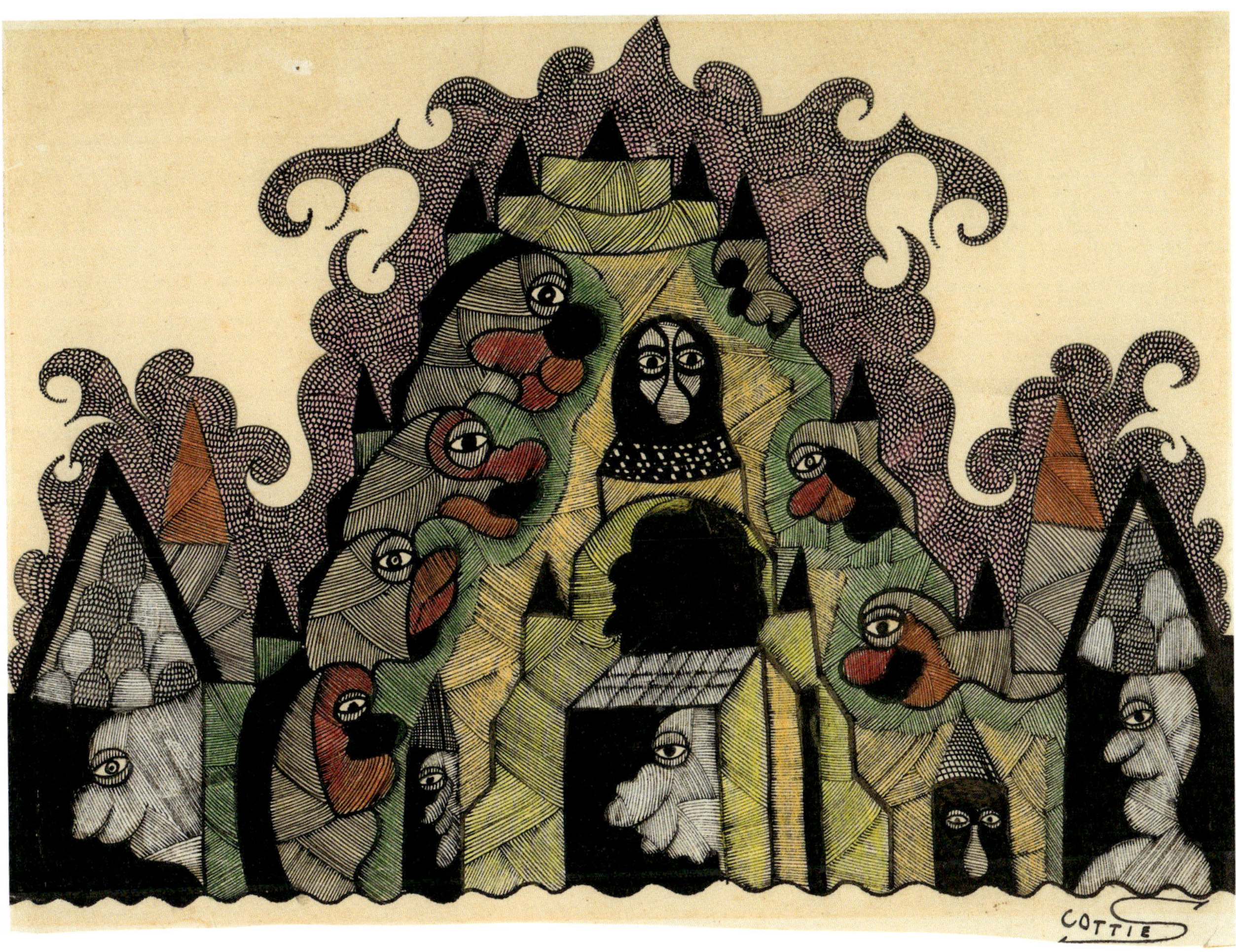

Scottie Wilson, *Untitled*, c. 1950s
Coloured ink on paper
28 × 38 cm

Canadian art. The crucial information, though, came from the artists themselves. Somewhere along the road a collector said to me, "You know, for me, it's always been about the story behind the art." That is true for many who admire outsider art, and I felt the weight of the personal details artists had shared with me—the search for meaning in their lives and the refuge art had provided on difficult days. Earlier in this book I offered an image of an archipelago of outsider art, with each artist inhabiting his or her own island. That proved to be a fitting description of the Canadian artists I met, for it was difficult to draw comparisons among them other than to bear witness to the intensity of their practice.

I started my research with SCOTTIE WILSON, one of the few Canadian outsider artists admired by the international art community. If there were an Outsider Art Hall of Fame, Scottie (as he is always called) would be inducted. Although he hails from Scotland, Scottie's mid-life calling as an artist began in Canada. The decade he spent in Canada is not well documented, but the Dunlop Art Gallery in Regina undertook that task in 1990 when it sponsored an exhibition of his Canadian drawings.

Scottie Wilson (Louis Freeman) was born in Glasgow, Scotland, in 1891.[2] The details of the first forty years of his life are somewhat sketchy, and Scottie may have contributed to the misinformation about his life. He apparently took great pleasure in putting forward a romanticized version of himself and his eccentricities, leaking fragments of personal information and leaving it to others to manufacture the rest.[3] He grasped the importance of appearing to be a "noble savage," as such peculiarities assured him a place in the art world.[4] What we do know about Scottie is that he grew up in poverty and left school by the age of nine, sold newspapers on the street, helped vendors set up market stalls, and peddled patent medicine with his older brother. In 1906, he joined the Scottish Rifles and was posted in India. He returned to Scotland around 1918 after serving in South Africa and the Western Front. Scottie deserted the Black and Tans in Ireland, apparently because he could not carry out the orders he was given.[5] He settled in London, hawking used goods from street stalls and shops.

Scottie's life in Canada began in the early 1930s in Toronto, where he ran a junk shop. Although he never explained his name change, it has been suggested that he wanted to blend into the predominantly British and Protestant population to avoid being a target of anti-Semitism.[6] He started his new life in Canada under the name Robert "Scottie" Wilson. He lived in Vancouver for a period of time (in the late 1930s and early 1940s), and that is where he saw totem poles of the coastal First Nations,[7] which he acknowledged as an influence on his work.[8] He had two exhibits there—one was self-promoted, the other was at the Vancouver Art Gallery in 1943.[9] He also lived in Winnipeg, where he met Douglas Duncan, who advocated for Scottie and helped him get established as an artist. But the story of Scottie Wilson the artist always begins in Toronto, where he found the famous bulldog pen:

> [I found a pen that] looked like a bulldog, with a nib as thick as my finger! Fourteen-carat gold it was and so unusual, so striking that I said I'm going to keep this pen. I didn't want to break up the bulldog pen with its nib so thick and beautiful. So I kept it. I took [it to] my shop in Young [*sic*] Street. A general store it was, and a few days after opening the shop I bought a large table with a thick cardboard top on which to stand my radio. I'm listening to classical music one day—Mendelssohn—when all of a sudden I dipped the bulldog pen into a bottle of ink and started drawing—

doodling I suppose you'd call it—on the cardboard tabletop. I don't know why. I just did. In a couple of days—I worked almost ceaselessly—the whole of the tabletop was covered with little faces and designs. The pen seemed to make me draw, and them images, the faces and designs, just flowed out. I couldn't stop—I've never stopped since that day.

Anyway, when the tabletop was full up I bought writing pads, drawing books, and cheap crayons in Woolworth's and began to develop my own style of working—the pen stroke and the crayon colouring. The drawings poured out, and I began hanging them up all over the shop and displaying them in the window. I couldn't stop, you see. It just went on and on. And I hadn't any time to look after the shop or the business either, and a friend of mind, a watchmaker named Billy, moved in to look after the business for me. I retired behind a curtain where I drew all day.[10]

Scottie continued to draw until his death in 1972. His first drawings were described as doodles, flowing organically from a centre point. Many featured distorted faces, while others depict vegetation, architecture, animals, or abstract patterns rendered in ink, coloured pencil, or wax crayon. He developed distinctive hatch mark strokes, not to suggest shading, but to fill in the empty spaces. It may be that the repetitive strokes quieted Scottie's mind, in the same way that others describe the soothing effects of rhythmic activities, like knitting. Scottie described the clarity his practice brought:

When I'm working I can see what's happening, and I can imagine what's going to happen. I see best when I'm finishing my pictures with a pen. When I'm making strokes; hundreds and thousands of strokes. I can see very clearly. But when I'm designing a picture, that's different. I can't see then. I'm too absorbed in creation.[11]

Scottie's freestyle doodles became organized images. As touches of graphite can be seen in some of his drawings, it is likely that Scottie sketched out his idea before starting the hatching process. He liked to work through an idea, producing a series of drawings on a theme. "The idea of a figure fills my mind and I have to get it down on paper, working it out in many variations," he said.[12] Scholars have proposed that Scottie's images were inspired by a fountain in Glasgow, lace curtains in his home, totem poles admired in Vancouver, British Columbia, Indian drawings and carvings seen on his military postings, and fretwork on furniture in his shop.[13] Scottie, however, claimed that his ideas came to him in dreams, and he refused to answer questions about the source of his images or their meaning.[14] Scottie later attached some names to the beings in his drawings: the Evils and Greedies were actors in an ongoing battle between good and evil. Nature images represented goodness and truth; human figures represented negative and destructive forces in the world. It's the faces that people remember most about Scottie's work. Sometimes alone, sometimes in groups, the faces glower and stare at us; they billow off each other like fungus on a stump. They are rather disconcerting. He seems to have abandoned the grand narrative of good versus evil in the 1950s, when he turned to drawing his private paradise.

Contrary to the stereotypical outsider artist as a reclusive, private individual, Scottie was keen for his work to be seen. Even when he had gallery representation, he would organize his own exhibitions and charge admission to view his work. One observer described a typical exhibit:

> Every inch of the walls were covered by unframed pictures held in place by drawing pins. The effect was overwhelming. None of the works seemed to be for sale, but there was a plate on a table appealing for a donation of silver. The show was crowded and Scottie moved among the public talking to them about his pictures and drawing their attention to the press cuttings which were on display.[15]

In 1945, shortly after the war ended, Scottie abruptly left Canada for Great Britain. He exhibited in Glasgow and then in London, where his work was shown concurrently with that of Picasso, Klee, and Miro.[16] He was soon picked up by a London gallery[17] but (undoubtedly, to the owner's annoyance) he would peddle his work for a few pounds on the street in front of the gallery.

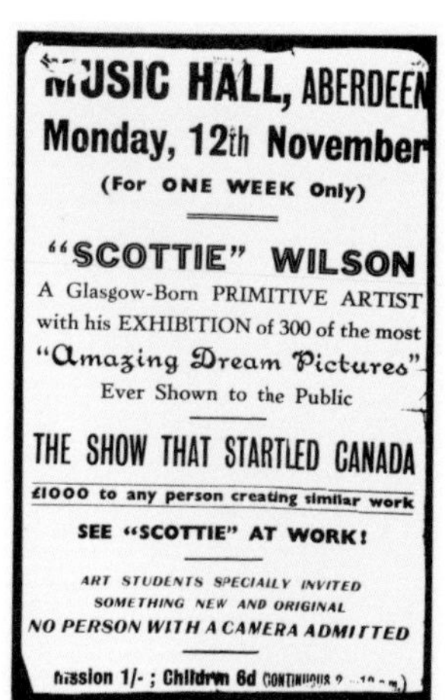

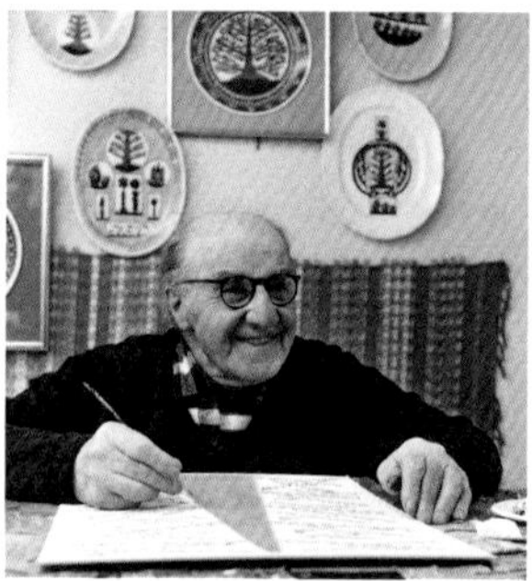

Scottie Wilson, exhibition poster, date unknown

Scottie Wilson working at home, Kilburn, 1967

Dubuffet saw Scottie's work at the Exposition Internationale de Surréalisme, organized by André Breton, and invited him to bring his art portfolio to Paris. Although Scottie did not know of or care about Dubuffet's status and reputation (referring to him as "that bloke Buffit") the meeting seemed to go well and Dubuffet added Scottie's work to his art brut collection.[18] Bill Hopkins, a London author and art critic who travelled to Paris with Scottie, recalled:

> When we arrived, not only was Dubuffet waiting, Pablo Picasso was with him. Both owned a few of Scottie's pieces, and Picasso had come to see—and perhaps buy—some more. I vividly remember both artists eagerly admiring Scottie's work, squabbling in their fierce, theatrical Gallic voices over who would buy which piece. Scottie accepted their homage with a grin but was somewhat matter-of-fact, as he would be with any interested buyer.[19]

Scottie's work changed over the years, particularly after 1950. The style remained constant, but his compositional technique became more decorative, and some say less interesting and emotionally compelling.[20] The sinister faces were replaced with peaceful nature images. However, his work remained popular and was exhibited in New York, Switzerland, and France. Scottie became interested in painting plates in the 1960s and, remarkably, this led to a contract to design tableware for the Royal Worcester Porcelain Company. His designs were later used on textiles made by the Edinburgh Weavers. He was also commissioned to create a mural for the headquarters of a Swiss bank. Scottie recalled a lunch in his honour, hosted by the bank president in his chalet. "There were the bankers with all their bags of gold, and me sitting there without the price of a kipper in me pocket."[21] Although Scottie was "uncultured" in some ways, he was highly sophisticated in the ways of marketing his own work. He made a modest income from his work and lived frugally; his only indulgences were expensive boots and hats.[22] Apparently, a suitcase full of money was found under his bed when he died.[23]

It has been hard to define Scottie's place in the art world.[24] In Canada, Scottie was grouped with primitive, naïve, provincial, and folk artists,[25] most likely because the label of outsider art had not yet entered our vocabulary. Before meeting Dubuffet, Scottie was grouped with modern primitive[26] or naïve artists, but most often with the Surrealists.[27] Although Scottie claimed the source of his drawings came from dreams (that is, his unconscious mind), he cannot rightfully be included among the Surrealists, an intellectual group that sought to set

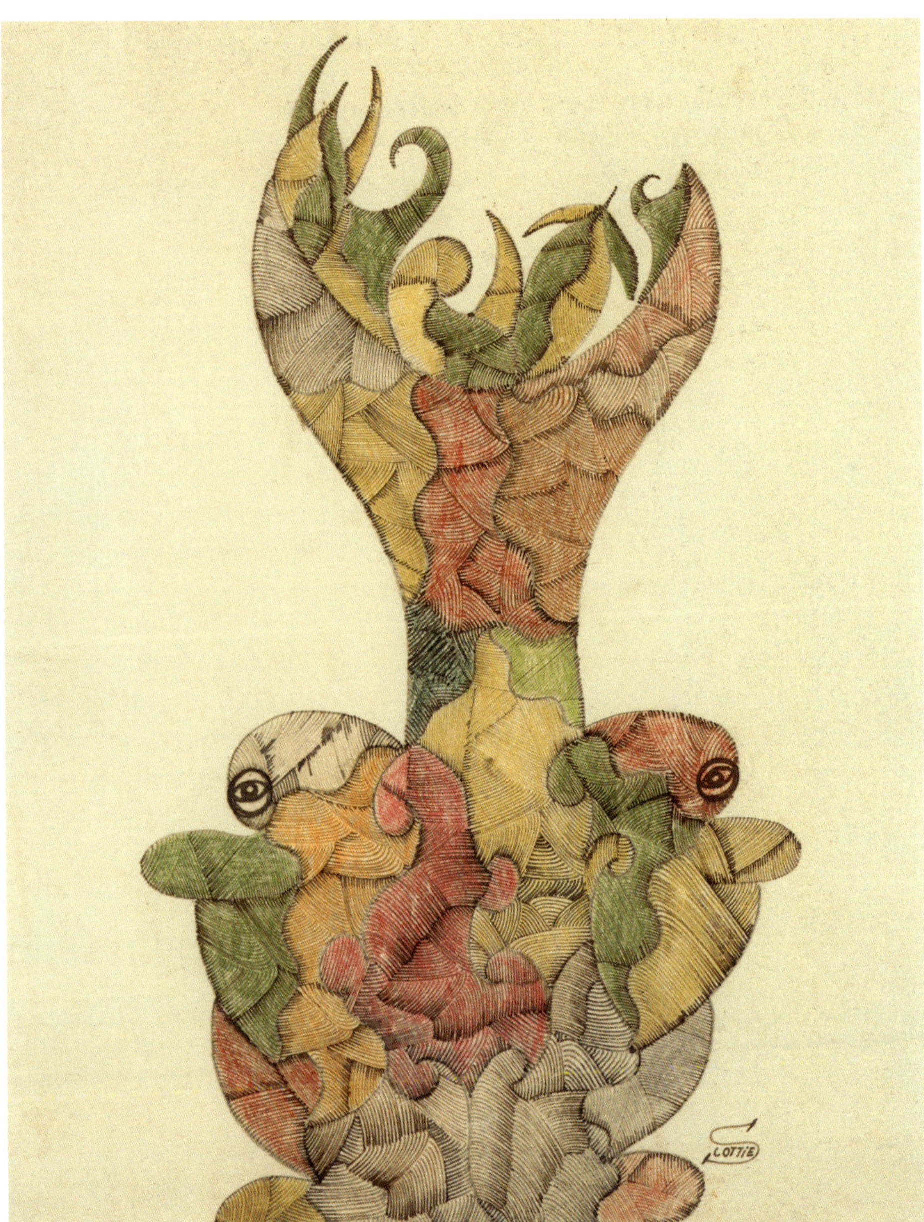

Scottie Wilson, *Yellow Fish and Faces*, c. 1938
Pen, ink, and crayon on paper
28 × 21.6 cm

aside logic and rationality in order to explore the spontaneous outpourings of the unconscious mind. The only "automatic" parts of Scottie's drawings were the hatching strokes he applied to blank areas after the design was in place. The rest of the piece was constructed in his mind before he started drawing, and there was no room for experimentation or chance.[28] Further, his chosen themes of good versus evil were certainly not ones entertained by the Surrealists. Nevertheless, Scottie's association with Surrealism brought him in contact with Dubuffet, who had a great deal of respect for him as a self-taught artist who had no knowledge of or interest in the traditions of art history.[29] Scottie was recognized as a remarkable creator and is now acknowledged as one of the leading outsider artists of the twentieth century.

British Columbia

After exploring Scottie's life and art, I had exhausted my knowledge of Canadian outsider artists. I began exploring outsider art in British Columbia, from the remote northern islands of Haida Gwaii (where *everyone* self-identifies as an outsider artist) to the city of Vancouver. Not surprisingly, British Columbia has a unique perspective on outsider art. A local artist published a book called *Who Needs Art When You Have a View Like This,*[30] inspired by a billboard advertisement for new condominiums. For some of us, it is a provocative statement suggesting that art has little value compared to the natural vistas to be seen from every window. For others, the statement reflects the priorities of the metropolis population. Yet the wonders of nature are a highlight of beautiful British Columbia and a point of pride for its residents.

I sought out interesting artists in my own community. I might be advised to look for them selling work on such-and-such a street corner. Sometimes I located them; often I did not. I wandered through local art exhibitions and talked to artists there. Kindred spirits occasionally popped up to share their views. I scoured flea markets and attended an exhibition that was said to feature outsider art.[31] Occasionally my art discoveries were made by happenstance, buried in bins at collectables shops. One shop proved to be an excellent resource, as its proprietor was both knowledgeable about the genre and supportive of neighbourhood artists. Not only did he introduce me to the work of these artists, he acted as an intermediary in relaying messages to the artists from me. It was a slow process, as an introduction was only the first step in building rapport. Some were reluctant to share their thoughts with me, and have remained so during my years of research. Few had heard of outsider art and

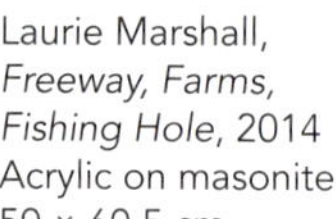

Laurie Marshall,
Freeway, Farms, Fishing Hole, 2014
Acrylic on masonite
50 × 60.5 cm

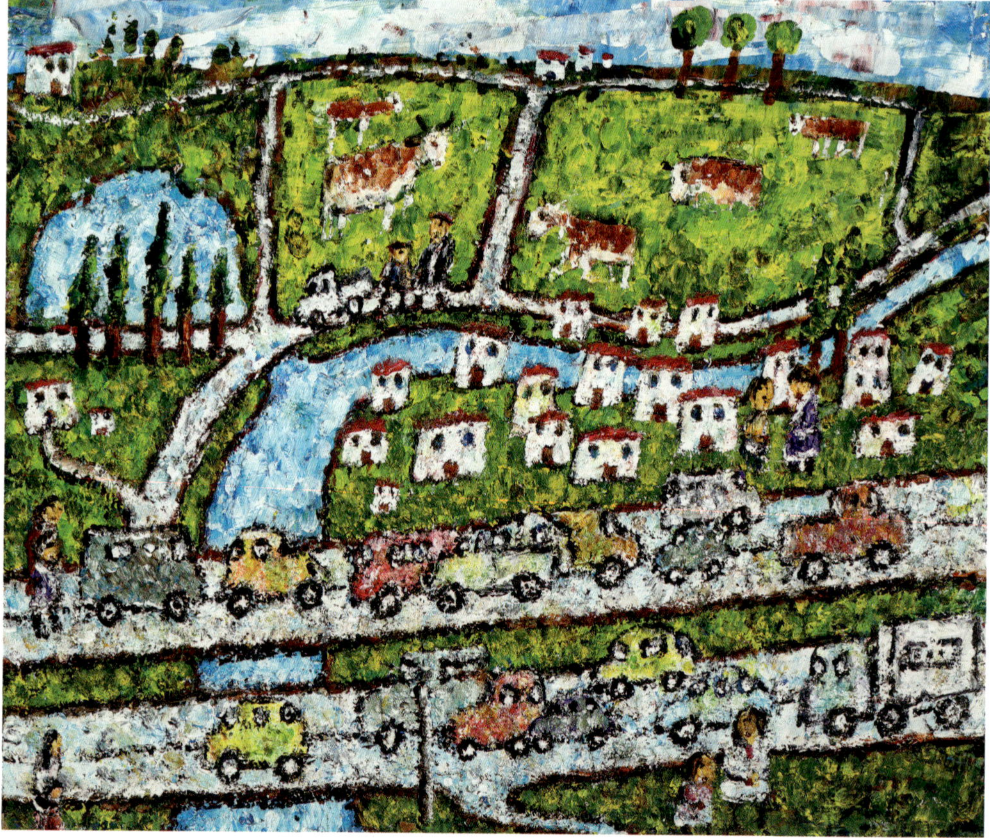

wondered how it related to their own creations. Most denied being artists because they had not been trained in art.

The hub of outsider art in Vancouver is an artist-run gallery in the Downtown Eastside, a neighbourhood that houses the city's marginalized population. It is a tight-knit community, known for its history of social activism. The gallery works towards social, cultural, and economic justice by supporting artists who struggle with mental health issues and socio-political marginalization. Art, it says, fosters survival, cultural participation, and human rights.[32] Although exhibition criteria are not limited to artists with mental health or marginalization issues, the subject matter of the artwork must address the gallery's mandate.

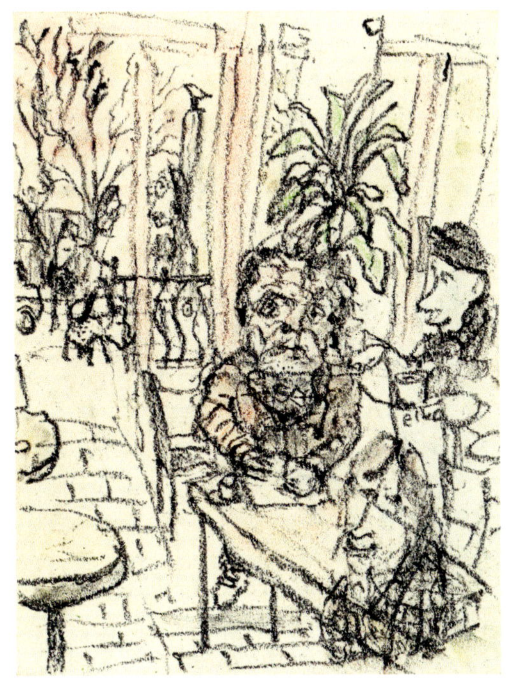

Laurie Marshall,
Self-portrait, 2015
Charcoal, chalk, and pastel on paper
40 × 30 cm

The gallery provides exhibition space to artists who struggle with issues that have led to their marginalization. It is a gallery of equal opportunity and social inclusion, and that alone makes it a commendable venture. But its definition of outsider art differs from that of the international art community, as it makes the artist's social status the central point of reference. As discussed earlier, a person's marginalization is a tragic circumstance of their life, but the fact that they create art does not necessarily mean their work falls under the rubric of outsider art. Just as there is no "art of the mad," there is no "art of the marginalized." However, a literal interpretation of the term "outsider," as Lucy Lippard suggests, puts social justice ahead of the art. There is no question that social inclusion is a worthy objective, but it comes with a caveat: How can one include people and groups into structured systems that have systematically excluded them in the first place? One author calls this "dancing the dialectic."[33] That is to say, the hierarchies that support these inequities must be challenged before fairness in the art world can be achieved.

I met some interesting artists at the gallery, including LAURIE MARSHALL, who is well known for his whimsical paintings. He describes himself as a doodler who first picked up a paintbrush at a drop-in centre when he was about fifty years old. He grew up in farming country, hence the proliferation of cows, horses, and other creatures in his paintings. His living space is crowded with artwork—stacks of it are piled on every surface. Sometimes he has an idea of an image he would like to paint, but usually he just starts painting and good things happen. He applies paint in thick layers then scratches through it to create images with a palette knife, a cloth, or his hands. He doesn't like paint brushes. Marshall stopped painting a few years ago, and has no explanation for why he abandoned a ritual he pursued with such passion. All he knows is that he is done with it and is now pursuing other creative ventures.

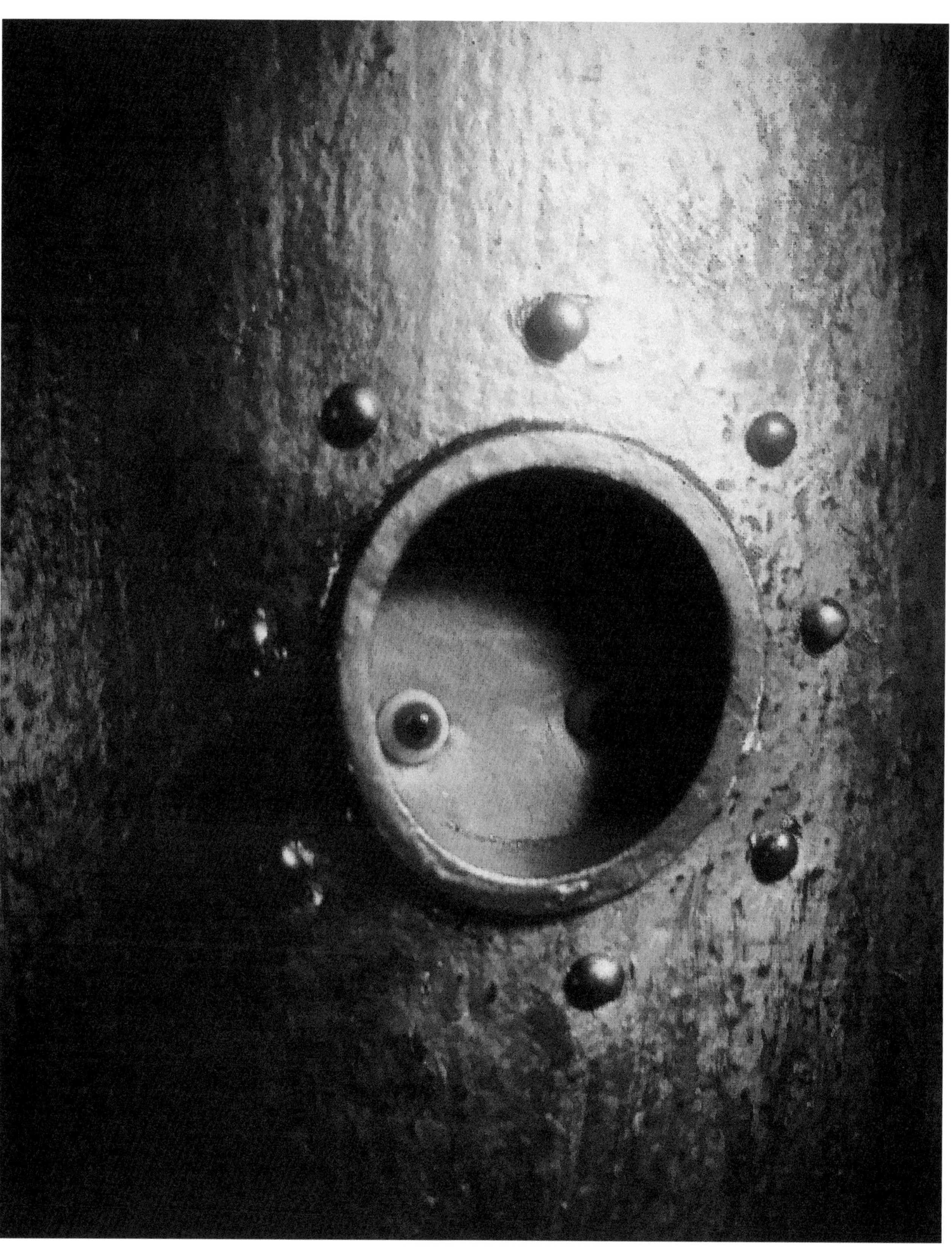

< Kevin House, *Portrait*, 2020
Wood, paint, plastic, metal
1:24 scale

KEVIN HOUSE was the first outsider artist I met in the mid-2000s when I began researching the genre. At the time, House was painting large canvases in the style of vintage carnival banners, and I admired one of American-Siamese twins, Chang and Eng Bunker. I lost track of House and bumped into him again only recently. He was buying a rubber toilet-plunger head to use in his creation of miniature (17 cm) carved crutches. This didn't surprise me. He has had many adventures since we first met.

House grew up in Edmonton and Vancouver. In his early twenties he endured a long spell of agoraphobia, which prevented him from leaving his home. Teaching himself to draw, paint, and play finger-style guitar was his way of coping with anxiety and feelings of entrapment. House flourished as a musician and landed a recording contract. He moved to New York City in 1998, intending to pursue a music career. He was down to his last twenty dollars when he found a used canvas on the street and, spending his last bit of money, bought paint to create circus banners that he sold in subway stations. It put enough money in his pocket to pay the rent. House eked out a living for a period of time, playing music and trading in antiques at the Chelsea Flea Market; that's where he met Rose Fontanella, who specialized in folk art, outsider art, and African-American memorabilia. It was the first time House heard about outsider artists and learned that he was one of them. One thing led to another, and he began painting portraits of pets in the style of sideshow banners. It was not the artist's life he dreamed of, but it afforded him an opportunity to hone his painting skills. He suffered a mental breakdown in the mid-2000s, putting an end to both his art and music. His only creative activity was painting on vinyl records, a project he called "Songs Without Music." In hindsight, he said, this was a pivotal point in his life. He decided he did not want to be part of the commercial world of making art for other people, but wanted to create only for himself. He set out to find his soul, and that he did, by returning to art and music. He has never looked back.

Talking with House is a dizzying experience—ideas burst out of his head like fireworks. He takes the germ of an idea and runs with it until it morphs into an entire universe. He describes himself as a monotasker, meaning that he becomes fully absorbed in an idea to the exclusion of everything else. His last grand project was called "Based on a True Story," a hoax museum he filled with the vestiges of imaginary people. Molly Crane, for one, was born in 1905 in Stony Plain Alberta and was the world's second largest female midget daredevil. She was the star attraction of the Bighorn Brothers Carnival: NO BIGGER THAN A COCKATOO, FASTER THAN A SPARROW, SWEET AS A CANDY BAR, SHARP AS AN ARROW. Lillian Ladybird Franklin, born in 1903 in Manhattan, gave an eyewitness account of the Chrysler Building robbery of 1936. Although she denied having consumed too many drinks at the speakeasy, she claimed to see a large airship hovering above the building. Then there's A. C. Lark, born in 1891 during an electrical storm. Also known as the Human Radio, he could transmit radio signals through this body. Sleep proved to be difficult until he mastered self-hypnosis techniques. Viewers at House's DIY exhibit could browse through memorabilia and listen to recorded interviews of people who knew these extraordinary characters. That exhibit was followed by "Shoe Side Story." Taking another deep dive into his imagination, House told the story of a woman through sculptures and drawings of forty-five fanciful shoes.

House has perfected the "art of obtainium," which he defines as a finder of things. And, indeed, he is a collector of ephemera—old magazines, letters, newspapers, books, and "stuff." But what interests him most are the (invented) stories attached to the objects he finds.

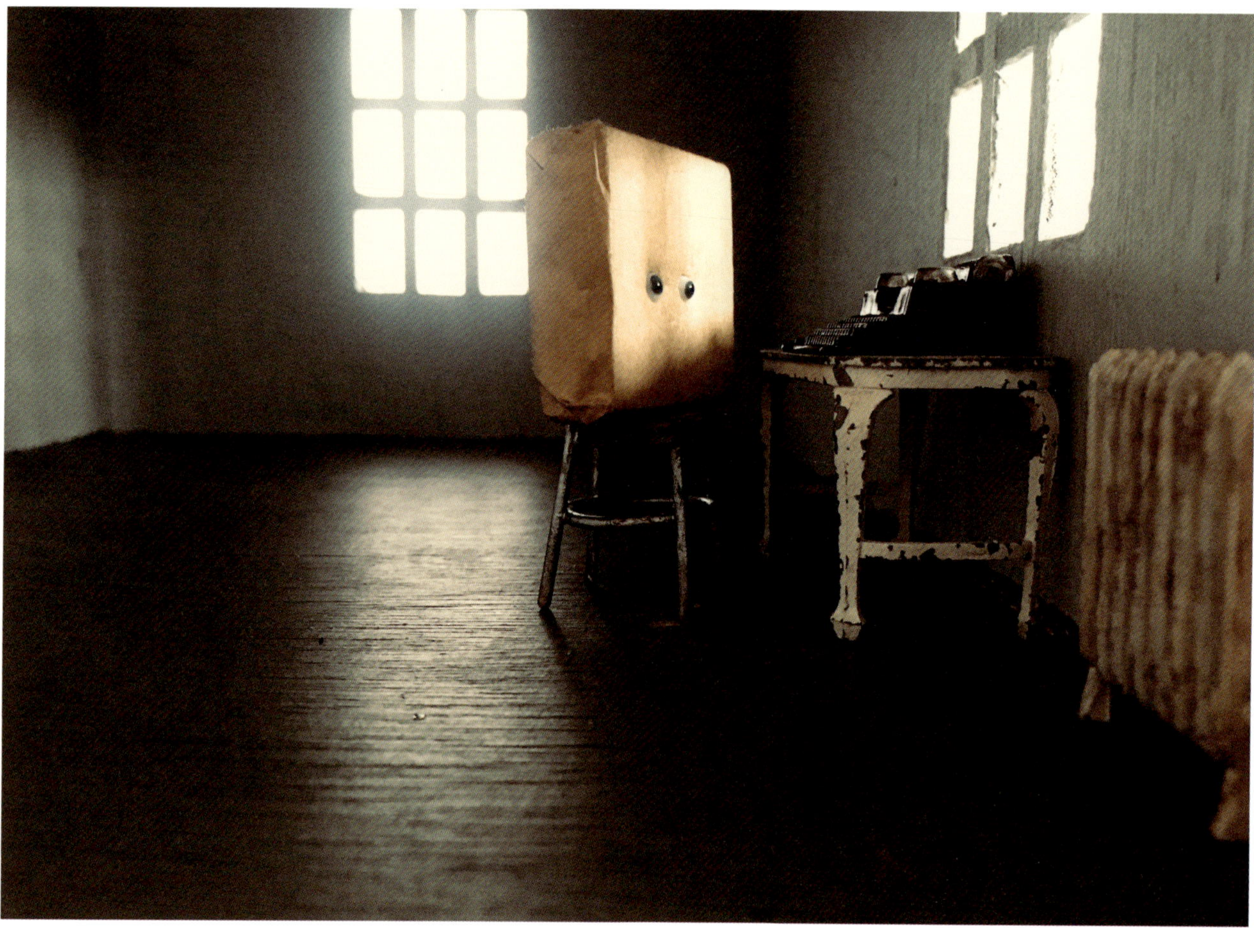

Kevin House, *Not So Alone as One Might Think, Just Look at the Light Mailed Right Through My Window*, 2020
Wood, paper, metal, paint
1:24 scale

He is, at heart, a storyteller and admits to being obsessed with narratives of people's lives. In his twenties, he was particularly interested in written biographies of artists. They helped him plan his life, giving him leave to consider what living the life of an artist could be like. Joris-Karl Huysmans's 1884 novel *À rebours* (*Against Nature*) made a significant impact on him. The ability to retreat into a world of his own invention was an intriguing proposition.

House is building a world for a young man forced to socially isolate during an epidemic. This miniature world, called *Isolation Boy*, springs from an idea he has been exploring for many years (that became reality during the COVID-19 pandemic). Isolation Boy peers out of his pod-like Isolatronium, protected from the outside world. He announces:

> Dearest Outside World,
> It seems I've made some progress with the Isolatronium. Some days are dreary as I get weighed down with small but crucial technical details. As time passes it increasingly becomes more apparent what the Isolatronium is capable of. It may turn out to be the ideal mechanism for venturing into outside environments. We will see. I will elaborate further as I get closer to completion. Will write soon.
> Yours Indelibly,
> Isolation Boy

A master of detail, House's miniscule pieces are skillfully constructed from repurposed materials. Isolation Boy himself is made of wood, paper, and doll eyes, and he measures five by five centimetres. The Isolatronium pod, twenty-three by ten centimetres, is crafted from a yogurt container, plastic, and a rubber sink stopper. The project originates from his personal experience with anxiety and seclusion and is, he says, a culmination of all the things he's created and all the skills he has acquired over the years, from antique restoration to creating art, writing music, and working on film projects. The dioramas allow Isolation Boy, the artist's alter-ego, to confront a world that is difficult to navigate. By manifesting situations in an imaginary world, House can better manage his experiences in the real world. Isolation Boy works on multiple levels for him: the musical and introspective aspects of the creative process as well as the psychological exploration and spiritual reflection that drive it. It is a meditation of sorts that is open to changing narratives. "There is an inherent musicality to all my creations," House says. "Finding the meditative and intuitive state of being is key to all I do; the unknowable mojo that happens when a series of notes or images come together to create a whole." He calls his process of discovery "the inward wilderness." He talks about the interconnection of music and art and how meaningful they are to him. I've never heard him talk about one without reference to the other. Working in either medium is a cathartic, meditative experience that helps him traverse the geography of his inner self. He is always searching for "what he doesn't know," that is, the mystery embedded in a phrase of music or a work of art. He compares it to a divining rod—a direct line to creating things that will resonate with others.

A few weeks into this project, House had built more than ten scenes of Isolation Boy at home: sitting before his typewriter, preparing to go onstage for "The Shut-In Show," sitting with a cup of coffee, and so on. In one scene, Isolation Boy looks into the mirror and muses, "I don't feel so good. No, I'm OK. No, I don't feel so good. I think I'm OK though." House is now working on Isolation Boy's laboratory. It is where the Solitarium will be built, a mobile pod that will allow Isolation Boy to travel into his own internal wilderness. I asked him how Isolation Boy's story will unfold. He doesn't know. He's learned to stay out of his own way when creating music and art. The narrative will evolve over time, like a work of improvised music. It could go on forever.

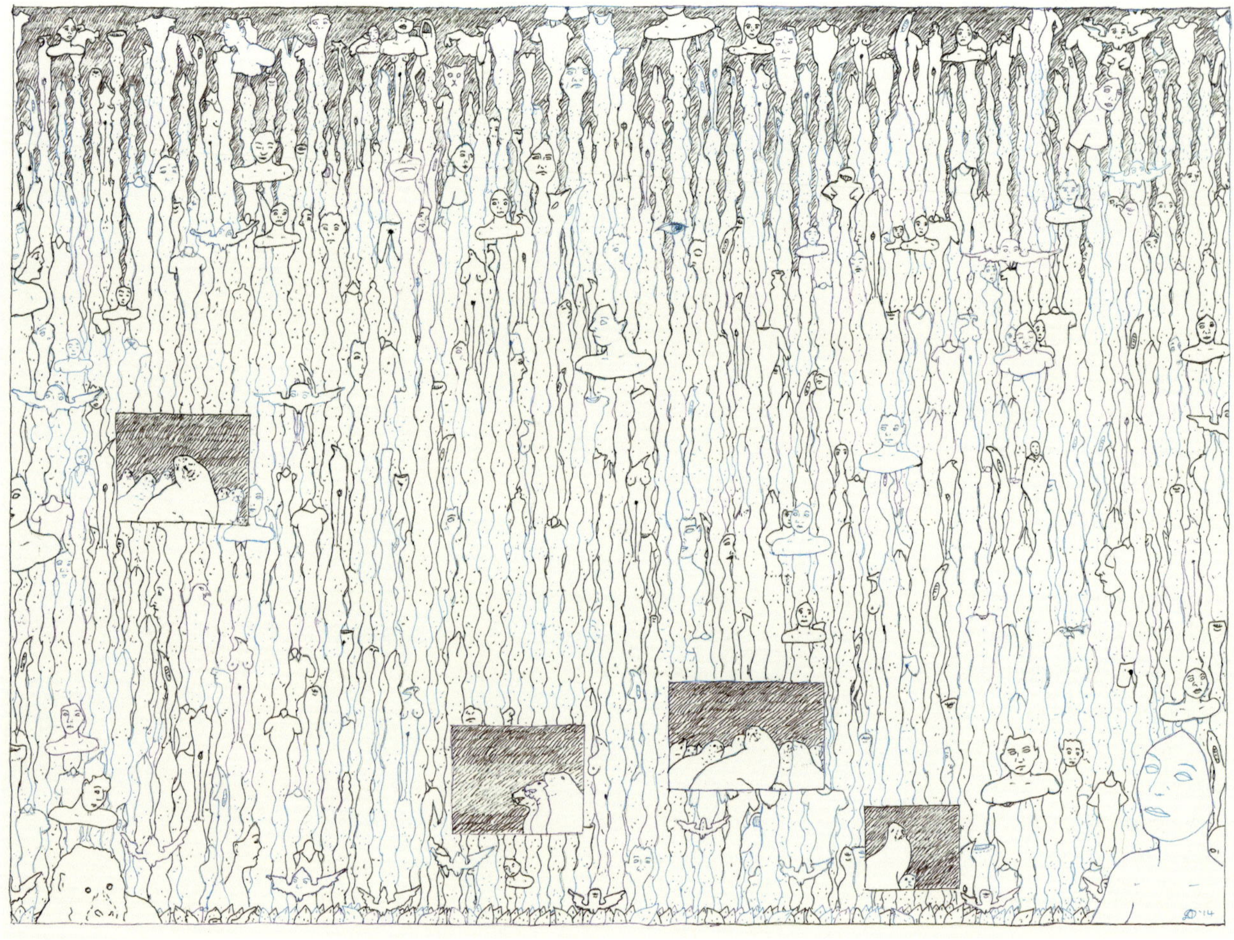

David Ogilvie, *Shores of Ulysses – Two*, 2014
Ink on illustration board
34 × 46.5 cm

When I first met DAVID OGILVIE in Vancouver some years ago, he was absorbed in mapping out a series of boxes on paper. His work was on display at a community centre and he was on site to talk to visitors. His work was compelling and I was curious about the pictures he had laid out so carefully on storyboards. Many conversations later, I came to understand these peculiar drawings were not stories but images dredged up from his subconscious. Ogilvie's explanation began with a discussion about *Forbidden Planet*, the 1956 film that inspired *Star Trek*.

Forbidden Planet is a science fiction film that features twenty-third-century space travellers who arrive on a distant planet to learn the fate of an expedition sent from Earth years earlier. Only two people from that expedition have survived, and one, Morbius, has been studying the Krell, highly advanced inhabitants of the planet who disappeared two hundred thousand years ago. The Krell built a machine that could create anything they could imagine; however, they forgot about monsters from the id—elementary forces of the subconscious mind. Not only did these monsters wipe out the Krell, they also killed most of the crew of the original expedition from Earth. Monsters from the id appear again, this time springing from the unconscious mind of Morbius, who feels threatened by his daughter's decision to leave the planet.

What does this have to do with Ogilvie's art? Well, his art is about the power of the id, Freud's description of the unconscious part of our psyche that responds directly to basic needs and desires. The id is the primitive, irrational, and fantasy-oriented part of our minds. In short, it is the master of our dreams. It is why Ogilvie calls his work "dream art."

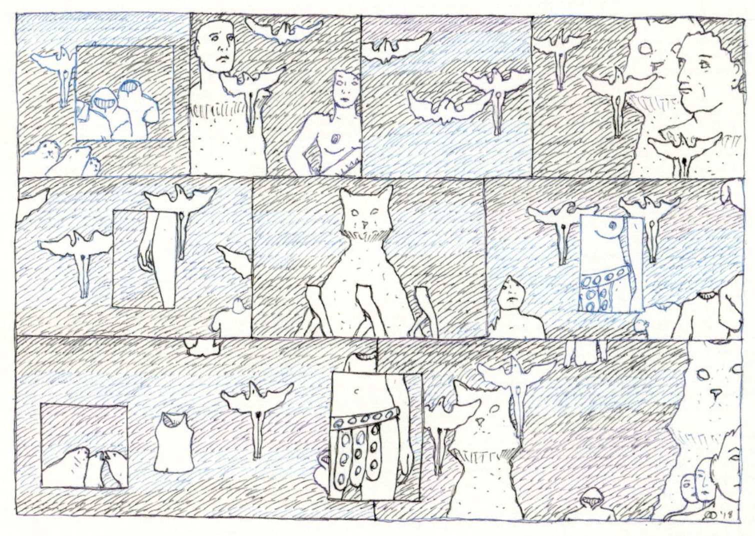

David Ogilvie, *Dreams of Circe – Three*, 2018
Ink on paper
16 × 23.5 cm

Ogilvie worked in a variety of jobs before he retired: dishwasher, cook, farmhand, millworker, infantryman, warehouseman, press worker, and janitor. He found it hard to fit in. He did a stint as a copyboy for a Victoria newspaper in the 1970s. When the paper went on strike, he had to supplement his income by doing odd jobs, one of which was drawing cartoons for small, local newspapers. He enjoyed those assignments, but sought more stable employment with the railway. His obsession with drawing began in his sixties, while recovering from a lengthy illness. He taught himself to draw, mainly with ink, and has surrendered to the imperative to create art all day. He paints when he is home, but always takes his drawing materials with him when he goes out. Although Ogilvie's creative imperative began later in life, he doesn't consider his early years to have been wasted. His everyday experiences were filed away for future reference. He cherishes memories of castles and antiquities he saw on his travels as well as the beauty of the Canadian landscape. Retirement has allowed him to chase his muse, indulge in his passion for drawing, and explore the work of the Surrealists.

Ogilvie begins each piece by drawing boxes on paper, which he then fills with figures and background markings. The page is not meant to be read as a story; each drawing is a complete picture. The figures are reminiscent of statues: nude, rigid, and expressionless. Indeed, he is particularly interested in classical sculpture, especially their blank eyes that stare disconcertingly at the viewer. He finds them to be wonderfully eerie. The bird-like figures are harpies, a mythical creature from Greek mythology with the body of a bird and the face of a human female. They bring another unsettling element to the scene, as they were employed to transport guilty people to Hades. Ogilvie sometimes refers to these creatures as Muggins—creatures that cannot be controlled. The disembodied clothing that floats on the page is another image brought forth by his subconscious, adding one more mysterious element to his images. Coloured squiggles fill the background. Like Scottie Wilson's hatched lines, they are used to fill empty spaces, not as shading.

Ogilvie's drawings became more intriguing when I learned to study them not as stories but as individual dream impressions. As discussed earlier, context is critical when engaging with outsider art. The result is a journey into the surreal realm of another person's psyche, where images have their own peculiar sensibilities, completely divorced from reason. It's a good place to dwell occasionally and, as other artists recommend, just let your imagination run free.

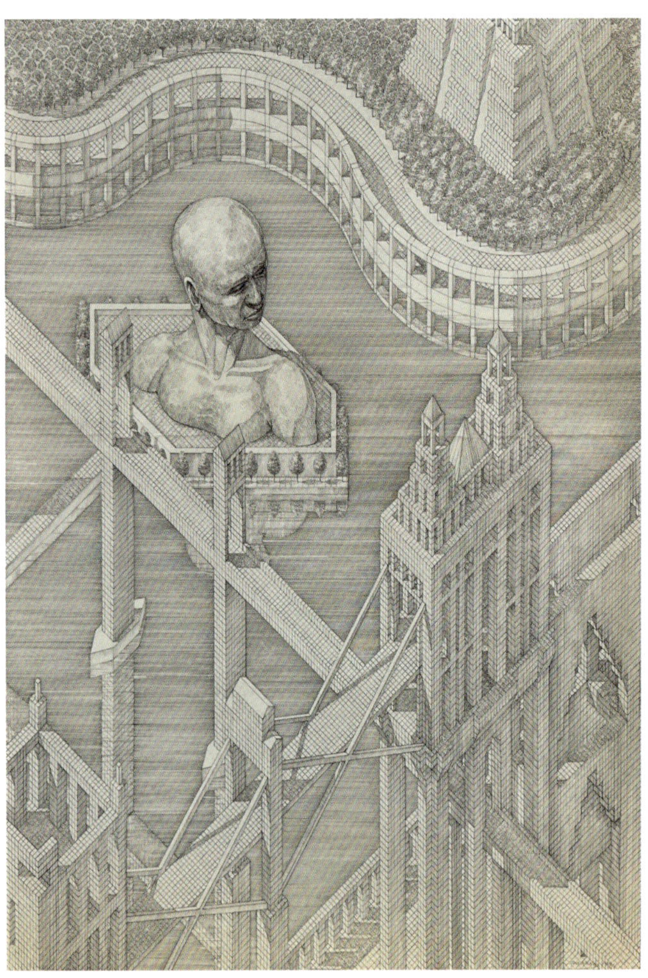

Ian McKay, "Tower of Babel" series, 1980s
Ink on paper
180 × 50 cm

I met IAN MCKAY in the mid-2000s. He started out as a mime artist and never lost his flair for the theatrical: full of life, quick to laugh, a friend to many. If you ever met him you would know, because he told *everyone*, that he was the opening act for a Led Zeppelin concert and performed with Cheech and Chong at a burlesque house called the Shanghai Junk. Around this time, he started a fundamentals art course but found it too academic and boring to pursue. Instead, he taught himself to draw by studying the old masters. Although he developed macular degeneration later in life, he didn't put down his artist's tools until it became too difficult to work. A member of the Blind Artist Society, McKay gained the admiration of many and was featured in *Visionary Architecture: Unbuilt Works of the Imagination*,[34] along with other renowned architects, including Piranesi, Rizzoli, and Frank Lloyd Wright. He was remarkably proud of that recognition.

I remember my first visit to McKay's home studio. Large surrealistic acrylic paintings lined the walls, but his current project lay on a drafting desk. A three-dimensional skyscraper was emerging from the surface of flat, white paper. How was this possible? He explained that it was part of his Tower of Babel project, which he had been working on for twenty years. Like the architectural drawings of Achilles Rizzoli's visionary, utopian world,[35] McKay's imagined cityscape was taking form in the quiet space of his living room. He called his fantastical, imaginary cityscape *Axonometropolis*, an infinite landscape of buildings that have no beginning and no end. Because he was nearly blind, he could create only one small area at a time, using a large magnifier that swung over his desk. The drawings were improvised directly on paper, in ink, freehand, without a plan. This is how McKay described his fantasy world:

> Axonometropolis is a city of the imagination; infinite in structures, roads, canals, and bridges as if in a daydream. I have been working on the Babel Project for twenty years. I was inspired by the writings of the blind author Jorge Luis Borges. Ironically perhaps, like him, I am nearly blind. When inventing the Library of Babel, Borges said that the universe is a sphere whose centre is everywhere and circumference nowhere. I am imagining the City of Babel. Babel was to be constructed to reach Heaven; and so, for me, it must be built to infinite scale.
>
> Axonometropolis is a term I invented to describe a city which can only exist as an axonometric drawing, which describes mass, volume, and spatial relationship without perspective. Therefore, there are no vanishing points or horizon. The buildings, pathways, lakes, and gardens are visible in their actual scale, in all directions, to infinity. Until 2010 I was drawing only the "districts" of Babel. Now the districts are expanding into each other, forming larger areas where the viewer can get a greater sense of my ultimate goal.[36]

McKay enjoyed describing Axonometropolis to me, pointing to the air above us and explaining how the sky would form a sphere around us—an interwoven, never-ending landscape. I would watch him pick up a pen and begin to draw without further ado. Nothing was mapped out, except in his mind, where he knew how to assemble the spires and columns like a miniature construction set. He could simultaneously hold multiple dimensions in his head and draw for hours, listening to CBC radio, the sunlight filtering through his window. I don't believe there was an end to the Axonometropolis project, a point at which the vast city would abruptly give way to open lands. If McKay were still alive, he would be bent over his desk, pen in hand, until the world ran out of paper to draw on. Even then, I imagine, he would extend the city over his walls, the ceiling above his head, and onto the sky itself.

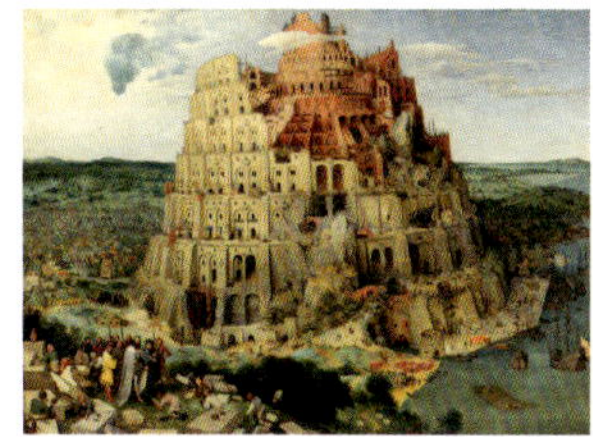

Pieter Bruegel the Elder,
The Tower of Babel, 1563
Oil on wood
114 × 155 cm
Vienna, Kunsthistorisches Museum

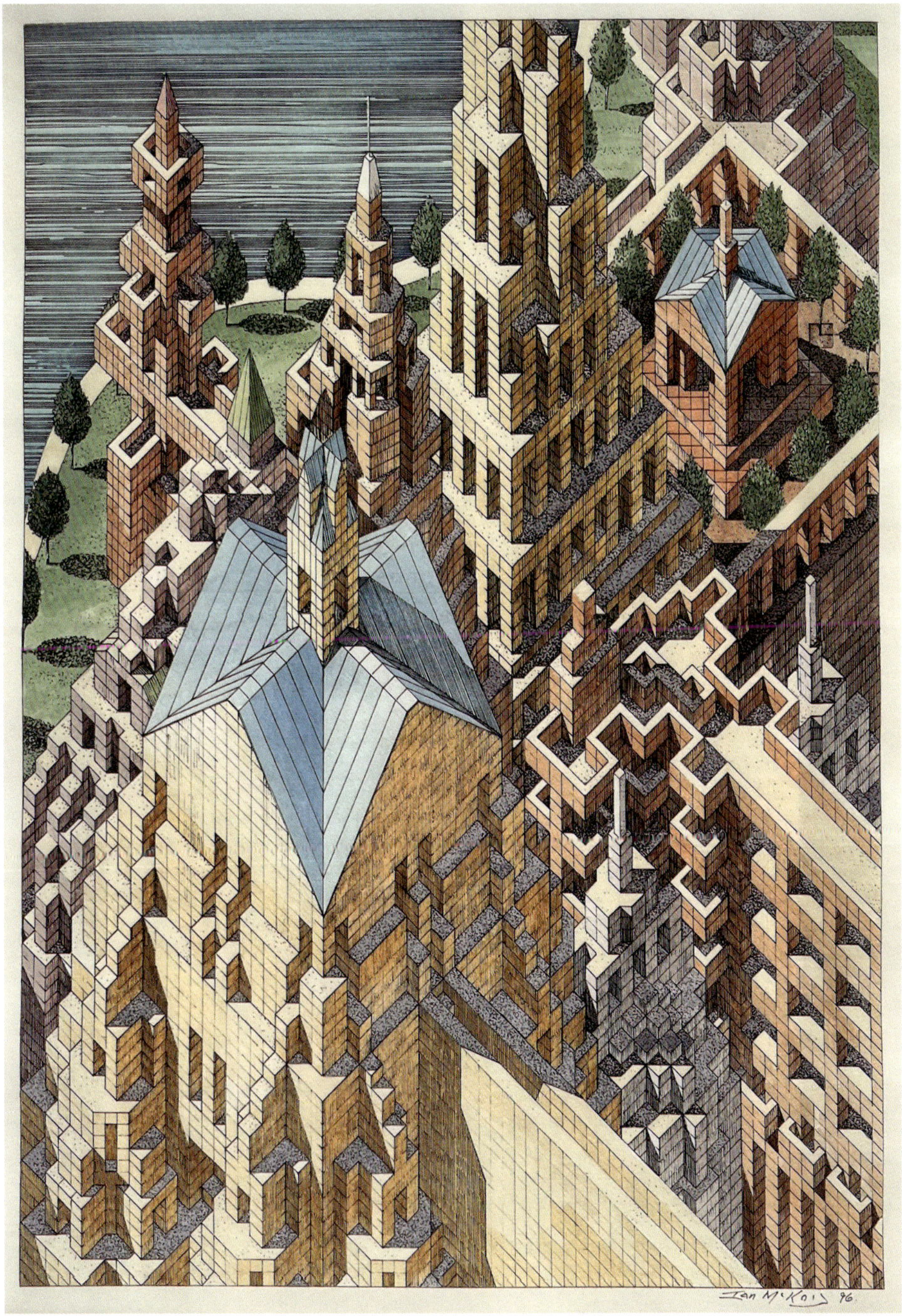

Ian McKay,
"Tower of Babel" series, 1980s
Ink and watercolour on paper
180 × 50 cm

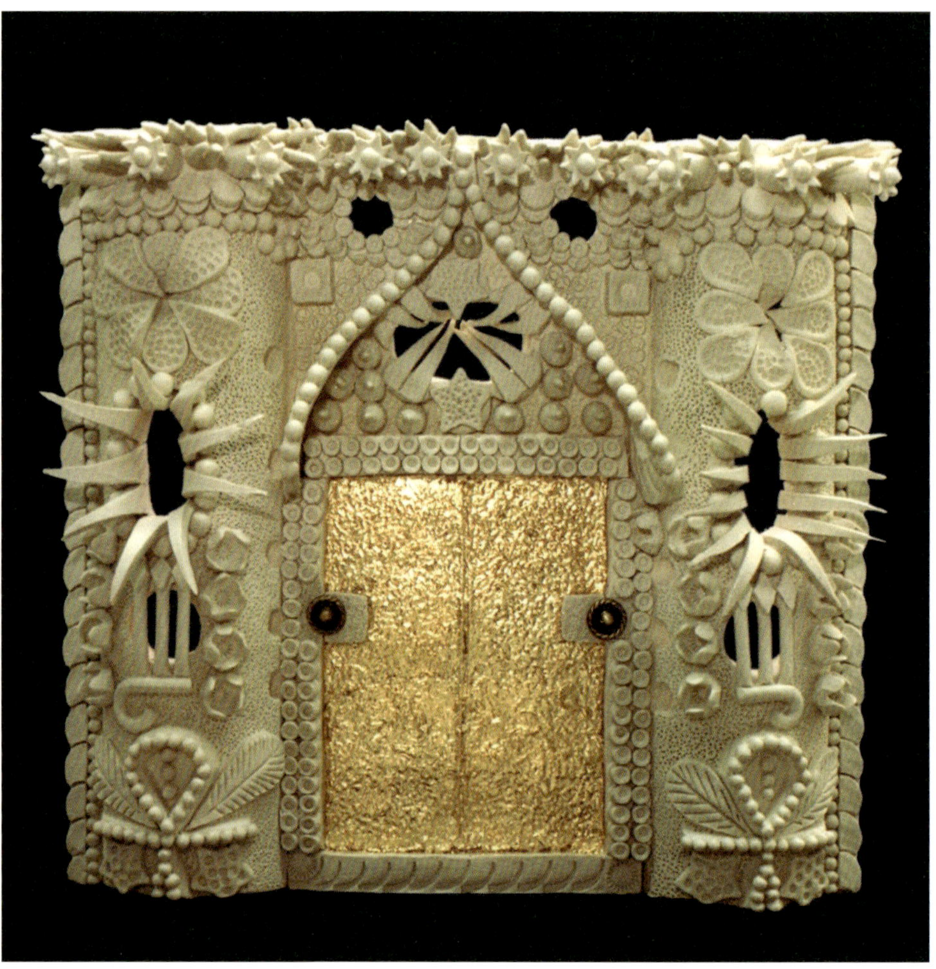

Frederick von Engelhardt,
The Main Gate (Atlantis), 1993
Porcelain on black hardwood
with electrical fixtures
and gold leaf
37 × 42 × 11 cm

I came to know SERGE VON ENGELHARDT through his daughters, who hold a treasured collection of their father's ceramic works and porcelain sculptures. His story is one of finding place and purpose in the new world. Like so many other Europeans in the first half of the last century, life for the von Engelhardt family was one of chaos and relocation. His parents were displaced from Estonia after World War I and sought refuge in Germany where he grew up. The arts were emphasized in school and sculpting lessons were part of the curriculum; that undoubtedly laid the foundation for his interest in becoming a sculptor. After World War II, now married with four children to support, von Engelhardt found employment in a mass-production ceramic factory, where he made models of animals and lamps for sale in gift shops. Because the owner was not able to pay him, von Engelhardt acquired a kiln in lieu of wages. He built a small studio behind his parents' apartment building from trees that he felled himself. Thus began von Engelhardt's calling as a ceramic artist.

Lured by films of life in Canada, von Engelhardt emigrated from Germany with his family in 1952. They landed in Northmark, Alberta, where he worked as a farmhand to support his family. Ill-equipped for prairie winters, they moved to Grande Prairie where he found work as a butter maker. As one of his daughters described to me, life was dire; they built a house from an old pig barn and eked out a basic living. They were a proud and dignified family who made the best of a difficult situation. Their life improved somewhat when they moved to Edmonton a few years later. Von Engelhardt continued to work at odd jobs to support

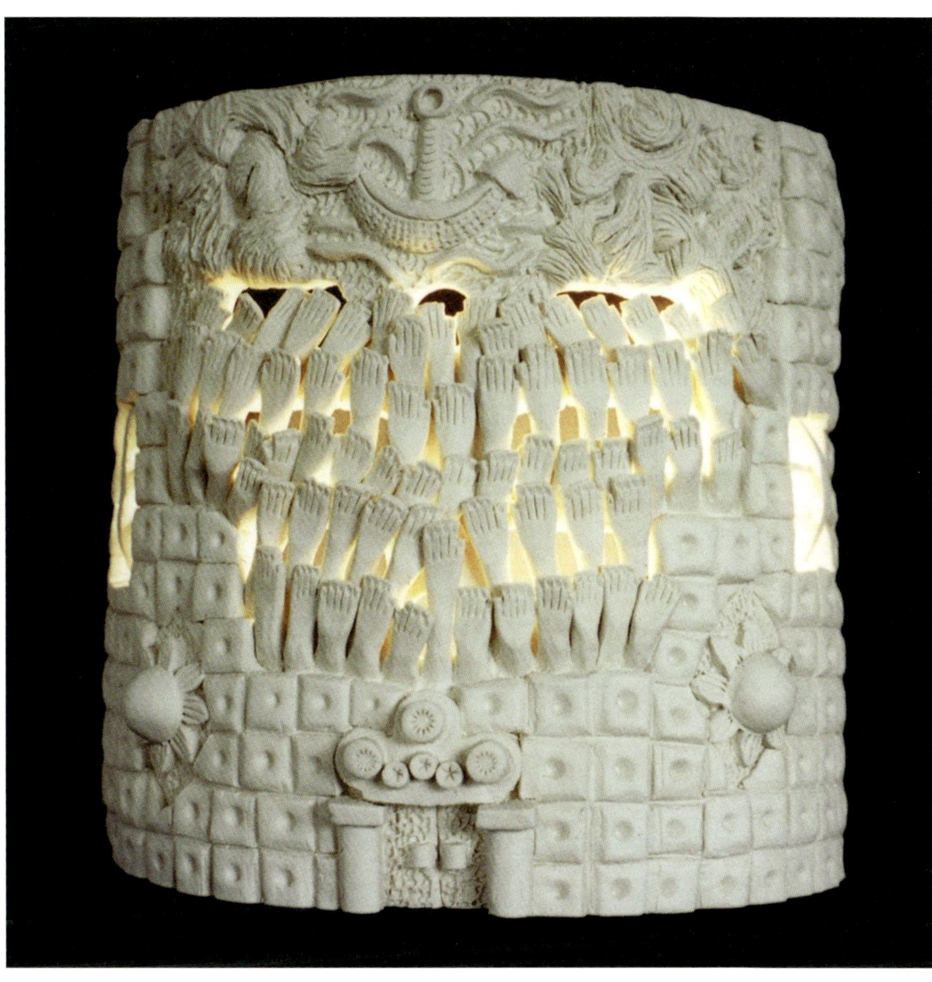

Frederick von Engelhardt, *Island of Atlantis, Wall Section of the West Gate: The Gate of Hope*, date unknown
Porcelain
28 × 17 cm

the family and spent the rest of his time in a ceramics studio he built in the basement of their house. While in Germany, he had taught himself to make ceramic and porcelain sculptures, and he was finally able to pursue his artistic vision. Through trial and error, he created forty different glazes from the Alberta mud for his ceramic bowls—a unique product that has never been replicated.

Von Engelhardt sold many ceramic pieces and a few sculptures, but it was difficult to build interest in his porcelain fantasy world of Atlantis, the most spectacular of his creations. Plato described the lost islands of Atlantis as a utopian nation, rich in precious metals, with a magnificent capital city. Unfortunately, its inhabitants turned greedy and lost their principled foundation; the gods became angry, and in one night of fire and earthquakes Atlantis sunk beneath the waves. Considering von Engelhardt's turbulent life in a world that had lost its moral compass, it's not surprising that the fate of Atlantis occupied his thoughts. He spent countless hours meticulously sculpting buildings that he imagined on the lost island, many illuminated with backlighting. Although he didn't particularly care if people liked his work, he hoped that the sculptures would generate some income. It wasn't a profitable venture. In 1980 the family moved to British Columbia and von Engelhardt opened another studio to make his ceramics and fantasy sculptures. He worked in his studio every day, alongside his wife who worked on her own ceramic creations, but the public failed to appreciate his vision.

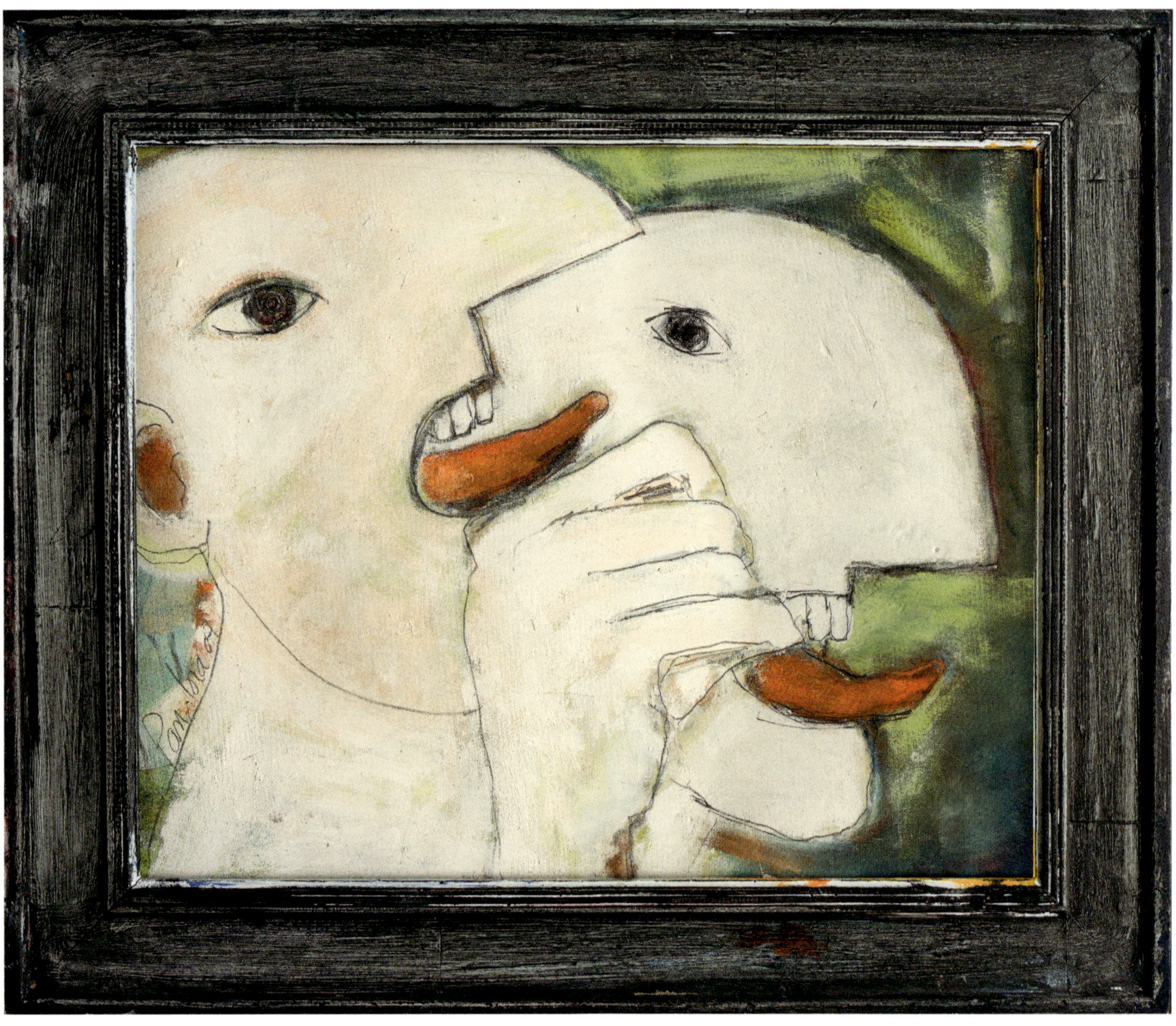

Pandora, *Untitled 17*, 2015
Acrylic paint on vinyl fabric
49 × 58 cm

I admired Randy McArthur's artwork at a Vancouver antique store overflowing with dusty treasures and paintings from local street artists. I learned he was a bit of a legend in both the art and music world. I was curious to meet this elusive man.

PANDORA (as he prefers to be called) is a tall, lanky figure; it's easy to imagine him on stage in his performance days. He was the lead singer of a punk band, the Generators, and I expected him to be garrulous and intractable. But Pandora is an unassuming type of guy, who has done a lot of living in his lifetime. He is reluctant to speak about himself but is frank and open about the injustices in the world, particularly among the poor and disenfranchised members of his community in the Downtown Eastside of Vancouver. His fifth-grade teacher wrote on his report card: "Randy could have used tact, but didn't." He admitted that comment is still applicable today, but he has a lot to say about those who live a marginalized existence. It is his reality.

Pandora's life reads like a grunge-lit novel—a transient youth, existing on the fringes of society, dabbling in music, art, and drugs. That was Pandora's life for many years. He hit the streets of Toronto at the age of fourteen to escape an abusive family situation, then

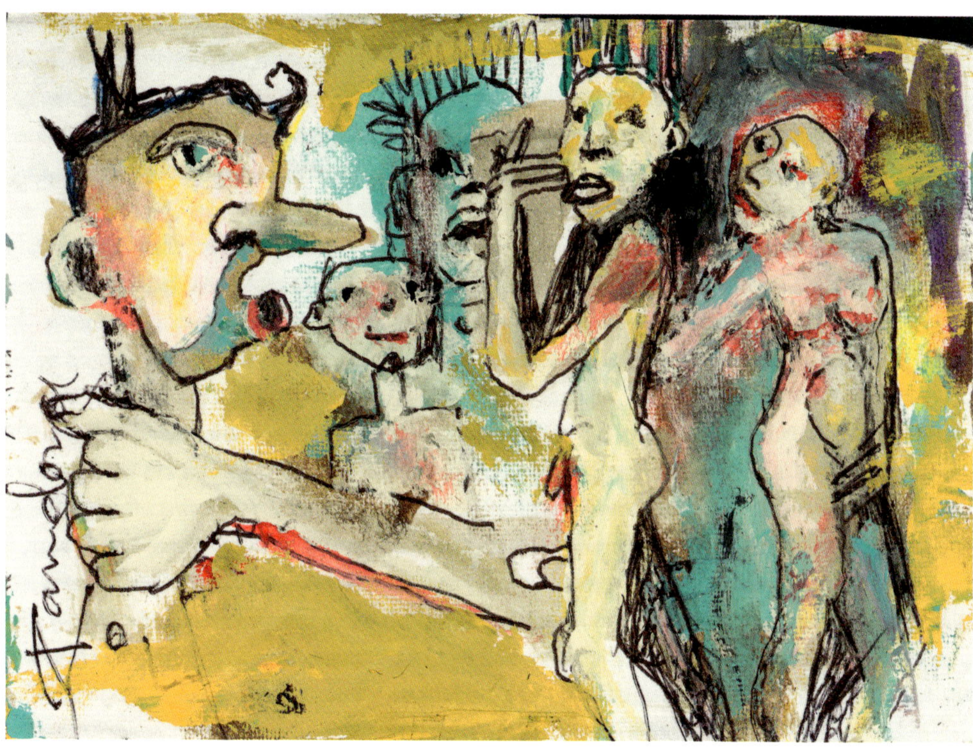

Pandora, *Untitled*, 2019
Acrylic on paper
11 × 14.5 cm

moved to Montréal where he worked in a drag bar for a few years. He acquired the name Pandora because he applied heavy black makeup to his eyes, making him look like a Panda bear. His name also references a small box of family memorabilia that his mother gave him—a Pandora's box of troubles and trauma, misplaced during his transient years. The mythical Pandora, he reminded me, is a provider of hope, and that is an apt description of the type of work he does at a needle exchange depot, the first harm-reduction centre in Canada. He is committed to making life safer for those who cannot help themselves. His legacy, he hopes, will be that he saved lives and made memorable art. He modestly admits to being an artist,* but eschews any kind of label.

Pandora has been a prolific painter for the past twenty years. He estimates he has produced at least a thousand works of art. He did a short stint at art school in his younger days, but didn't see the point of it all and left before he had to pay registration fees. He paints every day, with supplies from the dollar store, and describes his art practice as a necessity for his mental health. Without this outlet, he says he would become agitated and disoriented from sensory overload. He learns things through painting—things about himself and how he got to this place in life. His paintings are always about people because he finds them to be infinitely interesting. He describes his paintings as images from dreams. Asleep or awake, the images are already formed, waiting to be put on canvas. Faces peer out from the canvas, menacing or angelic, observing the viewer observing them. The demons don't always look evil, and that's the frightening part. Ordinary-looking folk can reach out to harm an unsuspecting bloke. You simply don't know where danger lurks. But neither can you predict where you will land in life's game of snakes and ladders. During the writing of this book, Pandora was offered a role in a Hollywood film production about the opioid crisis. Karma is like that, he says. You never know how it will manifest. Your Pandora's box might find its way back to you.

* Pandora prefers to call himself a "fartist," not an artist, as he regularly expels images from his overcrowded head.

Saskatchewan has a long-standing commitment to art and culture, and the tight community of artists, collectors, curators, and arts organizations mentored me in the history of art in their province. I was introduced to the work of prairie folk artists by the Dunlop Art Gallery, part of the Regina Public Library, which has been collecting and exhibiting artwork of provincial significance since 1948. The MacKenzie Art Gallery and the Saskatchewan Arts Board[53] also have large collections of historical folk art. While the work is preserved as a cultural record of the past, it is also valued for its aesthetic merit. The mid-century folk artists stand side by side with the province's contemporary artists. William McCargar, Ann Harbuz, Jan Wyers, and Dmytro Stryjek are just a few of the many who left their mark in that province's distinct art world.

It seems that both crops and artists thrive in Saskatchewan. A confluence of ideas in the mid-1900s created a unique setting for art to flourish in its own style. There was a vibrant art scene in Saskatchewan in the 1960s and '70s: Clement Greenberg took note of the Regina Five[54] and their take on modernism, which dominated the American art scene at that time.[55] Regina became known as a centre for ceramic sculpture, particularly after David Gilhooly (1943–2013), king of California Funk,[56] arrived to teach ceramics at the University of Regina in 1969. For those seeking an alternative to the structure and rules of modernism, Gilhooly's agenda was a welcome relief. The Regina Clay Group[57] established ceramic creation as art and, while it never developed into a formal art movement, their work was successfully exhibited both nationally and internationally. Most importantly, the clay artists rejected the modernist vision of uncovering abstract, universal truths. Instead, they explored concrete, local realities. Their belief in the importance of place and personal experience resonated with the back-to-the-land philosophy popular at the time.[58] The artists described having a double sense of place that resulted from growing up with rural and immigrant roots, leaving Saskatchewan to study art in the United States, and returning home to reengage with their own culture. They created art immersed in a place shared with others, both geographically and culturally.[59]

As in the rest of Canada, folk art peaked in Saskatchewan in the 1970s, and the province became immersed in exploring and preserving local knowledge. It was, in part, a reaction to modernism's internationalism, but it was also a "moment of self-awareness"[60] to realize that the region had a vibrant culture of its own. Artists spurned imported art opinions and lauded the rural class that gave rise to prairie socialism.[61] Emerging artists like Joe Fafard, David Thauberger, and Vic Cicansky found inspiration in their prairie roots[62] and fresh insights in the work of common folk.[63] David Thauberger (1948–) described his own relationship with folk art. Tasked with cataloguing the Saskatchewan Arts Board's collection, he became acquainted with the work of a generation of self-taught artists who communicated communal memory from the heart. It was a visual patois that blended "the accents and inflections of vernacular and popular culture with the syntax of modernism."[64] Folk artists offered a way to escape the influences of contemporary art dogma and reengage with local history and personal experience.

Thauberger recounts the impact of discovering the work of local folk artists, like WILLIAM MCCARGAR. His first impression of one painting with a vast orange sunset was that it was the most hideous painting he had ever seen. Over time, however, his aversion became a revelation:

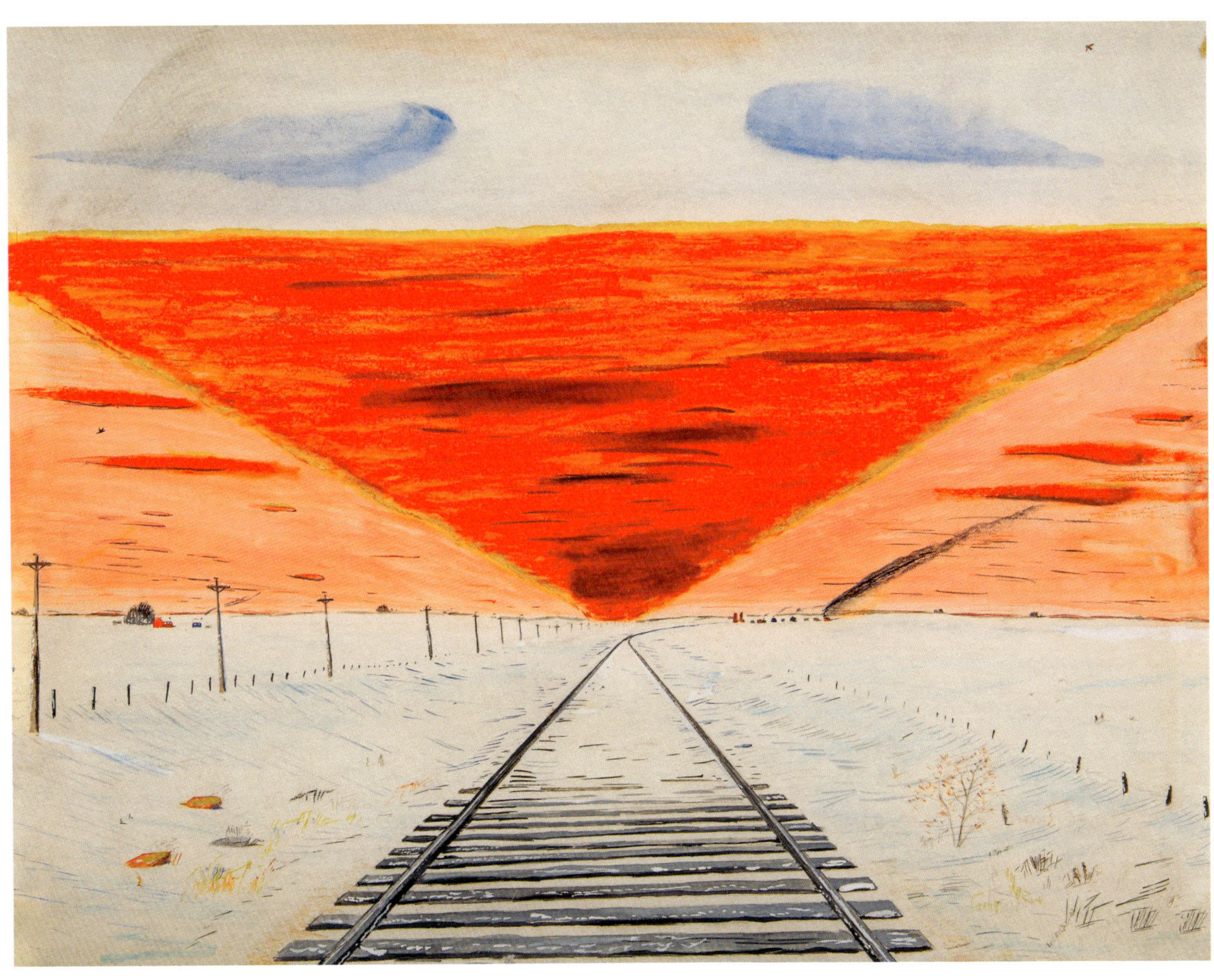

William McCargar, *Untitled*,
c. late 1960s
Tempera, pastel, ink on paper
52.5 × 69 cm

> I think the thing that opened the door was first of all the colour—the incredibleness of the colour. The outrageousness of the subject, the way it was, the stylization of it, the formal elements of it . . . And then the fact that it actually was here . . . this guy was actually painting this place! And it was outrageous and colourful and as inventive as anything that any trained artists in the art capitals were doing at the time . . . It gave me permission to deal with this place on my terms![65]

It was an *aha* moment for Thauberger. He realized that every personal experience, no matter how strange, could be explored through art. The ordinary becomes the extraordinary. Thauberger identified with every artist who struggled with questions of marginalization and unorthodox methods of production.[66] From the outside looking in, prairie life was as exotic as urban culture.[67] Meeting folk artists led him to understand that others like him—ordinary folk—shared his puzzling position as an outsider in possession of unacknowledged insider knowledge.[68] That is a thought-provoking statement. It describes a time when professional artists pushed back against the dictates of the art establishment and embraced folk artists as their colleagues.[69] In fact, it echoes Dubuffet's proclamation made thirty years earlier. In effect, those prairie folk artists played the same role as Dubuffet's art brut artists; untrained artists who painted from the heart were an antidote to the pretence of the academic art world. And, as many professional artists have told me, discovering the work of self-taught artists freed up their own practice. As one explained, it was inspiring to watch the local folk artists find their own way to and through art and discover unique solutions to technical problems that plague every professional artist.[70] Thauberger says that every generation invents the wheel it needs. I describe it as "a Dubuffet moment" on Canadian soil.

I make a general distinction between folk art and outsider art. Folk art proposes the commonplace as art;[71] outsider art proposes the personal and the idiosyncratic. It was, however, becoming an awkward exercise to squeeze creative expressions into prefabricated boxes. I had to accept there is a spectrum of art, with outsider art at one end and mainstream art at the other,[72] and folk art is somewhere along the line. Unfortunately, there are problems, too, with that approach. What factors determine where to place a work of art along the scale? There are many things to consider: the artist's biography; stylistic indicators (aesthetics); the artist's distance from the mainstream art world; and social factors such as marginalization. In painters' lingo, it is a wet-on-wet field,[73] with categories and styles blending into each other.

Before arriving in Saskatchewan, my contacts thoughtfully provided a roster of artists that might be of interest to me. I reviewed the list and looked for online images to acquaint myself with their work. The search for LEVINE FLEXHAUG called up an array of near-identical paintings. (Collectors call them Flexies: All the Same and All Different.) I was shocked. Surely, these were paint-by-number productions. This was early days in my research into outsider art in the prairies and I wondered what else was in store for me. But a day or two later, I was still thinking of those very peculiar landscape paintings and was compelled to look at them again.

Levine Flexhaug was a speed painter who made his living from the 1930s to the 1970s selling landscape paintings while travelling around Manitoba, Saskatchewan, Alberta, and

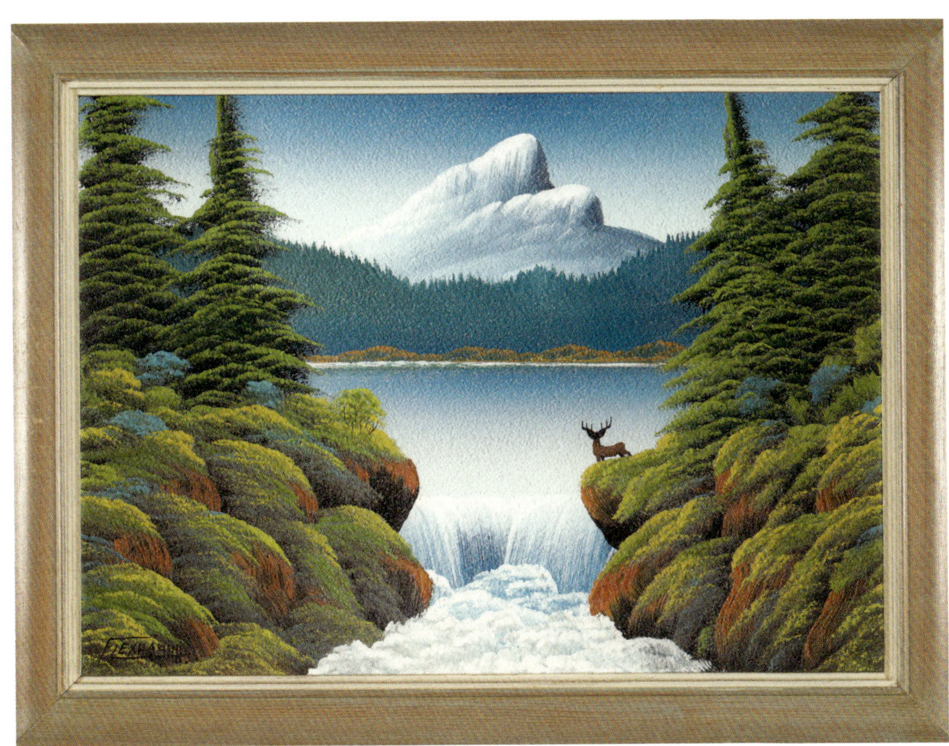

Levine Flexhaug, *Untitled*,
c. mid-twentieth century
acrylic on cardboard
25 × 34.8 cm

British Columbia. He typically worked on multiple easels in a public place, as admirers gathered to see images of iconic Canadian landscapes spring to life on canvas. He was said to spend only five to eight minutes on each painting, a remarkable feat for anyone but a carny entertainer. It was captivating to watch an artist work, as so many had done with Jon Gnagy[74] and Bob Ross,[75] celebrity television hosts who showed North Americans how to draw and paint. While today Flexhaug's practice might be described as performance art (that is, performing the act of painting), at the time his buyers were delighted to engage in a little landscape romance. An original painting was highly prized in a prairie home.[76] Despite (or perhaps because of) the almost surreal quality of Flexhaug's paintings, they have remained enormously popular, even becoming the subject of a touring exhibition. I am not alone in experiencing an ache of nostalgia when I look at a Flexhaug painting. All is well there. *O Canada, the True North strong and free.*

Flexhaug belongs in the chronicles of Canadian history, but I don't know where I would place him on the sliding scale of art, mentioned earlier. Although he was self-taught and his work is certainly out of the norm, Flexhaug created art solely for the purpose of eking out an existence during the Depression. It was his job. Flexhaug was a brilliant maker and marketer of a certain idea of Canada, a myth that sadly never existed.[77] I mention him here because his popularity is indicative of Saskatchewan's willingness to embrace his work as art, albeit with tongue in cheek. That in itself is important to note.

In general, the term outsider art was considered an historic category[78] and is not commonly used in the prairies, perhaps because artists and collectors are reluctant to categorize art in the first place. Maybe there is nothing to be outside *of* where high and low art have a place at the table. Vernacular art is a term more commonly used, suggesting use of a visual dialect that is understood by people of the region.[79] However, when I specifically inquired about outsider artists in Saskatchewan, I heard a chorus of people shouting, "Roger Ing!" I was curious to hear more about this legendary character.

ROGER ING was the owner, cook, and resident artist of the New Utopia Café in Regina. The walls were covered with Roger's artwork, the chaotic kitchen was in disrepair, and cans of paint littered the floor, which may explain why the city health department shut the place down in 1993. (A risqué picture in the dining area may have contributed to the decision.) Ing moved to Regina from Hong Kong in the 1950s. He studied traditional Chinese painting before he emigrated and took one art course on his arrival, along with welding and photography. He was a busboy at a downtown restaurant for many years before opening his own burger joint.

Ing was known for *Rogerisms*—traditional Chinese painting merged with Western abstraction and collage. No one can say how many paintings Ing produced; he was prolific and his choice of materials (like house paint and found canvases) meant that works of art could be created on the spur of the moment. Framed art was acquired for almost nothing at thrift shops, then painted over with Ing's own inventive ideas. A paint-by-number of Leonardo's *The Last Supper*, for instance, was transformed into a contemporary piece when Ing taped a magazine picture of Jimmy Swaggart over it, with arms outstretched over Jesus and his disciples.[80] Nothing was off limits: the Mona Lisa was a favourite subject, as well as Marilyn Monroe, pin-up girls, tigers, fish, UFOs, steaming cups of coffee, frying pans, aliens with antennae, and so on.[81] And anything at hand was a potential object to glue onto his paintings, including random kitchen utensils. Paintings spilled over frames and onto walls, or were sometimes painted over to create a fresh surface. Didn't like something about your chosen piece? No problem. Roger might repaint it to match your décor,[82] but more often he would show you the door.

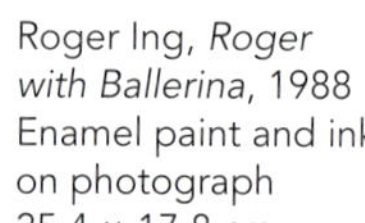

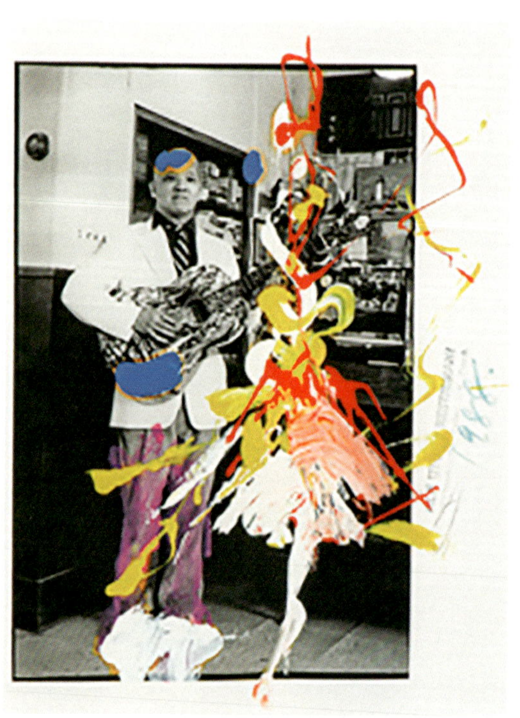

Roger Ing, *Roger with Ballerina*, 1988
Enamel paint and ink on photograph
25.4 × 17.8 cm

As with all outsider art, Ing's work is not easy to describe or categorize. The best description of "Roger style" I've heard was given by a local artist and friend of Ing, who described it as a cross between Chinese calligraphy and abstract expressionism.[83] I think that's the closest one can get to a formal description of work that is quirky, humorous, inventive, original, bold, and irreverent. One of the most interesting things about Roger Ing is that he was a local celebrity—loved and admired for being himself. Hundreds of people in Regina are proud to own a Rogerism, as they could be had for anywhere from five to fifty dollars. After leaving the café, Ing continued to paint for the rest of his life and enjoyed a few exhibitions, a retrospective of his work, and a short documentary film about his offbeat world. MuchMusic filmed a few events at the New Utopia. Perhaps the appeal of Roger's art is that it defied description.

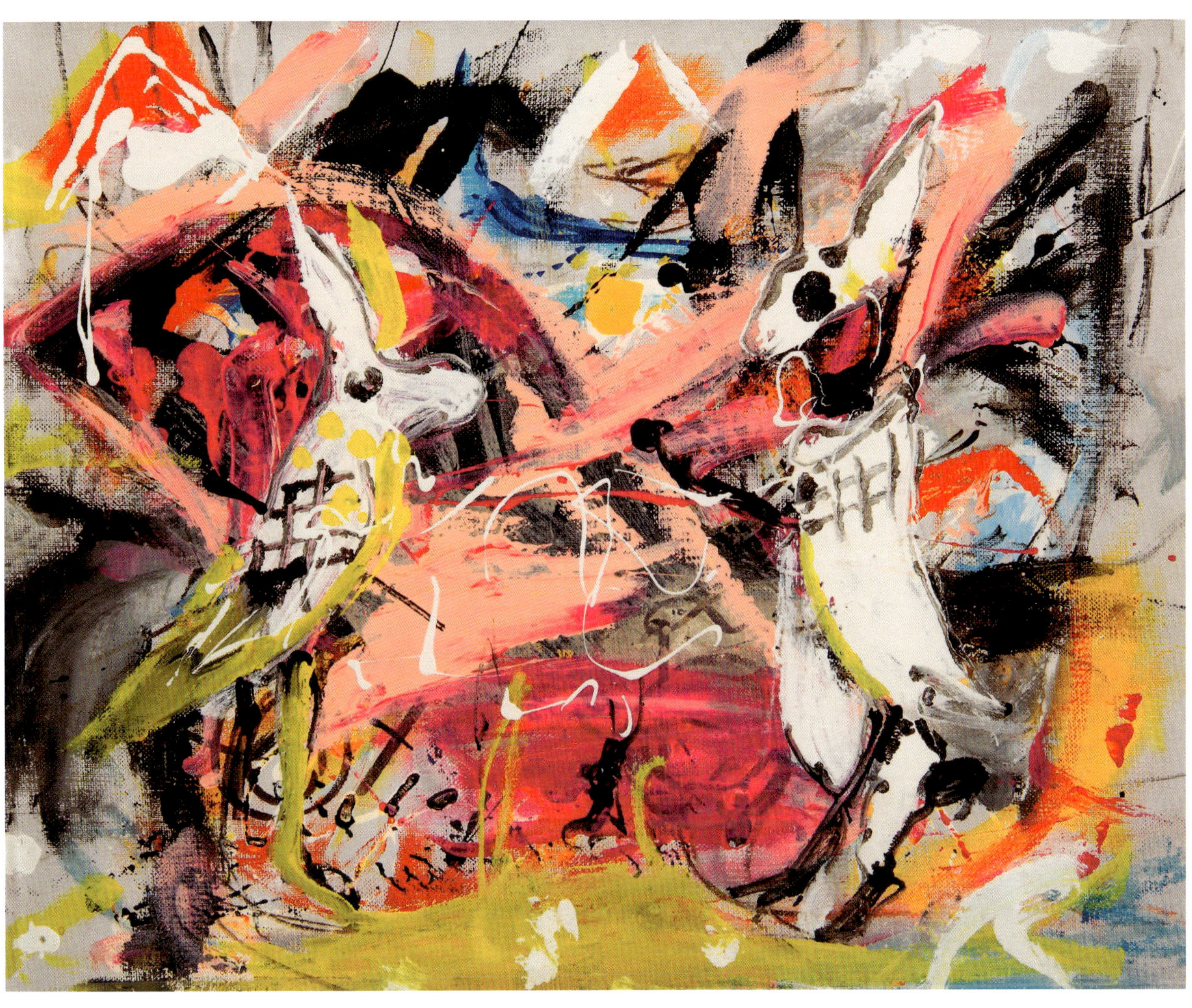

Roger Ing, *Untitled*, 1991
Enamel paint on canvas board
40.6 × 50.8 cm

Jahan Maka,
Untitled, c. 1980s
Chalk, pastels, and paint on paper
98 × 75 cm

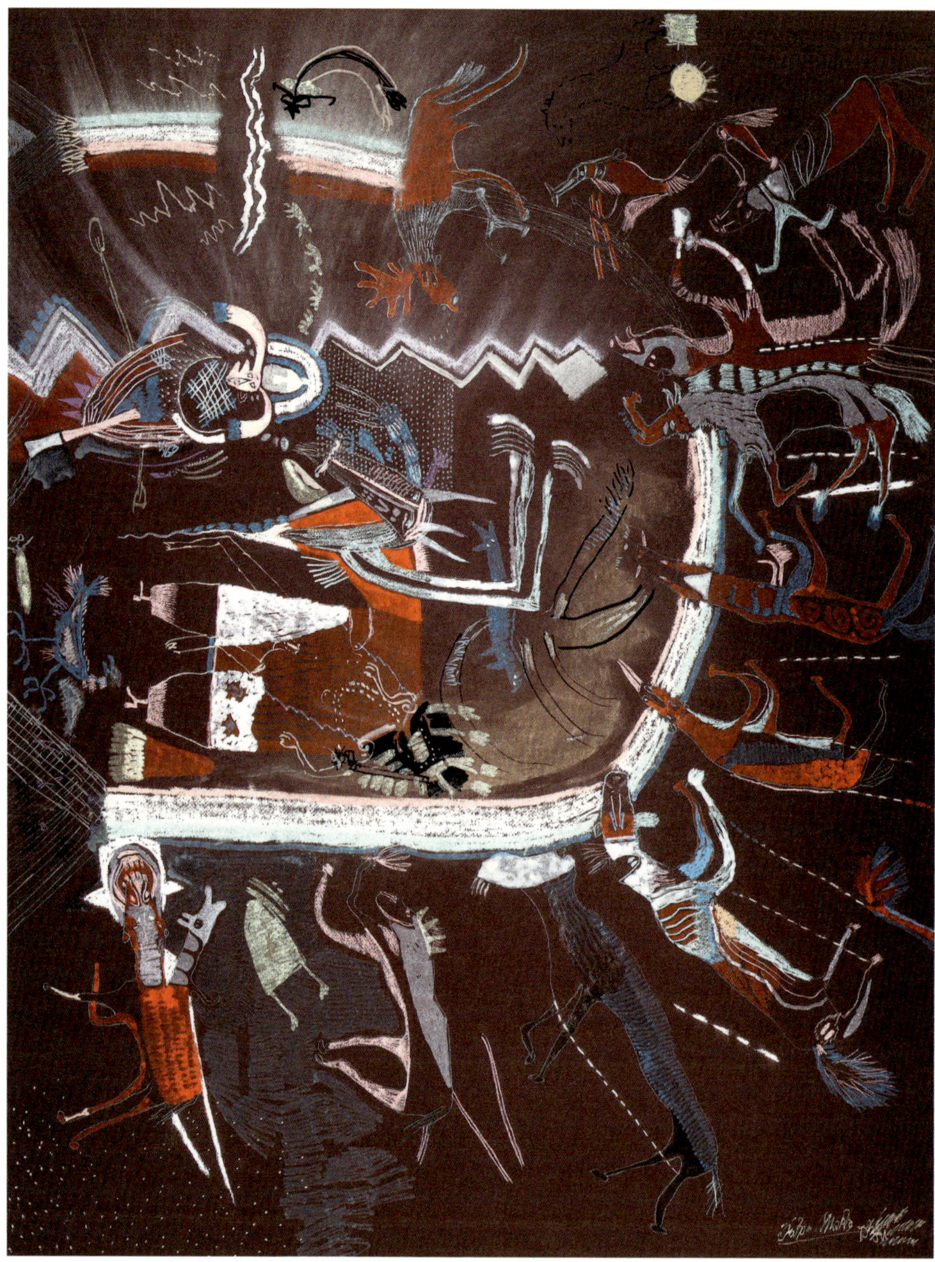

One of the most curious stories I heard on my journey was that of JAHAN MAKA, a notable prairie-settler artist. Although the details of his life are unclear, Maka was born on a farm in Lithuania; his family lost their farm during World War I, and Maka left for Canada in 1927, hoping to make enough money to return home and buy another farm. The Depression thwarted his plans and he found work as an itinerant labourer in the Prairie Provinces. He eventually settled in Flin Flon, Manitoba, where he worked as a miner for twenty-three years.

Maka's friends recalled him as a bit of a loner, introspective, but sociable with his close circle of friends. He began painting at age sixty-eight, improvising with products like commercial enamels, model airplane paint thinned with lighter fluid, appliance touch-up paint, wax crayons, and carpenter's chalk. He rebuilt worn paint brushes with hairs from his own moustache and painted on walls and doors of his home when he ran out of canvas. Motifs he wanted to recreate, like people or animals, were carved from wood or linoleum and stamped onto the canvas or board. Maka's close relationship with his godson, Tony Allison, was integral to Maka's development as an artist. Allison, himself an art student, encouraged Maka to paint and brought him professional art materials whenever he visited. In 1977 he convinced Maka to enter a juried art exhibition where he was awarded first prize. When asked about his work, Maka said they were "just paintings."[84] Allison promoted Maka's work and acted as intermediary between the artist and galleries. In 1983, Maka travelled with Allison to Mexico and the United States, where he discovered the black paper and drawing materials that distinguish his later, magnificent body of work.

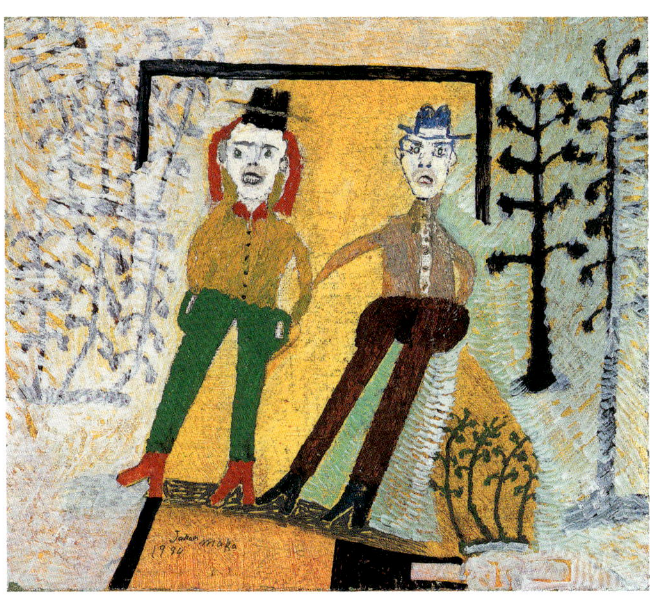

Jahan Maka, *The Prince Emigrates*, 1984
Oil on canvas
36.8 × 48.5 cm

Maka's work evolved over twenty years of production, from scenes of crudely rendered people and animals on an empty background to complex narratives on black paper. His development was noted but not questioned; validation flowed from a modernist myth that the greatest painters reach their peak in late career. Maka was praised as a great postmodern folk artist,[85] but I would call him an outsider artist for the highly idiosyncratic nature of his later work. Art critic Michael D. Hall described Maka as a great symbolist. Like Chagall, Maka's artwork is not expressive, but rather representative. The viewer has to do more than respond to the work; it has to be pieced together.[86] But, as it turned out, there was more than Maka's genius involved in the creation of his work.

Maka's art dealer, along with the curator of his retrospective in 1988,[87] went to visit Maka in Flin Flon. Maka's drawings on black paper were, they discovered, a collaborative effort. In one scenario, Maka's old friends, who came to visit and reminisce, picked up chalk and pencils and added marks to the drawings. In another and more likely version of the truth, Maka collaborated with Allison and Maggie Lenderbeck, a young Indigenous artist who helped around the house. Allison's interest in European military lore is said to be evident in the weapons and insignia on characters in the black paper paintings. Lenderbeck confirmed that Maka would instruct her to fill in the background of his works with colour. She complied. It is impossible to say how much of each artist's hand appears in the paintings. What remains are highly original and remarkable drawings.[88] Maka's career becomes no less interesting for its twists and turns, and the works remain extraordinary.

Was Maka a folk artist, outsider artist, great modern symbolist, or impostor? Did he compromise his art when others became part of the process or is this simply a story about the ruinous effects of a greedy art market?[89] I don't have answers for these questions. What is troubling is the need to elevate Maka from the marginalized status of a folk or outsider artist to that of master symbolist in order to honour his work. As Hall says, we can only compare his work to Chagall, Picasso, or Henri Rousseau when we remove the crippling outsider label and move him into the mainstream; his art deserves more than we have allowed.[90] That is to say, by calling Maka a symbolist, we can avert the patronizing chatter that keeps the artist outside the aesthetic and intellectual centre we call the mainstream.[91]

Ontario

While it was relatively easy to navigate through the art landscape in other parts of the country, exploring outsider art in Ontario was challenging, given its immense size and the range of opinions offered on art and its consumption. As I learned in British Columbia, raising the subject of outsider art was not a good conversation starter. I had heard of an exhibition in 2006, "Outside Coming In: A State of Freedom, Canadian Outsider Art," at the Art Gallery of Mississauga. It was a carefully curated collection and included some of the artists referenced in this book. The show garnered a modicum of attention, but nothing much came of it. Its curator[92] suggested that outsider art as a distinct genre has, perhaps, had its day. It may be that Ontario's market-oriented art industry doesn't have an interest in artwork that is out of the norm. One gallerist advised that he dropped the outsider label when he observed that collectors were not comfortable with this new and unfamiliar terminology. Other gallerists, however, felt that the public is very receptive to unconventional forms of art, but art institutions do not support work that falls outside the narrative of art history. None of these views were surprising, as I had heard them all in other cities and other contexts.

I was intrigued with the artwork of J. P. DANYS in Ottawa. I was unable to contact him, but pieced together his story from a gallerist, Guy Bérubé, who knew him well. In the 1980s, Danys cut his long hair, narrowed his pant legs, and joined the punk scene in Ottawa and Montréal. Completely absorbed in that lifestyle, he became a prolific painter of punk rockers, mainly fictional party-loving characters with spiked and coloured mohawks. A few of his effusive artist statements survive, this one from an exhibit in 2007:

> Hello art lovers from around the world. I'm J. P., self-taught unconventional artist from Bytown.
> Having a wide range of interests in art is good, I think.
> It's difficult to make choices sometimes.
> Because you can't do it all or have it all.
> But if you want to buy art, this gallery is perfect.
> I pretty much like everything here, even my stuff isn't [too] bad, I think.
> There wasn't much interest in my sculptures made from recycled materials.
> Maybe they were too weird. So here's five new more mainstream acrylic paintings.
>
> P.S. Sorry if you find my statement short. It was originally fifty pages.

While J. P.'s public persona was that of a painter, he was absorbed in a much bigger project—fabricating life-sized sculptures of people who shared his apartment. Bérubé was, perhaps, the only person to see the collection. He recounts his experience:

> It was common for me to see all types of people lingering outside my gallery.[93] They would peek through the window at the artwork but would never come in. Some were homeless. Some were addicts. Some dealt with mental health issues. Despite my invitations to enter the gallery, many were hesitant to venture in. One particular fellow, J. P., eventually came in. He entered boldly and immediately exclaimed, "I am an artist too, you know." After several weeks of getting to know J. P., I asked him to describe his work to me. He spoke of his paintings, which I would eventually exhibit

> J. P. Danys, *Untitled*, 2005
Found coat hangers, papier-mâché, discarded newspapers, white gesso paint
111.8 × 38 × 22.8 cm

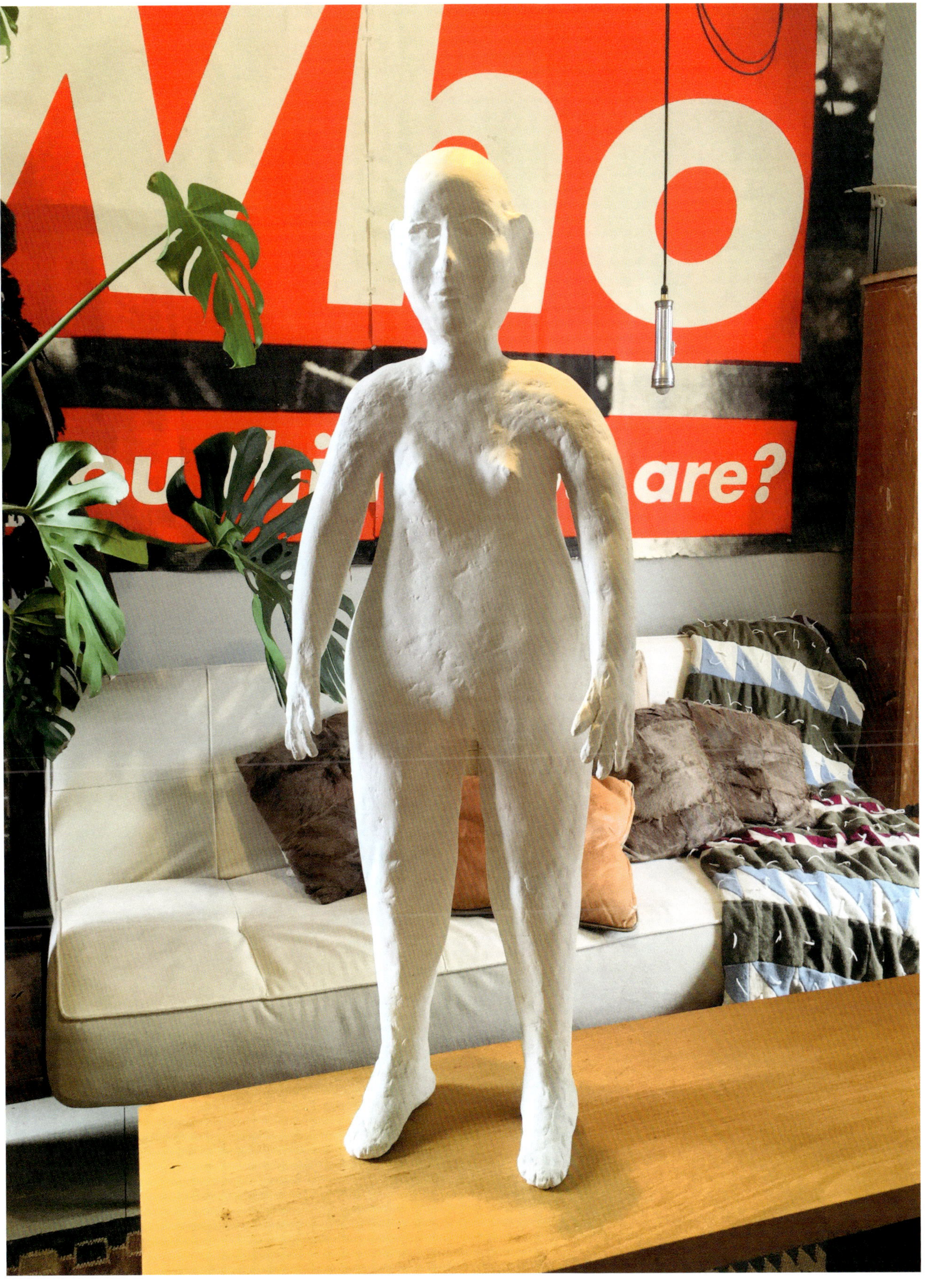
are?

> in group shows, much to the horror of several uptight locals. But it was the description of his sculptures that really captured my interest.
>
> J. P. said that he "lived with his creations." To me, this seemed to be what most artists were accustomed to. J. P. insisted I come to his home to see for myself. Studio visits are a common practice for art dealers or gallerists but I had a feeling that, in this case, I'd be up for a unique visual feast. I was not prepared for what I was about to see.
>
> J. P. lived in government subsidized housing. His unit was one of the smaller studio apartments in the basement. It was filled to capacity with life-size sculptures of people, all women, dressed in what seemed to be thrift shop finds, along with disheveled wigs and badly applied makeup. It was a blast to the senses. J. P. explained how they were constructed. He would use hundreds of manipulated wire coat hangers to shape the body, limbs, and head. He would then apply papier-mâché to cover the "bones" of the sculptures, paint them white with gesso, apply facial features and makeup, nail polish on some, add the clothing and wig, and would christen them with individual names. I do not recall any of the names of the wonderful creatures. Most of the sculptures were standing, but some were seated, and one was lying on the bed. I suspected that J. P. was questioning his gender identity and this may have been one way to create, adapt, and experiment his way through the issues. J. P. explained that the sculptures were not lovers. Rather, they were friends who helped him combat loneliness.
>
> J. P. decided to show me a special surprise. He removed the skirt and underwear of one of the standing sculptures. I braced myself for what was about to be revealed. J. P. lifted her bulky sweater and pointed to her belly and said, "Look, her baby." On each side of the sculpture's extended belly was an opening, covered in clear plexiglass. I peered into an opening to see a baby doll sleeping peacefully within her mother's full belly. I was simply overwhelmed. I knew I was seeing something at its purest form—an extremely raw emotion—something that may have been lacking in J. P.'s difficult life.
>
> I burst into tears immediately after leaving J. P.'s tiny apartment. I knew I'd witnessed something unique and intimate. I also realized that these sculptures had to remain his secret. I could not present them to the public and risk him be ridiculed.
>
> Soon after my visit, J. P. came to the gallery. He announced that he had destroyed all the sculptures, except for one, which he gave me. When I asked him why he had done this to all of his incredible sculptures, J. P. simply said, "I no longer need them."

Although J. P. never explained his reasons for creating these statues, it is possible that they helped him explore his sexuality. He lived as a woman for three years in the 1990s, and stated in a letter, "I'm still not sure if I'm transgendered or just lonely. The thing is I often have the desire to express my feminine side. I get very depressed when I don't or can't."[94] Perhaps they simply kept him company.

I was also introduced to FRITS RUHLAND, who created a magical world in his private corner of the forest. He resides in the Netherlands, but returns to his brother's farm in Ontario every summer. It's a routine he has maintained for the past forty years. Initially, Frits created fairy gardens of coloured stones, kitschy garden gnomes, and stone angels to amuse visitors. Bored with that project, he began creating mobiles from bits of painted wood in the style of Alexander Calder. His ideas came together when he saw a video of a miniature circus that Calder created to entertain friends. A logical continuation of this idea, according to Frits, was to create his own Cirque du Soleil with Barbie dolls. The dolls were easy to source, were all the same size, and were the only cheap aerial acrobats available to him. Given that the circus itself is a somewhat tasteless exhibition, Frits said, he embellished his actors with dollar-store glitter and nail polish. These performances, he warned, were not suitable for children or prudish people. Frits eventually banned visitors from his forest site, and now creates only for himself. The circus transformed into a flying circus, along with airplanes and gliders. It later featured space-girls with airships, space scooters, and a flying saucer. It became a kind of Moulin Rouge burlesque for a period of time. He is now working on his version of the Broadway musical *Cats*.

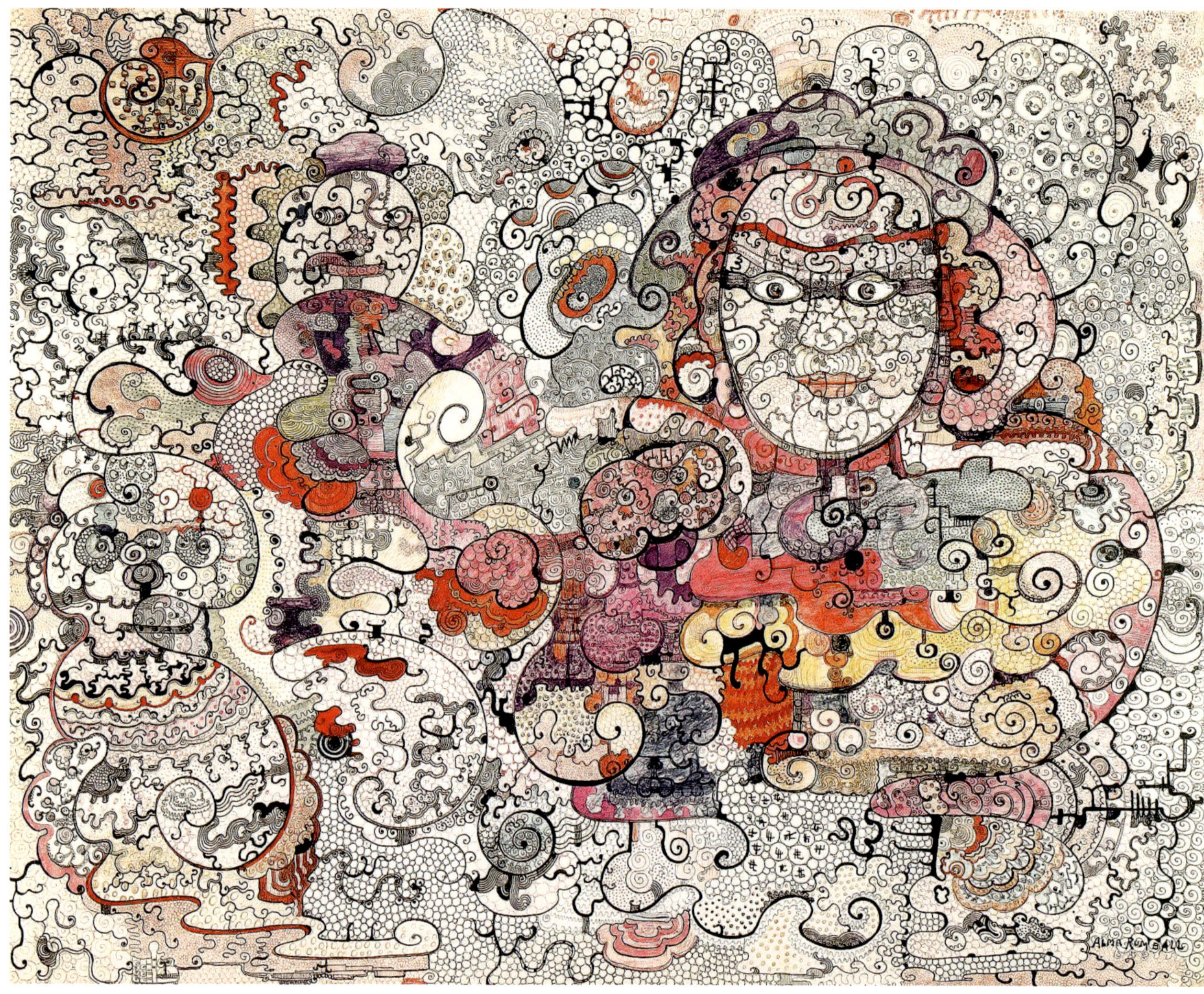

Alma Rumball, *Garden of the East*, c. 1965
Pen and coloured ink on paper
62.5 × 78.7 cm

Although outsider artists work in isolation and are unaware of what others are creating, I have noted similarities in their designs, their themes, and always the compelling force that drives their work. Two that come to mind are Ontario artist ALMA RUMBALL and legendary English artist Madge Gill (1882–1961). Gill created automatic (uncontrolled) drawings under direction from the spirit world. She drew while in a trance-like state and attributed her work to her spirit guide, Myrninerest,[95] signing her work with its name. Gill claimed to be merely a vessel though which the spirit world expressed itself.[96] Her alleged connection to the spirit world has been dismissed by some critics as nothing more than an alibi to account for her uncontrolled compulsion to draw.[97] Nevertheless, there was a period of history in which it was fashionable to consult mediums as conduits for messages from the supernatural world. Communications that came from the spirit world arrived through automatic speaking, writing, and drawing. When I heard about Rumball's spiritual drawings, I was curious to learn about her art practice.

Rumball spent a lot of time drawing as a child, and eventually left the family farm in Ontario to work as a painter in a ceramics factory in Toronto. She returned to Huntsville in the 1950s and her life took a dramatic and unexpected turn. She lived the life of a recluse and did not venture out except for family functions. About that time, Jesus appeared to her, with a panther, and commanded her to draw and write in order to help humanity.[98] She then realized there were other levels of spiritual existence and began to communicate with a turbaned spiritual guide named Aba Pasha, who identified himself as a genius. Most importantly, "the Hand," which she believed was the hand of God, made its presence known to her. She watched as it chose art materials and drew detailed drawings and images on its own. Rumball said, "I'm as excited to see what the Hand will do as you are. I can't accept credit for them [the drawings]; you see, I don't do them."[99] She watched as the Hand drew images of unfamiliar forms and faces, as well as Joan of Arc, Tibetan gods, and images of Atlantis. Her drawings are intricate and charming. The Hand did not completely take over her consciousness; Rumball was always present, as herself, and others could speak with her while she drew. The distinction, her family advises, is that Rumball's creations were mystically guided, not merely the product of automatism, where the artist taps into the unconscious mind.

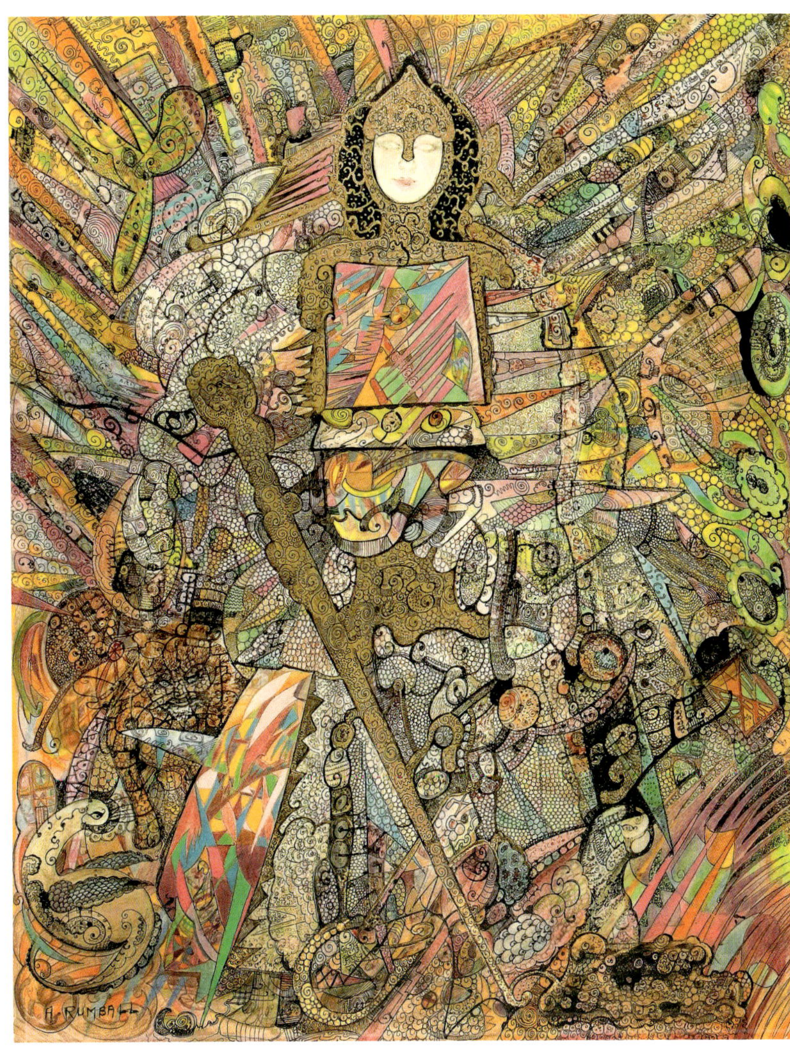

Alma Rumball, *Joan of Arc*, c. 1960s
Pencil, crayon, and coloured ink on paper
78.7 × 62.5 cm

Rumball created a remarkable number of drawings—nearly five thousand in all. She also left more than one hundred pages of spiritually inspired writings describing life in Atlantis. Her family have sought the opinion of spiritual leaders, one of whom identified certain Tibetan deities. The foreign hieroglyphics present in some of her drawings are said to predate early Tibetan writing. Contradictory opinions have been offered on the source of Rumball's art, from mental illness to an advanced state of consciousness. Rumball's family believes the drawings are the "Sacred Language of Light, activation drawings with codes embedded in them for the elevation of humanity, at this time."[100] I can only present them to you as the wondrous fantasy creations of an artist completely absorbed in a world of her own making.

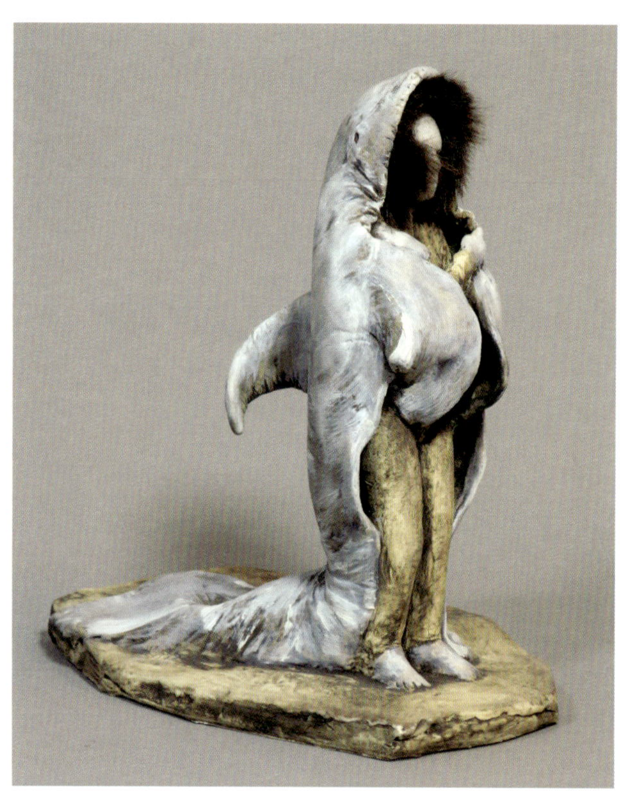

Jordan McLachlan, *Orca Trainer*, from the "Zoo Living" series, 2015
Clay, paint, synthetic hair
25 × 23 × 15 cm

For JORDAN MACLACHLAN, making art is a way to explore life's troubling issues. Never able to skilfully negotiate the demands of the outside world, clay and kiln are always there to ease the passage. She probes a subject for years, creating fantasy worlds of clay that ask, "What if *this* happened?" *This* might be a nosy peek into the lives of a condominium building's occupants (*Condo Living*), engaged in mundane and intimate activities, from visiting with friends to indulging in acts of passion. As we trespass into their private lives, one of them peers back at us with binoculars: the voyeur confronts the voyeur. Or it might be a world that examines the complex relationship between humans and animals, where boundaries between species begin to blur (*Zoo Living*). Creatures morph into fantastic beasts like rhino-elephants; others spew golden locks from their snouts. Above all else, she is a storyteller, showing us what *could* be.

MacLachlan has worked with clay since she was a child, a practice that sprung from her affinity with animals. She created an imaginary family for herself, believing she was an orphaned mountain lion cub who was adopted by humans. Her parents indulged her fantasy, allowing their speechless, feral child to walk on all fours and eat from a dish on the floor. Having to attend school was a rude awakening and she had trouble fitting in with her classmates. Reluctantly, she stopped "being an animal" around the age of twelve. Still preoccupied with animals, she drew pictures and taught herself how to sculpt them from clay. They were her darlings, and their presence provided a safe refuge as life fell apart around her. She explored the genera of animals: Equus, Canis, Loxodonta, and so on until she was satisfied that she understood them all. Her feeling for animals, she says, is an uncomplicated love. Her aim is not to make beautiful reproductions, but rather to capture the essence and ineffable spirit of each creature.

MacLachlan taught herself how to sculpt with clay, a simple and ubiquitous medium made of earth and water. It was an accessible material that didn't have the technical demands of ceramics. She still prefers the primitive and expressive qualities of clay; it triggers memories of working with her mother's pie dough—bits that were discarded when her mother baked for her friends at coffee gatherings. She was there, a silent spectator to the talk and laughter of women, finding safe harbour from the real world for a cloistered hour or two. Everyday materials embellish her clay sculptures as if they were plucked fresh from a child's oven: nail polish, varnish, paint, and glaze are her shiny sprinkles on baked goods. Clay is considered a low-brow material in the art world, associated with artisans rather than artists. It is a problem that also plagued the Regina Clay Group over the years, isolating the movement from the mainstream of Canadian art.[101] But for MacLachlan, clay is an obvious medium for creating things in the natural world. It wouldn't make sense to craft animals out of anything else. I have observed the artist with her clay creations, and it would be hard to imagine her working in another medium, like paint, for that would put her hand at the end of a brush. She must feel the clay, warm it in her hands, and breathe life into her creations.

MacLachlan says she didn't choose to be a sculptor; rather, she succumbed to it. It has not been an easy life. Sculpting is an imperative for her, and she models figures every day. A single figure is born after days of labour, a grouping materializes several weeks later, and years pass before another world of her own making is realized. This image—*Dogs Attacking Man*—is from a series called "Unexpected Subway Living," which contemplates a world after a catastrophic event where people and animals have been forced underground. The piece is crafted in plain red clay with only the dogs painted black with dabs of white, mimicking life pared down to the bare essentials. The world would be a hellish place with no food or housing; societal norms as we knew them would disappear. Survivors would take refuge in the literal and metaphorical space of subways, where they could disembark at any station or stay on forever, riding the track through interminable scheduled loops and infinite ways of being. MacLachlan says it is a frightening and challenging place, where nightmares and dreams proliferate and collide. A headless woman strolling with her pet pigs has become the new normal. But others seem unphased by the new order: dudes chill with cigarettes and drinks, a woman gives birth on the floor, and lovers embrace. The world *doesn't* end; people adapt to the most calamitous catastrophes in unforeseen ways. A Santa doppelganger holds a bag of the most wondrous things. A faith healer performs a baptism and someone else has set up a barbeque to grill some creature that, perhaps, a dog has managed to catch. That, I think, is the precious message informing her installations. Life goes on. Human ingenuity wins the day.

Jordan McLachlan, *Dogs Attacking Man*, from the "Unexpected Subway Living" series, 2010
Clay and oil paint
17.8 × 17.8 × 25.4 cm

MacLachlan is currently working on a new series, as yet unnamed, that sums up "what she thinks she knows" about the world—the undeniable truth that everything in nature is connected.

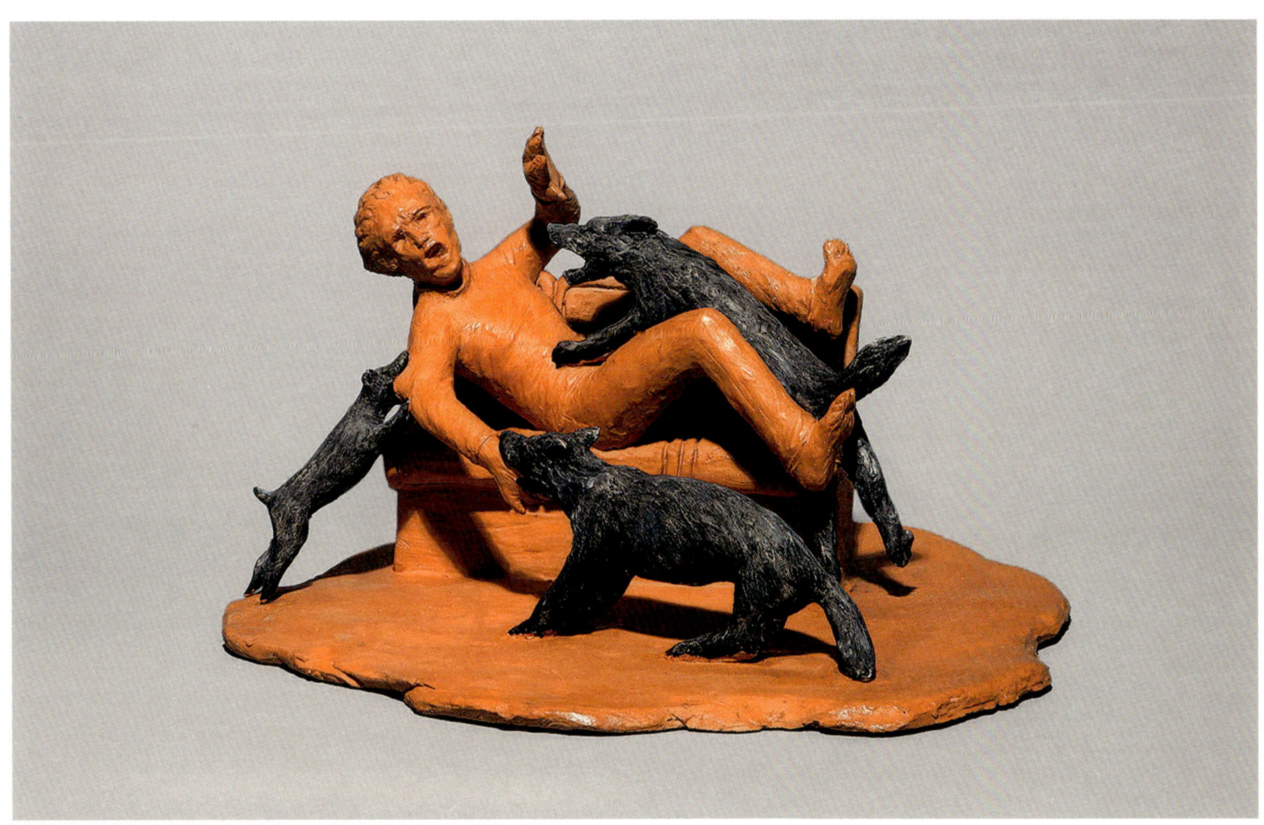

Whatever you thought you knew about MENNO KRANT and his art is probably wrong. It's a recurring problem with outsider art; that is, ascribing meaning to the work of secluded self-taught artists without knowing their intent. It gets complicated when an artist is "outed" and asked to account for the output of his personal activities. It's been a struggle for Krant to balance his all-consuming need to paint with the demands of those who want to share his work.

Krant recalls that as a child he was always drawing. Sometime in elementary school, a teacher informed him that he didn't have the talent to be an artist and he pretty much gave up art, except for a few wood carvings, for the next thirty-five years. His private, creative world started up in the early 1990s when he decided to live in his car. The outsider art world laps up stories like this, and much is made of this period of Krant's life. It echoes the stereotypical image of an eccentric and marginalized artist who goes off grid. But, he explains, he wasn't homeless; rather, it was a choice he made in order to live the life he wanted. His job provided enough income to meet his needs, but rent was expensive and he didn't want to spend his salary on a place that he would inevitably fill with stuff he didn't need. He loved being alone in his car, locked in a private space with the freedom to drive away at a moment's notice. But time drags, he says, when you're living in a car, and he took up drawing to fill the long, dark evenings. On days off he headed to the lake where he was free to experiment with art supplies. Wondering what to paint first, he chose a lighthouse across the way. That proved to be a disappointing and dull project, but it made him realize that he had to tap his imagination rather than replicate images from the outer world. What others would learn in art school, Krant learned by trial and error or, more accurately, through his total immersion in art. He spent his days playing with paint and colour—floating canvasses in the lake to discover the effect of water on paint and using his fingers and tools to drip, scrub, and scratch images onto surfaces. This is when his passion to create took priority over everything else in his life. Nothing else mattered.

Initial reactions to Krant's work were negative. He didn't share his work for six years. The public part of the artist's life began when a friend took some of his paintings to a local flea market. A folk-art collector bought a few and took them to New York, where other dealers and gallerists took notice. His career took off but things got out of control, as Krant describes, when he was flooded with exhibition invitations and he was painting at an impossibly frenetic pace. He was sometimes labelled an outsider artist, a term he had never heard before. (Was he a cowboy or something?) Other times he was just Menno Krant, the artist. Although he avoided all publicity and never disclosed his art persona to neighbours and acquaintances, it was still difficult to remain invisible. The final straw, he says, was when a busload of art enthusiasts showed up at his door, asking to tour his home studio. Since then, Krant has guarded his privacy carefully. He lives a modest life, shielded from the corruption and greed of the art world. Perhaps those are values he inherited from his parents.

Krant's family moved from the Netherlands to Toronto when he was five years old. It was an escape, he says, from memories of unspeakable personal tragedy, a brutal war, and fear of another. He is sincere when he describes a perfect childhood with loving parents. There were no expectations imposed on him other than to do his best and be a good person. It's a theme that comes up often in conversations with the artist. Raised in an environment of kindness and charity, he radiates empathy for others. In fact, his concern for the suffering of others is what informs his art.

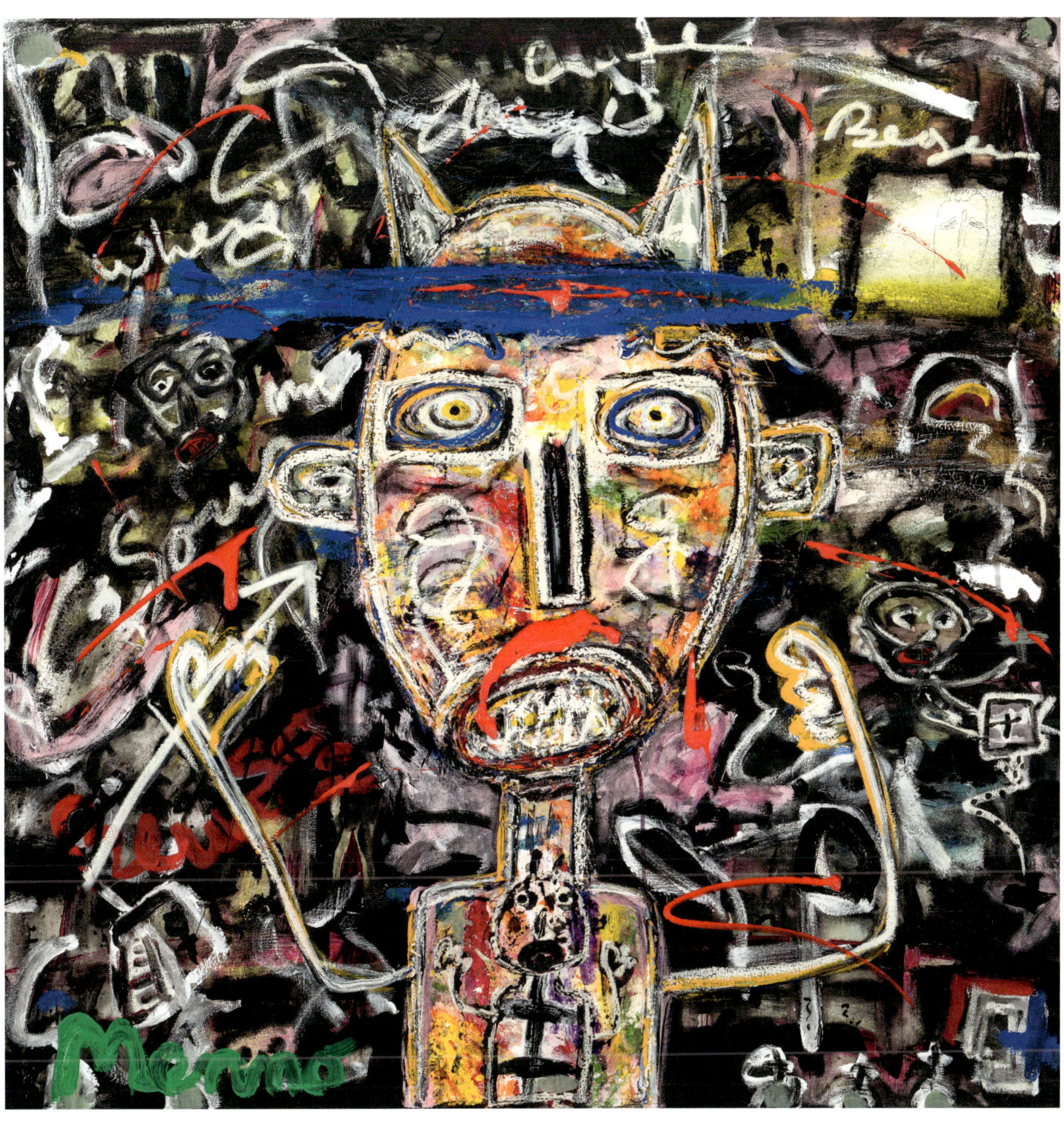

Menno Krant, *Untitled*, 2000
Acrylic and oil on canvas
91.4 × 91.4 cm

Menno Krant, *Untitled*, 2005
Acrylic and oil on canvas
30.5 × 30.5 cm

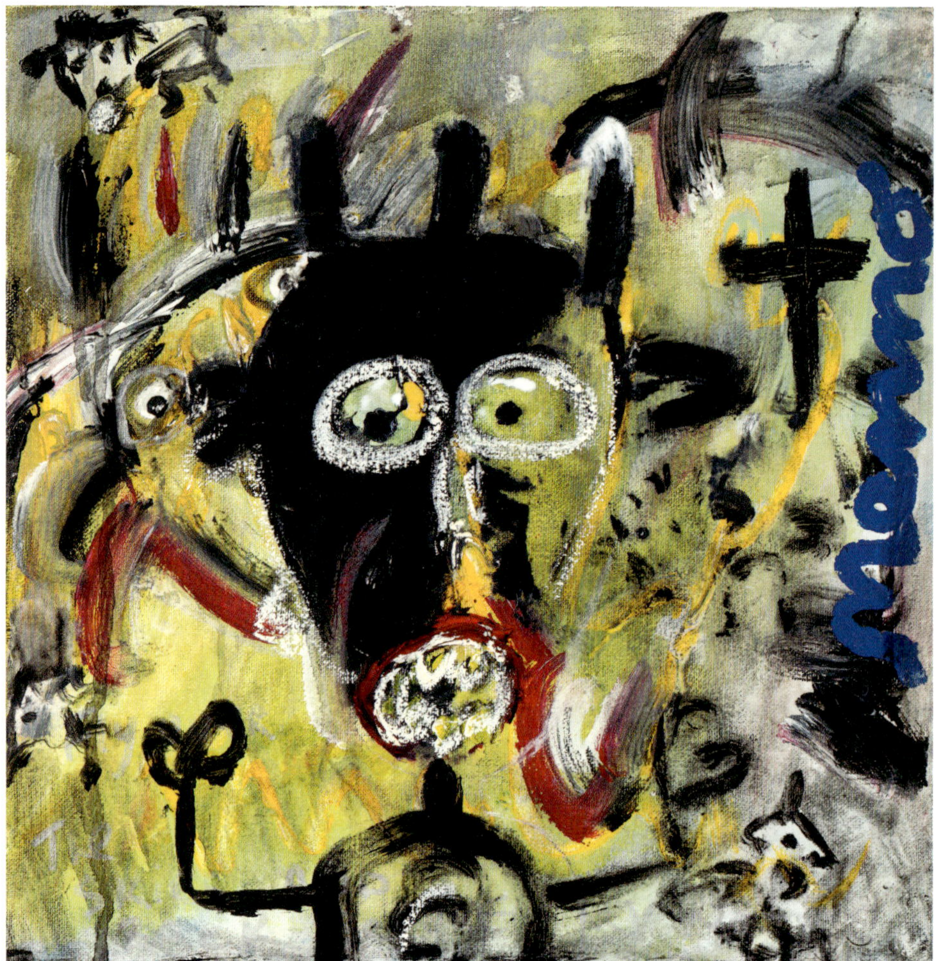

Of all Krant's work, it is the portraits that stand out—wild-eyed creatures with flailing arms and mouths agape. Like encountering Francis Bacon's contorted figures with yawning jaws, initial incomprehension soon turns to admiration for the rich and vivid compositions. Always untitled, viewers are left to ascribe their own meaning to the work. Some recoil in disgust, calling Krant a devil-painter. But these punch-you-in-the-face portraits that leap off the canvas were never intended to portray evil. If the colours are dark, it's simply because black paint happened to be on sale that day. The patient observer discovers the truth that lies beneath the riot of colour. The caged mouths and barred teeth tell of repression, not anger. Unable to articulate the circumstances of their lives, these lost souls are mute with despair.

A keen observer of others, Krant studies those around him. His paintings, he explains, are not portraits of particular individuals, but rather the emotions that exude from ordinary people he sees riding the bus or walking down the street. Limp with exhaustion, lost in their own thoughts, their feelings of hopelessness are impossible to miss. Rich folk, poor folk: they are all the same, trapped in lives they unwittingly fell into. It's those evocative expressions he strives to capture on canvas. The viewer can, for a moment, step into the shoes of a fellow traveller. For a time Krant worked archiving historical photographs, and he describes the impact of those images on him. The expressions of prisoners clinging to barbed wire fences in concentration camps were identical, he noticed, to those of refugees gripping chain link fences fifty years later—utterly lost, terrified, and confused. It's the archetypal story of human tragedy, repeating itself ad infinitum. Through Krant's paintings, we are invited to bear witness to the pain of unlived lives. Perhaps it's his unflinching portrayal of those raw emotions that startles viewers; as he explains, he understands the world only through images, and this is what he sees. He acts as a telepath of sorts, recording the subject's feelings directly on canvas. Visitors to Krant's home are confronted with this reality in the thousands of paintings that line the walls. While some find this off-putting, others grasp the meaning immediately. He is painting everything wrong in the world.

But there is beauty in Krant's paintings—layer upon layer of it. Beginning with an abstract painting on canvas, he adds thick, textured acrylics and oils, the spontaneous first stroke suggesting the next and so on until the canvas is heavy with shapes and colour. The painting reveals itself at that point and shows the way forward. He prefers an aerial view of work in progress and lays his canvas on the ground to paint. Texture provides the only perspective he needs. He often paints in the dark, pointing out that red is still red even if he can't see the true colour on canvas. As a final step, he shines a light behind the piece to view it from another angle.

It has taken many years for Krant to reach this level of artistic confidence, moving from what he describes as primitive blockhead figurative paintings and fluid drawings on paper to his complex multilayered six-by-nine-foot canvasses. And twenty years ago he had to teach himself to paint again. He recalls going to the hospital when he felt unwell and waking up five days later after heart surgery. He is still puzzled about those missing days and the subsequent years of recovery. Even now he can't recall events from that period of his life; looking at photographs of himself over "the missing years" is a bewildering experience. He worked it out on canvas in a series called "Whacked," portraying himself in various discombobulated states of recovery.

Krant paints every day, even if it is a small work on a cigarette package or cereal box. Like other artists I've met, painting is just something he needs to do. It's a spontaneous and all-consuming activity that brings him much joy and comfort, especially when his walls are completely covered in his own artwork. There is no ulterior motive in his daily practice. By that I mean his work is not directed to the goal of an exhibition or potential sales. If an exhibition is scheduled, he chooses from among hundreds of finished paintings and quickly creates more when they are gone. If ten paintings leave his house, he creates ten more to replace them. A certain balance must be maintained. Like Danielle Jacqui, who covered every available surface of her home with mosaics, Krant sees an empty space as a place for another painting. While he paints, life stands still and he floats in timeless space. That is exactly where he wants to be.

I met Krant again after I had put my pen down, so to speak. I had prepared the final draft of this book without reconnecting with the artist, whom I had briefly met ten years ago. He seemed to have vanished into the hinterland of the art world and I could not locate him for a meaningful discussion about his art practice. But then he reappeared and, because the tough research and writing was behind me, I had the luxury of time and familiarity with the topic to probe a little deeper into the motivation of an artist who is compelled to create, to the exclusion of almost everything else in life. In talking with Krant, I realized that I had overlooked a significant trait of outsider artists—that is, self-determination and self-actualization. I use this psychological lingo loosely in describing the artist's drive to become himself, not through external rewards but through his own internal impulse to create. What a man *can* be, he *must* be.[102] It is, perhaps, Krant's recognition of the unfulfilled lives of others that makes his work so poignant.

Québec

I didn't hear much about folk art in Ontario, although significant collections are held there. But, as in other parts of Canada, the 1970s was also the heyday of folk art in Québec, and I learned how it informed all self-taught art that followed. Early collections of local folk art were built through the efforts of mainly anglophone individuals, like Nettie Sharpe,[103] and a Québécois perspective was never presented in a national museum. Collectors of early Québec folk art reconstructed the portrait of a culture to match their own perceptions of it; that is, the mental image the English had of a certain Québec. Our appreciation of the collection must begin, then, with acknowledgment of our own filters.[104] In an effort to take back their own cultural narrative, three researchers set out in 1972 to investigate the "culture of the common people" in their own province with a view to decolonizing their history and culture.[105] The result was the bible of Québec folk art, *Les Patenteux du Québec*. (A *patenteux* is a handyman, an inventive tinkerer.) Works that had been described only in aesthetic terms by others were now introduced by the makers themselves, restoring a voice to those who were entitled to it.[106] The authors documented the vast landscape of Québécois folk art, all of it highly inventive, some of it quirky, imaginative, and amusing. It is not a forgotten genre; its status as a viable art form in the contemporary art world continues to be explored.[107]

Folk ceramicist ÉDOUARD JASMIN of Montréal is one of the most celebrated *patenteux*. He began working in red clay after his retirement, creating tableaux of his fondest childhood memories: the general store, a school classroom, his mother spinning yarn in the attic. His whimsical re-creations of local scenes are treasured for their humorous depiction of characters and situations. Not only do these pieces trigger nostalgic memories for all of us, they are an important record of Canadian history.

The topic of art by self-taught creators is close to the surface in discussions about art in Québec, and, for some, outsider art is an extension (albeit a long-reaching one) of folk art. It is also fundamental to understanding Claude Bolduc's story of becoming an artist. Although not widely known in Western Canada, ARTHUR VILLENEUVE was a self-taught painter from Québec.

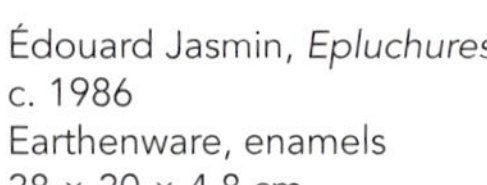

Édouard Jasmin, *Epluchures*, c. 1986
Earthenware, enamels
28 × 20 × 4.8 cm

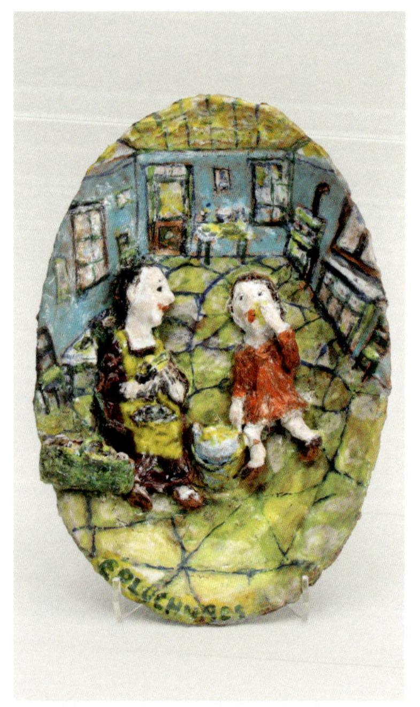

Villeneuve, like Scottie Wilson, was classified as a primitive or naïve painter.[108] Raised in a working-class town, he settled on a career as a barber when he was sixteen years old. He prospered, married, and had four children before his wife died in the 1940s. He remarried soon after and had three more children. The family lived in a small house in Chicoutimi, Québec. In 1946, Villeneuve had a revelation during a church service that urged the congregants to make full use of their God-given abilities. Believing he had been remiss in developing his artistic talent, Villeneuve began experimenting with drawing, collage, and sculpture.[109] In 1957, he began painting images on the walls of his house, a project that spanned nearly two years. Not only did he cover the outside of the house,[110] he also painted the interior walls, the ceilings, and even the windows. It seems that Villeneuve never looked back; he was a prolific artist who created thousands of paintings in his lifetime.

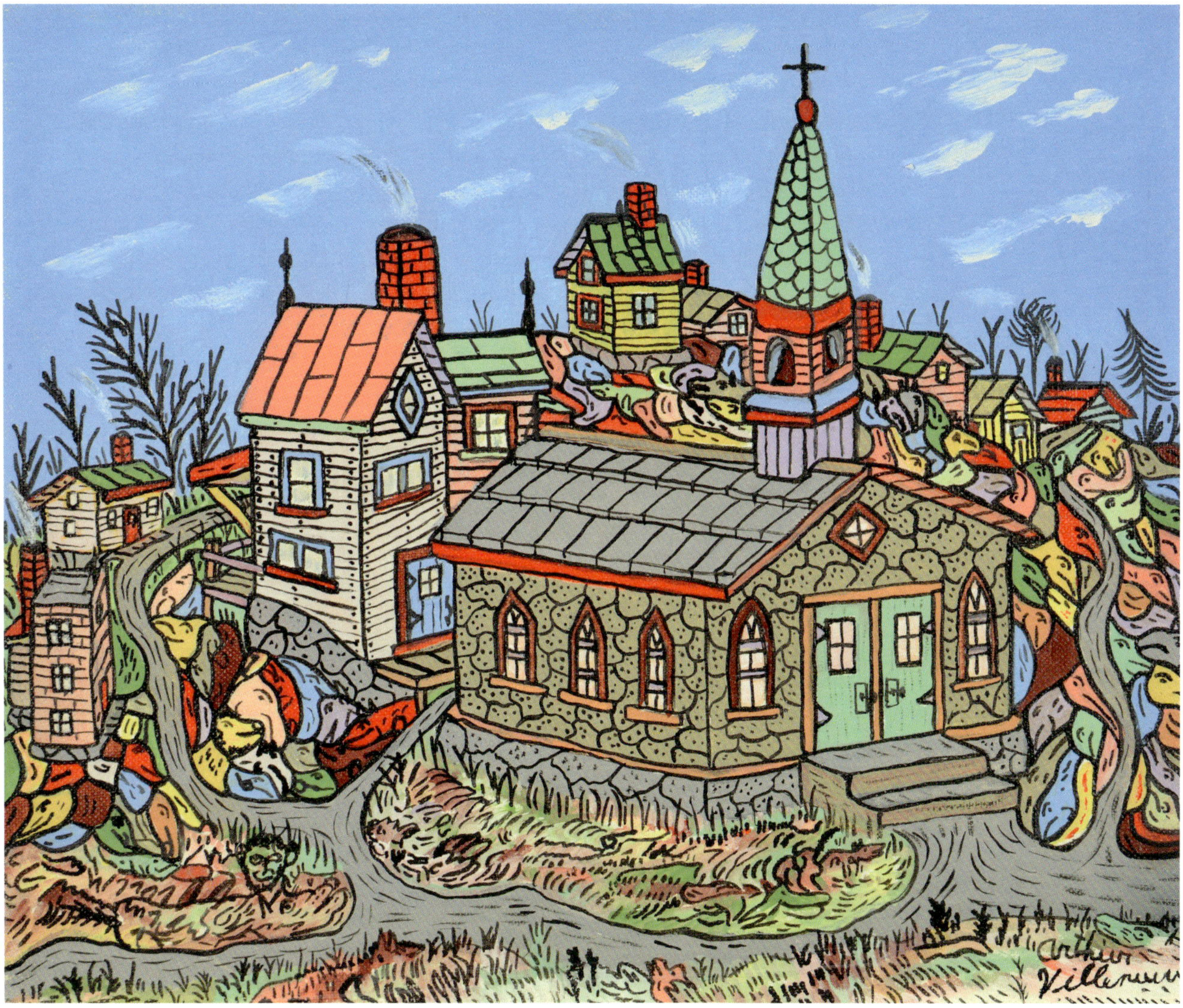

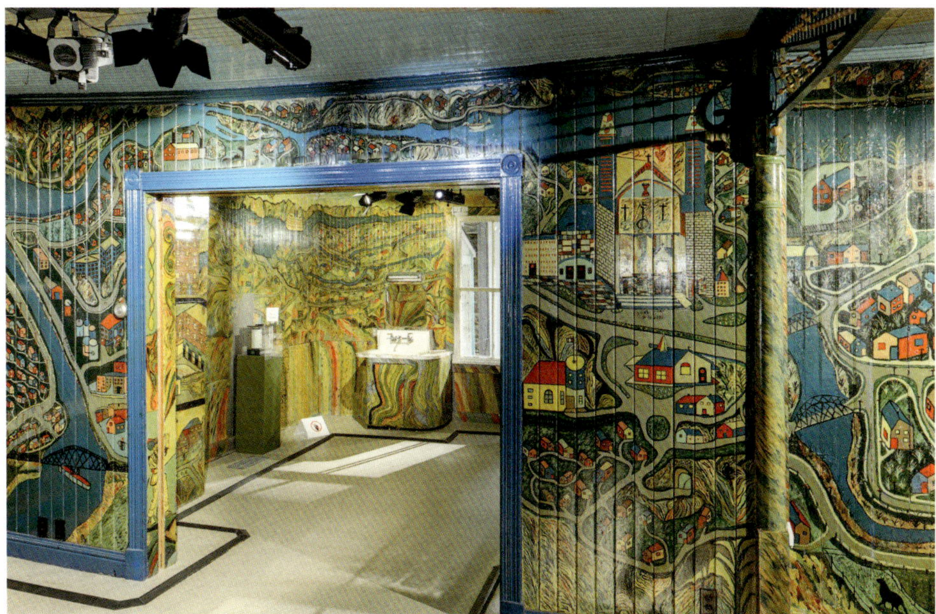

Arthur Villeneuve, *La Vieille église*, twentieth century
Oil on canvas board
25 × 30 cm

Interior of the Arthur Villeneuve home

Meeting Villeneuve was an epiphany for Québec artist CLAUDE BOLDUC. Bolduc's first art memory is watching a movie about Van Gogh, *Lust for Life*, on his black-and-white television set when he was five or six years old. It wasn't the beautiful paintings, though, that stuck in his mind. It was the scenes of struggling coal miners and Van Gogh's uncompromising commitment to living with them, sharing their crude housing and frugal meals of potatoes. The injustice of the situation revolted him but inspired him to draw. He drew a lot. Bolduc's father used to compare his drawings to those of local painter Arthur Villeneuve, who was the brunt of many jokes in rural Québec. Although it wasn't meant as a compliment, Bolduc was proud of his burgeoning artistic talent. This painting *L'Instant de Grâce* depicts the moment of his rebirth, when he became conscious of art.

Bolduc pursued music for many years. It wasn't until 1985, when his work as a postman led him (literally) to Arthur Villeneuve's door in Chicoutimi, that he made the decision to dedicate his life to art. Bolduc would stop to chat when he encountered Villeneuve in his garden. Most of their encounters were brief, as Villeneuve's ever-watchful wife would call him away if the conversation went on too long. But the magic happened when Villeneuve and Bolduc were alone and could talk about art. Bolduc says those moments were a rare privilege, and he treasures the memories. Sometimes Villeneuve would invite him into his house to see his unorthodox paintings and the frescoes that covered the walls and hallways. Villeneuve was a man of few words, and would answer Bolduc's questions by simply saying that the answers lay in the artwork itself. Villeneuve was a proud and confident man, who had no doubt of his artistic mission. He believed he was the reincarnation of artist Henri Rousseau.[111] "God gave me this talent," he often said. "I must make it fruitful." But what fascinated him the most, Bolduc says, was to hear Villeneuve talk about the inspiration for his paintings—his fears and fantasies expressed through Indigenous and Judeo-Christian images. Villeneuve stressed the importance of the subconscious (which he called the sus-conscious) that was always present in his work. "It's the reincarnation of life," he said.

After meeting Villeneuve, whom he calls his liberating idol, Bolduc made the irrevocable decision to start painting again. Although he was unaware of the significance of the date, he began to paint on January 4, 1987, at the age of thirty-two. He later discovered that was Villeneuve's birthday. Bolduc describes his early years, when he absorbed himself in art in response to a troubled relationship:

> From 1987 to 1990, I painted a lot. It was extremely liberating for me. A self-therapy in every sense of the word. I did not care at all about the various derogatory or ridiculous comments I received from people around me. As soon as I got home from work, I locked myself in a room in the house that I had set up as a workshop and painted. Often until exhaustion . . . I hardly took time to eat. I devoted all my free time to painting.

Bolduc had his first exhibition in Chicoutimi in 1990. He modestly described it as rather well received.

When I first encountered Bolduc's work, I was immediately reminded of the mid-fifteenth-century Dutch painter Hieronymus Bosch. Sometimes called "the devil's painter," Bosch's fantastical imagery portrayed heretical religious narratives; the most memorable are those that depict his nightmarish images of eternal damnation. Bosch's paintings are instantly recognizable, for it

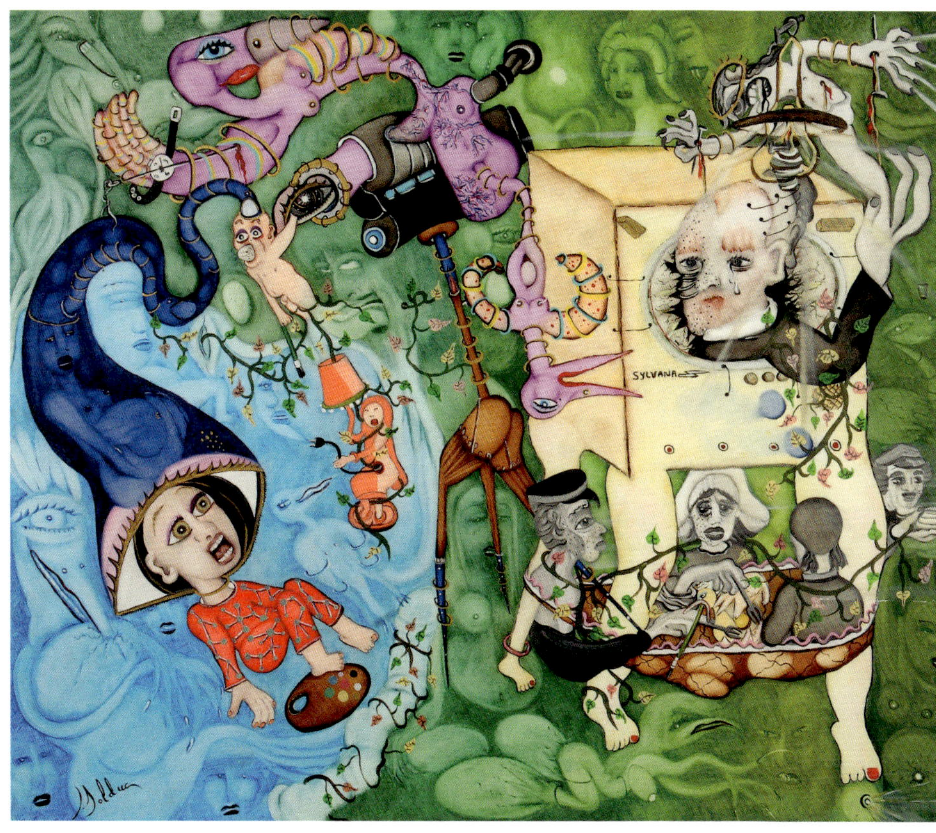

Claude Bolduc, *L'instant de Grâce*, 1997
Oil on canvas
50 × 60 cm

would be impossible to see one without stopping to stare, in trippy wonder, at the abominable events that await us in Hell. It's not that Bolduc's artwork is heretical. It is not, especially from the perspective of today's viewer. Rather, his work is Bosch-like because it commands us to stop and consider his proposition from an anything-but-orthodox perspective. He describes his own work as *art singulier*, a French term describing self-taught artists who are entirely outside the fine art system, either by choice or by circumstance. His unconventional images are an intensely personal form of self-expression. And, as Bolduc says, it gives him the right to be himself. It is necessary for his survival. This accords with Dubuffet's category of *neuve invention*—a somewhat gray area between the strict parameters of traditional art brut and mainstream art. It is a looser, less rigid category and it allows for a wide diversity of forms and styles. Its artists are typically self-taught, many live marginalized lives, but their works are not necessarily spontaneous outbursts of creativity. Rather, their body of work reflects a methodical exploration of the artist's identity.

Bolduc's early work was in a naïve style that depicted his personal memories or social issues. He began exploring "the invisible" a few years later, drawing inspiration from his own interpretation of the world and the limits of the parallel universes of consciousness and unconsciousness. There, a plethora of strange creatures inhabit a sensual and dreamlike world, among mythical and religious imagery. Bolduc skewers the church, literally and figuratively, in many of his paintings. It's not that he has lost his faith; in fact, he is a deeply spiritual person, who believes in the fundamental teachings of the Bible. It is the failings of the church that trouble him and fuel his prolific art practice.

I asked Bolduc to take me into his paintings, to explain the main themes in his work. In a general way, he says, his art addresses our place in the divine creation. The instinct to live—

Claude Bolduc, *Transe-porteur d'éternité (Le Clonage)*, 1998
Oil on canvas
70 × 60 cm

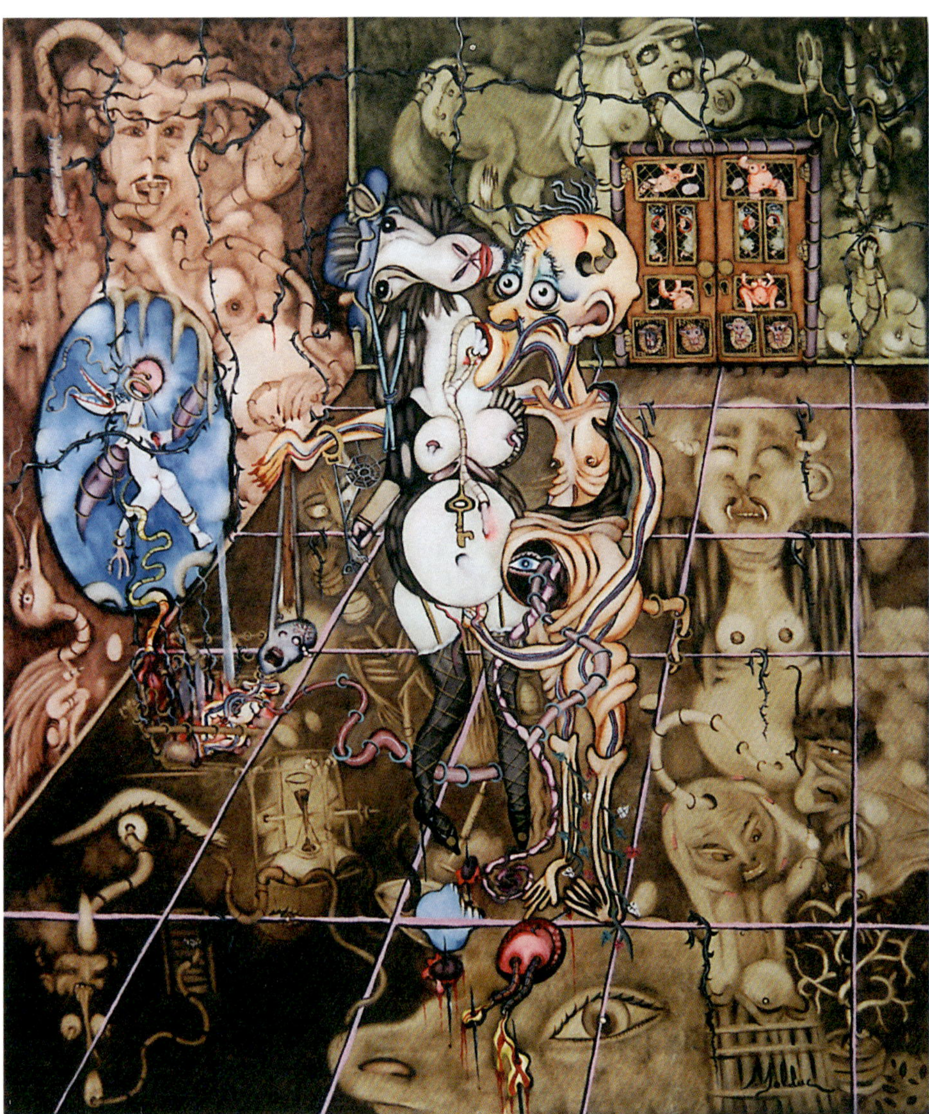

sexuality—is always in opposition to death. Eros is perpetually in a death dance with Thanatos. He uses Christian symbolism to illustrate this infinite and base struggle: seductive Eve at the Tree of Knowledge, human suffering as represented by Christ on the cross, humanity in all its deviancy. He reflects on how far we have moved away from the original message of tolerance and compassion. The challenge, he says, is to recover the mystery of creation.

In many ways, exploring Canadian outsider art was an easier task in Québec, and Bolduc was only one of many local artists who shared their story with me. Les Québécois are open to the idea of art outside the fine art system, perhaps because of their fondness for the work of the common man as well as their cultural ties with France, where the concept of art brut was first articulated. Although I am warned that it is an uneasy acceptance, it appears that outsider art is alive and well in Québec. While the subject of art brut or outsider art did not come up spontaneously, many people, when asked, offered their views on the genre. A few galleries support the artists[112] and the province boasts the only museum of outsider art in Canada. The Musee d'Art Singulier Contemporain [113] (Museum of Outsider Contemporary Art) is the creation of a collector who is passionate about *l'art singulier.*[114] It is housed in a renovated church in Mansonville, a village in the Eastern Townships of Québec near the American border. The artists are described as singular artists who live outside the territory delineated by art markets and art history. The singular artist is one who explores his own borders and is a migrant in his inner world.[115] They are self-taught, sometimes marginalized creators, who have put much thought and effort into their work.[116] The museum, both in its setting and its meticulous presentation of artwork, is a love letter to the genre.

Every city, it seems, has an offbeat resident who is celebrated for their eccentricities. Like Roger Ing in Regina, everyone knew the pope of Montréal, SORGENTE PALMERINO (PAPA PALMERINO). Palmerino immigrated to Canada from Italy in 1956 with his wife and children. He worked as a janitor, cook, and factory worker until a work accident forced him to retire early. In 1970, Palmerino had a vision of the Virgin Mary, who told him that he was the pope and that his mission was to serve God. Palmerino opened a shop on the ground floor of his home and filled it with both handmade and ready-made religious artifacts. He made rosaries decorated with plastic jewels, paintings of religious images, as well as papal tiaras and headwear made with red sticky tape, fabric, beads, and sequins, some reaching over a metre in height. His creations were spectacular, inspiring fashion designer Christian Lacroix to feature some of Palmerino's headwear in a fashion show.[117] His remarkable body of devotional works included photographs of himself in the role of the pope and as Jesus re-enacting the stations of the cross.

To those who remember him, Palmerino didn't merely think he was the pope; he *was* the pope. His purpose, he believed, was to share a message of peace and love and to encourage devotion to God among those who came to receive his blessing and pray with him in a room at the back of his shop. In 2000, a fire destroyed his shop, and little remains of his life's work.

While few Québec artists were as highly visible as Papa Palmerino, the province is home to many artists equally passionate about inventing diverse and offbeat universes according to their own individual visions. Some were solitary makers who were reluctant to announce their presence to the art world. Others were delighted to have an audience interested in their work.

Sorgente Palmerino,
Jésus de Nazareth (Papa Palmerino), c. 1990
Photo on paper
21.6 × 27.9 cm

Sorgente Palmerino,
Chapeaux, c. 1990
Mixed media
50.8 × 25.4; 20.3 × 10.2;
38.1 × 20.3 cm

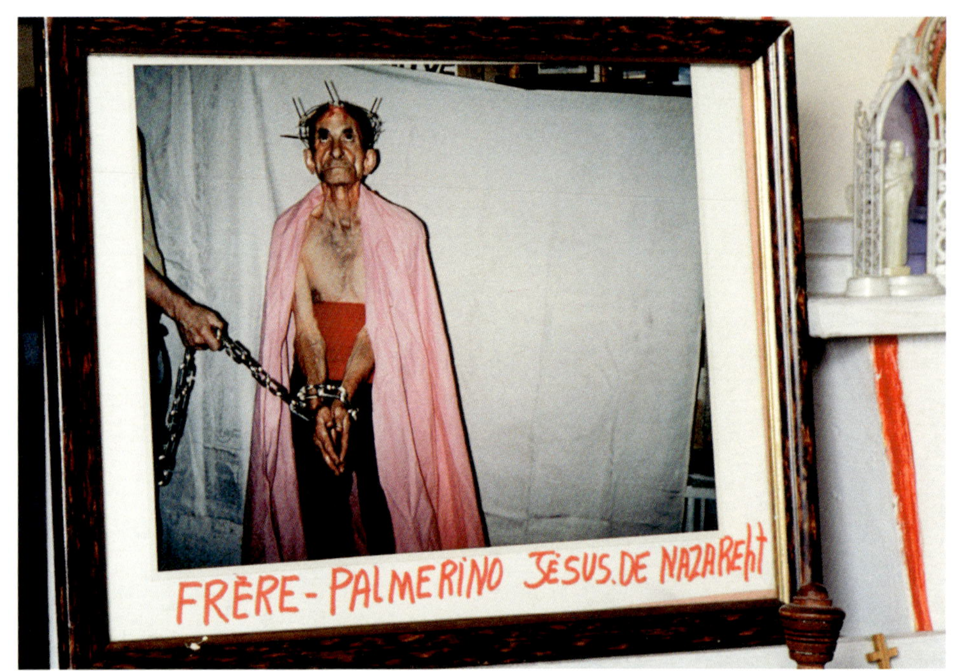

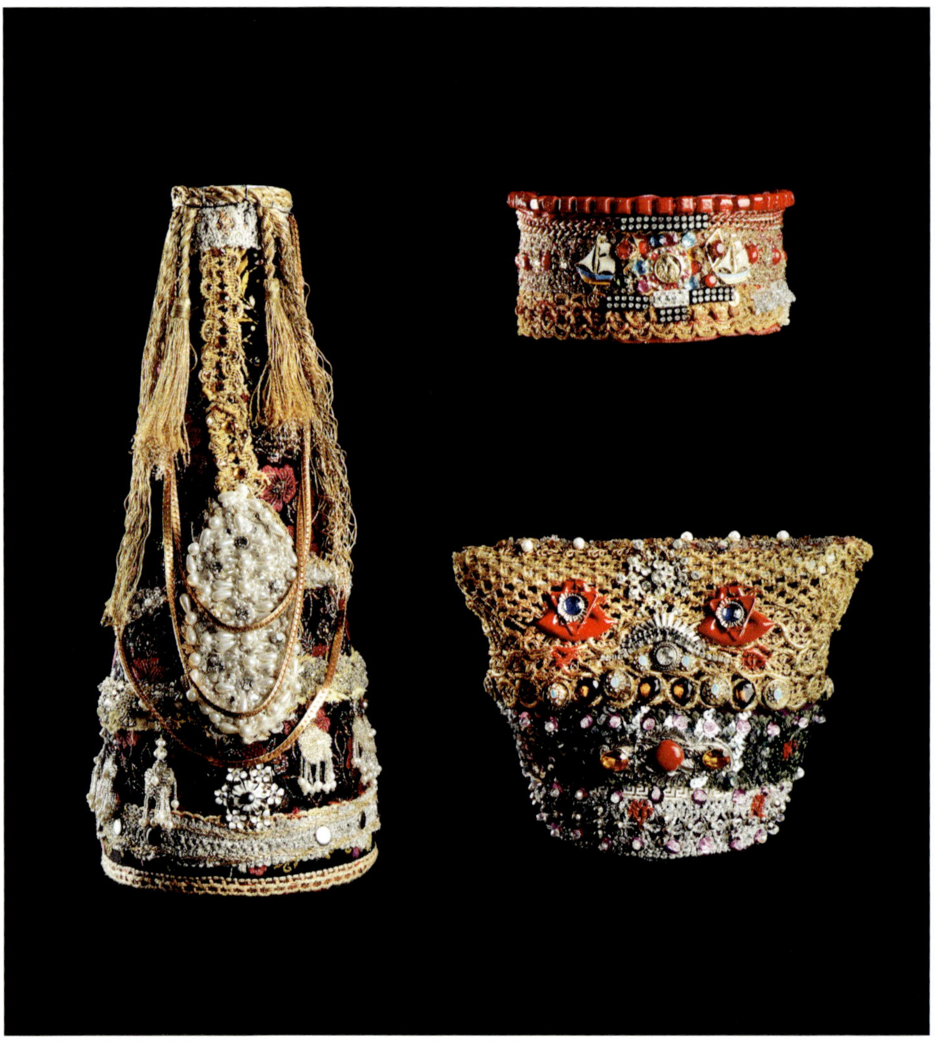

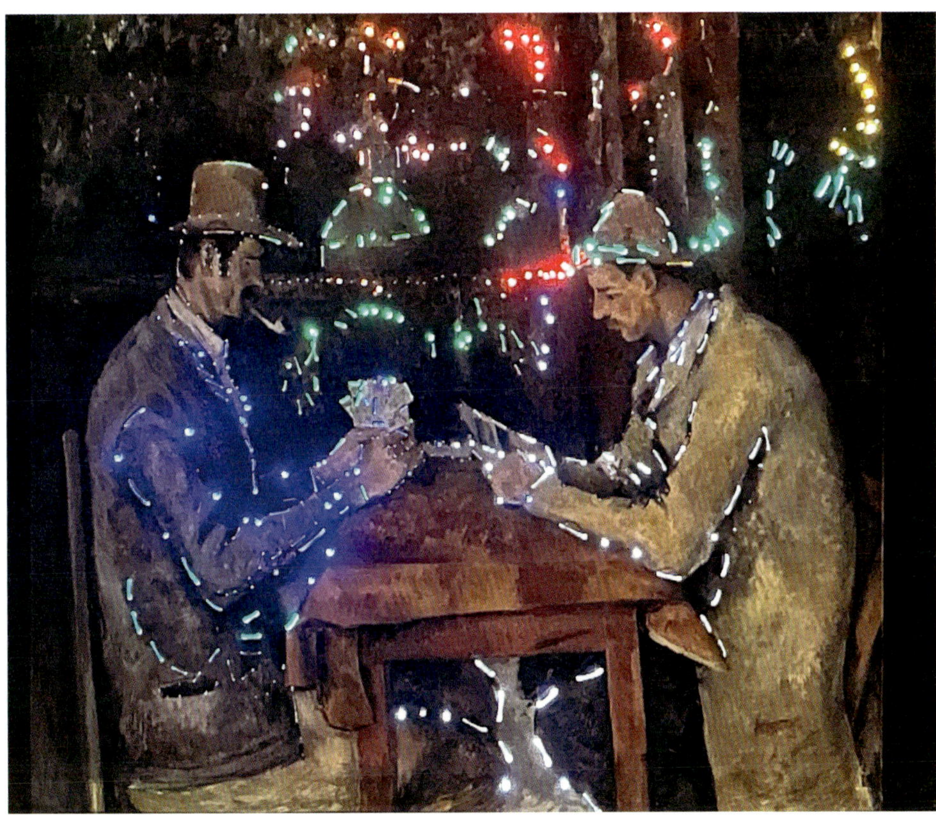

William Anhang, *Cezanne's Card Players*, 2013
Acrylic paint, light-emitting diodes, optical fibres, microprocessors
53.3 × 63.5 cm

Some years ago I met an artist in Billsville, Montréal. The "Bill" who lives in Billsville is WILLIAM ANHANG. I've never met anyone like Bill, nor seen work like his, perhaps because I don't know any other electrical engineers who have become artists. Anhang's complex creations involve fibre optics, fractals, and the Mandelbrot set. I don't profess to understand the mathematical theory behind his work, but Anhang's vision is to illuminate artwork with fibre optic lighting. It is a dazzling and dizzying experience to walk into his space; artwork covers every possible surface, including the ceiling.

Anhang describes himself as a typical Polish farm boy. His family immigrated to Canada in the 1930s and his early years were spent on a dairy farm. They moved to Winnipeg after the war and Anhang pursued a degree in engineering. He worked in a few different engineering jobs, but his story as an artist began in February 1974 when, by chance, he walked by a university classroom where copper enamelling was being demonstrated. He returned the following week to take a class, and this led him to install a kiln in his home to make small pieces, including copper-enamelled light switches and electrical-outlet covers. Thus began Anhang's fascination with marrying light and art. The pivotal point, Anhang recalls, was later that year when he showed his artwork to spiritual teacher Ram Dass,[118] who proclaimed, "You are an artist," and encouraged Anhang to pursue art. Anhang felt he had no option but to follow this instruction, and so he abandoned engineering and began his new life. He has been experimenting with copper, painting, and fibre optics ever since.

Anhang is guided by his spiritual beliefs. He explained how he heard the voice of God, who instructed him to spread His word through art. In a sense, Anhang believes he is a messiah, as God singled him out for a purpose. However, his spiritual beliefs are far more nuanced.

> William Anhang, *China (Fractal Piece)*,
front and back view, 2006
Acrylic paint, light-emitting diodes, optical fibres, microprocessors
45.7 × 63.5 cm

If Anhang announces, "I am God," it is followed by a more universal statement: "And so is everybody else. God is in all of us." Like Einstein, Anhang's desire is to "experience the universe as a single significant whole."[119] With no definite notion of God or theology, the function of art and science is to awaken these feelings in those who are receptive to it.[120] Anhang has had several divine visitations and knows that God is always with him. He does not dwell on his connection to God; he accepts it as a fact of his life and the source of his creative energy. It is not uncommon for outsider artists to credit God with their motivation to create art. But unlike spiritually inspired artists like street-preacher Sister Gertrude Morgan (1900–1980) and Baptist minister Howard Finster (1916–2001), Anhang's creations do not have a religious theme. His spiritual beliefs give him incentive and purpose, but they are not the subject of his creations.

Anhang's work is technically complex and he works with assistants to achieve his vision. A helper may paint a canvas under Anhang's guidance, then turn it over to him to drill holes and thread it with fibre optics. Anhang tends to work in series, like "Crépin Illuminated,"[121] which are fibre-optic versions of Crépin's paintings. Fractals feature in another series of illuminated paintings. (Fractals are shapes that retain their characteristics despite their size. Viewed infinitely close or very far away, the pattern remains the same. Think snowflake.) The paintings are beautiful and organically fluid. Other illuminated paintings include grand themes like the Last Supper and celebrity portraits of Oprah Winfrey, former Prime Minister Jean Chrétien, and, of course, himself. More recently, Anhang has been creating wearable art, including large painted collars that rest on the wearer's shoulders like an oversized ecclesiastical ruff. Anhang enjoys modelling these wondrous fashion statements, turning static works of art into performance pieces. His enthusiasm is contagious.

Anhang's signature work is a series that reimages Cézanne's Post-Impressionist masterpiece *The Card Players*. It is the cornerstone of Anhang's career—a self-referential work that reflects themes of his earlier creations. It's no accident that Anhang feels a kinship with Cézanne, an artist known for depicting light in a novel way. In Cézanne's world, forms exist in a universal light—static, timeless, and free from the variations of season and weather. Anhang's work is not about card players, but about Cézanne's paintings of card players. It is a conversation between masters of light. Like Cézanne, Anhang's conception of light is an essential element of his paintings and vital to their beauty. It is like he was saying to Cézanne, "Have you thought of *this*, Paul?"

While all the artists I met shared a passion (bordering on obsession) to create, some were born storytellers. Anick Langelier and Henriette Valium are two skilled raconteurs.

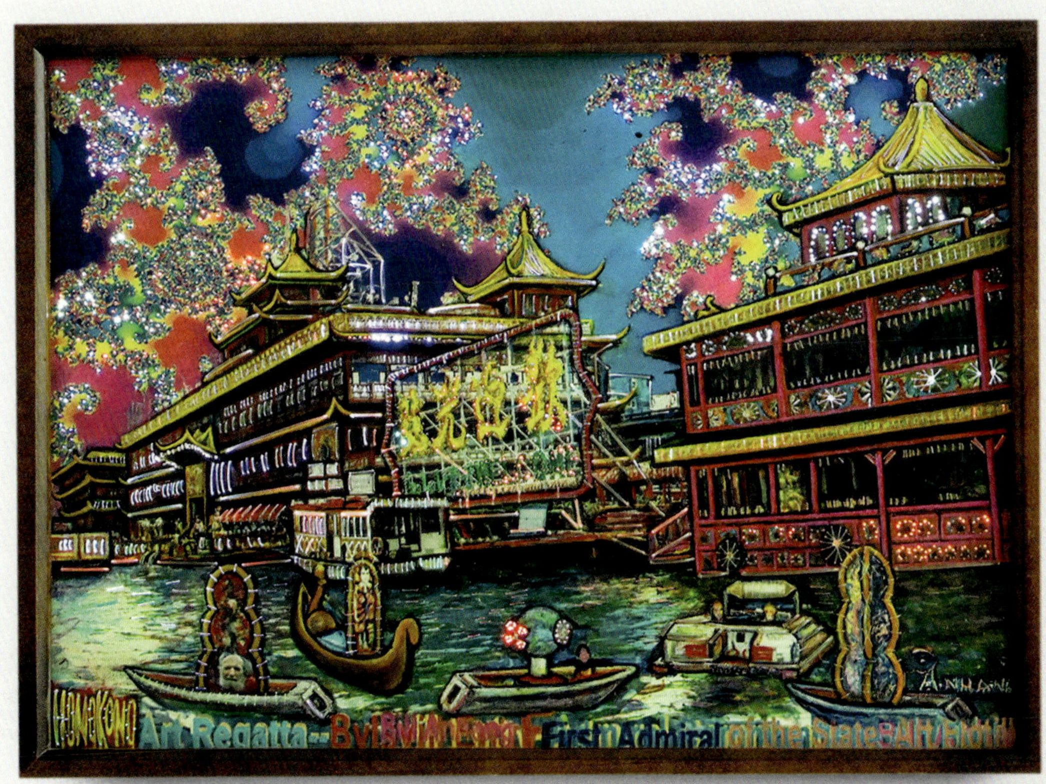

125

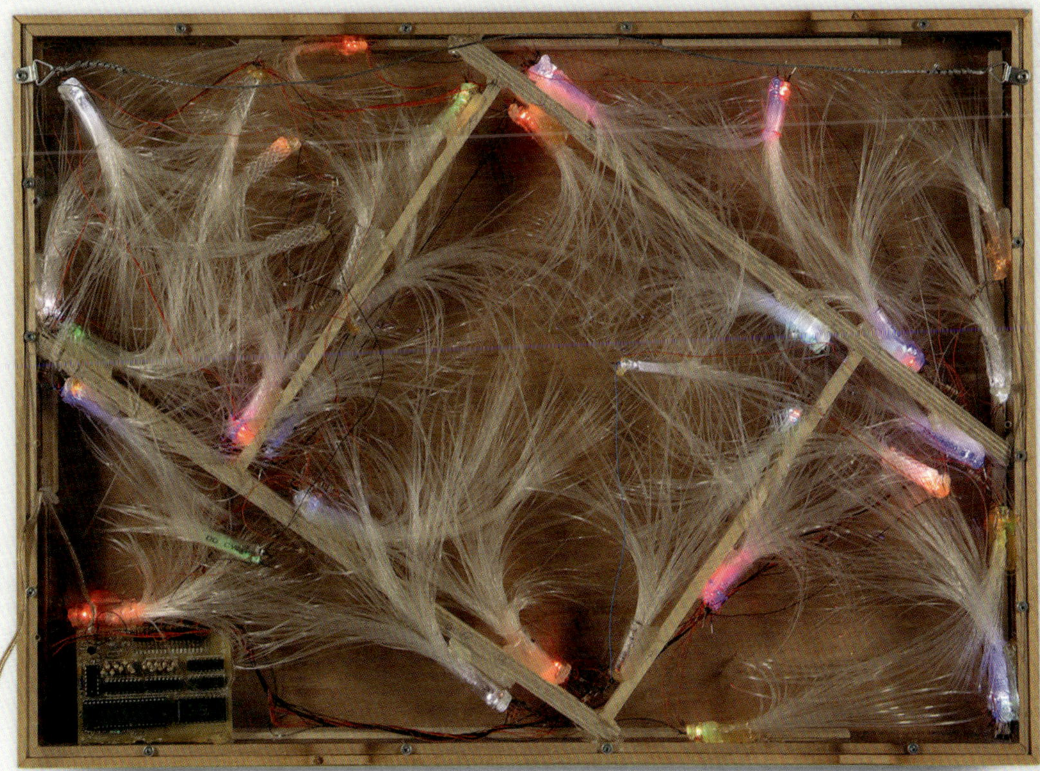

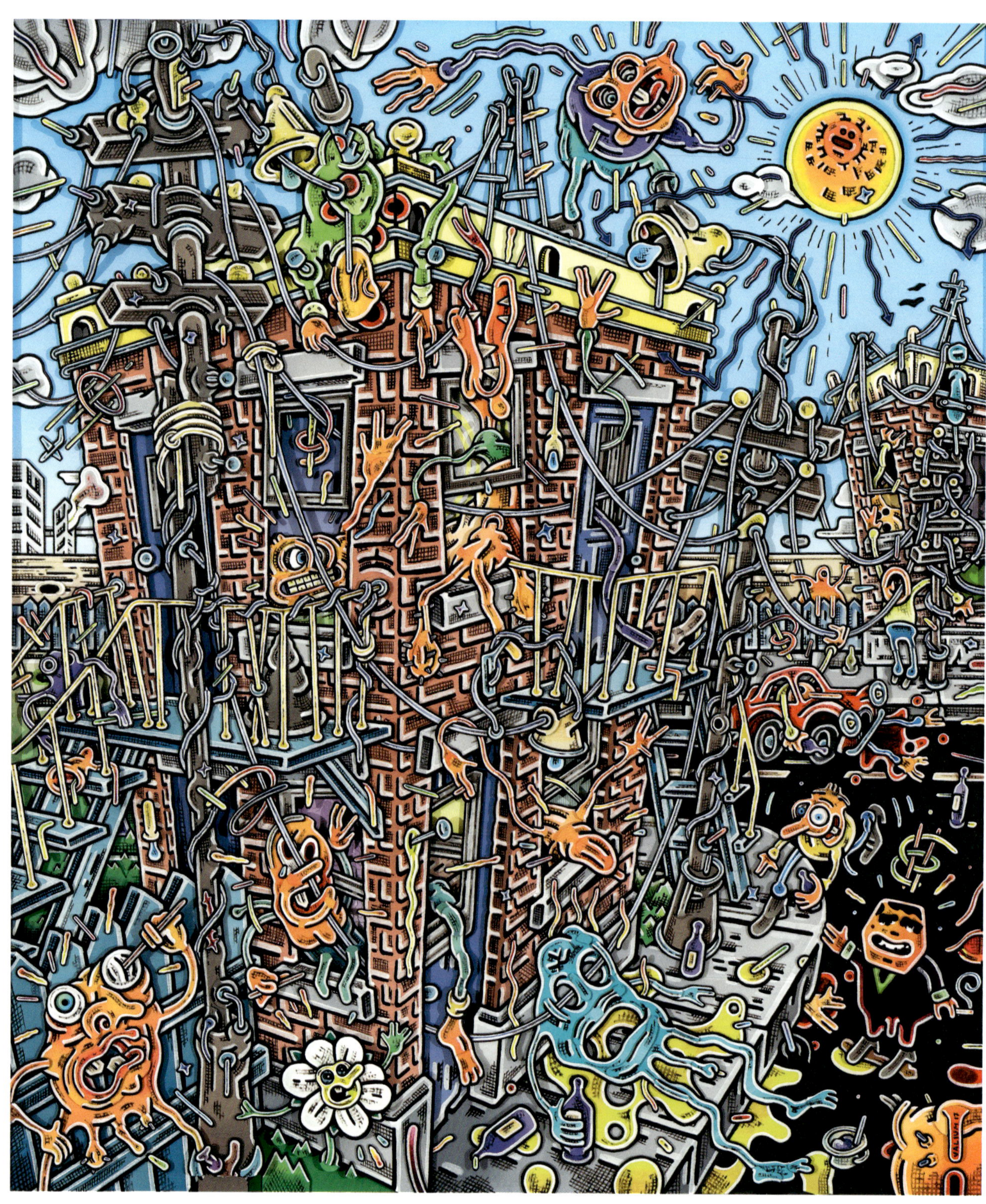

Henriette Valium (Patrick Henley), *Rachelle Berry*, 2017
Mixed media on wood
122 × 100 cm

It is difficult to describe the work of HENRIETTE VALIUM (Patrick Henley). When I asked him to tell me about his work, he happily announced, "I hate everyone equally. My work is so inflammatory that everyone—and no one—is offended." He calls himself "a big ball of nihilism." He is the epitome of political incorrectness.

Called the Pope of Comics[122] and the greatest French-Canadian cartoonist, Valium chose his name when he started working with a self-published fanzine called *Iceberg* in the 1980s. To shake things up, the women took men's names and the men took women's names: Henriette Valium was born. Valium says he has been drawing since he was in diapers and making comics since his teens. Things started happening at the CÉGEP[123] in Vieux-Montréal in the 1980s, the height of the underground scene in Québec. His crowd wanted to emulate the European style and began with folded sheets of copier paper. At first, Valium worked on small-format comics and fanzines with other artists, but found it difficult to collaborate on creative ventures. He eventually started to produce his own large-format silkscreened comics. His work is treasured in the underground comic world, but it is nearly impossible to make a living creating extravagant comics. He does it anyway. Valium lives in a garage and draws all day because that's just what he does. He has come to terms with the choice of having a job, which would provide a steady income but no time to create, versus having time to draw all day but no money. He has chosen the latter.

In an insightful interview that puts his work into context, Valium was asked about his artistic approach. He says he's never really had one and describes his creative drive as an obsessive-compulsive disorder. If he didn't create, he would throw himself off a bridge. He acknowledges the influence of punk, Robert Crumb, and artists like George Grosz, Hans Bellmer, Bosch, and Escher. Contrary to Dubuffet's description of the art brut artist as a solitary being who is responding to an authentic creative impulse, Valium doesn't believe that describes his practice. He says he is incredibly disciplined in his approach to art, to the point of being a control freak. In fact, he sees himself as quite the opposite of a spontaneous creator. In his opinion, a pure and authentic creative impulse is a utopian vision that derives from a need to attach labels to art. He questions whether solitude is a common characteristic of outsider artists. "Does one believe in this when one is alone, in order to ease the loneliness, or does the creative act itself isolate us from others, from the clan."[124]

Valium's projects have become grander in scale and complexity over the years. His most recent book (the first in English), *The Palace of Champions*, took him about ten years to complete. Every page started as a thirty-three-by-fifty-centimetre painting. To examine the details on each page is nothing short of mind-boggling. To give you a sense of the type of fantastic tales Valium weaves, his first story is called "Lâcher de Chiens" (Let Go the Dogs). Two Rottweilers (that is, two killing machines) are loose in an alley and head towards him. Their jaws exert 1753 pounds of pressure per cubic centimeter. He kicks the first one in the mouth with his army boots (with metal clasps). "Cervical surroundings burst on spot! Vertebral column swings up in the air. Intestines and bowels follow, I guess." Soft canine projectile meets human wall of steel. AAAAAAAAAAAAAAAAA. SKWAIIIIILYKR!!! Someone calls the police and things deteriorate even further.

The second story, "Québec is a Schizophrenic," comes with a warning: "Never open the door of this wardrobe . . . or else . . ." And, of course, the "or else" unfolds in a gory, dripping

> Henriette Valium (Patrick Henley), *La Main Couleur Peau #04*, 2006
Mixed media on paper
40 × 25 cm

mass of guts. Other stories in the book are equally gruesome: "If you dig a hole in a forest and later, an animal fall down in it and die, will it be your fault?" features a cartoonist who lives in a shitty art hole and does not win an Oscar; "Money clean what is dirty and dirty what is clean; Money is the ciment of the fractal incestuous clanic pyramid; Money is the meta-injustice" describes life at #07 – 8374 St-Laurent Street; a one-page comic called "Art is both the raft and the storm" is self-explanatory; "Al Qaida: an artificial war against a synthetic enemy" is about a man who discovers a homeless person living under his sink; "There's better than lying: restrain the truth" features Dr. Fuckenstein; "It's gonna be everyone or nobody" features a game of hate and death (with complicated rules and regulations); and "To blaspheme is to name the unspeakable: we should silence the god/devil" is a story about those who damn the useless artist.

All of it is dizzyingly weird and wonderful. And as Valium says, there is bad and good, but neither wins; there is always a sequel. When we met, his current project was about a big, fat, ignorant guy (Pattou), who goes to live on another planet after watching the depressing news on TV. Like many of his stories, it is autobiographical, made against his will by a mean muse.

I thought I had never known anyone like Valium or seen work quite like his, but then I recalled meeting American artist Joe Coleman (1955–) and his unclassifiable oeuvre of paintings and performances. Like Valium, Coleman emerged on the underground art scene the 1980s. Mixing a flair for theatrics and technique that bordered on the obsessive, he was hailed as a modern-day Salvador Dalí.[125] Both are consummate storytellers who expose the dark side of humanity.

Outsider art purists would like to exclude Coleman from that category, and I suppose they would make the same argument against Valium. They refer to Coleman as a "crossover" artist: one who has moved into the world of mainstream art. After exhibiting at the Outsider Art Fair for six years, Coleman was barred from exhibiting because, it was announced, he briefly attended (and was expelled from) art school in his youth. This was ostensibly the reason for his exclusion; one critic, however, pointed out that another exhibiting artist was an art professor.[126] Others complained that Coleman had become too commercial (that is, successful and self-promoting) to be considered an outsider artist. He's just "too much" for outsider art purists who prefer their artists to produce impenetrable work while living a socially isolated existence.

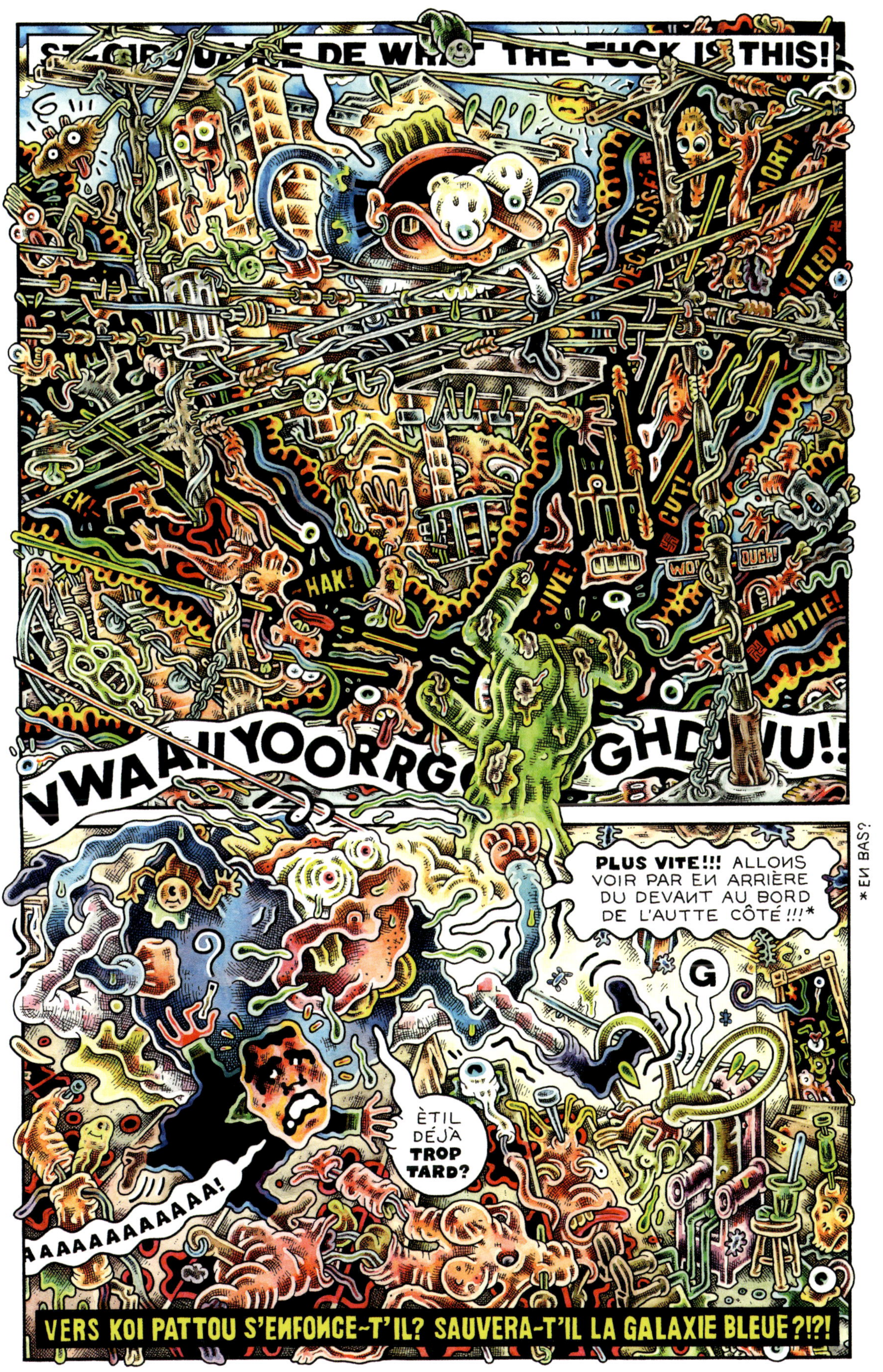
DE WHAT THE FUCK IS THIS!
MORT!
KILLED!
DÉCALISSÉ!
EK!
HAK!
JIVE!
CUT!
WO!
OUCH!
MUTILE!
VWAAIIYOORRG
GHDUUU!!
PLUS VITE!!! ALLONS VOIR PAR EN ARRIÈRE DU DEVANT AU BORD DE L'AUTTE CÔTÉ!!!*
* EN BAS?
G
ÈTIL DÉJÀ TROP TARD?
AAAAAAAAAAAAAAAA!
VERS KOI PATTOU S'ENFONCE-T'IL? SAUVERA-T'IL LA GALAXIE BLEUE?!?!

Anik Langelier, *La Chute d'Icare*, 2016
Acrylic on canvas
76 × 91 cm

> Anik Langelier, *Cauchemar Aux Tigres*, 2008
Oil on canvas
76 × 102 cm

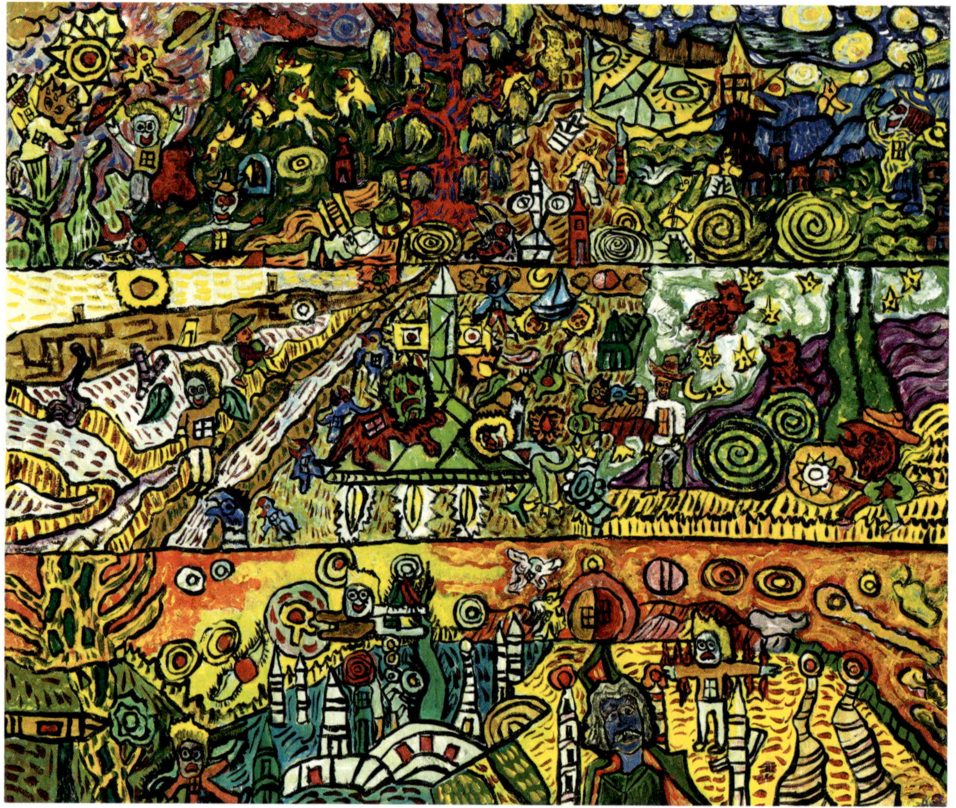

ANICK LANGELIER is a different kind of storyteller. She began painting in her teens as a way to manage her mental health and hasn't stopped since. Her canvasses are densely packed with images and her home is crammed with paintings. Working on six to eight paintings at a time and finishing ten or more a month does, she admits, create storage problems.

Langelier is a quiet woman who says that talking about herself is talking about her art. Her dialogue with God is manifest in her paintings; He is constantly with her. But sometimes hellish demons are with her, too, and that makes for interesting artwork. For Langelier, it's all about the narrative and the stories that her paintings tell. As in all good storytelling, there is always tension: a struggle between good and evil, the lure of temptation, the possibility of betrayal. It is the tipping point, I think, that fascinates her—the moment when the hero's fate is sealed. The Last Supper, for example, is a favourite theme. She manipulates characters in the scene; sometimes the apostles have the faces of famous artists or writers, in others they wear masks to obscure their identity. But in every painting they are depicted at the iconic dining table just after Jesus has announced the impending betrayal. The wheels have been set in motion. The story line takes a dramatic detour. For Langelier, it's all about the narrative of a life that is disintegrating.

Edgar Allan Poe and Stephen King are two of Langelier's favourite authors. Both are expert storytellers who hold the string taut until it snaps. Life can be like that, she thinks. Ordinary lives can be held in the balance until one event unravels the entire narrative. Take King's story of Cujo, for instance. A beloved, gentle pet dog is bitten by a rabid bat, which transforms him into a vicious beast. Or Icarus, who suffers the consequences of one

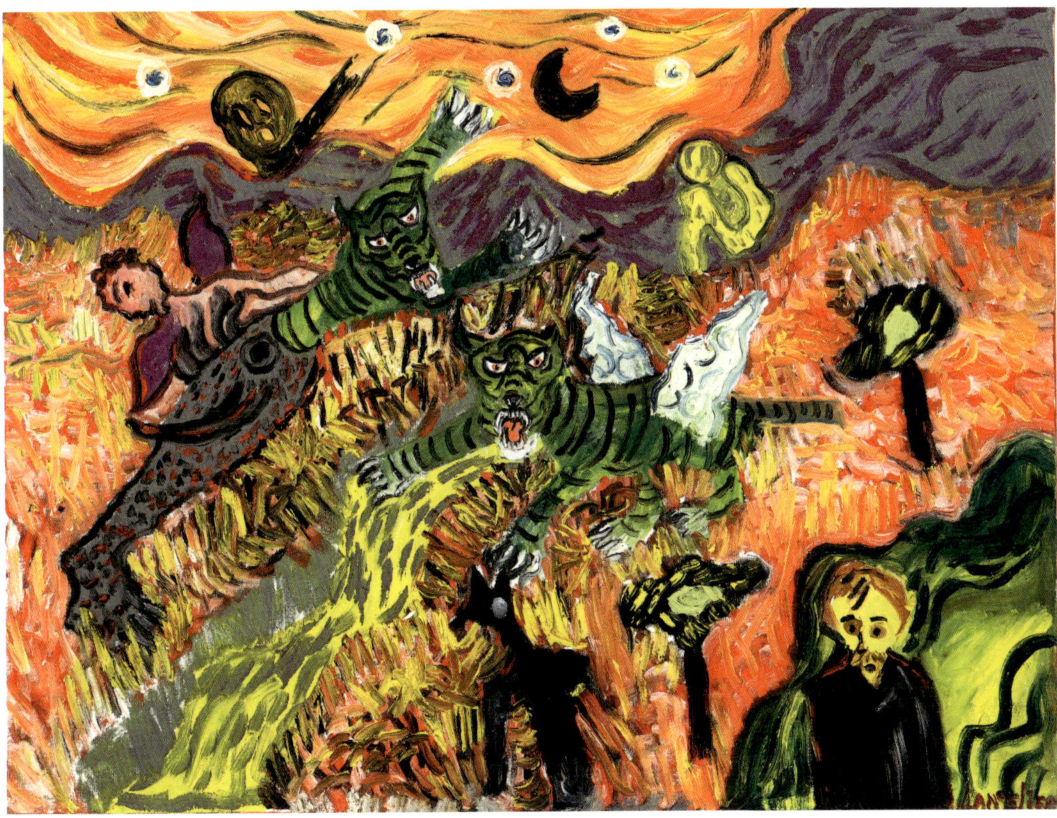

reckless decision. Giddy with the gift of flight, he soars too high, the heat melts his wings, and he plummets to his death.

Langelier's painting of Icarus is set out in three layers and reads like a book. Icarus jumps for joy when he hears of his father's plan to escape the island. Birds flock around him as if to demonstrate the wonders of flight. Icarus gets his new wings but the animals look alarmed and the birds appear more threatening. Perhaps they are warning him that humans are not meant to fly. Icarus dons his wings, soars gleefully above the town, and finally crashes to earth with his wings on fire. In every scene, cypress trees thrust into Van Gogh-like skies of whorls and stars. In fact, there are very few paintings in which some residue of Van Gogh is *not* visible: his face, bright sunflowers, glinting stars.

Langelier discovered Van Gogh's work when she was young, unwell, and recovering in a halfway house. Those blue, blue skies opened up a world of art to her. But it was Van Gogh's letters to his brother that truly resonated with her. She understood Van Gogh's struggle to come to terms with the darkness in his life, and she was sure he would understand her own troubles. Life was bleak, but looking at art books inspired Langelier to paint. She took a few art courses but didn't find much help there. She couldn't attend art school because she hadn't completed high school. She had to figure it out on her own. Her hero, Van Gogh, peers out at us from various paintings, along with other cultural icons, like Picasso, Dalí, and Shakespeare. They are, perhaps, a nod to those who nurtured her creative spirit.

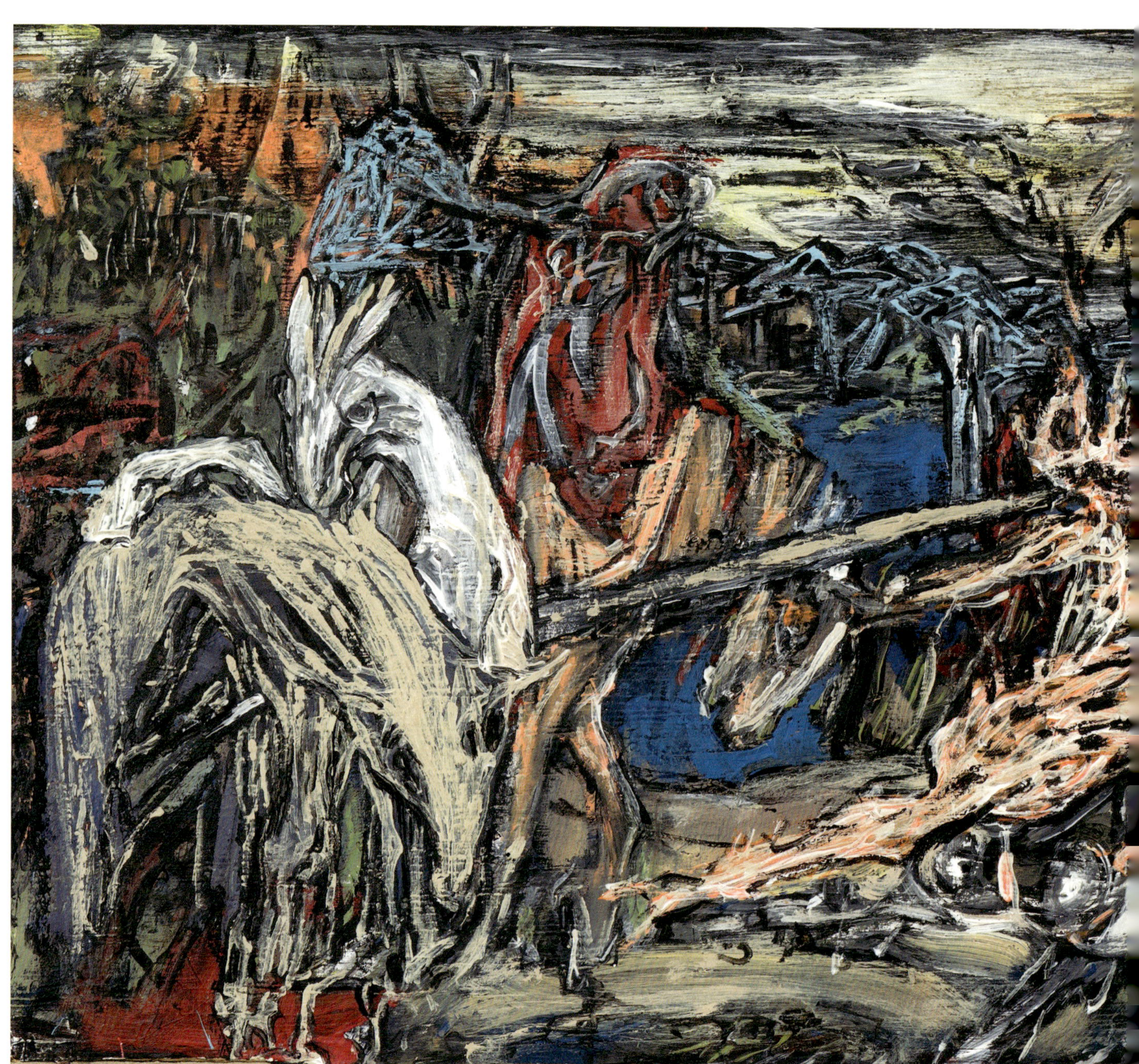

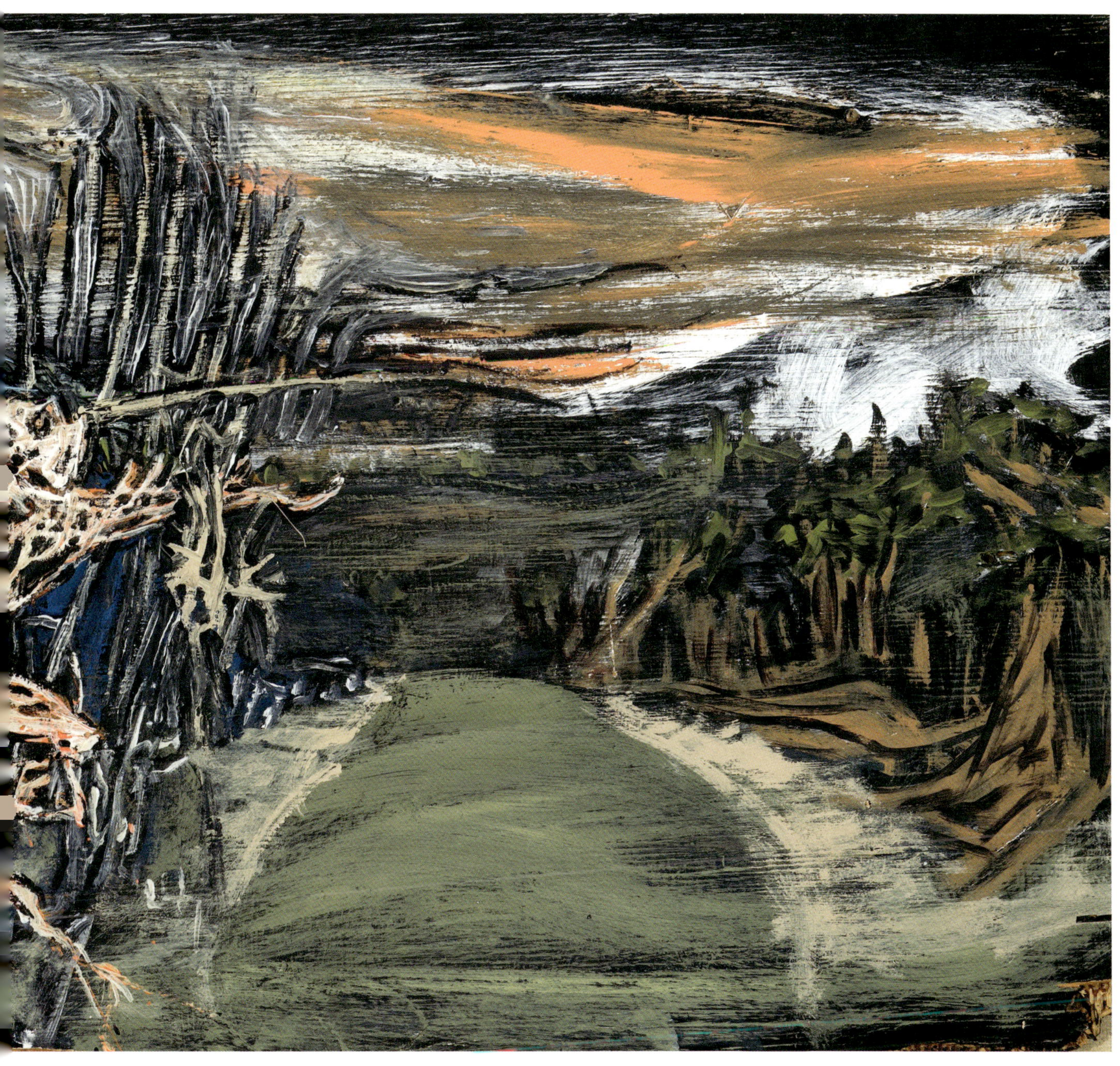

Nancy Ogilvie, *Circuit*, 2013
Acrylic on wood
53 × 123 cm

Meeting Anick Langelier led me to revisit the work of Van Gogh. Not just portraits of the artist and his starry skies, but the feel of them—the thick paint, stabbing brush strokes, and mix of colours. When I first saw NANCY OGILVIE's work, I again thought of Van Gogh, but for a different reason. It was as if Van Gogh had collaborated with H. R. Giger, applying his painting techniques to Giger's airbrushed biomechanical beings. But more than her technique, it's Ogilvie's images that are arresting. At first glance, they appear to be tangled tree roots in the master's style, but as with other outsider artists, there is never an attempt to mimic another's work. It is the viewer who connects the dots to that end, not the artist.

If Van Gogh is Anick Langelier's muse, Joe Davis is Ogilvie's. Joe Davis (1951–), a leader in the field of bio art, is an artist-scientist and research affiliate in the Department of Biology at MIT and the George Church Laboratory at Harvard Medical School. Brilliant and offbeat, he engages in mind-boggling projects like creating silkworms that extrude golden threads and encoding Wikipedia into an apple, therein infusing a literal tree of knowledge into the proverbial forbidden fruit. Ogilvie met Davis in 2004 and has kept in touch since then, even apprenticing in his laboratory. Although she feels compelled to paint, she doesn't believe in restricting herself to art. Doing that would find her stuck in a loop, "regurgitating her own nonsense" over and over again. I would like to be privy to an Ogilvie-Davis conversation and observe how their ideas weave together. I can't imagine the universe they would bring to life, but it would be unlike anything I have seen before.

Ogilvie doesn't see herself as an artist. She is just someone who makes paintings. It keeps her grounded, she says, and is a kind of therapy to help navigate her insomnia-filled nights. She began drawing and painting as a child and then more intensively after a bout of depression at the end of high school. She worked as a live sound engineer for many years to support herself while she painted. Both, she says, were full-time occupations. She recounts a life of isolation, often self-imposed to minimize the stress of work and social interactions. But it's painting that consumes her days and nights—sometimes up to twenty hours at a stretch. It allows her to confront her demons head-on. They lurk in her paintings, tangled in the deep underbrush, keeping the viewer at bay. It is the work of a solitary person, a painter of visions. Ogilvie typically works on about thirty canvasses at a time, and each group can take six months or more to complete. She explained that the canvasses work together to make a whole. It's like looking through a wall of small windows that reveal the entire scene. Sometimes she stops painting for a period of time, either because she's driven herself to the point of exhaustion or needs to take time off to reflect on the world around her. Although she is reluctant to call herself an artist, I beg to differ.

It is not easy for Ogilvie to speak about the subject matter of her art or explain how an idea develops into a painting. It is a clear and orderly process, she says, that begins with images and forms that have all been studied and practised in her head. To her, reaching into other dimensions is an obvious technique, but one she cannot communicate to others. It would be like trying to teach someone how to think with her own mind, how to navigate her own landscapes with her personal tools and experiences. That is an impossible task. She doesn't care if no one appreciates her work; it is a healing practice that is necessary for her well-being. Imagination cures, she says. "Let the train run off the track."

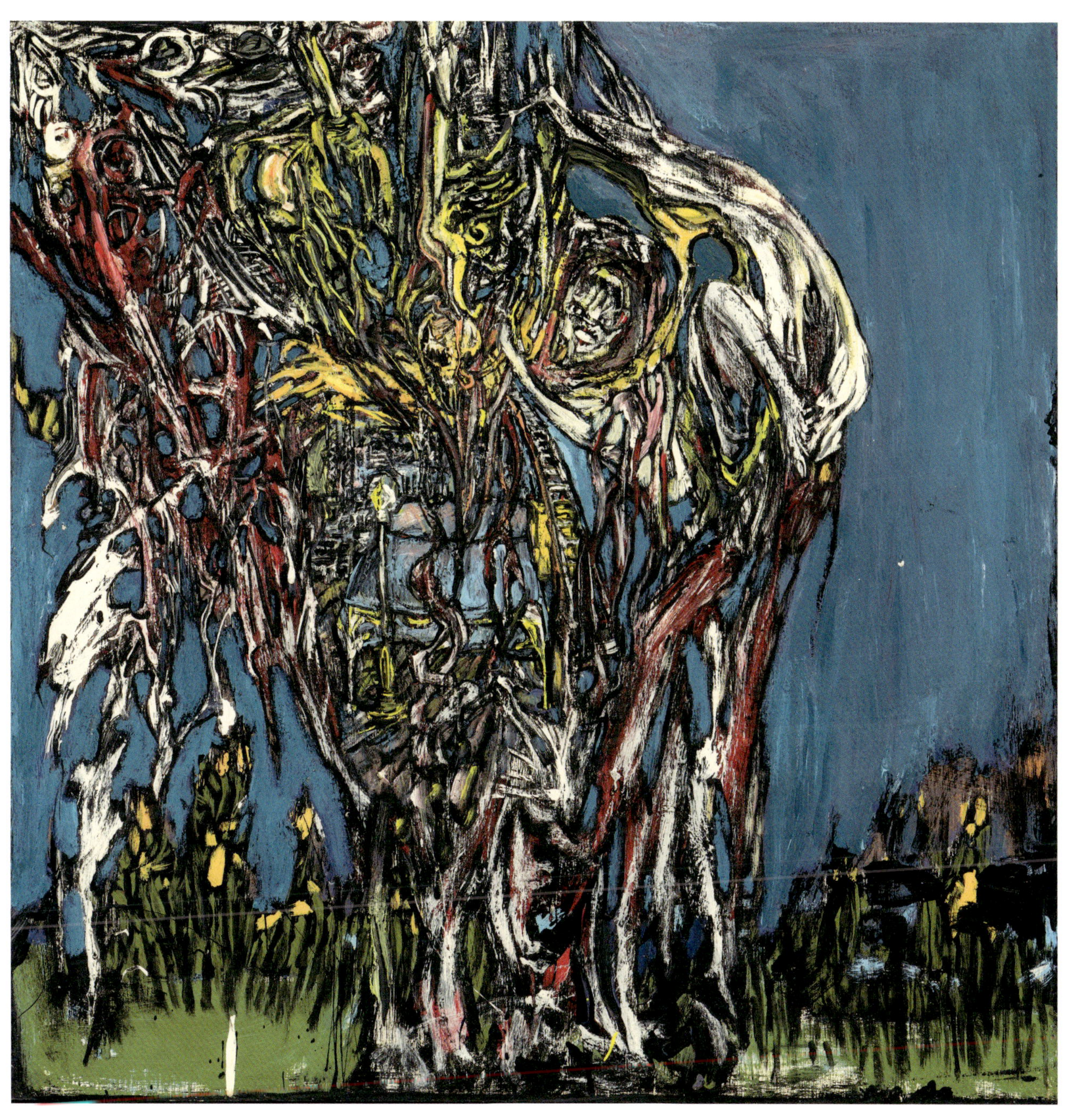

Nancy Ogilvie, *Le Cerveau de la Hanche*, 2013
Acrylic on wood
61 × 51 cm

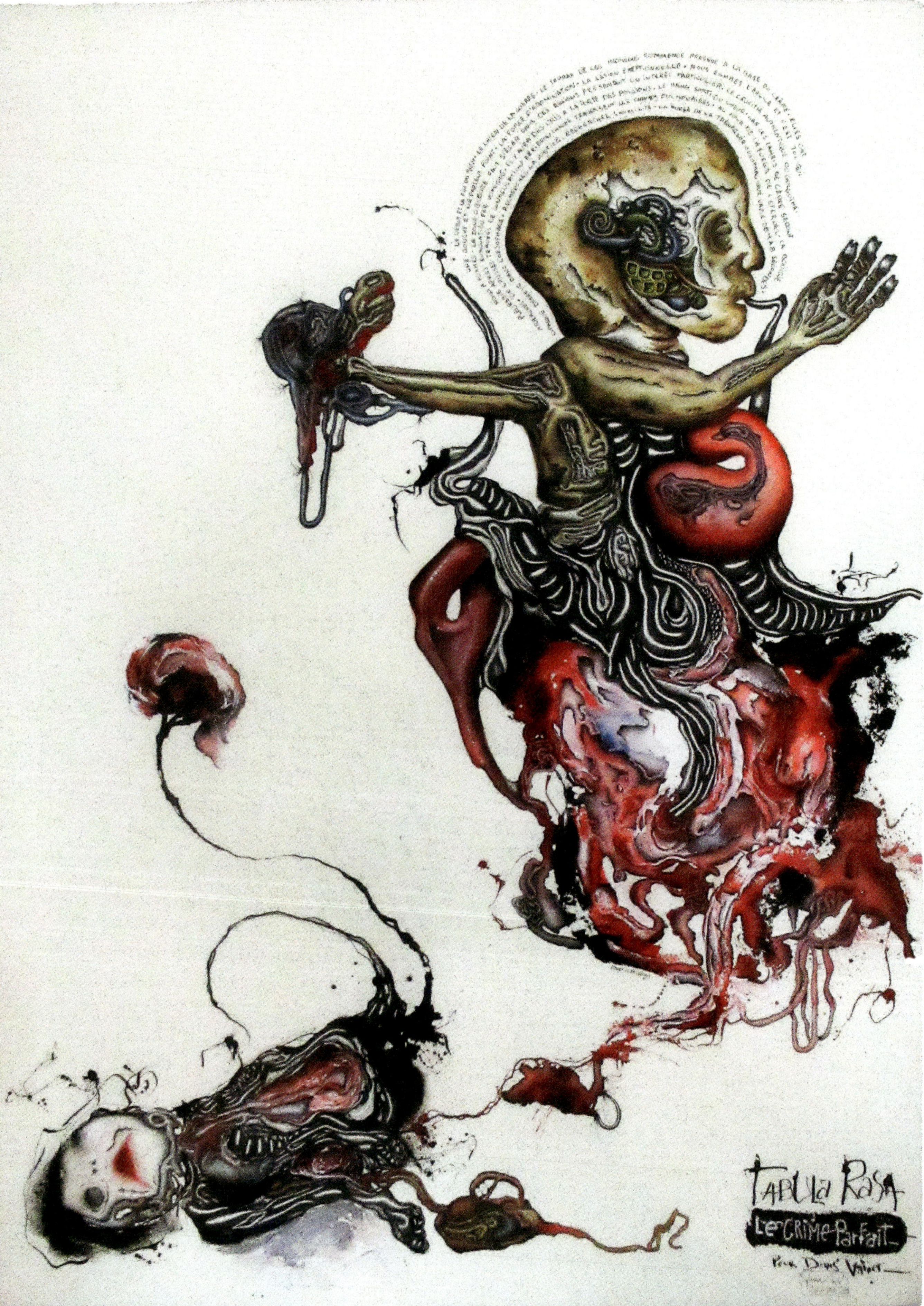
TABULA RASA
Le CRIME PARFAIT

Like Nancy Ogilvie, SYLVAIN MARTEL doesn't call himself an artist. He just likes to draw. And draw he does, every day. It's the only thing that makes sense to him. He has archived thousands of sheets of intricate ink drawings which are rarely seen unless he invites someone to view his work. The drawings are at once shocking and beautiful, human anatomy splayed for full view. Martel says they are about "life," and their beauty lies in their texture and colour. You can change many things about yourself, he says, but you can't change your interior. It is one of the few things that remain constant in life.

< Sylvain Martel, *Tabula Rasa*, 2015
Ink and acrylic on Arches paper
76.2 × 55.9 cm

Martel doesn't remember a time when he didn't draw. It is the focus of his life, consuming almost every free hour when he is not working at a printing shop. It is hard to describe his work. The word that springs to mind is *visceral*. His drawings reveal both the inward mechanisms of the body and the deep workings of the mind; they resist description but are open to infinite interpretation. The drawings are exquisitely detailed—some in vivid colour, some in black ink. Thick swirls of ink and fine feathery wisps come together to form foreboding anthropomorphic shapes. Cross-hatching fills the empty cavities and pools of colour spill onto the paper. And there is red. A lot of red. Perhaps red is the lifeforce of these organisms. Perhaps it is blood leeching away, taking life. I cannot penetrate these drawings alone. I need Martel's guidance, but he is a man of few words. I am speechless. I am in awe.

Drawings and books fill Martel's home, and there is a stack on his drawing table: the Bible, an anatomy book, a medical manual, a zoological guide. Taking a deconstructivist approach to the text, his practice is to open a book at random, copy a phrase, open another, pick a sentence, and so on. The juxtaposition of ideas is absurd but intriguing. He describes it as a *cadavre exquis* (exquisite corpse), an expression made up of words instead of images.

This drawing, *Tabula Rasa, Le crime parfait*, was dedicated to the poet Denis Vanier.

> Le début et la fin du rien.
> Le chien de la guerre.
> Le thorax de ces individus commence presque a la base du crâne.
> Elles ont une bouche et ne parlent point.
> La force d'abomination.
> La lésion exceptionelle.
> Nous sommes l'argile et c'est toi qui nous a formés.
> La zone obscure peut siéger dans des régions présentant un intéret particulier.
> Ce crucifié authentique du Golgotha.
> Pleurésie après évacuation par vomique.
> Il y aura des cris a la porte des poissons.
> Le sang sortie du coeur.
> Car les lambris de cèdre seront arrachés.
> De grosses travées de condensation péribronchique traversent les champs pulmonaires.
> Au jour de la fureur de l'éternel.
> La bouillie opaque descend dans l'oesophage.
> Recherchez la justice, recherchez l'humilité.
> La durée de la traversée oesophagique varie de 4 a 8 secondes.

The beginning and the end of nothing.
The dog of war.
The thorax of these individuals begins almost at the base of the skull.
They have a mouth and don't talk.
The force of abomination.
The exceptional lesion.
We are clay and you are the one who formed us.
The murky area may sit in areas of particular interest.
This authentic crucified from Golgotha.
Pleurisy after vomit evacuation.
There will be screams at the fish door.
Blood coming out of the heart.
Because the cedar lambris will be torn off.
Large span of peribronchic condensation pass through the lung fields.
On the day of the fury of the eternal.
The opaque porridge descends into the esophagus.
Seek justice, seek humility. The duration of the esophageal transit varies from 4 to 8 seconds.

This fragmented, reconstructed statement invites the viewer to link ideas. But unlike the great collage artists of modernism there are no references to pop culture or historical events to weave meaning into the work. That may be the beauty of Martel's word salad. Make of it what you will. When asked to put his art practice into context, he could only offer this: "I was born in 1967. I don't know the date of my death. While I'm waiting, I draw. Time stops."

I regret not meeting DANIEL ERBAN before he died. I did, however, spend time with his family in Montréal and learned about his life from them. From all accounts, I would have liked him.

Erban had some early art training that came to naught. He worked as a carpenter before becoming a math teacher in 1980 but spent all his free time creating art; he slept little and passed most of the night hours in his studio. Unused now, the studio still bears his presence. Evidence of his prolific output is piled on tables and stacked in bins; there is a lot of artwork to admire. A bookcase crammed with CDs sits in the middle of the room, and I imagine Erban listening to his jazz collection as he painted through the quiet hours of the night.

His family describe him as larger than life. Gregarious and outspoken, Erban was passionate about people, society, and his art. He was a generous, kind man who was quick to defend marginalized populations. He declared that he would never paint flowers, and indeed, he did not. In fact, speaking for the oppressed was what drove him to create. He insisted on talking to those who viewed his art, hoping to engage them in a discussion about the inequities of life and shock them out of complacency. The artist's early work featured the seedy underworld of Montréal, but, over time, his themes became even darker and grimmer.

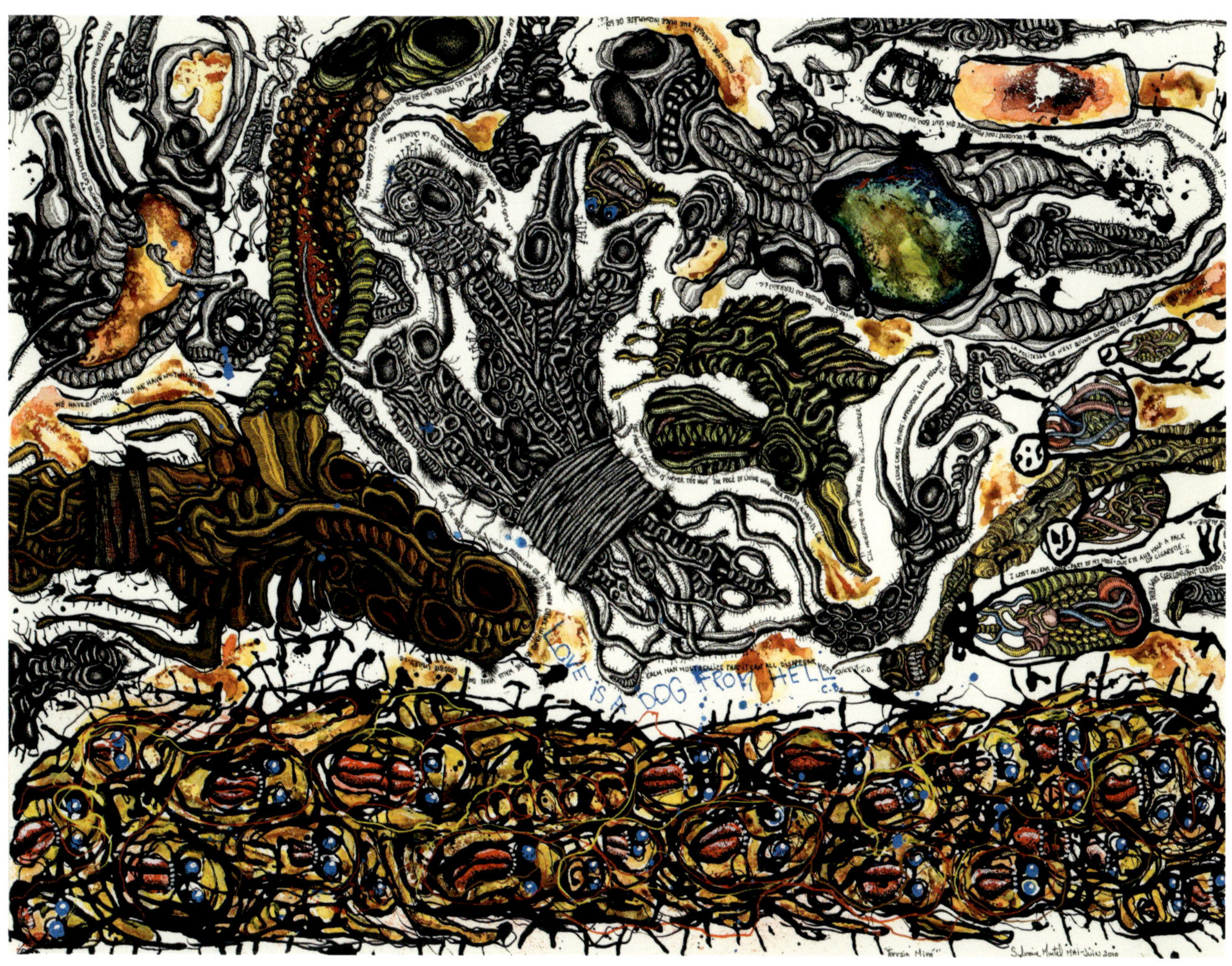

Sylvain Martel, *Terrain miné,*
2010
Watercolour, acrylic, ink
30.5 × 40.6 cm

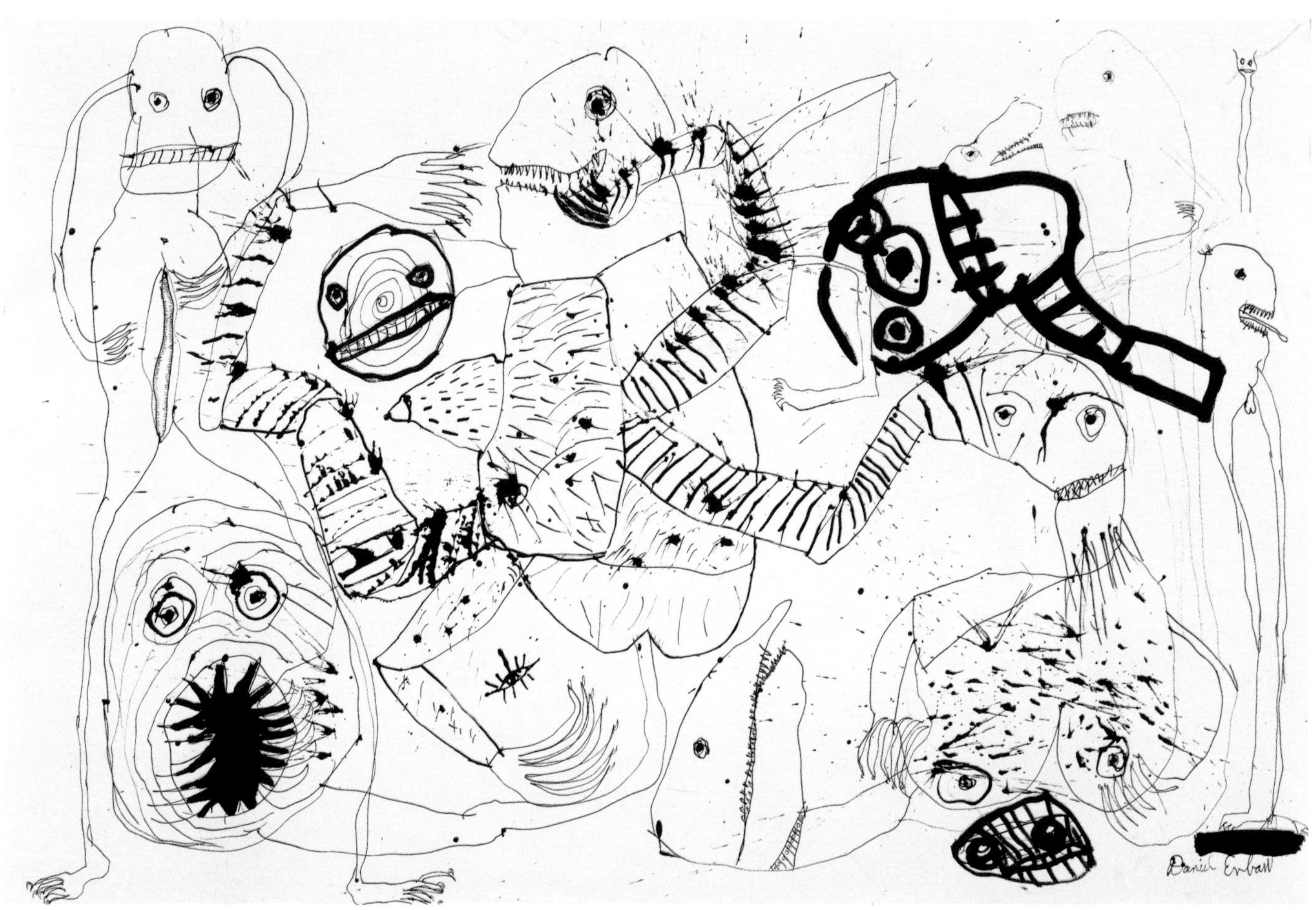

Daniel Erban, *I Know What you Did Last Night*, 1994
Mixed media on paper
102 × 152 cm

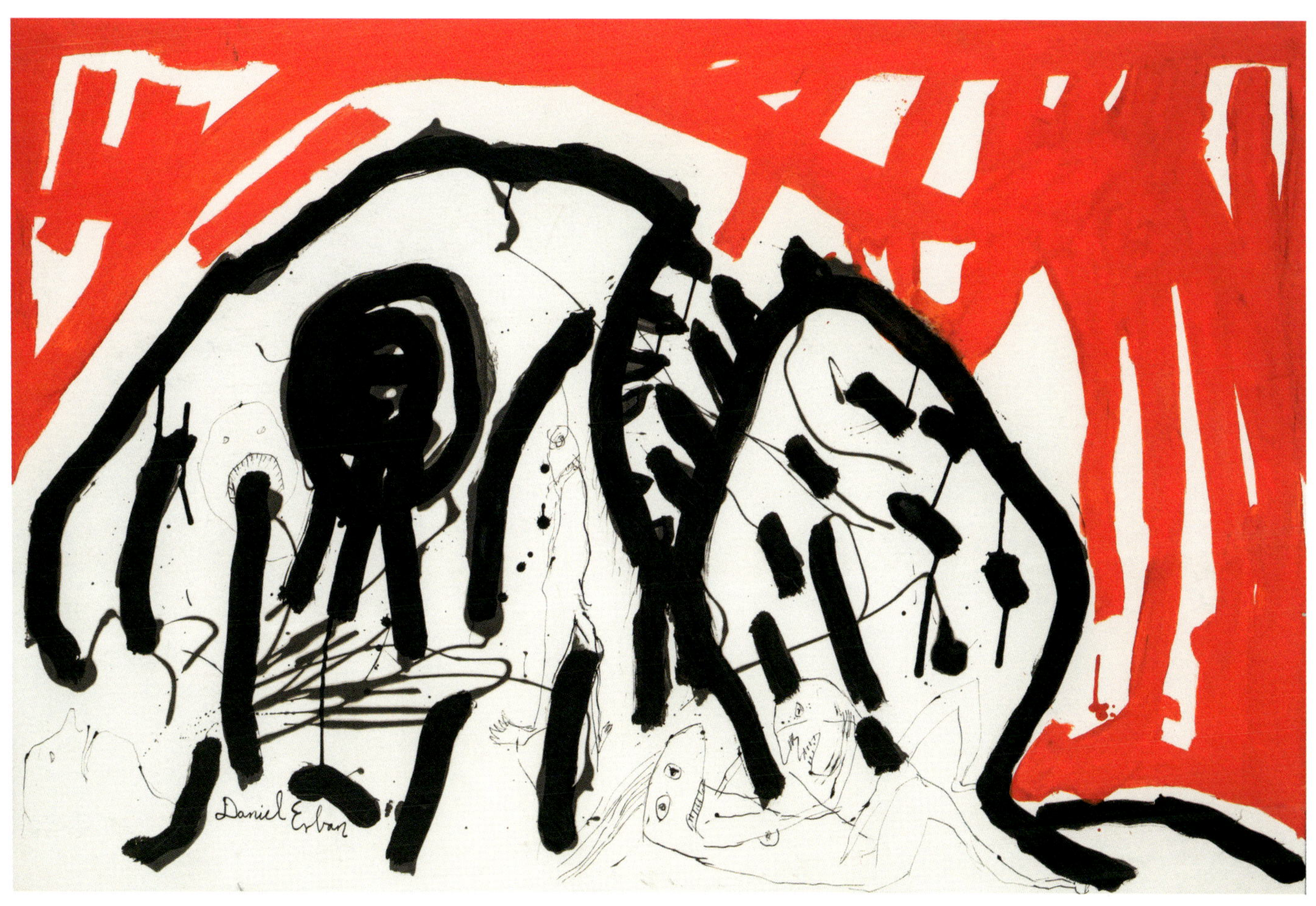

Daniel Erban, *Midsummer's Night Dream*, 2006
Mixed media on paper
102 × 152 cm

> Daniel Erban, book cover for *Thou Shalt Not Kill*, 2009

Erban worked quickly; he drew or painted directly onto canvas, with any materials at hand. Large paintings were often completed in one sitting. His work is powerful and compelling, and I am drawn to the boldness and confidence of his lines. It's only on closer inspection, though, that my eyes translate those brush strokes into disturbing images. I am left in a state of cognitive dissonance—aware that I am simultaneously beholding beauty and brutality. As with Sylvain Martel's drawings, I find it difficult to rationalize my attraction to the work.

Like many provocative artists before him,[127] Erban intended his artwork to jolt the viewer from complacency. But he was not part of a celebrated art crowd, nor did he dash a one-off statement piece to express his personal views of a particular event. His entire body of work is one declarative expression of man's inhumanity to man. I gained some insight into Erban's work when I learned his mother was a Holocaust survivor. As one writer explained, documenting her own mother's story of the Holocaust was a way to confront her own monsters.[128] To be silent about the past was not an option, nor was it possible to exorcise those ghosts. It was only possible to examine and understand her relationship to them. She used her writer's skill to articulate those deep wounds, but those tools are not available to everyone. As one artist said, "If I could say it in words, there would be no reason to paint."[129] And so I imagined Erban wrestling with his own demons, hoping to reach a state of provisional peace.

Erban generally explored themes in his work, like the underworld of Montréal or the mistreated, marginalized populations of the city. He felt compelled to depict the ugly side of life. It is not possible in these few pages to display the breadth of his work. But one piece, in my view, sums it all up: *Thou Shalt Not Kill*, his handmade book of art. He describes it as follows:

> This is a collection of 502 eleven-by-eight-and-a-half-inch drawings decontextualizing the pre-postmodern interpretation of $E = mc^2$ and contradicting the right-wing agenda that life is not worth living because time is money and we are doomed to eat our children.

Erban's book is a collection of his black ink illustrations of Kenneth Rexroth's poem "Thou Shalt Not Kill." The poem, written in 1953–54, is a long, elegiac work mourning the death of Dylan Thomas, who drank himself to death on his last poetry tour of the United States. Although it mourns the loss of a great poet, it deplores the destruction of creativity by the dominant culture of power, violence, and death. The poem begins:

> They are murdering all the young men.
> For half a century now, every day,
> They have hunted them down and killed them.
> They are killing them now.
> At this minute, all over the world,
> They are killing the young men.
> They know ten thousand ways to kill them.
> Every year they invent new ones.
> In the jungles of Africa,
> In the marshes of Asia,
> In the deserts of Asia,

Thou
Shalt
not
Kill

Daniel

In the slave pens of Siberia,
In the slums of Europe,
In the nightclubs of America,
The murderers are at work.

This is Erban's constant lament: every day, atrocities are taking place all over the world: people are murdered, voices are silenced, creativity is stifled by hyenas with polished faces and bow ties, sitting in billion-dollar offices. How many have died at the hands of political parties or in the back wards of provincial madhouses, he asks. How many lie in the canyons of death?

It is a sobering plea for accountability.

Creating art is not something artists do; rather, it defines who they are. A few go on to pursue art careers through formal avenues, like art school, while others are driven to create with no thought for the outcome. Their life's work seldom leads to public recognition, but that was never their intention. LUC GUÉRARD is one of those people.

Guérard remembers being fixated on drawing in his teen years. He desperately wanted to study art at L'École des Beaux-arts de Montréal, but his father had other ideas. So he forged his father's signature on the enrollment application and was accepted to art school. It seemed that he won the battle, but his father refused to fund his seventeen-year-old son's escapade and the plan was abandoned. Instead, Guérard began exploring art himself at the expense of his studies. His grades plummeted. His father relented the following year and agreed to let his son attend art school, but by then Guérard had changed his mind. He had no interest in producing art that looked like photographs. He taught himself to paint and has been pursuing his passion ever since.

It has not been an easy life for Guérard: children, the death of his partner, and financial struggles took their toll on his emotional resources. But he feels he's lived a blessed life because he is free to paint. He doesn't envy those "flavour-of-the-month" artists who end up repeating the same painting in an endless number of permutations in response to public demand. He is free to experiment with paint whenever he feels like it. Recognition can be fleeting, and Guérard is philosophical about his life's work. "You need to know that your work is valid. Recognition would flatter your pride, but do you really need it? You really need support and stability. If I didn't have a family, if I had been alone, maybe I would have been drunk all the time."[130]

Guérard describes his practice as a sensual experience, and the subject of his paintings is just a pretext to manipulate colour on canvas. *Nude on a Sofa*, for example, started with a concrete idea that became something else when it hit the canvas playground. The "something else" is an odalisque, an Olympia, a Picasso nude, painted in vivid gem tones. Flattened and abstracted, she reveals herself as a multifaceted jewel. Guérard points out the use of black outlines in his paintings, a technique left over from his paint-by-number days.*

* I have met a surprising number of artists, both professional and self-taught, who fondly recall their first paint-by-number efforts.

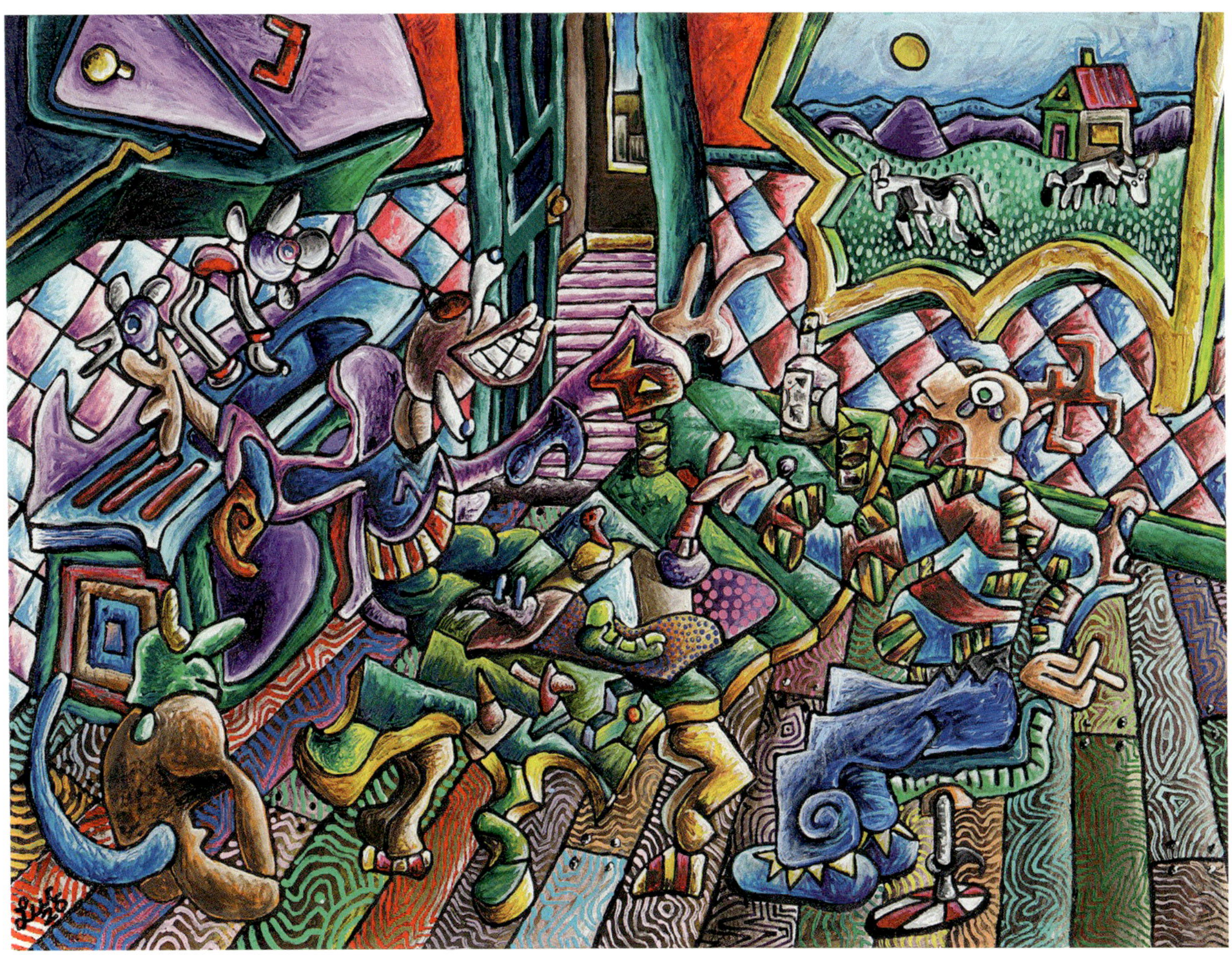

Luc Guérard, *Échec et mat*, 2020
Acrylic on canvas
77 × 102 cm

Luc Guérard, *Nue au Sofa*, 2018
Acrylic on canvas
77 × 98 cm

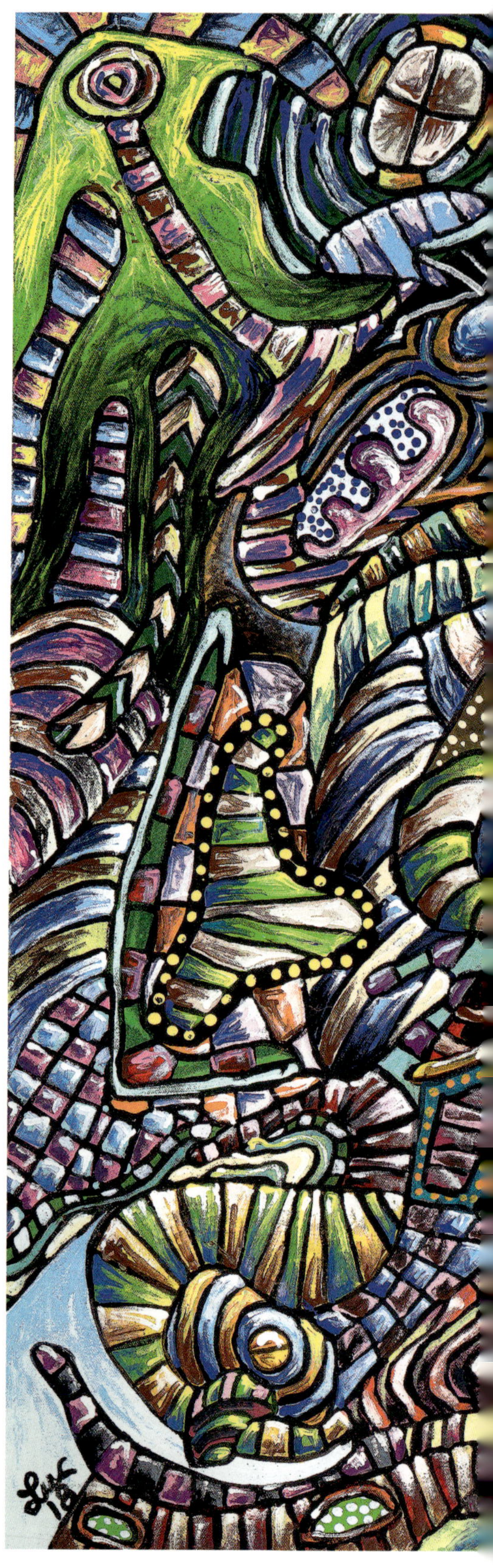

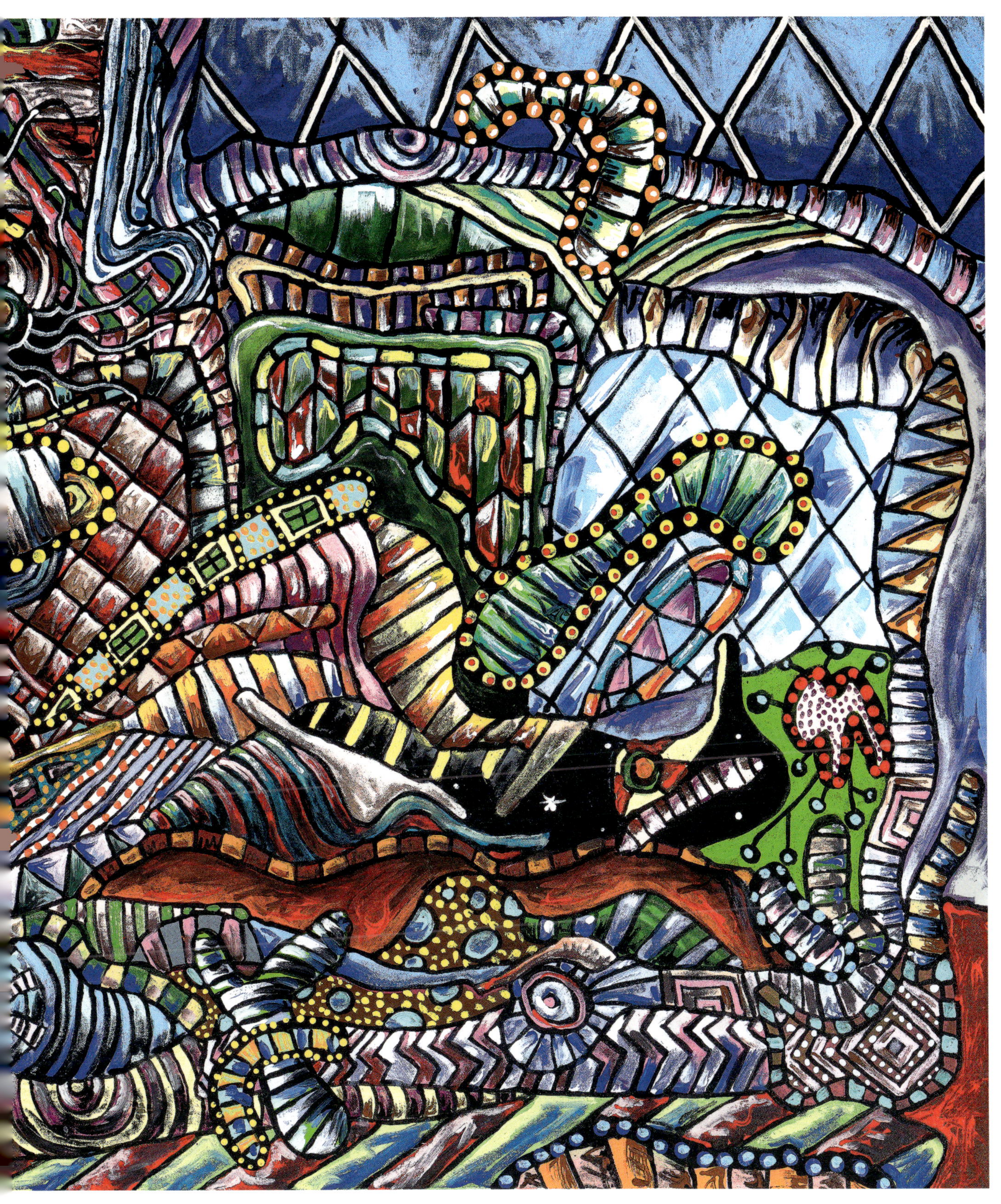

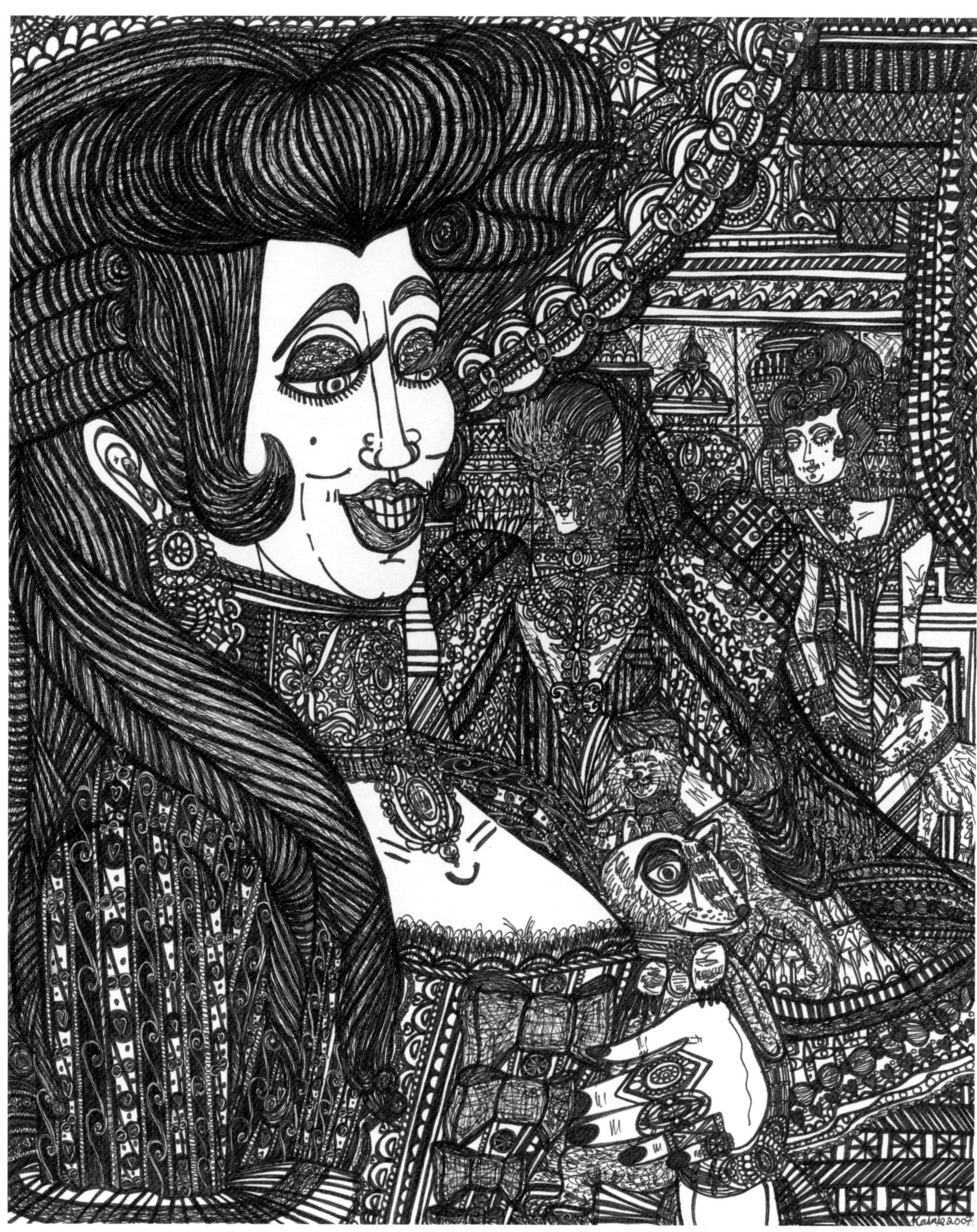

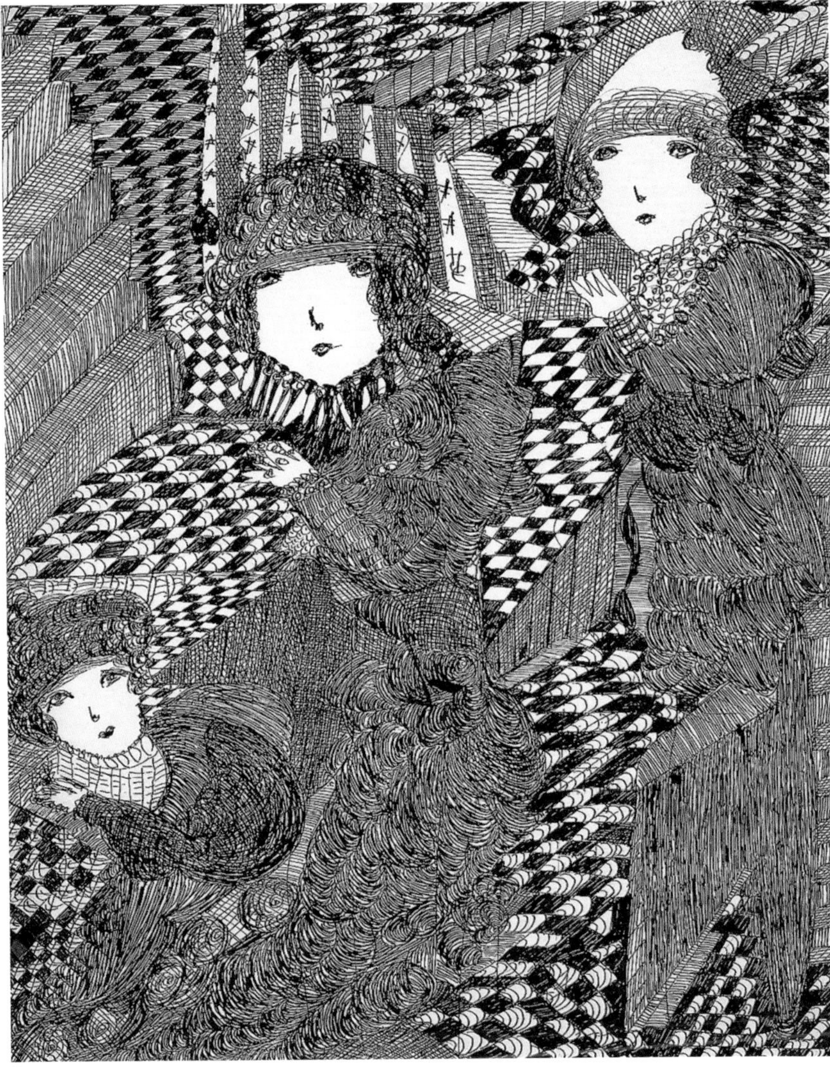

Madge Gill, *The Three*, c. 1945
Ink on card
63.5 × 50.8 cm

< Karine Labrie,
Marie-Antoinette et sa petite chienne, 2010
Ink on paper
43 × 36 cm

Chiaroscuro is word that comes to mind for artist KARINE LABRIE. In art lingo, *chiaroscuro* refers to the contrast between dark and light, bringing drama and life to the composition. In Labrie's story, it describes her own emergence from dark to light—from withdrawn child to confident artist.

I met Labrie at a small gallery in rural Québec and was introduced to her work at Vincent et moi in Québec City.[131] What first struck me was the similarity of her drawings to those of British artist Madge Gill, a well-known visionary and outsider artist recognized for her pen-and-ink drawings of fashionable ladies. But while Gill's inspiration came from the spirit world, Labrie's art springs from her own imagination. She hasn't stopped drawing since she first picked up a pen as a young child. Congenitally deaf, drawing is her way of connecting with the world. Labrie's parents observed her creative activities at an early age and were concerned about the growing piles of heavily marked, dark drawings in her room. Most drawings, they said, were more ink than paper, and marked so deeply they threatened to tear through the page. But eventually she shared her work with her family and later with the staff at Vincent et moi. It was difficult for her to step out of the shadows because her life had been marred by bullying and humiliation.

> Karine Labrie, *Untitled*,
c. 2015
Ink on paper
24 × 19.5 cm

Labrie depicts the bedecked and bejeweled fashionistas of her daydreams. Her greatest inspiration comes from the royal courts of the eighteenth century. She says this of the image titled *Marie Antoinette*:

> One day the idea came to me to create characters and royal settings. Right away I thought of queen Marie Antoinette. For her, I drew a chic salon and her companions. I placed a small dog in her arms and, above it, a kitten who is not very visible. I created for her the jewels that I would have liked to wear if I had been queen at that time.

Labrie draws all day, even while doing other things, like watching television. Her universe is one of fashionable people, usually women, who dress like royalty and sport *Le Pouf*, an extravagant, towering hairstyle made popular by Marie Antoinette. They stand proudly before the viewer in all their resplendent attire: bedecked, bejeweled, and revelling in the attention. The highly decorative patterns of their clothing blend in with the equally decorative background. It is hard, sometimes, to tell where the clothing ends and the wallpaper begins. Other details reveal themselves if you take time to study the piece. What looks like patterned fabric turns out to be a dog or a delicate teacup. The women always wear five rings on each hand. Look closer and you will see titles on the spines of books on the shelf. It's a world of infinite detail. Labrie cannot count the number of hours she spends on each drawing because she works on four or five at a time. The hours, she says, add up to "many." She usually draws with ink and a felt pen on standard letter-size paper, but she occasionally creates larger pieces. When she runs out of ideas for a new drawing, she makes collages. She also picks up trinkets at thrift stores and transforms them into jewellery. (The only downside to Labrie's excessive creative energy, she says, is that her apartment is a mess.)

I have observed a rippling effect within art communities such that one artist inspires another to explore their own creativity. The inspiration doesn't come in the form of a motivational speech, but something deeper than that. It comes from watching another artist create simply for the joy of creating. François Bertrand, the former director of Vincent et moi, found satisfaction in helping other artists achieve their artistic vision. He had done some clothing design in his youth, but never had an opportunity to explore his own creativity. Like the prairie folk artists who "gave permission" to contemporary artists to push the boundaries of creativity and imagination, the pieces fell into place as Bertrand watched Labrie draw. Artistic freedom is contagious; it gave Bertrand licence to "just create." A joint exhibition of their work—Labrie's drawings and Bertrand's textile sculptures—was held in 2018.

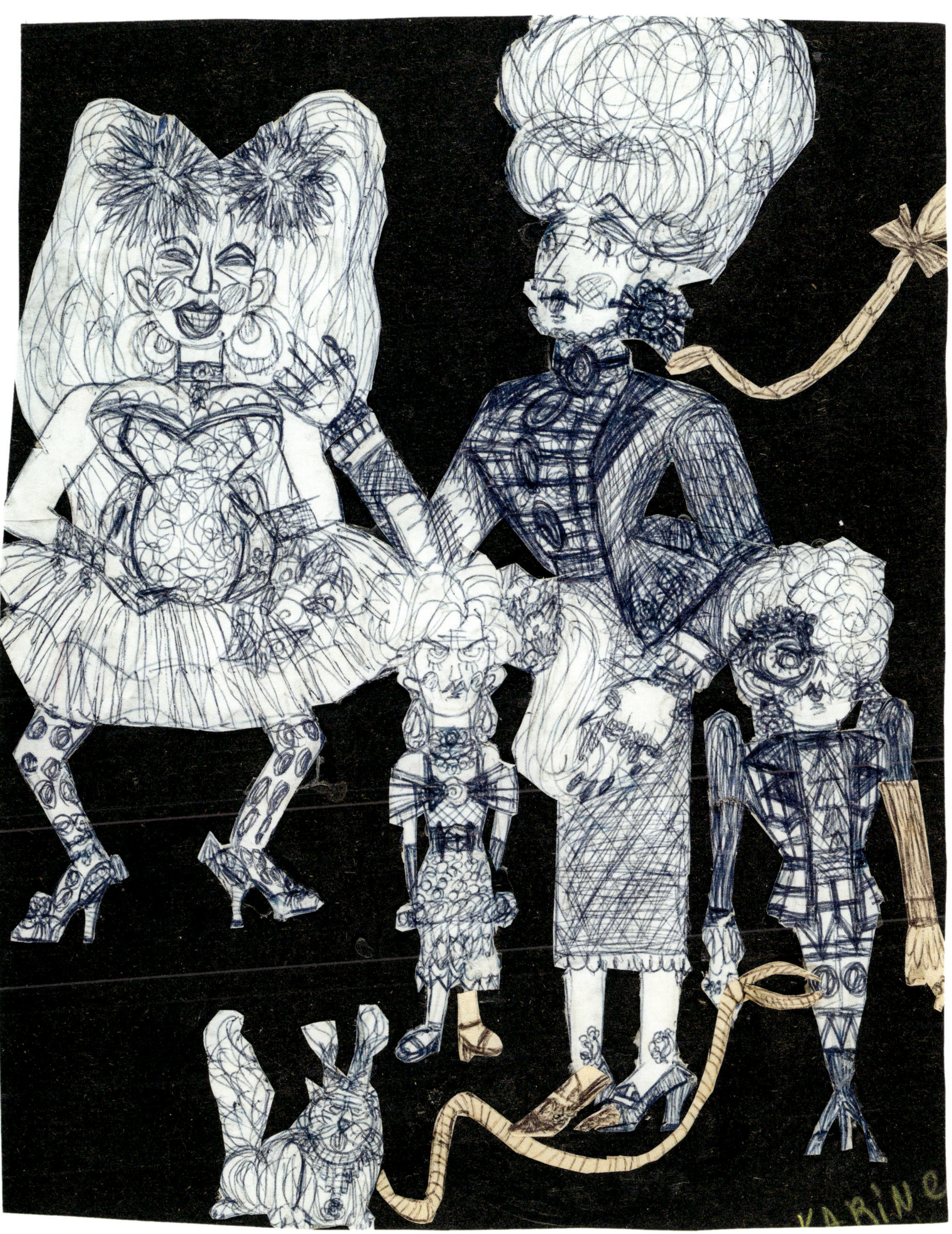
KARINE

Lessard brothers, *Sculptures*, c. 1990s
Mixed media with wood, fabric, hair, cosmetics
23 cm to 42 cm

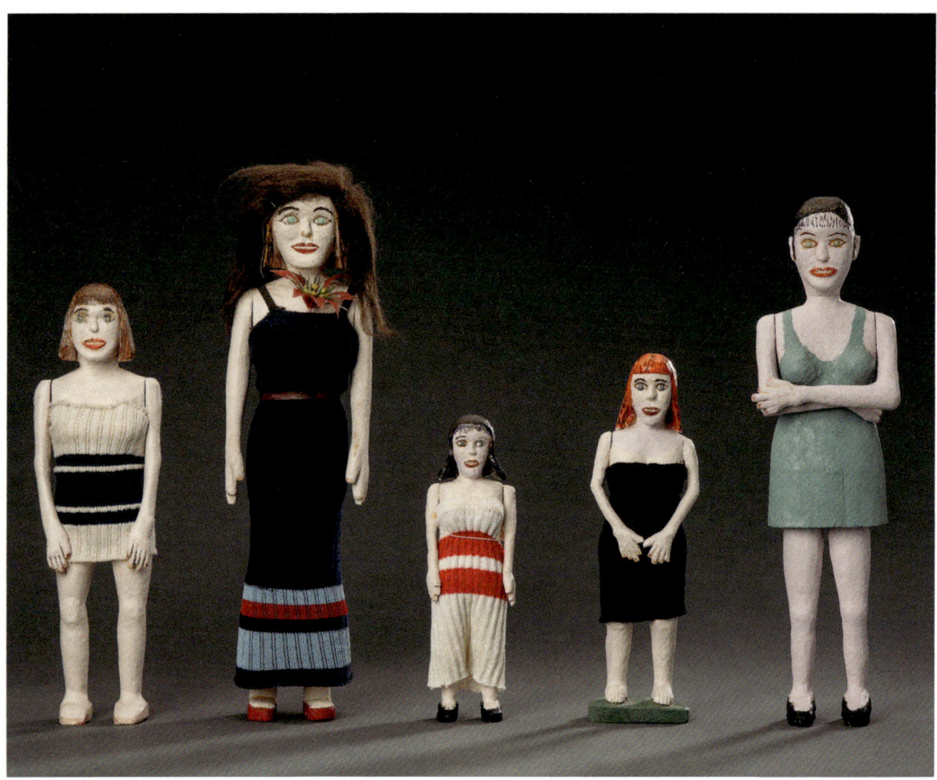

I am sometimes at a loss for words to describe the art that I encounter. In some cases, it is best experienced on an affective level, where words are less important. In other cases, the artwork defies categorization. What label would I apply to wooden figures made by the LESSARD BROTHERS, farm workers in a small town in Québec's Eastern Townships?

In the late 1990s, a local folk-art collector noticed whirligigs and other odd sculptures in front of the home of Hervé, Lucien, and Roger Lessard. He stopped to ask if any were for sale. While visiting, the collector noticed some nicely carved animals on display in the house, as well as wooden carvings of women wearing clothes made from old socks and other discarded material. He learned that the statues were made by two of the elderly brothers to decorate their home. Some were modelled after exotic dancers from the local bar, some were merely fanciful ladies. What is remarkable about these figures, aside from the surprise at seeing a crowd of them standing together, is the artists' attention to detail. The women's arms are articulated, their makeup and nail polish are applied with care, their jewelry is assembled from found objects, and some sport real hair donated by members of the Lessard family. No one can really say why the brothers created the dolls, but they are delightful in their bold quirkiness. Although the carvings originate from a region steeped in folk-art tradition, and are made with traditional carving tools, the brothers have strayed far beyond the parameters of folk-art themes. While it is relatively easy to identify traditional folk-art pieces, it becomes harder to classify idiosyncratic creative works —that is, those in a singular, unique style—because they share many characteristics with outsider art. If a label is necessary, they may fall into the category of contemporary folk art because they emerge from the hands of folk-art carvers. But the pieces are so distinctive and delightfully individualistic that it's hard to give them a name. They just are.

Atlantic Provinces

Some years ago I began blogging about outsider art in Canada as a way to record my research and to connect with fellow art enthusiasts. I had read conflicting information about MAUD LEWIS and was puzzled to learn that she was sometimes described as an outsider artist. I referred to Lewis only to say that I had always considered her to be a folk artist who painted in a naïve style and I would not be researching her legacy in the context of outsider art. That spawned a flurry of emails questioning my sanity, but it gave me a clue that perhaps Canadians did not distinguish between the broad categories of folk art and outsider art. I did not revisit this issue until I was forced to consider the relationship between the genres in Canada and then again when I discovered that Scottie Wilson and Arthur Villeneuve's work had been categorized, for lack of more precise terms, as naïve and primitive art. So, it did not come a surprise that I was being challenged on the label I applied to Canada's Grandma Moses.[132]

If you are Canadian, you may know something about Maud Lewis, and if you are a Nova Scotian, you probably know a lot. For those not familiar with Lewis, she was born in 1903 in Yarmouth County, Nova Scotia. She had a physical condition that left her physically deformed and impaired her mobility and dexterity.[133] She dropped out of school when she was fourteen, after completing the fifth grade. After the death of her parents in the 1930s, her brother squandered their inheritance and, around that same time, she had a child out of wedlock, whom she gave up for adoption and never saw again. Lewis moved to Digby

Maud Lewis, *Oxen and Logging Wagon*, c. 1960s
Oil on pulpboard
26 × 35.8 cm

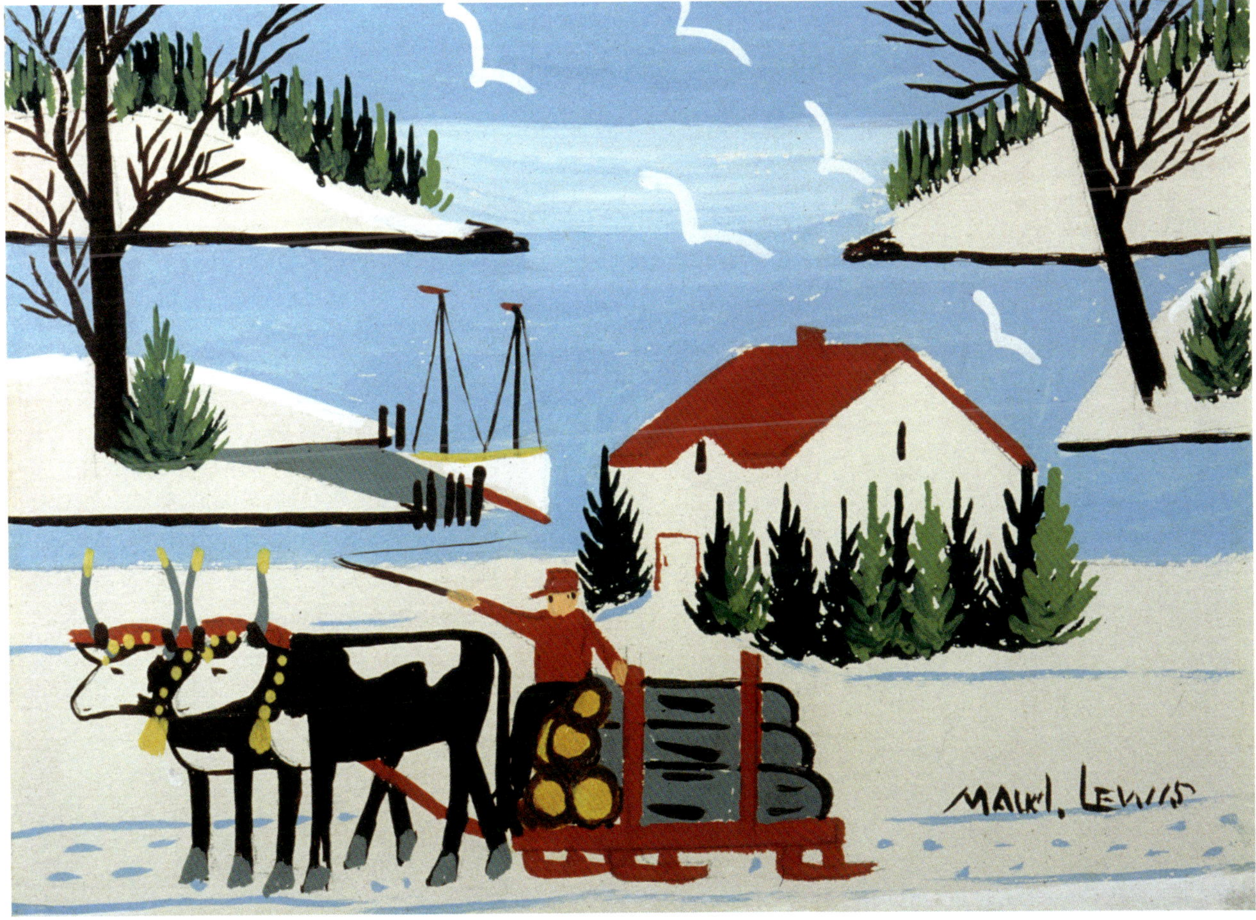

to live with her aunt. She worked for Everett Lewis as his housekeeper and they married in 1938. She lived the rest of her life in his tiny one-room house, with no electricity or plumbing. In the early years, she dabbled in art by selling hand-painted Christmas cards while Everett peddled fish. As she became more absorbed in her artwork, she painted every surface inside her home with bright images of flowers, butterflies, and the like. She also painted colourful landscapes on wooden panels that she sold to local residents and tourists.

Lewis gained notoriety as a folk artist during her lifetime, but achieved fame after her death in 1970. Her death coincided with a revival of folk art and, it is said, Lewis's artwork was used as a vehicle to reimagine the rural Nova Scotia experience, both past and present.[134] Her life was reframed as one of noble poverty that spurred her need to create.[135] She became a folk-art icon and the subject of projects to venerate her life and art, including books, documentaries, and a retrospective of her work at the Art Gallery of Nova Scotia. Her home was reconstructed in the museum. This response to Lewis and her work was part of a general movement in Canada, the USA, England, and Australia in the 1970s to visualize a future that was full of optimism. Cultural heritage tourism became an industry, and Nova Scotia fully embraced it; even poor rural folk, like Lewis, could triumph over hardship and be content with simple things.[136] Life was full of possibilities. Such was the cultural optimism of folk art.

Today, however, local artists and historians are bringing the darker truths about Maud Lewis's life to light.[137] The reality of an unwed mother who gave her child up for adoption and marriage to an allegedly abusive husband is the opposite of the sunny optimistic biography that was being promoted. The critics describe how a story that's been so closely intertwined with provincial tourism, an art institution, and a corporate sponsor has been sanitized.[138] And recently, the Art Gallery of Nova Scotia has been accused of exploiting her legacy.[139] In the midst of this controversy, the Gallery reports unwavering support from visitors to the Maud Lewis exhibit. From a feminist perspective, Maude's story can be framed another way: she was a mid-century female artist who was so successful that she was able to support her family, in spite of her debilitating physical condition. That, in itself, was a remarkable achievement. Visitors continue to be inspired by Maud's work and her personal story; they connect with her on a spiritual level.[140] In many ways the biographical details of both folk and outsider artists are used to support or deny their status in a category of art. The gatekeepers may be unnecessarily vigilant; perhaps the viewer's connection with the art is all that matters.

ANTHONY JOSEPH AUCOIN is a master of two things: sonnets and crepuscular sunsets. He didn't genuinely appreciate sunsets until he started painting them. Every sunset is unique and ever-changing, he says, as a gust of wind can change the view entirely. A. J., as he prefers to be called, didn't plan to be an artist. It just happened. As he explained, he was always a doodler, but he happened to draw a rabbit in eighth-grade art class. His teacher, Mother St. Charles, looked at it and exclaimed, "Is it ever proportionate!" That comment stuck in his mind, and fifty years later he took up art again.

An RCAF veteran and former member of a road-paving crew, A. J. started painting as a way to pass the time. For many years he got together with a group of local artists at the Inverness Legion in Cape Breton, Nova Scotia, every Thursday afternoon. They called themselves "The Colour-Blind Collective," and it was a pleasant way to socialize with art and beer. A. J. doesn't know any rules of art, and doesn't care to know about them either. The best advice he received from another artist is how to hang his paintings so they sit flat on the wall. He says he doesn't aim to produce a perfect painting, nor does he aspire to be a professional artist. Because he once heard that viewers look for flaws in paintings, he decided to give them a lot to find. His philosophy towards creating art is something he learned in grade school: try for one hundred, make sixty-two. When he started painting, he used whatever material was at hand—cardboard, glue, and cheap paint. Then, to his delight, he found the dollar store in his town offered everything he needed to make art, including canvas and acrylic paints. That discovery was inspiring, although he continues to paint on cut-up cardboard boxes from time to time. He could never afford to frame his work, so the frame had to become part of the painting. He still prefers this style. A. J. explained that he takes a spontaneous approach to artmaking. He doesn't plan ahead; he just starts painting and the image evolves. He paints with his fingers, using a brush only to reach into the corners of the work. He always signs his work "A. J./A. J." The first A. J. represents the id (the creative part of himself), while the second one represents the ego (the active part of himself that makes the painting).

Although he is known for his sumptuous sunsets, which he paints from memory, A. J. explained that language is his forte, not art. He is a Latin scholar, but doesn't have much use for it now. He speaks English, but incorporates French and Gaelic phrases into his artwork, as they are also spoken in his community. Painting is an enjoyable pursuit, but sonnets are what he likes to talk about. He considers himself to be first and foremost a poet. A lifetime of writing sonnets has given him great pleasure, and he claims to have the system down pat. He reveres Shakespeare ("the granddaddy of 'em all") and can recite the stanzaic structure of a sonnet at the drop of a hat. He recalls walking out of a poetry class when the instructor announced they would be working in free verse. That's not his thing; sonnets are. A. J. has ingeniously combined his love of words and paint by adding informative plaques onto his work that provide details about himself, the artwork, and the frame. These extra features are sometimes composed from capital letters that he cuts from race-track programs and glues onto cardboard. He might also add a sonnet because he is foremost a poet.

A. J.'s messages embellish the canvas like another coat of paint, adding texture and meaning to his work. Contemporary artists may use words to deliver a provocative message, but A. J., a master of crepuscular sunsets and sonnets, is simply inviting us to pause and contemplate the beauty of nature.

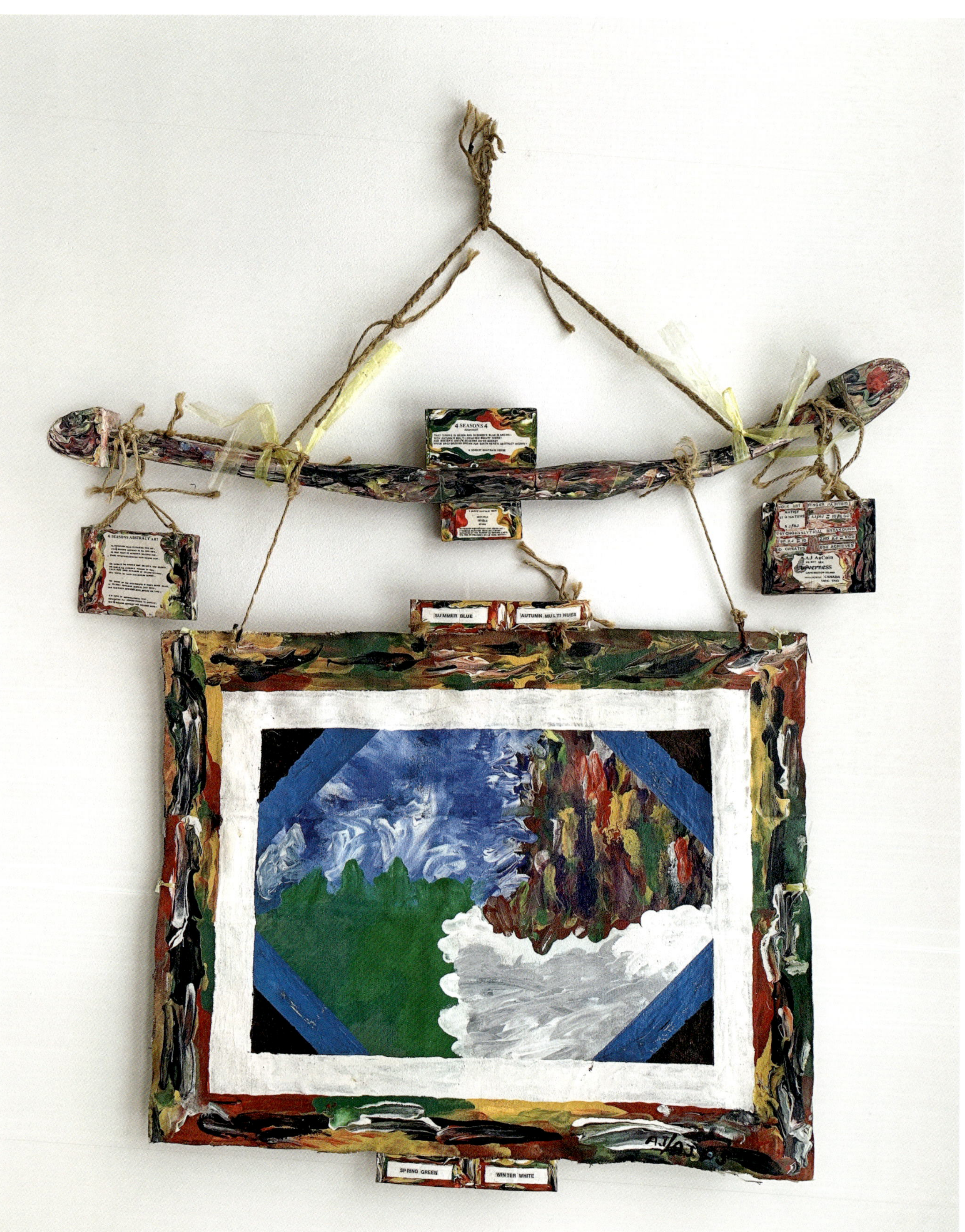
4 SEASONS 4
4 SEASONS ABSTRACT ART
FINGER PAINTING
ARTIST
AJ/AJ
ID CREATES
EGO ACHIEVES
AJ AuCoin
Inverness
CANADA
SUMMER BLUE
AUTUMN MULTI HUES
SPRING GREEN
WINTER WHITE

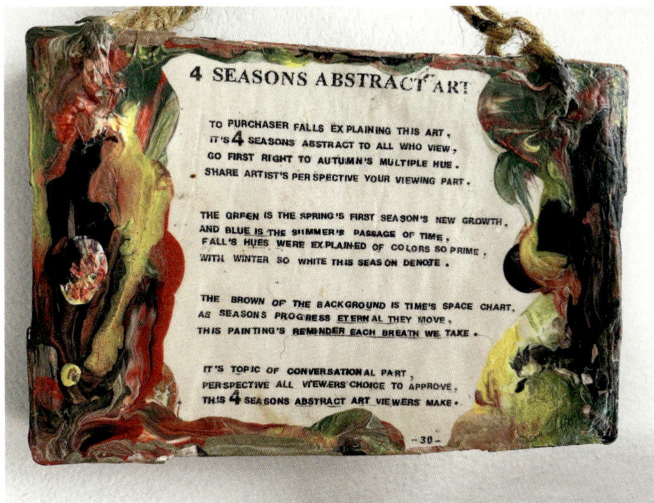

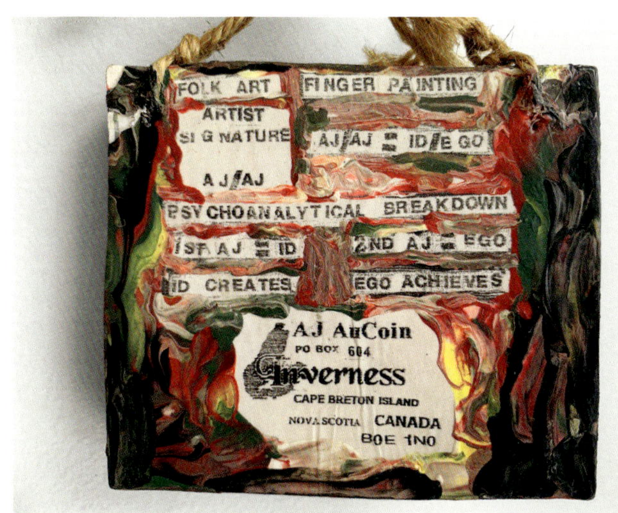

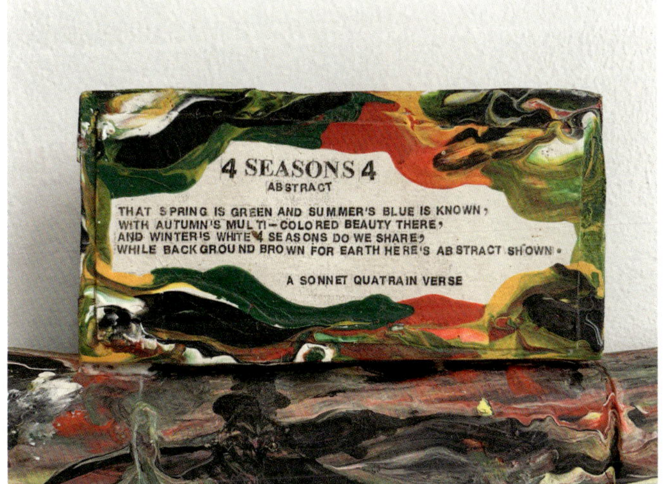

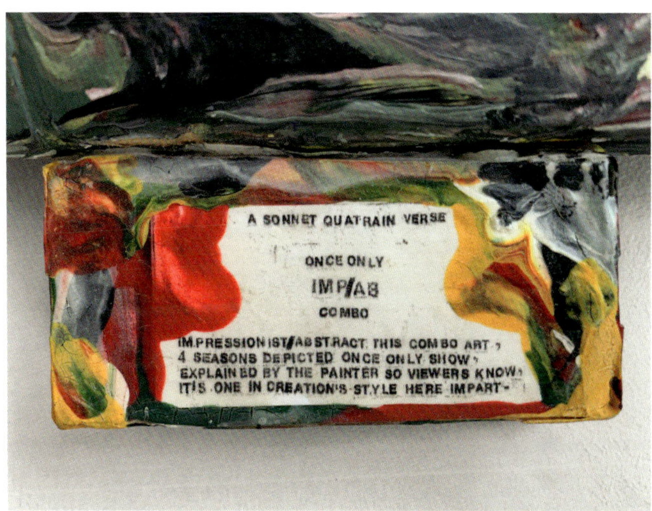

< A. J. Aucoin, *Untitled*, 2005
Acrylic paint and mixed media
on canvas and cardboard
60 × 70 cm (details above)

Indigenous

My exploration of outsider art began in Europe and the United States, where I learned from those who had considerable experience with historical collections of art brut as well as contemporary outsider art. What I found most surprising was how little is known about Canada—not just our art scene, but our country in general. It is assumed that we lack an identifiable culture because we are a young nation. While it is true that Canada's first colonies were unified less than two hundred years ago, North America has been inhabited by Indigenous populations for many thousands of years, and those cultures have informed and shaped our national identity. It is only our record of European settlers and colonization that is short in comparison with the history of other countries. What is puzzling to those "from away" is that Canadians are both homogenous and diverse. We accept that we are a mosaic of cultures, not a melting pot like our American neighbours. Multiculturalism is not only an ideological objective; it is an official policy. While our vision is to respect the individuality and identity of all cultural and ethnic groups among us, the policy has been criticized as reflecting only the views of Ontario's anglophone elite[141] and for failing to acknowledge the unique rights of Canada's First Peoples.[142] Needless to say, we are a work in progress, as all countries should be.

It would be remiss in not discussing the cultural quilt of Canada without reference to Indigenous communities.[143] In every province I visited, I heard a great deal about the flourishing of contemporary Indigenous art. I was eager to engage in those discussions because I am often asked about Indigenous art when I am outside Canada, as many equate it with outsider art, perhaps because it is foreign and exotic to their eyes. They say they have not seen anything like it before, especially art from Canada's Inuit communities. But novelty is not synonymous with outsider art, and it would be unfortunate if such views reflected outdated notions of so-called primitive art. That would serve only to perpetuate the stereotypes of cultures that differ from our own. As one Indigenous writer suggests, turning cultural artifacts into tourist attractions simply re-enacts the unbalanced power relations established at first contact when Europeans believed they discovered the "noble" or "ignoble savage."[144] Within the narrative of Western art history, the re-naming of tribal objects as art is "the aesthetic equivalent of decolonization, as bringing Others into the 'mainstream' in a way that ethnographic studies, by their very nature, could not."[145] Such renaming or status elevation mimics the dynamics of colonialism in the aesthetic realm and prevents the objects from speaking for themselves.[146]

The move to apply the outsider art label to Canadian Indigenous art is puzzling, as the label is not attached to the work of Indigenous artists in other countries. The artwork of Native Americans, Indigenous Australian peoples, or New Zealand Māori, for instance, is not considered outside of anything—it is respected as art in its own right. Yet some seek to place Canada's Indigenous artists in the outsider art category, arguing that the effects of colonialism are directly responsible for the marginalized status of their people.[147] While the same argument can be made with respect to Indigenous peoples in other countries, there has been no move to attach the outsider label to their artwork. While the trauma of Canada's Indigenous population through centuries of oppression is an undisputed fact, the artwork of a marginalized population ≠ outsider art.

The very idea of Indigenous art is problematic. Some scholars instruct that Indigenous art is a concept constructed by non-Indigenous academics; the term *art* has been externally imposed on objects that hold cultural significance to members of the Indigenous population.

The problem itself is one of naming, for every name is burdened with meaning.[148] Daisy Sewid-Smith, a member of the Kwakwaka'wakw nation, advises that the word *art* is not in the vocabulary of her people.[149] Custom dictates that she speak only about her own traditions, practices, and doctrines, but she believes that members of other Indigenous groups identify with her views. There are two ways to approach Northwest Coast cultural objects, she says, depending on one's perspective (that is, one's Indigenous or non-Indigenous status). Sewid-Smith's ancestors and members of her community consider these works to be inherited treasures; they are precious because they hold the secrets of the past. The non-Indigenous population, on the other hand, may appreciate the work for its aesthetic features. Lacking a holistic understanding of the culture's beliefs and values, they analyze the physical qualities of the work as if it were a Rembrandt, then interpret it in Western art terms.[150] The work becomes one-dimensional when interpreted this way, and its meaningful origin becomes obscured.[151] To members of Sewid-Smith's nation, these items are much more—they carry meaning that cannot be articulated in words.[152] The objects are alive: they teach about the past and explain the existence of the universe. "They reveal who we are, where we originated, who our ancestors were, and whom and what they encountered."[153] A Mohawk art historian sums it up this way:

> It is as though thousands of years of Indigenous peoples constructing, interacting with, interpreting, and reflecting cultural metaphors (on the land, in North America) never really happened or is somehow "unknowable" because it is articulated from a different intellectual tradition reflecting different knowledge structures. Along with the devaluation of (our) history, colonialism has also devalued Indigenous intellectual thought, and in many cases fails to see it as an intellectual tradition at all.[154]

The "no word for art" argument was promoted in the 1980s. Apache scholar Nancy Marie Mithlo observes that it was a useful tool to promote the needs of various constituents. It supported declarations of multiculturalism, Indigeneity, and the authenticity of decorative art market items, but it also released scholars from the obligation to take native knowledge systems into consideration.[155] These perspectives suggest it may be unwise to impose any label on Canadian Indigenous art, particularly historical cultural objects. It is fair to say that Indigenous art is neither mainstream art nor outsider art; it inhabits a unique art world of its own creation. Dubuffet himself recognized its unique status. And, although it may be different from the art of other cultures, it is nevertheless a highly developed and mature expression of culture within its own context.[156]

Newly crafted works intended for sale in the art market, such as paintings and pottery, may incorporate symbols, designs, and techniques handed down through generations. Although they are made "today," they do not necessarily belong to the world of contemporary art. Nor do they fall into the category of outsider art, as they do not reflect the private, personal views of their makers. In fact, Indigenous designs do not belong to individual artists because they did not create the designs; rather, the designs belong to the community.[157] It is a collective cultural narrative. Its symbology is obscure only to those who are not attuned to the underlying discourse.[158] It is I who am an outsider to this particular world.

Of course, not all contemporary Indigenous artists adhere to traditional art forms in their creative ventures. Norval Morrisseau (1932–2007), for example, was a self-taught Ojibwe painter who founded the Woodland School of art. Sometimes described as a legend painter, his images referenced the myths and customs of his people and the Midéwiwin society of shamans.[159] He invented his own vocabulary to communicate his dreams and visions in vivid paint, outlined in black, like the stained-glass windows of the Catholic church he attended in his youth. Susan Point (1952–) is a Coast Salish artist who explores the boundaries of her nation's traditional art by incorporating her own stylized imagery. She, like others, reaches new heights of contemporary expression. As she says, her people are rooted in their history yet face the future.[160] Like all contemporary artists, she invites viewers to form their own opinions and interpretations of her work. Others, like artist and activist Lawrence Paul Yuxweluptun (1957–) of Coast Salish and Okanagan ancestry, employ European painting techniques to illustrate both Indigenous and global issues. Combining Northwest Coast designs[161] and surrealism, Yuxweluptun's stylized characters confront viewers with issues of colonialist suppression of Indigenous peoples and their struggle for rights, land, resources, and sovereignty. He is a contemporary artist in his own right, having inherited, reinterpreted, and disrupted the historical (Western) narrative of Northwest Coast art.

One cannot make sweeping generalizations about Canadian Indigenous art and artists. Doing so fails to recognize the different cultural narratives of each nation and the artistic vision of individual creators. Contemporary Inuit drawings (of the past twenty to twenty-five years) continue to offer a fresh perspective on life in Canada's North, but their place in the art world—Inuit, outsider, or contemporary—is controversial. It is the naïve-style[162] drawings from Inuit communities that draw the admiration of international outsider-art collectors, particularly those who embrace folk and naïve art as part of the outsider-art genre. But the drawings are not part of traditional Inuit culture; they are a new art form with a remarkable history. In the 1950s, the government of Canada relocated the nomadic Inuit population to permanent community settlements.[163] With diminished means to support themselves, Japanese printmaking was introduced by Qallunaat (non-Inuit) to the Inuit community of Kinngait, Nunavut,[164] as a way to boost the local economy.[165] Sometimes referred to as a colonial solution to a colonial problem, the introduction of Inuit drawings to the art market in the 1950s has been described as a "cultural miracle of the twentieth century."[166] Today, production of prints is a significant source of income for Arctic communities, and the prospect of financial independence is the impetus for many Inuit artists.[167]

It is a mistake, I believe, to attach the outsider label to the work of Inuit artists, as some have proposed. Although the artists have had no formal art training, the artmaking project was an initiative brought from the south, the artists are paid for their output, and they are receptive to public critique.[168] Departing from conventional imagery does not necessarily make one an outsider artist. Perhaps it is more accurate to say that their work has matured beyond the borders of more traditional first- and second-generation Inuit art.[169]

The autobiographical drawings of Annie Pootoogook (1969–2016),[170] for example, often depict the day-to-day realities of life in the north, from mundane scenes of families watching television in their living rooms to horrific illustrations of domestic abuse and drug addiction. Stylistically, the narrative realism of her drawings is in keeping with her elders, but she was open to new areas of inquiry. Encouraged by the Kinngait co-operative staff to draw what she felt, her highly personal and raw "psychological drawings" focused on her private concerns and the social ills of her community.[171] Pootoogook was nominated for the Sobey

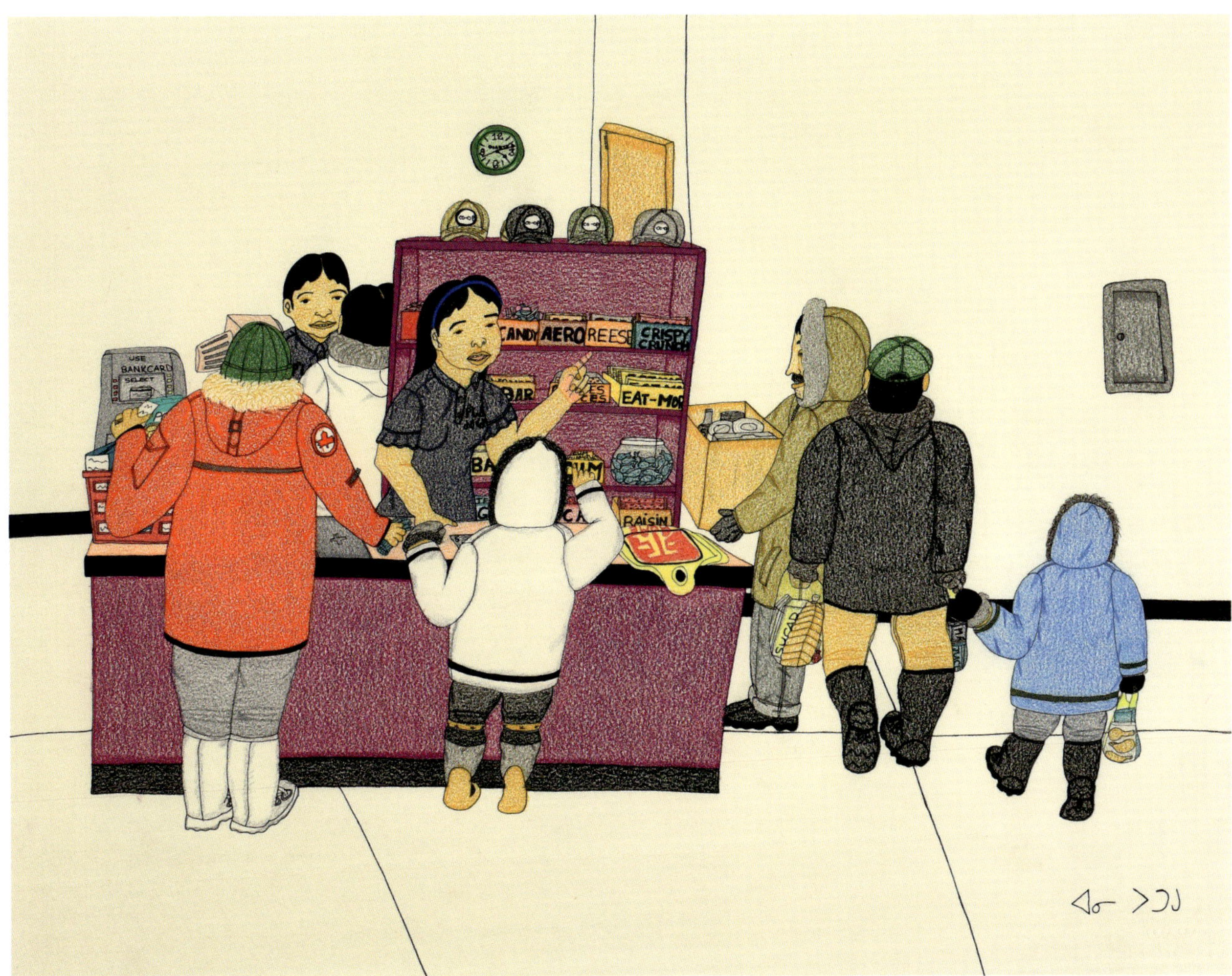

Annie Pootoogook,
Untitled, 2002
Coloured pencil and ink on paper
51 x 66 cm

Art Award, Canada's pre-eminent prize for contemporary Canadian art.[172] After her nomination, the eligible geographical regions were expanded to include the Yukon and Northern territories, which marked a significant shift in Canada's conceptualization of Inuit art. Recognized as one of the most significant Canadian artists of her generation, Pootoogook received the Sobey Art Award in 2006. She permanently transformed the landscape of Inuit art by breaking through the "ethnic art" glass ceiling and firmly establishing contemporary Inuit art in the mainstream.[173]

In blurring reality and fantasy in surrealistic depictions of Arctic life, Shuvinai Ashoona (1961–) has also departed from northern nature images.[174] Although her knowledge of the traditional Inuit lifestyle is the foundation of her art, her images veer into the fantastical, combining scenes of daily life, Inuit mythology, and Western popular culture where zombies, octopuses, and rainbow baleen whales (inspired by a Skittles commercial) might inhabit a polar landscape. Life is reimagined just enough to make her drawings quirky and captivating.[175] She is an artist at the peak of her performance. By incorporating personal, enigmatic iconography, she challenges the expectations of southern viewers of what images of the North *should* look like. Her collaborative work with Canadian artist Shary Boyle is an extraordinary testament to her status in the contemporary art world. Boyle describes her first impression of Ashoona's artwork:

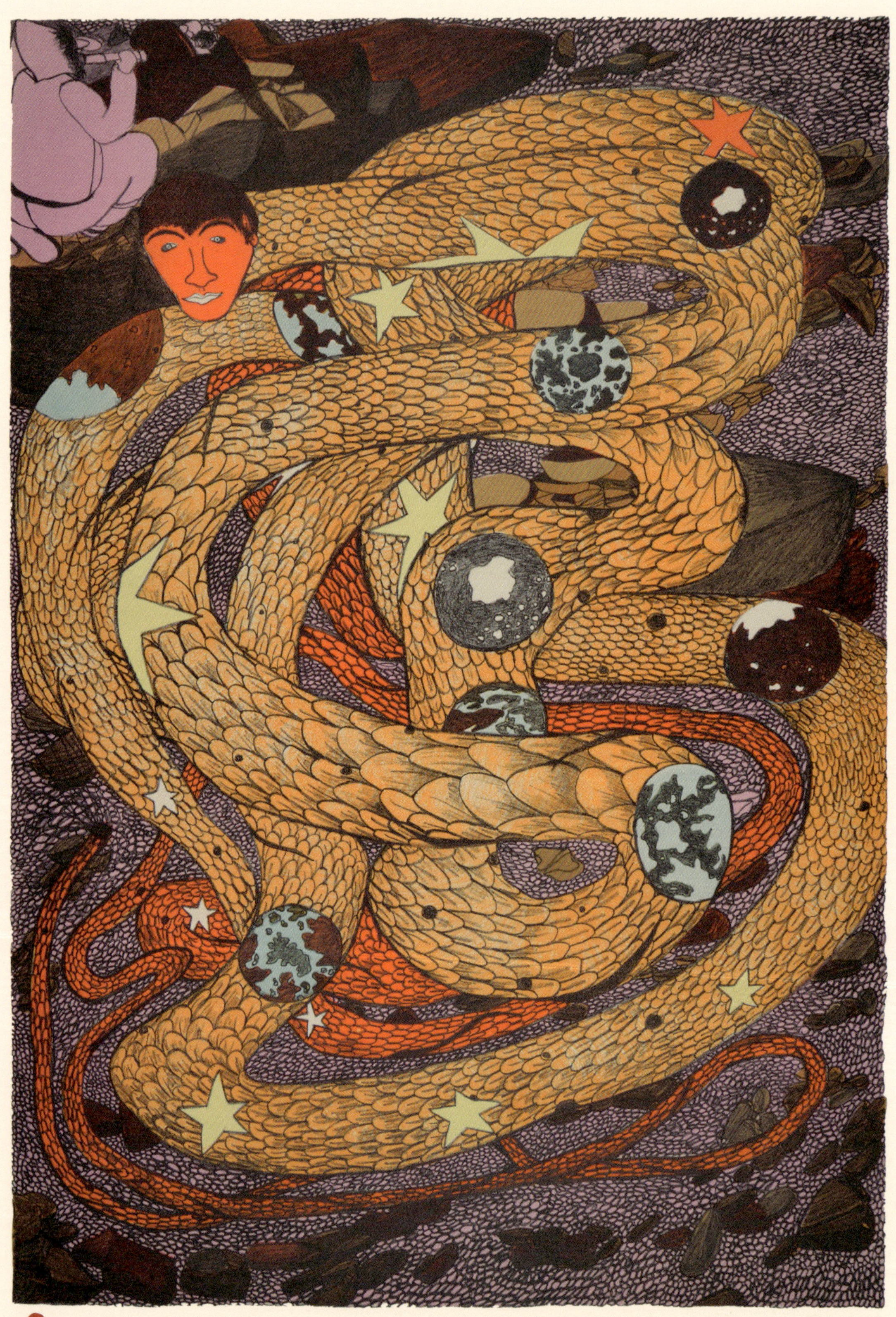

> I intuited the energy of her drawings as flying; when an artist is deeply lost in their work and it's going very well, they fly. These drawings were high as a kite. I had never seen anything like them and I immediately felt, this is home. This is the shared home of imagination.[176]

< Shuvinai Ashoona,
Inner Worlds, 2014
Lithograph
193 × 55.8 cm

Bridging the worlds of Inuit and international contemporary art, Ashoona has shattered colonial expectations of indigeneity and expanded the place of Inuit art in contemporary Canadian art history.[177]

I had the opportunity to meet with one Inuvialuit[178] carver from Cape Parry in the Northwest Territories and talk with him about leaving his traditional home, both literally and artistically. FLOYD KUPTANA shared his story with me, from childhood memories to his turbulent life on the streets of Toronto—hospitalizations, police encounters, and rehab centres. He fondly recalled fishing and hunting with his grandfather, but he also talked about darker, troubled times at home and at residential school. As a member of Canada's Indigenous population, Kuptana survived a lifetime of systemic discrimination. Life was challenging.

Kuptana was already a skilled carver when he arrived in Toronto in 1996. While traditional stone carvings marketed through the Inuit co-operatives had become representative of Inuit culture, his carvings were unique—humans, animals, and entities from the spirit world transformed into new three-dimensional beings. His move to Toronto offered more than a new way of life; it gave him an opportunity to observe other artists working with paint and collage.[179] It was a revelation for him to realize that he could create in two dimensions instead of three, and he set out to bring the invisible Inuit world to life on canvas. Kuptana simply followed his intuition in manipulating paint instead of stone. His early work is extraordinary: the surfaces are highly textured, the colours pop from the canvas, and the complex shapes he depicts seem to mutate into new images. Drawing from his repertoire of Inuit mythology and shamanic tales of transformation, Kuptana stands with the Surrealist masters. They are, indeed, the work of a contemporary Inuit artist exploring a new medium.

Kuptana was a quiet man, prone to periods of silent contemplation. But another side of him, playful and animated, described the humorous escapades and terrifying acts of Inuit mythological creatures. When I visited him, he had just completed a painting of his beloved Sedna, the half-woman, half-fish sea goddess, leaping out of the water to escape a blue water creature. It was a tender link to the life he'd left behind. A white polar bear on Sedna's back struggled to maintain its balance as she leapt away from the monster. Perhaps the fight to stay above water was a revealing metaphor for Kuptana's transition to big-city life.

Kuptana was sometimes inspired by Western art. Sitting in his home studio, I watched as he admired a Picasso masterpiece featured in a magazine, a bold and colourful portrait of a woman. He propped a blank canvas on his stand, moving his hands in front of it, shaping out his vision before picking up a paint brush. He appeared to be carving the empty space before touching brush to flat surface. The instinct to carve, whether stone or air, runs deep. Kuptana drew one sweeping yellow line before putting down his brush to talk about his life as an artist. Although his carvings are in the collections of Canada's major museums, he didn't consider himself a national treasure. Recalling a time when he was asked to demonstrate his carving skills before a museum audience, he likened himself to a trained monkey.

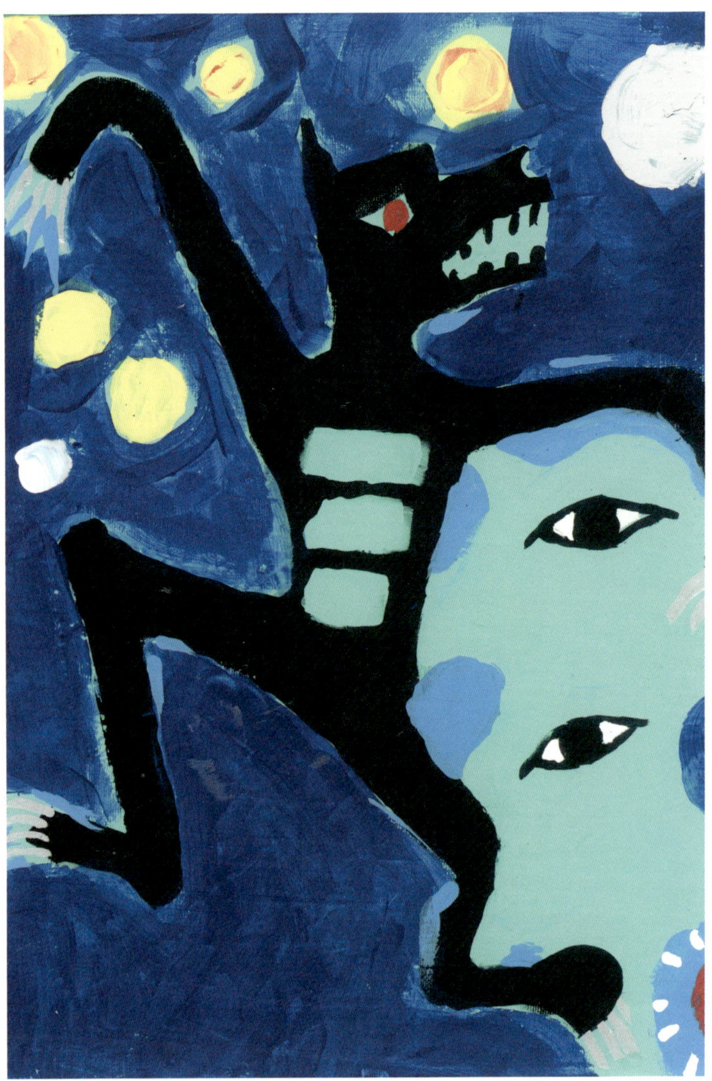

Floyd Kuptana, *Untitled*, 2015
Acrylic on canvas
38.1 × 27.9 cm

I recalled Dubuffet's description of the monkey-like aspects of cultural art and I feared that Kuptana felt the pressure of creating on command, performing yet another party trick for the audience. It's not that he didn't enjoy painting; his face lit up when he sat down to paint, thinking about the tales his characters would tell. It's that he felt pressure to produce paintings to earn a living. I didn't see that portrait finished over the course of my visits; I had undoubtedly disrupted the solitude of his workspace and distracted him with conversation. It would eventually be finished and bought by a passerby at the Toronto lakeshore where Kuptana sold his paintings on the street. I wondered what the crowds thought of Kuptana as they hurried by. I hoped they would slow their pace to greet the man behind the art and ask about his long journey "from home to away," from carver to painter. Floyd Kuptana died at age fifty-seven, alone in a park, during the writing of this book.

Some call Kuptana an outsider artist, perhaps because his fantastical painted creatures magically morph into otherworldly beings. He did, indeed, paint such creatures, but the good souls, evil demons, trickster spirits, and nonhuman beings spring from Inuit mythology and shamanistic beliefs. They inhabit the imaginations of Inuit peoples and are ever-present in their art.[180] Far from his ancestral home and community, Kuptana's paintings were an expression of his culture and, perhaps, an affirmation of his identity. But to apply the outsider label to his work undermines his agency as an accomplished artist—his right to grow, explore, and experiment in a new medium. That is what artists do. Blindness to creativity and individuality in conditions different from our own is often a fiction of Western culture and scholarship.[181]

The slow acceptance of Inuit art into the contemporary art world is in part, perhaps, because of our colonialized views of what it means to be Inuit. To view Inuit art through an anthropological or ethnographic lens promotes ethnocentrism, isolationism, and provincialism; it also primitivizes the work.[182] Recognizing the relevance and importance of contemporary Inuit art is to acknowledge that both Inuit and non-Inuit live in a shared world, experience a shared present, and occupy a shared globe.[183] The Arctic regions are a place of fluid cultural hybridity and diversity, where a mutual dialogue runs between north and south about contemporary issues and aesthetics.[184] This conversation becomes ever more important as Inuit art gains recognition in the international art world. It should not be relegated to the nebulous category of outsider art, leaving it to struggle for recognition and credibility as "real" art.

When All Is Said and Done

This journey began with Dubuffet's anti-hierarchical approach to art and his call to relinquish our culturally conditioned and stereotyped opinions of what art *should* be like. In coining the term *art brut* in the 1940s, Dubuffet proposed a cultural shift in the way Western society receives and values art. Although this is a far less radical proposition now than in Dubuffet's day, it nonetheless remains relevant, particularly in an era that raises philosophical questions about art itself—what it is and who defines it as such.[185]

At the outset, my approach to outsider art was guided by Europe's pursuit of creative authenticity and the extensive collection of work by self-taught artists in the United States. My views shifted as I explored the genre with other Canadians. I was forced to let go of definitive statements on outsider art crafted by foreign scholars and construct my own based on artwork and opinions presented to me in different regions of the country. While some felt that outsider art was passé and others were slow to accept the distinctive work of these creators, many were quick to share stories about self-taught artists in their own communities who created with intensity and devotion, only because they felt compelled to do so. Art that lives outside the fine-art system spoke to viewers on an emotional level—intriguing, unforgettable, and sometimes disturbing. While purists lament the demise of authentic outsider art, there is an easy acceptance from the public of non-academic art and an openness to what Cardinal called an alternative kind of art.[186] While an artist's biography tends to be the main focus in the international realm of outsider art, it is less so in Canada. By that I mean that Canadians are not fixated on the frailties and vulnerabilities of artists as a defining feature of outsider art; rather, what is of interest is the artist's pressing need to create art, for no one but herself, despite her lack of training. It is not necessary, I learned, to go to a museum to discover art, nor am I obliged to accept the opinion of art professionals about what art *is*. Perhaps all that is needed in Canada to foster a conversation about outsider art is a theoretical framework and vocabulary to discuss it.

There is a call to abandon all labels for art. It is said that self-taught art is always the bridesmaid for fine-art brides; it is considered only when it "looks like" something recognized in the mainstream canon and deemed serious art only when it is elevated to that status.[187] The dearth of critical analysis on works of outsider art has been construed as a dismissive gesture—an assertion that it is unworthy of academic scrutiny.[188] Some artists have dodged the amorphous label of outsider art through the vision of progressive curators and the insistence of the art community,[189] but most have not. However appealing it would be to drop the outsider label and just call it *art*, the proposition brings other challenges: it implies that *all* outsider works of art can be taken at face value, subject to the same critical analysis as mainstream art. But not all idiosyncratic artworks easily submit to conventional analysis, particularly when the work was never intended for public consumption.[190] To judge outsider art through the same lens as mainstream art may not be the road to acceptance. The genre of outsider art is best considered from a theoretical perspective. And rather than subjecting individual artworks to the scrutiny of art criticism, new language may be necessary to discuss it. The work can be appreciated on aesthetic and affective levels and, where the artist's internal dialogue is not readily understood, his biography may bring meaning to the work.[191] The truth of the work lies in its quality, the power of the artist's story, and his skill in communicating what he was compelled to record in visual form, saying, perhaps, "This happened to me."[192] Moving forward, there is a need to balance biographical and aesthetic approaches to exploring outsider art.[193]

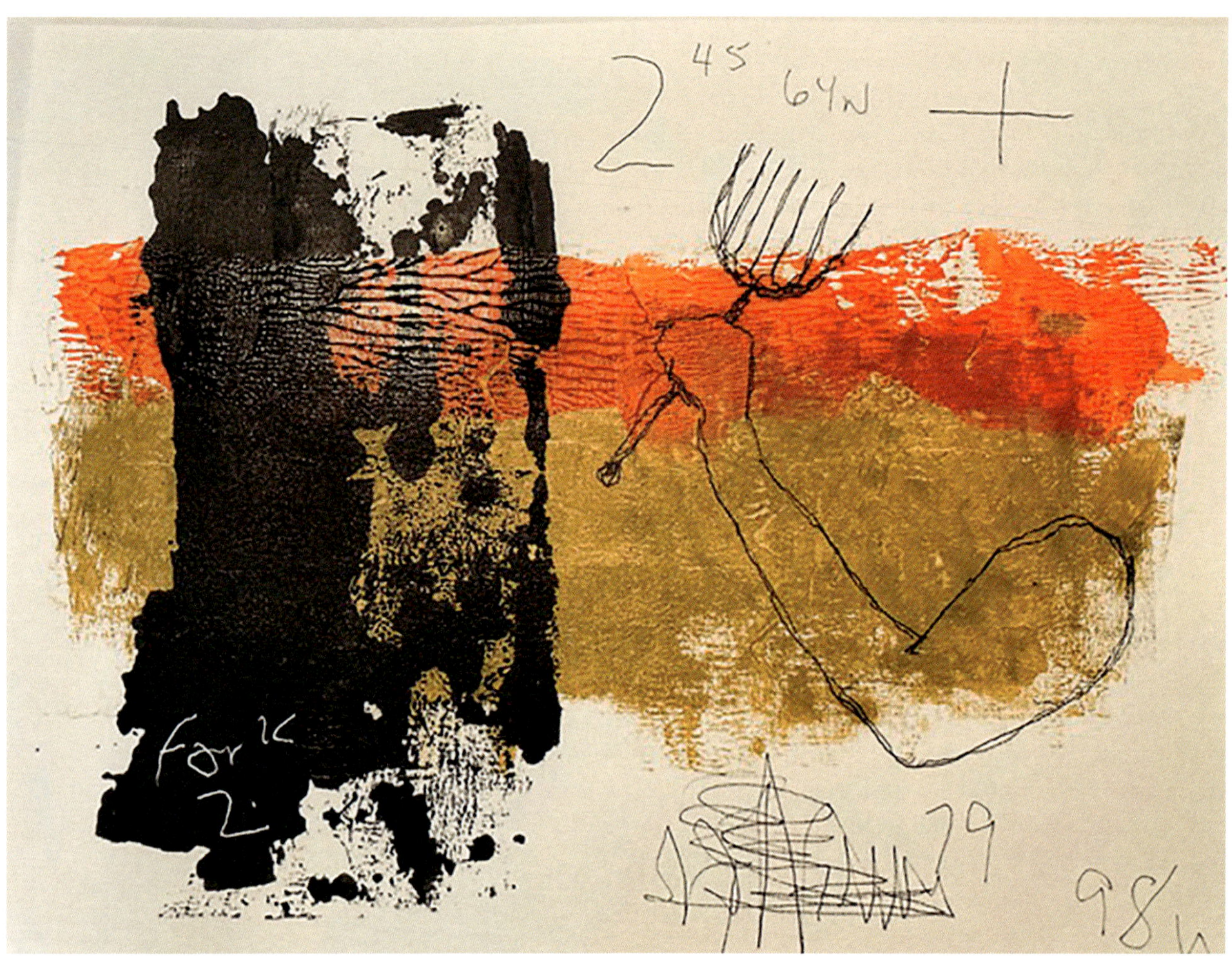

The Dodo Bird, *Fork with Trembling Hand*, 2022
Ink, food colouring, acrylic on paper
28 × 35 cm

Our role, as viewers, is to bear witness to the artist's story. As Cardinal proposed, the viewer must take a risk and commit to looking:

> When looking at the work, you are in a sense collaborating with what the artist was trying to do. You are not inhabiting his psychic space—you are imagining and projecting into it, and if you have an attentive imagination you will see things going on in the picture over and above the aesthetic choice of colour or form, etc. It is not an exercise in formal symmetry, it is a bloody miracle of explosive, violent mind effort. It is a mental property that is being put onto paper and it is now outside of your normal relative experience. In that flash moment when you are taking a mental photograph, you can begin to see where the artist was trying to go. At that point you are on the edge of your own revelation about outsider art. There is an area which we can't map very clearly and we argue about it and fret around the edges and are looking for fragments as opposed to total demonstrations.[194]

However we choose to frame the "art of the artless,"[195] it carries the strength to share the stage with mainstream work. "Pictures talk to each other,"[196] presenting opportunities to experience art in other ways. We must call on curators to continue their tradition of literacy and function as moderators in contextualizing outsider art: who made the artwork and why, what is special about the work, and how it is artistically meaningful.[197] Roger Cardinal advised that however much we think we know about a work of outsider art, there are always blind spots that harbor the richness.[198] A fresh approach is required when viewing outsider art; what appears to be an overt expression may hide multiple meanings. Cardinal tells us to be ready for that journey. Embrace ambiguity. As Robert Irwin said, "It's not about answers. It's the constant pursuit of the possibilities of what art is."[199]

[1] John Fleming and Michael Rowan, *Canadian Folk Art to 1950* (Edmonton: University of Alberta Press, 2012), 524.

[2] Scottie's life is carefully documented in Anthony Petullo and Katherine Murrell, *Scottie Wilson: Peddler Turned Painter* (Milwaukee: Petullo, 2004), 9. Scottie's birthdate is often recorded as 1888. However, his birth certificate states that Lewis Freeman was born February 28, 1891 in Glasgow. Scottie often boasted that he was born in Glasgow, which none of his siblings or anyone else ever disputed.

[3] Helen Marzolf, *Scottie Wilson: The Canadian Drawings* (Regina, Saskatchewan: Dunlop Art Gallery, 1990), 26.

[4] Marzolf, *Scottie Wilson: The Canadian Drawings*, 26.

[5] Marzolf, 8.

[6] Petullo and Murrell, *Scottie Wilson: Peddler Turned Painter*, 25.

[7] "First Nations" is the term most, but not all, reserve-based communities in Canada use to refer to themselves.

[8] Petullo and Murrell, *Scottie Wilson: Peddler Turned Painter*, 26.

[9] Petullo and Murrell, 29.

[10] Mervyn Levy, *Scottie Wilson* (London: Brook Street Gallery, 1966), 8.

[11] Levy, *Scottie Wilson*, 228.

[12] Marzolf, *Scottie Wilson: The Canadian Drawings*, 20.

[13] Marzolf, 22.

[14] Marzolf, 22.

[15] Marzolf, 28.

[16] Marzolf, 26.

[17] Petullo and Murrell, *Scottie Wilson: Peddler Turned Painter*, 37.

[18] Petullo and Murrell, 38.

[19] Petullo and Murrell, 42.

[20] Petullo and Murrell, 44.

[21] Petullo and Murrell, 46.

[22] Petullo and Murrell, 46.

[23] Petullo and Murrell, 41.

[24] Marzolf, *Scottie Wilson: The Canadian Drawings*, 26; Petullo and Murrell, *Scottie Wilson: Peddler Turned Painter*, 37.

[25] Russell Harper, *A People's Art: Primitive, Naïve, Provincial, and Folk Painting in Canada* (Toronto: University of Toronto Press, 1974).

[26] Levy, *Scottie Wilson.*

[27] Petullo and Murrell, *Scottie Wilson: Peddler Turned Painter*, 37.

[28] Marzolf, *Scottie Wilson: The Canadian Drawings*, 16.

[29] Marzolf, 26.

[30] Davida Kidd, *Who Needs Art When You Have a View Like This* (Burnaby, BC: Burnaby Art Gallery, 2011).

[31] It proved to be an uncurated collection of work that did not accord with my understanding of the genre.

[32] Gallery Gachet, https://gachet.org/. A second gallery, Outsiders and Others, opened more recently. It is a non-profit art Society with a focus on bringing non-traditional artists to the forefront. The artists identify as outsider, folk, self-taught, visionary, intuitive, and artists with disabilities.

[33] Ronald Labonté, "Social Inclusion/ Exclusion: Dancing the Dialectic," *Health Promotion International* 19, no. 1 (2004): 115–21.

[34] Ernest E. Burden, *Visionary Architecture: Unbuilt Works of the Imagination* (New York: McGraw-Hill, 1999).

[35] Achilles G. Rizzoli (1896–1981). Born in Marin County, California, Rizzoli studied mechanics and engineering for several years, then worked as an architectural draftsman. From the 1940s he worked on a series of architectural visions (heavenly inheritances) that were discovered upon his death.

[36] Retrieved from artist's website, no longer extant.

[37] For example, cuckoo clocks or textiles. See Roger Cardinal, "Introduction," *Primitive Art* (New York: St. Martin's Press, 1979).

[38] Under the umbrella of folk art there is primitive art, naïve art, provincial folk art, and folk-art artifacts.

[39] See "Tales of These Halcyon Days: The Centralized Decentralization of Regional Culture Making," in Erin Morton, *For Folk's Sake: Art and Economy in Twentieth-Century Nova Scotia* (Montréal and Kingston: McGill-Queen's University Press, 2016).

[40] Ken Lum, "From the Archives: Ken Lum on Canadian Cultural Policy," *Canadian Art*, June 10, 2013, accessed November 22, 2019, https://canadianart.ca/features/ken-lum-canadian-culture/.

[41] Lum, "From the Archives."

[42] Joanne Cubbs, "Rebels, Mystics, and Outcasts," in Michael D. Hall and Eugene W. Metcalf Jr. (eds.), *The Artist Outsider: Creativity and the Boundaries of Culture* (Washington, DC: Smithsonian Institution Press, 1994), 86.

[43] Terry Kobayashi, "Introduction," *A Compendium of Canadian Folk Art* (Ontario: Boston Mills Press, 1985).

[44] Morton, *For Folk's Sake*, 4.

[45] John Fleming and Michael Rowan, *Canadian Folk Art to 1950* (Edmonton: The University of Alberta Press, 2012), xxiv.

[46] Nancy Tousley, "A Dream of More," in *Welcome to Our World: Contemporary Canadian Folk Art* (Kleinburg, Ontario: The McMichael Canadian Art Collection, 1996), 31.

[47] Charles Keil, "Who Needs the Folk?" in Journal of the Folklore Institute 15, no. 3 (September–December 1978): 263.

[48] Johannes Fabian and Ilona Szombati-Fabian, "Folk Art from an Anthropological Perspective," in Ian M. G. Quimby and Scott T. Swank (eds.), *Perspectives on American Folk Art* (New York and London: W. W. Norton, 1980), 291.

[49] For example, the Nettie Covey Sharpe collection at the Canadian Museum of History.

[50] Pascale Galipeau, *Les Paradis du Monde: l'Art populaire du Québec* (Ottawa: Musée canadien des civilisations, 1995), 30.

[51] Galipeau, *Les Paradis du Monde*, 29.

[52] Galipeau, 30.

[53] The Saskatchewan Arts Board was established in 1948 and was the first organization of its kind in Canada (and, it is claimed, in North America). It served as a model for the Canada Council for the Arts established some nine years later. Its mandate is to encourage participation in the arts through funding initiatives, consult on community development, and manage a large collection of art created by Saskatchewan artists. The Dunlop Art Gallery engages the community with a diverse range of visual artwork, its main focus being contemporary culture.

[54] Ted Godwin, Douglas Morton, A. F. McKay, R. L. Bloor, and Kenneth Lochhead.

[55] Modernism refers to a social and cultural movement in the early decades of the twentieth century. It sought to align the experience and values of modern industrial life. Artists rejected realistic images and experimented with form. There was an emphasis on materials, technique, and process. In general, it was associated with ideal visions of humanity and society. See the Tate definition: https://www.tate.org.uk/art/art-terms/m/modernism.

[56] Funk art was a popular art form in the California Bay Area in the 1960s and '70s. It was an anti-establishment movement and a reaction against non-figurative, abstract art. The artists used unconventional materials such as ceramic hobbyist glazes and found objects.

[57] Joe Fafard, Vic Cicansky, and David Gilhooly of the funk art movement.

[58] The Regina experience is described in Timothy Long, *Regina Clay: Worlds in the Making* (Regina: MacKenzie Art Gallery, 2005).

[59] Long, *Regina Clay*; see also Nancy Tousley, "Prairie Vernacular," *Canadian Art* 4, no. 3 (Fall 1987): 90–91.

[60] Helen Marzolf, "Art's Geophysics," in Amanda Cachia, *Cynthia Girard: The Black Glove and the Peacock* (Regina: Dunlop Art Gallery, 2010), 2.

[61] Long, *Regina Clay*.

[62] Long.

[63] Cachia, *Cynthia Girard: The Black Glove*.

[64] Nancy Tousley, "Putting Things in Place: David Thauberger's Vernacular Style," in Peter White, *David Thauberger: Paintings 1978–1988* (Regina: Norman Mackenzie Art Gallery, 1988), 7.

[65] David Thauberger, quoted in Michael D. Hall, *David Thauberger and the Art of the Genuine Simulation* (Moose Jaw: Moose Jaw Museum & Art Gallery, 2002), 9.

[66] Timothy Long, "Cabbage Rolls and Perogies for Hedgehogs: The Origins of David Thauberger's Insider-Outsider Art Collection," in Patricia E. Bovey et al., *Road Trips and Other Diversions: David Thauberger* (Regina, MacKenzie Art Gallery, 2014), 42.

[67] Long, "Cabbage Rolls and Perogies," 46.

[68] Long, 48.

[69] Tousley, "A Dream of More," 44.

[70] Jack Severson, Regina.

[71] Fleming and Rowan, *Canadian Folk Art to 1950*.

[72] Roger Cardinal, "Toward an Outsider Aesthetic," in Hall and Metcalf Jr., *The Artist Outsider*, 21–43.

[73] A painting technique in which layers of wet paint are applied on top of previously laid layers.

[74] Jon Gnagy (1907–1981), host of *Learn to Draw*. NBC, 1950–1955.

[75] Bob Ross (1942–1995), host of *The Joy of Painting*. PBS, 1983–1994.

[76] Nancy Tousley, "Levine Flexhaug and the Ideal Landscape," in Nancy Tousley and Peter White, *A Sublime Vernacular: The Landscape Paintings of Levine Flexhaug* (Alberta: Art Gallery of Grande Prairie, 2015), 24.

[77] Elena Lamberti, "Imaginary Postcards: Flexi(ble) Storytelling of a (Lost and Found) Canadian Mythmaking," in Tousley and White, *A Sublime Vernacular*, 119–28.

[78] Conversation with Timothy Long, chief curator at Mackenzie Art Gallery, Regina, January 30, 2019.

[79] A 2019 exhibit of historical folk art at the Moose Jaw Museum & Art Gallery, called "A Prairie Vernacular," showcased historic and contemporary vernacular pieces from prairie artists who used their common experiences, culture, and sensibilities as their source of inspiration.

[80] Patricia Lupton, "Prolific city artist churns out wild range of unique works," *Regina Leader-Post*, May 12, 1988.

[81] Sheila Robertson, "Ing cooks up artwork," *Saskatoon Star-Phoenix*, August 13, 1988.

[82] Lupton, "Prolific city artist."

[83] Jack Severson, "Finding the New Utopia," in Lorne Beug, Anne Campbell, and Jeannie Mah (eds.), *Regina's Secret Places* (Regina: University of Regina Press, 2006), 72.

[84] Michael D. Hall, "Jahan Maka: Symbolist on the Precambrian Shield," in Hall and Metcalf Jr., *The Artist Outsider*, 128.

[85] Tousley, "A Dream of More," 46.

[86] Hall, "Jahan Maka: Symbolist on the Precambrian Shield," 135.

[87] Susan Whitney and Helen Marzolf.

[88] Hall, "Jahan Maka: Symbolist on the Precambrian Shield," 134.

[89] Hall, 134.

[90] Hall, 140.

[91] Hall, 138.

[92] Duncan Farnan.

[93] La Petite Mort, Ottawa, 2005–2015.

[94] Letter to La Petite Mort Gallery, September 5, 2008.

[95] My inner rest.

[96] Cardinal, *Outsider Art*, 135.

[97] Roger Cardinal, "Madge Gill Biography," accessed January 15, 2020, https://madgegill.com/biography.

[98] Interestingly, the panther totem represents spiritual knowledge and presents itself to those who are intuitive, psychic, and artistically inclined.

[99] Alma Matters website, accessed January 21, 2020, http://www.almamatters.ca/articles-2/an-artistic-pioneer/.

[100] Author in conversation with Wendy Oke, April 18, 2018.

[101] Long, *Regina Clay*.

[102] American psychologist Abraham Maslow's (1908–1970) hierarchy of needs, the top of which are self-actualization needs, the desire for self-fulfillment.

[103] Her collection includes sculptures, religious objects, paintings, prints, ceramic and glass pieces, and textiles from the nineteenth and twentieth century. It is currently housed in the Canadian Museum of History, Gatineau, Québec.

[104] Galipeau, *Les Paradis du Monde*, 5.

[105] Louise de Grosbois, Raymonde Lamothe, and Lise Nantel.

[106] Galipeau, *Les Paradis du Monde*, 39.

[107] In 2018, the Musée d'art contemporain de Montréal mounted "Fait Main/Hand Made," which explored the world of popular art, handicrafts, and contemporary art. The exhibition examined the gulf that has always divided craft (hand-made objects) from the fine arts and dispelled the belief that contemporary artists (particularly conceptual artists) have no technical art skills.

[108] D. G. Carter, *Les chroniques du Québec d'Arthur Villeneuve* (Montréal: Montréal Museum of Fine Arts, 1972), 15. La Pulperie de Chicoutimi calls the permanent exhibit of Villeneuve's work "Far from Being Naïve!"

[109] Jean-Louis Gagnon, *Arthur Villeneuve: Le Génial* (published by the author, 1994).

[110] Villeneuve found inspiration in French-Canadian history, the Saguenay River, popular legends of the region, and ideas from his subconscious. See Micheline Marion, *Une Maison Pas Comme Les Autres* (Saint-Nazaire: Editions JCL, 1984), 20–23.

[111] In discussion with Claude Bolduc.

[112] Gallerie Robert Poulin and 106U in Montréal and La Gallerie des Nanas (now closed) in Danville, Québec.

[113] http://masc.com.co/.

[114] Patrick Cady.

[115] Patrick Cady, "The M.A.S.C," Musee d'Art Contemporain Singulier website, accessed December 7, 2019, http://masc.com.co/.

[116] Unlike the spontaneous creations described by Dubuffet in his strict definition of art brut.

[117] The Collection de l'Art Brut, Lausanne, Switzerland: https://www.artbrut.ch/en_GB/author/sorgente-palmerino-1.

[118] Also known as Baba Ram Dass (born Richard Alpert, 1931–2019), an American spiritual teacher, psychologist, and author.

[119] Albert Einstein, "Religion and Science," *New York Times*, November 9, 1930.

[120] Einstein, "Religion and Science."

[121] Fleury-Joseph Crépin (Joseph Crépin, 1875–1945) was a French businessman who believed he was a divine healer. Inspired by his guardian angels, he began painting in earnest and created 345 oils on canvas. Most depict temples seen in his dreams and were composed by dropping spots of paint onto the canvas. He created in a trance-like state and believed World War II would end when he made his three-hundredth painting. Strangely, his three-hundredth painting is dated May 7, 1945. He garnered the interest of the Surrealists and was admired as a great art brut artist.

[122] James D. Campbell, "Here be Dragons!: The Devilish Deliria of Henriette Valium," *Whitehot Magazine*, June 2019, https://whitehotmagazine.com/articles/dragons-devilish-deliria-henriette-valium/4325.

[123] CÉGEP is a French acronym that stands for Collège d'enseignement général et professionnel, known in English as a general and vocational college. Most Québec students start at age seventeen.

[124] Mathieu Beausejour, "An Interview with Henriette Valium," *The Palace of Champions* (Wolfville, Nova Scotia: Conundrum Press, 2016).

[125] Disinfo TV, "Joe Coleman's Cosmic Retribution," YouTube video, 9:15, December 5, 2012, https://www.youtube.com/watch?v=J-vLlFpjz6Y.

[126] Jesse Walker, "But Is It Outsider Art? A Prominent Painter Flunks a Purity Test," *Reason*, December 19, 2002, accessed January 15, 2020, https://reason.com/2002/12/19/but-is-it-outsider-art-2/.

[127] Such as Goya's *Saturn Devouring his Son*, Picasso's *Guernica*, and later the Young British Artists.

[128] Alix Kirsta, "The Trauma of Second-Generation Holocaust Survivors: Interview with Rita Goldberg," *Guardian*, March 15, 2014, accessed January 15, 2020, https://www.theguardian.com/lifeandstyle/2014/

mar/15/trauma-second-generation-holocaust-survivors.

[129] Attributed to Edward Hopper.

[130] Discussion with the artist, May 2019.

[131] The goal of Vincent et moi is to abolish notions of difference, disease, and disability. Its mission is to support its artists through a professional exhibition process.

[132] The comparison of Lewis to Anna Mary Robertson, or "Grandma Moses" (New York State, 1860–1961), is apt. Both were untrained artists who created sentimental work reflecting a "once-upon-a-time world" when life was uncomplicated and peaceful. See Morton, *For Folk's Sake*, 184, 185.

[133] Variously identified as the after-effects of polio, arthritis, or multiple birth defects. See Morton, *For Folk's Sake*, 181.

[134] Morton, 198.

[135] Morton, 198–199.

[136] Morton, 185.

[137] Nova Scotia artists Steven Rhude and Laura Kenney have been working since 2016 to bring some of the darker aspects of Lewis's biography to light and tell how her story has been sanitized. See Laura Kenins, "Think You Know the Story of Maud Lewis? Two Nova Scotia Artists Want You to Reconsider the Myth," *CBC Arts*, March 1, 2019, https://www.cbc.ca/arts/think-you-know-the-story-of-maud-lewis-two-nova-scotia-artists-want-you-to-reconsider-the-myth-1.5038991.

[138] The Art Gallery of Nova Scotia. Scotiabank helped fund the restoration and relocation of the Lewis house.

[139] Morton, *For Folk's Sake*, 216.

[140] In conversation with Dale Sheppard, Curator of Education & Public Programs, Art Gallery of Nova Scotia, November 8, 2019.

[141] "From the Archives: Ken Lum on Canadian Cultural Policy," *Canadian Art*, June 10, 2013, accessed November 22, 2019: https://canadianart.ca/features/ken-lum-canadian-culture/.

[142] Some Indigenous theorists and political leaders have challenged aspects of Canadian multiculturalism and propose an approach to help Canada move beyond colonial multiculturalism. See David B. MacDonald, "Aboriginal Peoples and Multicultural Reform in Canada: Prospects for a New Binational Society," in *Canadian Journal of Sociology* 39, no. 1 (2014).

[143] In Canada, the term "Indigenous people" refers to First Nations, Metis, and Inuit peoples, the original inhabitants of the land that is now Canada.

[144] Material culture and use of valuables such as totem poles and potlaches. See Isabelle Schulte-Tenckhoff, "Potlatch and Totem: The Attraction of America's Northwest Coast," in Pierre Rossel, *Tourism: Managing the Exotic* (Copenhagen: International Working Group for International Affairs, 1988), 117–47.

[145] Marianna Torgovnick, *Gone Primitive: Savage Intellect, Modern Lives* (Chicago: University of Chicago Press, 1990), 82.

[146] Grace Rogers, "Shallow Reflections: William Rubin, Modern Art and the Aestheticized Primitive," *Compass*, spring 2018, https://wp.nyu.edu/compass/2018/04/24/shallow-reflections-william-rubin-modern-art-and-the-aestheticized-primitive/.

[147] See Leah Sandals, "When Is First Nations Art Also Outsider Art?" *Canadian Art*, January 22, 2016, accessed January 5, 2020, https://canadianart.ca/features/when-is-first-nations-art-also-outsider-art/.

[148] Charlotte Townsend-Gault, Jennifer Kramer, and Ki-Ke-In, "Introduction: The Idea of Northwest Coast Native Art," in Charlotte Townsend-Gault, Jennifer Kramer, and Ki-Ke-In (eds.), *Native Art of the Northwest Coast: A History of Changing Ideas* (Vancouver: UBC Press, 2013), 2.

[149] Nor it is in the vocabulary of Inuit peoples. See Karen Selesky, "'Singing of what they no longer are'?: The Role of Traditional Inuit Myth and Legend in Contemporary Inuit Narrative and Visual Art," *The Northern Review* 17 (Winter 1996): 71–84.

[150] Townsend-Gault, Kramer, and Ki-Ke-In, "Introduction," 11.

[151] Townsend-Gault, Kramer, and Ki-Ke-In, 2.

[152] Deborah Doxtator and Lynn Hill, *Godi'nigoha': The Women's Mind* (Ontario: Woodland Cultural Centre, 1997), 37.

[153] Daisy Sewid-Smith, "Interpreting Cultural Symbols of the People from the Shore," in Townsend-Gault, Kramer, and Ki-Ke-In, *Native Art of the Northwest Coast*, 16.

[154] Isabelle Schulte-Tenckhoff, "Potlatch and Totem: The Attraction of America's Northwest Coast," in Pierre Rossel (ed.), *Tourism: Manufacturing the Exotic* (Copenhagen: IWGIA, 1988), 116–145.

[155] Nancy Marie Mithlo, "No Word for Art in Our Language? Old Questions, New Paradigms," *Wicazo Sa Review* 27, no. 1 (Spring 2012): 111–26.

[156] Cardinal, *Outsider Art*, 38.

[157] Cardinal, 17.

[158] One's position is defined by one's perspective: a person can be inside one group and outside another at the same time. There is nothing inherently inside or outside, positive or negative, about a specific location. See bell hooks, "Choosing the Margin as a Space of Radical Openness," *Framework: The Journal of Cinema and Media* 36 (1989): 15–23. See also Joan Borsa, "Towards a Politics of Location: Rethinking Marginality," *Canadian Woman Studies* 11, no. 1 (1990).

[159] Morrisseau (1932–2007) initiated the Woodlands School of Canadian art, a genre among First Nations near the Great Lakes, including southwestern Manitoba and northern Ontario. He was also a member of the Indian Group of Seven.

See Janet C. Berlo and Ruth B. Phillips, *Native North American Art* (Oxford: Oxford University Press, 1998), 230.

[160] Becky Rynor, "An Interview with Susan Point," National Gallery of Canada, March 14, 2017, accessed January 15, 2020, https://www.gallery.ca/magazine/artists/an-interview-with-susan-point.

[161] Formline is a design element characterized by the use of ovoid shapes, U forms, and S forms: continuous, flowing lines that swell and diminish in a prescribed manner.

[162] While folk art is often associated with a particular culture or tradition, naïve art does not necessarily have distinct roots. It is characterised by childlike simplicity of execution and vision.

[163] The relocation initiative to the High Arctic remains highly controversial. The government described it as a humanitarian gesture to save the lives of a starving population. The Inuit claim it was a forced migration to exert sovereignty in the north during the Cold War.

[164] Formerly Cape Dorset.

[165] Whales had been overhunted by whalers and traders, the fur trade collapsed in the 1930s, and caribou numbers were declining. The Canadian Guild of Crafts in Montréal commissioned artist James Houston to work with the northern communities. He introduced Japanese printmaking techniques to the Cape Dorset community and championed co-ops, which allowed the communities to manage and operate their own business enterprises. For more information on the government's relocation initiative, see Sarah Bonesteel, *Canada's Relationship with Inuit: A History of Policy and Program Development* (Ottawa: Indian and Northern Affairs Canada, 2006).

[166] Nancy Campbell, *Annie Pootoogook: Cutting Ice* (Fredericton, New Brunswick: Goose Lane Editions & McMichael Canadian Art Collection, 2018), 36.

[167] Kathryn Florence, *Tail/Tale/Tell: The Transformations of Sedna into an Icon of Survivance in the Visual Arts Through the Eyes of Four Contemporary Urban Inuit Artists*, master's thesis, Concordia University (2019), 31. The financial incentive is in contrast to the world of outsider art, which is populated by those who are compelled to create, regardless of outcome.

[168] For example, popular themes, images, and designs are repeated.

[169] First-generation artists were from Kinngait (formerly Cape Dorset) in the 1940s and '50s and mainly sold carvings to Baffin Island Trading Company. The second generation became involved in printmaking.

[170] Born into a family of artists in Kinngait, Annie Pootoogook portrayed scenes from her community and her own life in pen and coloured pencil drawings. She continued to produce art that reflected the reality of contemporary Inuit life despite being advised that collectors wanted depictions of nature or Inuit mythology.

[171] Nancy Campbell, "Cracking the Glass Ceiling: Contemporary Inuit Drawing," PhD dissertation, York University, 2017, 82.

[172] The Sobey Art Award is for Canadian artists under the age of forty who exhibited in a public or commercial gallery within eighteen months of their nomination. Five artists are shortlisted from each region of Canada: West Coast and Yukon; the Prairies and the North; Ontario; Québec; and the Atlantic Provinces. A jury selects a winner and four finalists, one from each region of Canada. See Campbell, "Cracking the Glass Ceiling," 60. Some jury members were resistant to Annie winning the award, claiming she was not "informed" enough, had not been exposed to modernism, and had no formal art training. There was also a perception that Inuit art is artificial because it is a commercial venture while contemporary art from the south comes directly from the artist's spirit. See also Patricia Feheley, "Modern Language: The Art of Annie Pootoogook," *Inuit Art Quarterly* 19, no. 2 (Summer 2004): 10–15. Annie's visual narrative, meticulous draftsmanship, and contemporary subject matter stand out against fifty years of graphics and idealized drawings of how life used to be.

[173] Heather Igloliorte, "Annie Pootoogook: 1969–2016," *Canadian Art*, September 27, 2016, https://canadianart.ca/features/annie-pootoogook-1969-2016/.

[174] Shuvinai Ashoona (1969–) is from a family of artists in Kinngait, Nunavut. Her early drawings reflect the Arctic landscape. By the 1990s her work became more personal, combining scenes from Inuit culture and mythology, Christianity, and southern culture.

[175] Ashoona also captures images from popular films and television, such as *Godzilla*, *Avatar*, and *The Walking Dead*. See, for example, her 2019 exhibition "We End Up Dreaming" at Feheley Fine Arts.

[176] Shary Boyle, "Shary Boyle and Shuvinai Ashoona Discuss their Collaboration," *Canadian Art*, November 25, 2015, https://canadianart.ca/features/shary-boyle-and-shuvinai-ashoona-discuss-their-collaboration/.

[177] Campbell, "Cracking the Glass Ceiling," 106.

[178] The Inuvialuit or Western Canadian Inuit are Inuit people who live in the western Canadian Arctic region.

[179] He was offered studio space at Gallery Arcturus, Toronto.

[180] A helpful overview is offered in "Your Guide to Monsters in Inuit Art," *Inuit Art Quarterly*, February 15, 2021, https://www.inuitartfoundation.org/iaq-online/your-guide-to-the-monsters-in-inuit-art.

[181] Campbell, "Cracking the Glass Ceiling," 26.

[182] Campbell, 24.

[183] Campbell, 62, quoting Dr. Norman Vorano, assistant professor and Queen's National Scholar.

[184] Florence, "Tail/Tale/Tell," 49.

[185] Michael D. Hall, "William Hawkins: Navigating Realities," in *William L. Hawkins: An Imaginative Geography*, (Milan: Skira, 2018).

[186] Roger McDonald, "An Interview with Roger Cardinal, the Father of Outsider Art," *Diversity in the Arts Today*, June 7, 2019, accessed February 12, 2020, https://www.diversity-in-the-arts.jp/en/stories/12639.

[187] Hall, "William Hawkins," 6–7. And consider the works of Jahan Maka, discussed in this chapter, and Matthew Wong, referenced in the chapter "Outside of What?", note 13.

[188] David Davies, "On the Very Idea of Outsider Art," *British Journal of Aesthetics* 49, no. 1 (January 2009): 25–41.

[189] For example, Thornton Dial (1928–2016), a Black artist from Alabama, was heralded as a powerful contemporary artist in his own right in a retrospective of his work at the Indianapolis Museum of Art, curated by art historian and cultural critic Joanne Cubbs. The Souls Grown Deep Foundation, which holds a collection of works by Black artists from the Southern United States, advocates for the contributions of these artists in the canon of American art history and eschews any kind of label to their work.

[190] The art of Henry Darger, for example.

[191] Eric Donald Hirsch, *Validity in Interpretation* (New Haven: Yale University Press, 1967).

[192] Roger McDonald, unpublished interview with Roger Cardinal, February 2017.

[193] McDonald, unpublished interview with Cardinal.

[194] McDonald.

[195] Roger McDonald, "An Interview with Roger Cardinal, the Father of Outsider Art."

[196] McDonald.

[197] Hall, "William Hawkins," 8.

[198] McDonald, unpublished interview with Cardinal.

[199] Pace Gallery, "Robert Irwin: Unlights," press release, January 2020, https://www.pacegallery.com/media/documents/Robert_Irwin_Press_Release_FINAL.pdf.

Artist Biographies

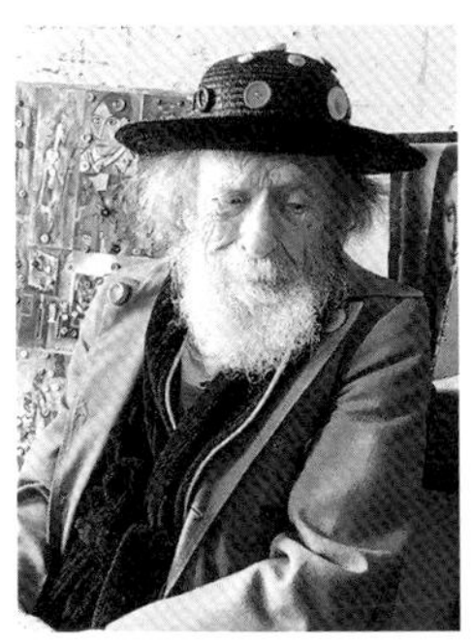

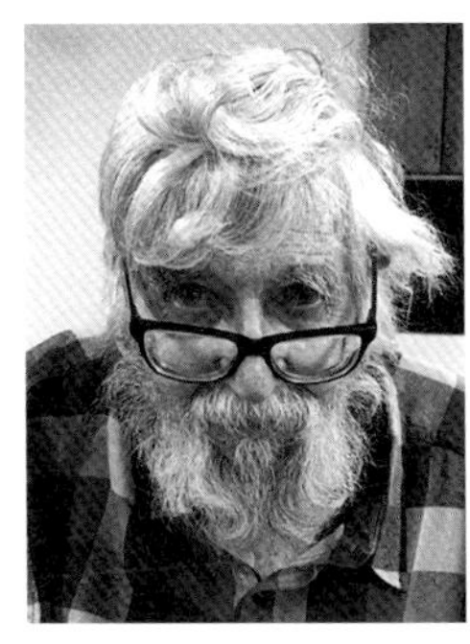

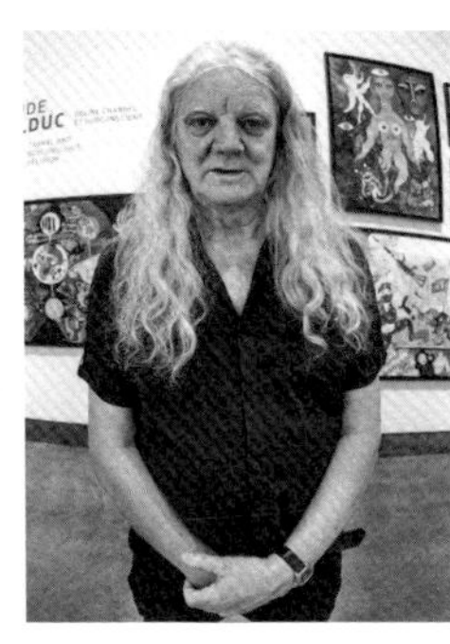

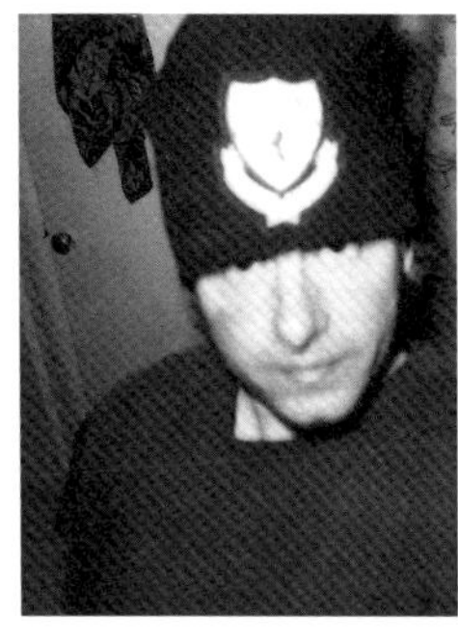

William Anhang
(1931–)

William (Bill) Anhang immigrated to Canada from Poland with his parents in the 1940s. After attending university in Winnipeg, Manitoba, he worked as an engineer in Canada and Israel. Although he had no exposure to art, he abandoned engineering in 1975 to dedicate his life to fibre-optic art. He lives in Montréal, Québec.

In 2015 Anhang was a featured artist in the exhibition "When the Curtain Never Comes Down" at the American Folk Art Museum, New York. He is the subject of a 2016 CBC short documentary titled *Billsville*.

Collections: La Fabuloserie, Dicy, France; Museum of Modern Art, New York.

A. J. AuCoin
(1933–)

Anthony Joseph AuCoin began writing poetry in his teens and took up painting at the age of sixty-six after retiring from his job as a raker on a road-paving crew. He lives on Cape Breton Island, Nova Scotia, and is a devoted harness racing fan.

Claude Bolduc
(1955–)

Claude Bolduc is a self-taught artist who began painting in 1987. He is also a citizen of Switzerland and lived in Geneva from 1997 until 2010. He lives near Montréal, Québec. His work has been collected and exhibited internationally.

Collections: Musée d'Art Singulier Contemporain, Mansonville, Québec.

J. P. Danys
(1966–)

J. P. Danys lives in Ottawa, Ontario, where he repairs bicycles and creates art. A self-taught artist without a resume, little is known about his life. He painted punk rockers and street scenes of city life and made life-size human sculptures that filled his apartment. Unable to adhere to social conventions, Danys found acceptance at La Petite Mort Gallery, Ottawa.

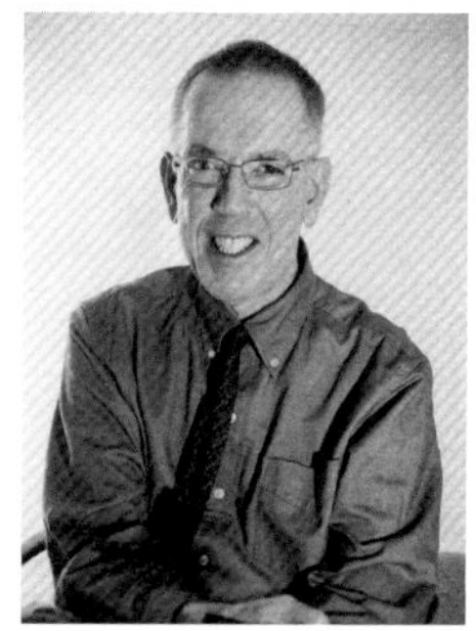

John Devlin
(1954–)

John Devlin was born in Halifax, Nova Scotia, and lives in Dartmouth, Nova Scotia. He studied architecture at the Nova Scotia Technical College in the 1970s, moving on to Cambridge University, England, to study theology in 1979. He began creating art in 1984 while living at home with his parents. In 1989 he moved into a group home where he lives still.

Collections: Art Gallery of Nova Scotia, Halifax; Centre Pompidou, Paris; abcd/Art Brut Collection Bruno Decharme, Paris; Collection de l'Art Brut, Lausanne; Treger Saint Silvestre Collection, Portugal; Antoine de Galbert Collection, Paris.

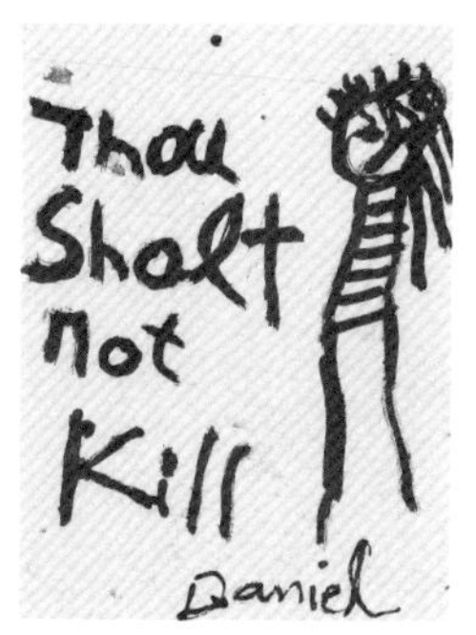

Daniel Erban
(1951–2017)

A child of Holocaust survivors, Daniel Erban was born in Israel in 1951. His family immigrated to Canada in 1954. A math teacher by day and artist by night, Erban explored the dark side of Montréal. He was known in both the underground art scene of Montréal as well as contemporary art venues.

Collections: Musée d'Art Singulier Contemporain, Mansonville, Québec.

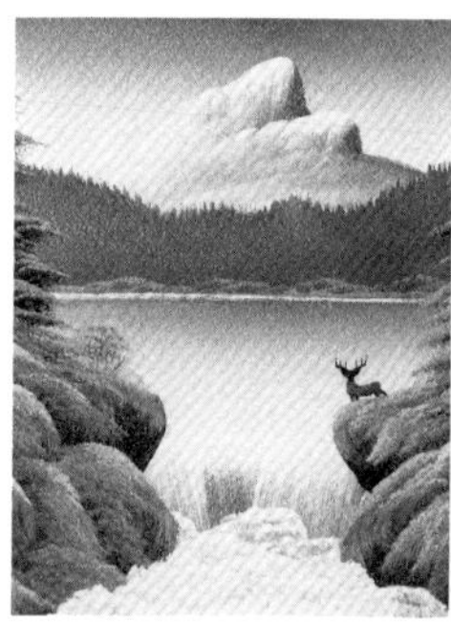

Levine Flexhaug
(1918–1974)

Levine Flexhaug was born in 1918 in Climax, Saskatchewan. He travelled through Western Canada, selling his paintings of fantasy Canadian landscapes. In 1955 he moved to Bridesville, British Columbia, and then to Fairmont Hot Springs in 1962, where his wife, Peggy, was a chef at the Fairmont Hot Springs Resort. He died in Invermere, British Columbia.

Full details of his life and art can be found in Nancy Tousley and Peter White, *A Sublime Vernacular: The Landscape Paintings of Levine Flexhaug* (Grande Prairie, Alberta: Art Gallery of Grande Prairie, 2016).

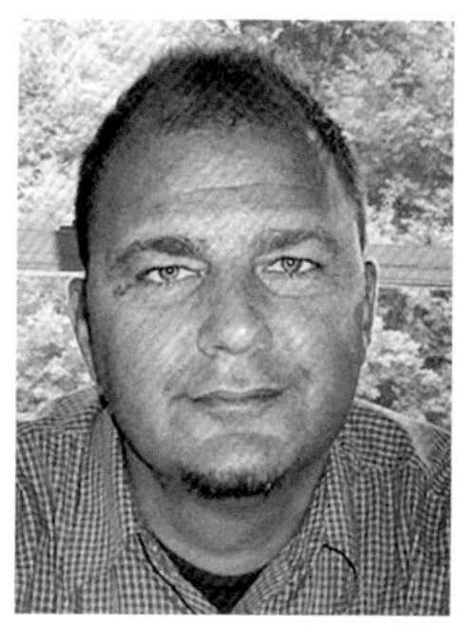

Karl Goertzen
(1971–2012)

Karl Goertzen was born and lived in Ottawa, Ontario. He was a fingerprint specialist as a civilian member of the RCMP. Goertzen started drawing comics as a teenager and progressed to painting in later years when he was unable to work because of his deteriorating mental health. He died of cancer at the age of forty-one.

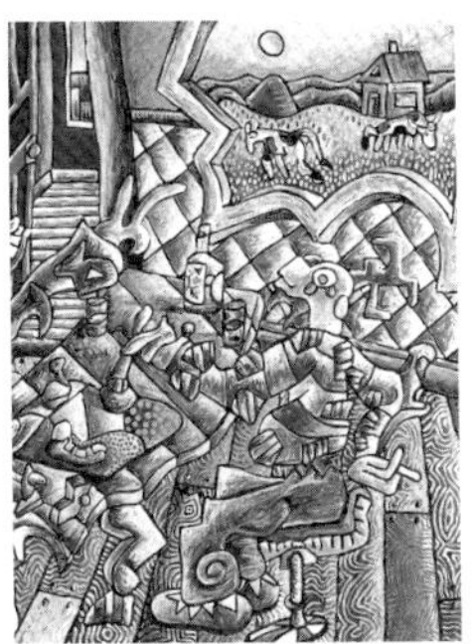

Luc Guérard

(1950–)

Luc Guérard was born in Montréal, Québec, and still resides there. He has been creating art since he was a child and taught himself to paint.

Collections: Musée Pop, Trois-Rivières, Québec; Musée des beaux-arts de Sherbrooke; Musée du Bas Saint Laurent, Rivière du Loup, Québec; Musée de Charlevoix, Pointe au Pic, Québec; Musée Canadien de l'histoire, Gatineau, Québec.

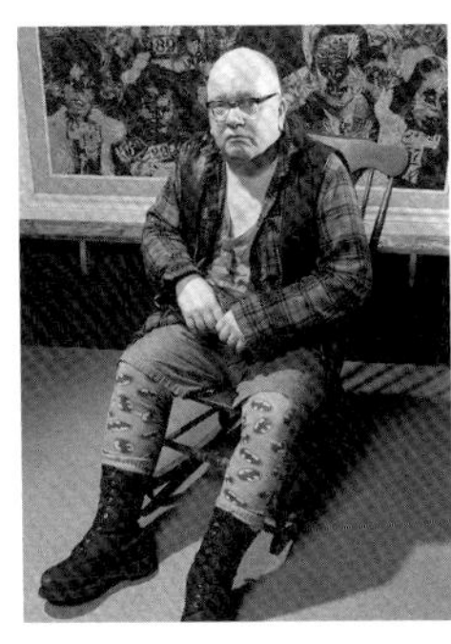

Patrick Henley, aka Henriette Valium

(1959–2021)

Known professionally as Henriette Valium, Patrick Henley was a comic book artist and painter of unsurpassed strangeness based in Montréal, Québec. He started drawing as a child and gained recognition in the underground comic scene in Europe and North America at the start of his career in the 1980s. His outrageous and hallucinogenic style kept him from the mainstream of the comic book industry.

Henley won the Pigskin Peters Award at the 2017 Doug Wright Awards for his graphic novel *Palace of Champions* (Conundrum Press, 2016). His art has been published in numerous anthologies as well as his own books: *1000 Rectums, It's an Album Valium!* (self-published, 1987); *Primitive Cretin* (self-published, 1994); *Elle Est De Retour !* (1989); *Maladies* (1991); *The Clinical Visit* (1995); *La Prison Anale des Freres Rouges* (1996); *Curées Malades* (2000); and *Mother's Heart* (2000).

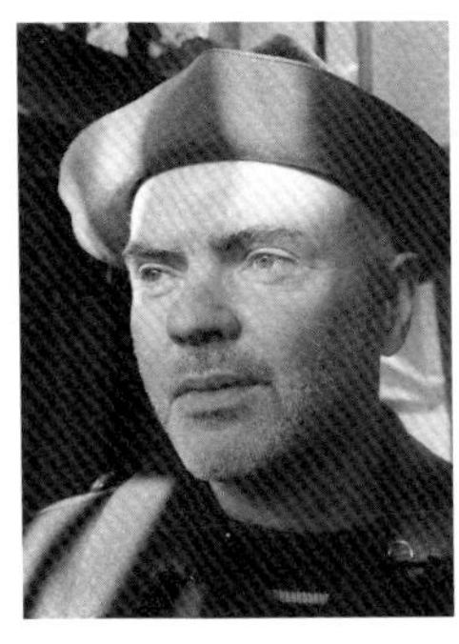

Kevin House

(1966–)

Kevin House was born in the UK, raised mainly in Alberta, and now resides in Vancouver, British Columbia. His work includes drawing, painting, writing, sculpture, stop-motion animation, and music. He finds inspiration in personal experience, storytelling traditions, ephemera, found objects, and history. House describes his practice as an imaginary roadside museum of the mind, in which he builds worlds and creates work to inhabit these worlds.

House has had numerous exhibitions in British Columbia and the United States. He has been featured in publications including *The National Post*, *Bark Magazine*, *Geist*, *Globe and Mail*, and *Uncut*.

Awards: 2014 Leo Awards nomination for Best Musical Score, Motion Picture, for the feature film *Down River*; NPR radio top ten of the year for the album *World of Beauty* (2009).

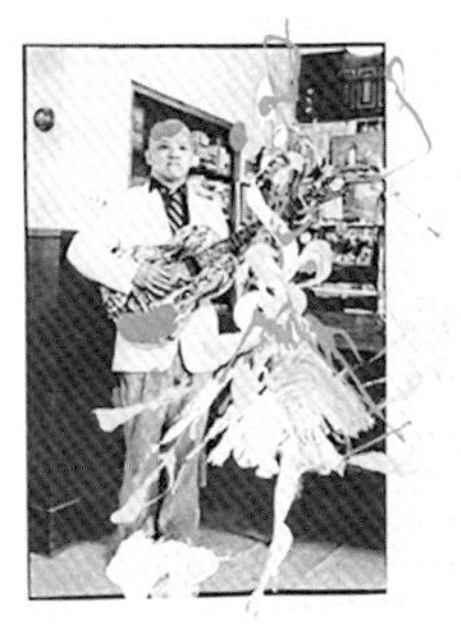

Roger Ing

(1933–2008)

Roger Ing was born in a village outside of Guangzhou, China, and immigrated to Regina, Saskatchewan, in 1950. He worked in his father's restaurant before he opened the New Utopia Café, a popular hangout for artists and locals in Regina. Ing learned traditional bamboo brush painting as a child, and local artist Kenneth Lochhead introduced him to abstract expressionism, all of which led to his unique "Roger style." He painted at the café and at home. Ing participated in many exhibitions and had his first solo exhibition at the MacKenzie Art Gallery, in conjunction with a screening of the documentary *Roger Ing's Utopia (1998)*, about the artist and his work.

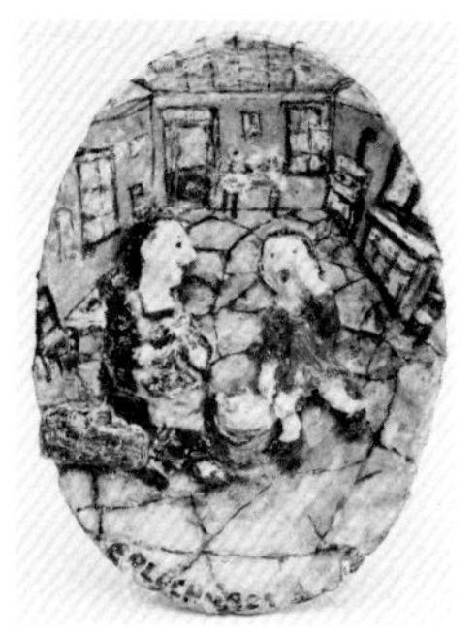

Édouard Jasmin
(1905–1987)

Born in Montréal, Québec, to a farming family, Édouard Jasmin worked a variety of jobs, including running a restaurant that he opened in the basement of his home. Jasmin invented his own techniques and methods in the 1970s. When asked to comment on his artwork, he said, "I am always looking for the funny side of the life, the pleasant one. I prefer the imaginary things, to make people laugh, to try to put some humour in my things."

Collections: Jasmin's work is in many private and public collections, including the Gardiner Museum, Toronto; Museum of Fine Arts, Houston; Musée national des beaux-arts du Québec, Québec City; and the Musée Canadien de l'histoire, Gatineau, Québec.

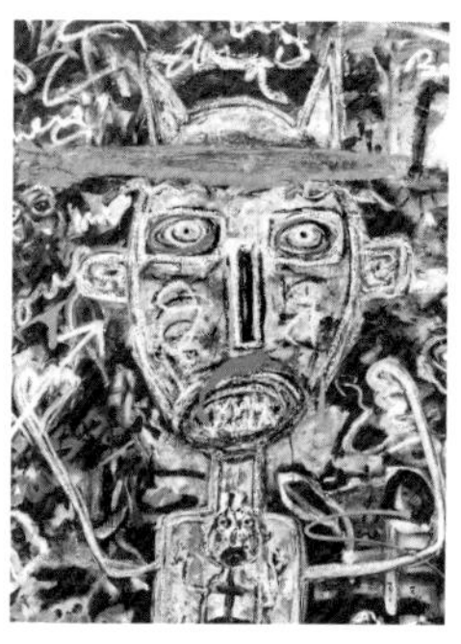

Menno Krant
(1950–)

Menno Krant was born in Hilversum, the Netherlands, and immigrated to Canada in 1955. He lives in Ontario. His work has been exhibited widely in Canada and the United States.

Collections: Art Gallery of Ontario, Toronto; Royal Ontario Museum, Toronto; Glenbow Museum, Calgary, Alberta; Art Museum at the University of Toronto, Justina M. Barnicke Gallery; MacLaren Art Centre, Barrie, Ontario; American Folk Art Museum, New York; American Visionary Art Museum, Baltimore; Frances Lehman Loeb Art Center, Vassar College, New York; Disney Asia, Hong Kong.

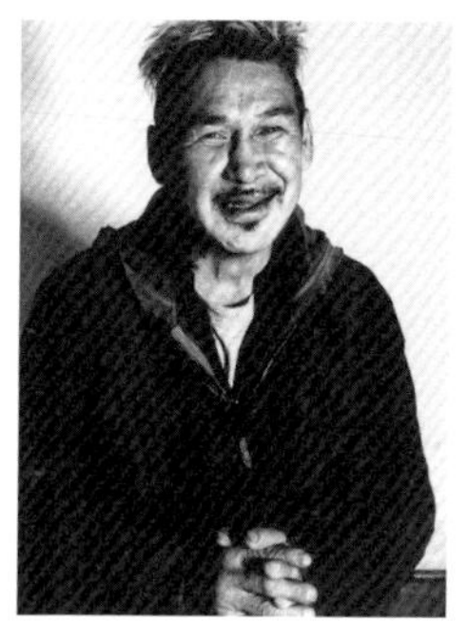

Floyd Kuptana
(1964–2021)

Floyd Kuptana was born in Cape Parry, Northwest Territories of Canada, and lived a traditional life of hunting and fishing with his grandparents. He learned to carve from family members and he became a skilled and imaginative sculptor of stone. Later in his career Kuptana began exploring two-dimensional work in painting and collage. He lived and worked in Toronto, Ontario, for the last thirty years of his life.

Collections: Museum Cerny, Inuit Collection, Bern; National Gallery of Canada, Ottawa, Ontario; Winnipeg Art Gallery, Manitoba; Gallery Arcturus, Toronto, Ontario.

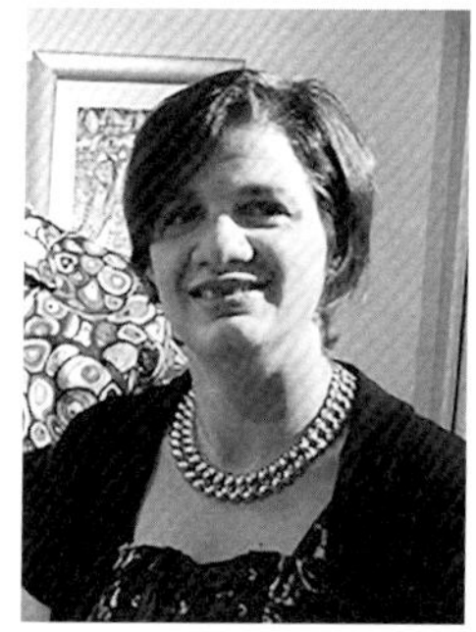

Karine Labrie
(1976–)

Karine Labrie lives and works in Québec City, Québec. She enjoys featuring clothing in her artwork, from drawings of extravagantly dressed socialites to masks covered in beads and jewels. Drawing has been an important tool for communication and a way to express herself artistically.

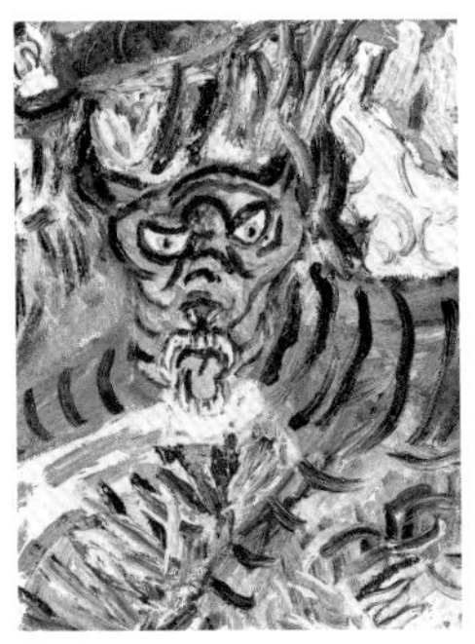

Anick Langelier

(1981–)

Born in Maria, Québec, Anick Langelier lives and works in Montréal, Québec. She is a self-taught artist who has been painting compulsively since adolescence. Her personal interpretation of the Bible and love of God drive her quest for truth and inspire her art. Langelier appropriates images from artists who inspire her and integrates them into her paintings.

Collections: Musée d'Art Singulier Contemporain, Mansonville, Québec.

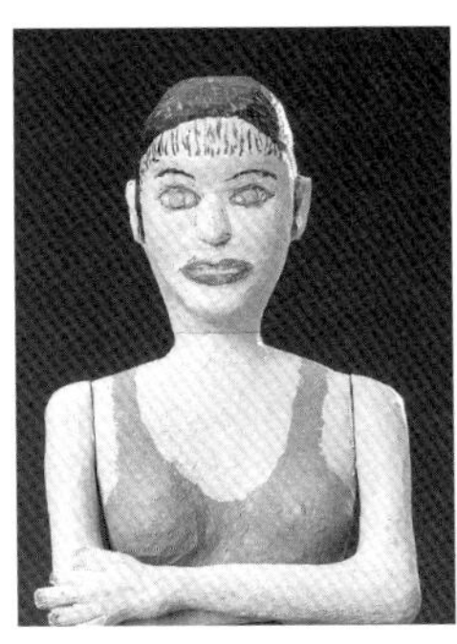

Lessard brothers

The Lessard brothers—Hervé, Lucien, and Roger—were farm labourers who shared a home in the Eastern Townships of Québec. Their carvings were discovered in 1998 by an antique dealer, but the brothers declined to sell them until 2012. The carvings functioned as decorative items in the brothers' home. They were not intended for public viewing. Roger, who is the only brother still alive, is not a carver.

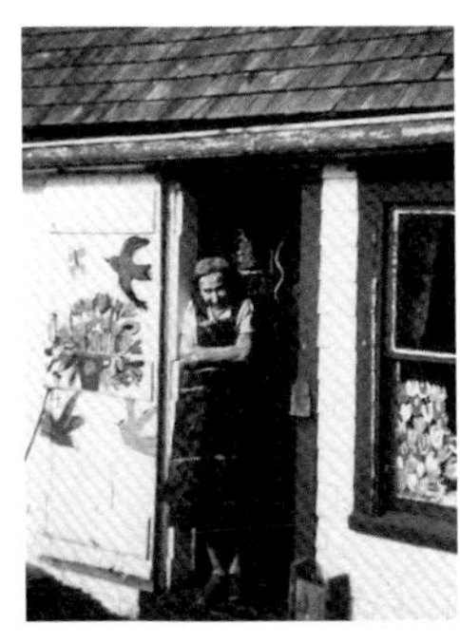

Maud Lewis

(1901–1970)

Maud Lewis (née Dowley) was born in South Ohio, Nova Scotia. Her mother taught her how to paint Christmas cards, which she created and sold during her married life. She married Everett Lewis, a fish peddler from Marshalltown, Nova Scotia. They lived in poverty in a one-room house with a sleeping loft. Lewis died of pneumonia in 1970. Everett was killed in 1979 by a burglar attempting to rob their house. The painted house was sold to the Province of Nova Scotia. It has been restored and installed in the Art Gallery of Nova Scotia.

Main collection: Art Gallery of Nova Scotia, Halifax, Nova Scotia.

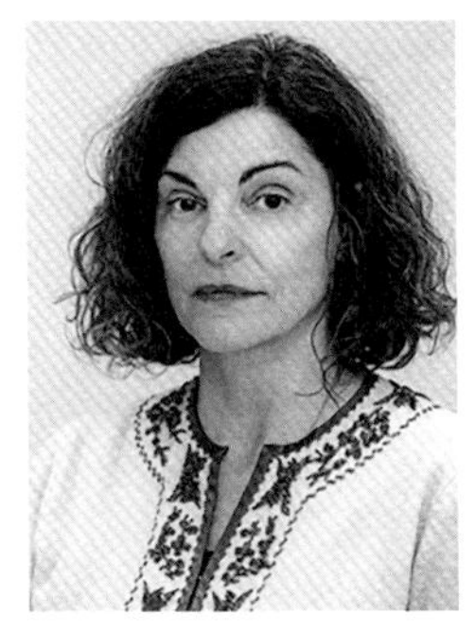

Jordan MacLachlan

(1959–)

Teaching herself to create figuratively in clay and mixed media, Jordan MacLachlan seeks to understand the world through multiple psychological and fantastical narratives. The output of her labor-intensive forty-five years of making art has been exhibited in Canada, the United States, and Europe.

Collections: Canadian Clay and Glass Gallery, Waterloo, Ontario; Art Gallery of Burlington, Ontario; Robert McLaughlin Gallery, Oshawa, Ontario; Confederation Centre for the Arts, Prince Edward Island; Stiftelsen Sør-Troms Museum, Norway.

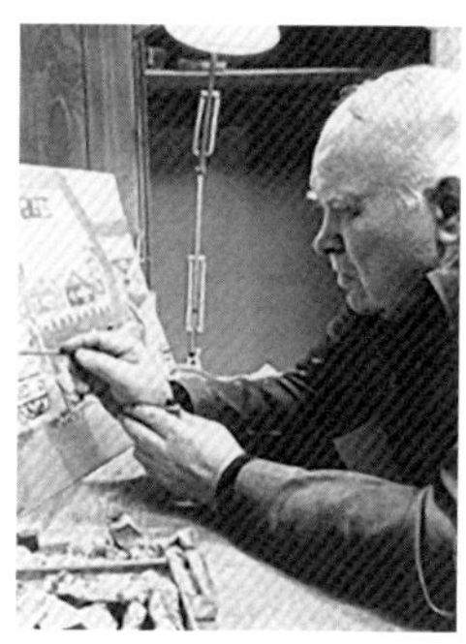

Jahan Maka
(1900–1987)

Jahan Maka was born on a farm in Svėdasai, Lithuania. His family lost their farm during World War I, and Maka left for Canada in 1927, hoping to make enough money to return and buy another farm. The Depression thwarted his plans and he worked as a labourer in the Prairie Provinces. He eventually settled in Flin Flon, Manitoba. He began painting at sixty-eight, improvising with commercial enamels, airplane paint thinned with lighter fluid, appliance touch-up paint, wax crayons, and carpenter's chalk.

Collections: Canada Council Art Bank, Ottawa, Ontario; Winnipeg Art Gallery, Manitoba; Mackenzie Art Gallery, Regina, Saskatchewan; Anthony Petullo Art Collection.

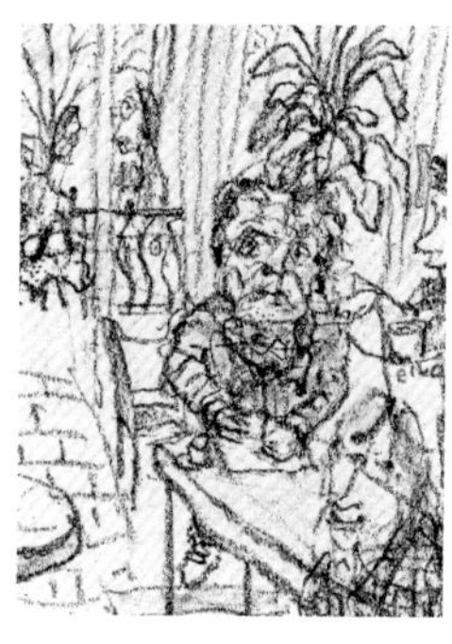

Laurie Marshall
(1956–)

Laurie Marshall was born in Kamloops, British Columbia, and now lives in Vancouver. He was a prolific painter for many years but stopped several years ago, for reasons he cannot explain. His work is treasured by many local collectors.

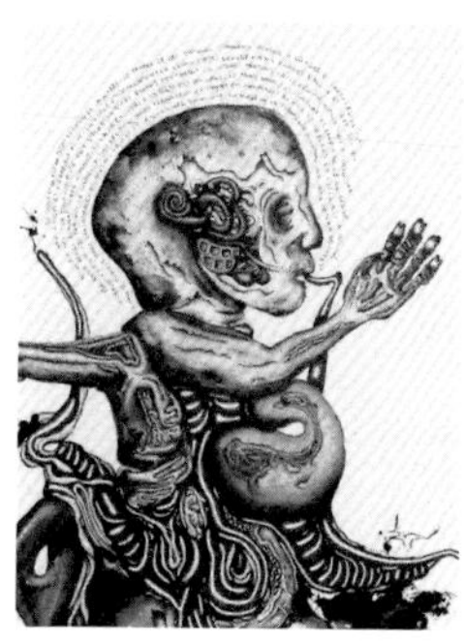

Sylvain Martel
(1967–)

Sylvain Martel started drawing as a child and went on to study graphic design at Cégep du Vieux Montréal. He has been working at a silkscreen shop in Montréal for thirty-five years and spends all his free time drawing. He will never stop drawing.

Collections: Musée d'Art Singulier Contemporain, Mansonville, Québec.

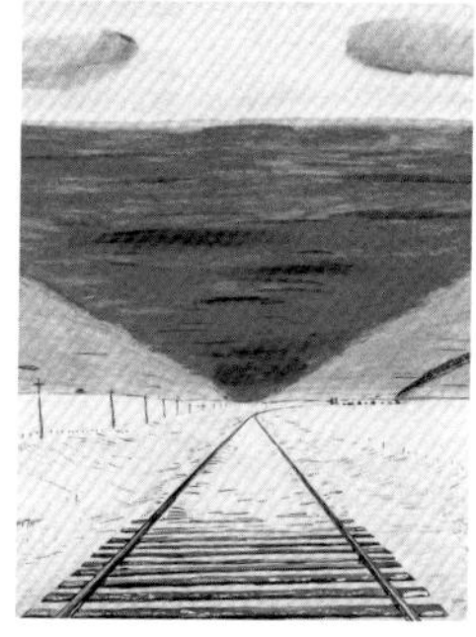

William McCargar
(1906–1980)

William McCargar was born in Newcastle, Ontario, and grew up in Moose Jaw, Saskatchewan. He was a station agent for the Canadian Pacific Railway for several decades. He began painting in 1958, taking advice from his neighbour, artist Kenneth Lochhead. He was part of touring exhibitions around the province and had a solo show at Regina's Rosemont Art Gallery in 1975. McCargar's work was featured in a 1979 issue of *ArtsCanada* magazine. The Dunlop Art Gallery in Regina held a retrospective of his work in 1987.

Collections: Musée Canadien de l'histoire, Gatineau, Québec; Mendel Art Gallery, Saskatoon, Saskatchewan; Saskatchewan Arts Board, Regina; University of Saskatchewan, Saskatoon.

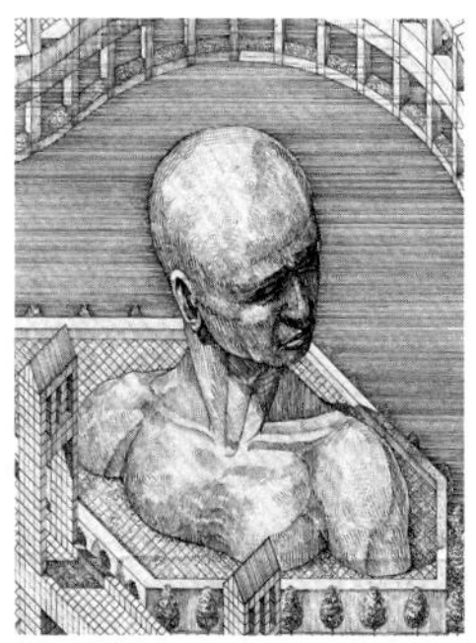

Ian McKay
(1949–2014)

Ian McKay's drawings were included in the book *Visionary Architecture: Unbuilt Works of the Imagination* (McGraw-Hill, 1999), which also featured the famous eighteenth-century architect Giovanni Piranesi. In 1992 he received the American Society of Architectural Perspectivists Award of Excellence. He was also a member of the Blind Artists Society.
His work was exhibited at the Outsider Art Fair in New York in 2008.

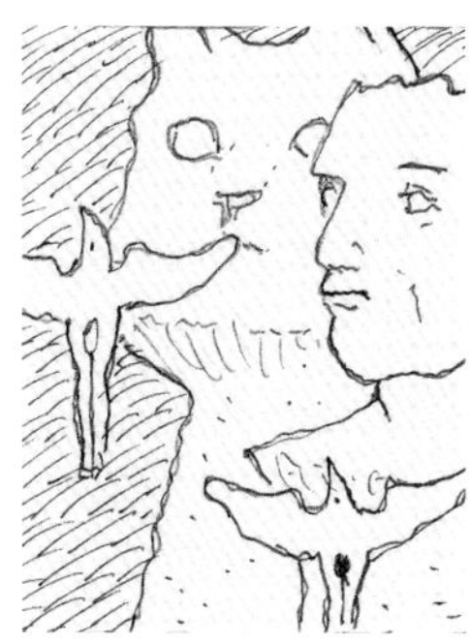

David Ogilvie
(1948–)

David Ogilvie worked in a variety of jobs in British Columbia before he retired. His obsession with drawing began in his fifties while recovering from a lengthy illness.
Ogilvie taught himself to draw, mainly with ink, and has surrendered to the creative imperative. He lives in New Brunswick, Canada.

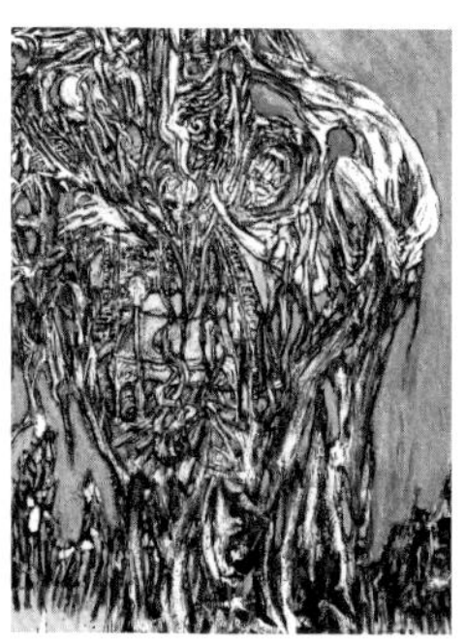

Nancy Ogilvie
(1976–)

Nancy Ogilvie started painting when she was a child and later attended art school at Sheridan College, Ontario, for a few months. She withdrew to manage her mental health.
She worked as a sound engineer for many years. "The death of the imagination," she says, is the greatest tragedy. Ogilvie spends time in Ontario and Québec.

Collections: Musée d'Art Singulier Contemporain, Mansonville, Québec.

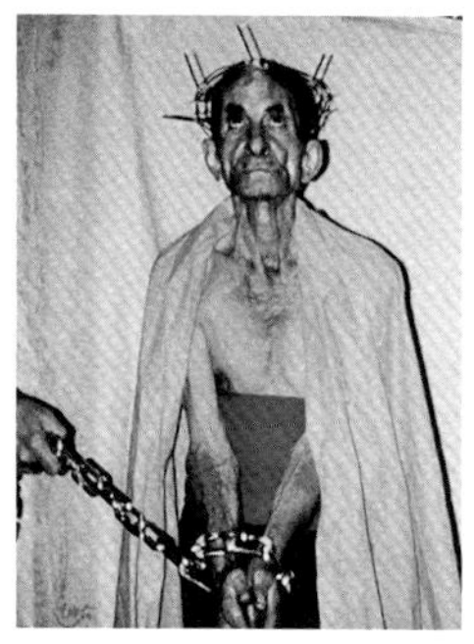

Sorgente Palmerino
(1920–2005)

Papa Palmerino (Sorgente Palmerino) was born in Umbria, Italy, and immigrated to Canada in 1954 with his wife and children. He worked as a janitor, cook, and factory worker in Montréal to support his family.
After retiring in 1970 following a work accident, he established a workshop and store on the ground floor of his home to sell religious artifacts.
In 2000, a fire destroyed thirty years of work.

Collections: Collection de l'Art Brut, Lausanne.

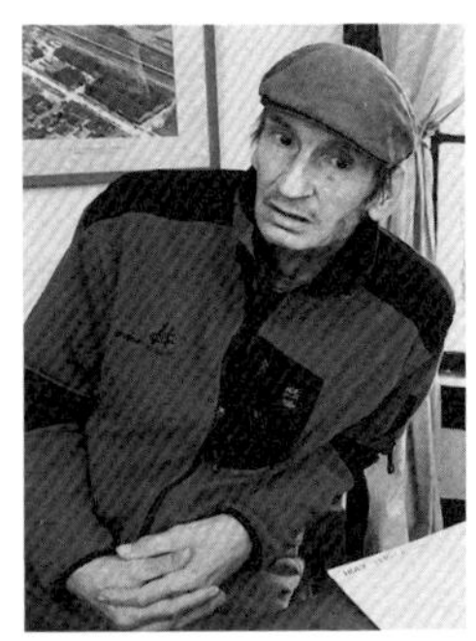

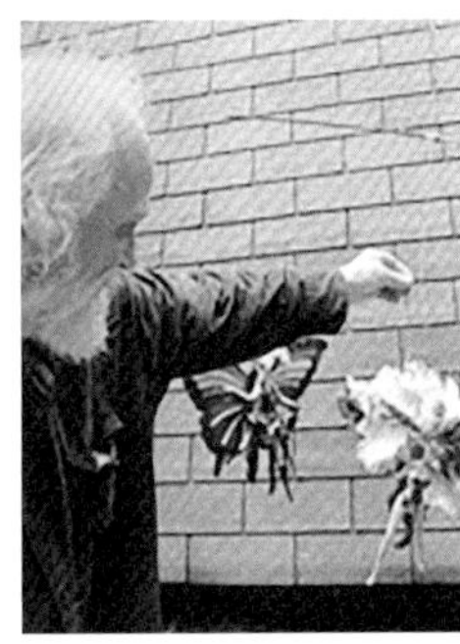

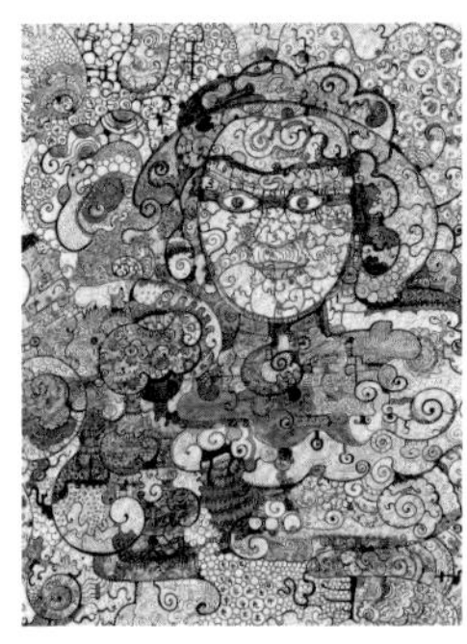

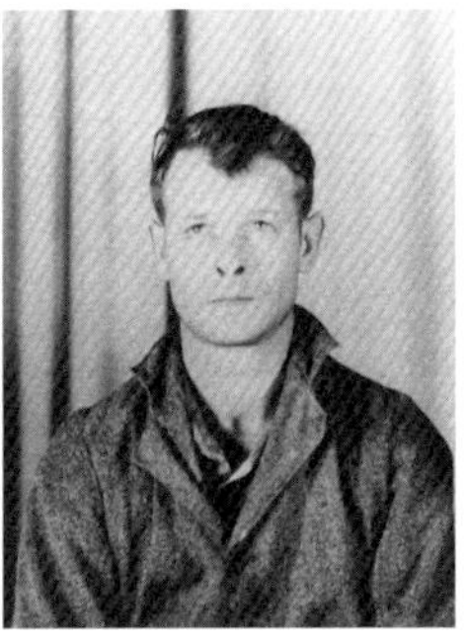

Pandora, aka Randy McArthur
(1956–)

Pandora left his home in Ontario at the age of fourteen and lived on the street for much of his life. He was part of the punk music scene in Vancouver, British Columbia, in the late 1970s but gave it up for painting. He works at a harm reduction centre in the Downtown East Side of Vancouver, a cause he is passionate about. Pandora paints almost daily, working on multiple canvases at the same time so his brain doesn't get too crowded.

Frits Ruhland
(1953–)

Frits Ruhland was born in Zaandam, the Netherlands, and still lives in his family home. He divides his time between Zaandam and Ontario. Influenced by his brother, Herman, an established artist who lives near Ottawa, Ruhland began creating enchanted gardens in the forest near Herman's home. Unable to make figures of his own, Ruhland used Barbie dolls to create miniature fantasy worlds.

Filmography: *Art, Faeries and Gnomes* (forthcoming from Aventus Films).

Alma Rumball
(1902–1980)

Alma Rumball grew up in a pioneering family in Muskoka, Ontario. She became a clairvoyant recluse at the age of fifty after seeing a vision of Jesus. Under the direction of a spirit guide, she became a prolific creator of coloured pen-and-ink spiritual drawings.

Rumball's work has been exhibited in Canada, the United States, Mexico, England, China, France, Austria, Italy, and Australia. A documentary film, *The Alma Drawings* (2005), won an award at the Hot Docs Canadian International Documentary Festival.

Frank Travis
(1914–1976)

Frank Travis was born in Toronto, Ontario, and grew up in a Catholic orphanage. He began drawing at the age of eleven and later studied technical drawing but did not complete his training. He worked in a variety of jobs until he joined the Canadian Air Force in 1941. He began art studies after the war but his mental health deteriorated. Travis was diagnosed with schizophrenia when he was thirty-five and was confined to a psychiatric hospital where he produced hundreds of drawings in graphite and chalk.

Collections: Collection de l'Art Brut, Lausanne; Western University, London, Ontario.

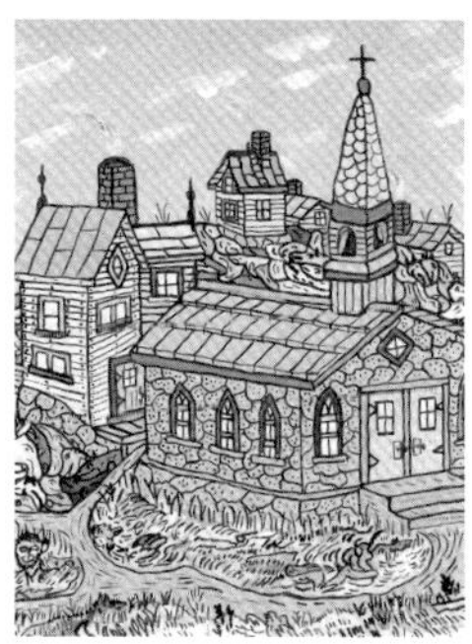

Arthur Villeneuve
(1910–1990)

Arthur Villeneuve was raised in a working-class family in Chicoutimi, Québec. Leaving school at age fourteen, he worked at a paper mill before becoming a barber. Villeneuve focussed on teaching himself to paint and, from 1950, created thousands of paintings. He received the Order of Canada in 1972.

Collections: National Gallery of Canada, Ottawa; Musée national des beaux-arts du Québec, Québec City; Villeneuve House, Pulperie de Chicoutimi, Québec; Musée d'Art Singulier Contemporain, Mansonville, Québec.

Filmography: *Villeneuve : peintre-barbier* (National Film Board of Canada, 1972).

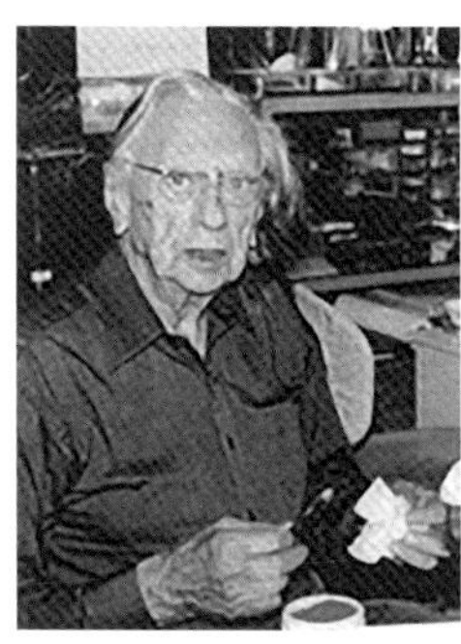

Serge von Engelhardt
(1913–2007)

The von Engelhardt family was displaced from Estonia after World War II and sought refuge in Germany. Serge von Engelhardt immigrated to Grand Prairie, Alberta, with his family in 1952 and eked out a living as a farmhand. They moved to Edmonton, Alberta, where he worked at odd jobs and constructed a ceramics studio in his basement. They moved to British Columbia in 1980, where he opened another studio to sell his ceramic work.

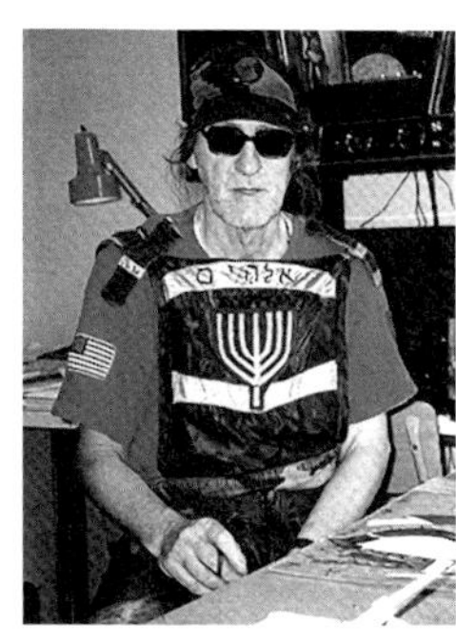

Roland Claude Wilkie
(1939–2017)

Born in Québec City, Québec, in a family of five siblings, Roland Wilkie survived an abusive childhood. Most of his youth was spent in foster care in Montréal. In his late teens, he returned to Québec City to live with his mother and stepfather. Wilkie had six children, three of whom were given up for adoption. Wilkie voluntarily admitted himself for psychiatric treatment in 1995. Although he was diagnosed with schizophrenia, he declined drug treatment.

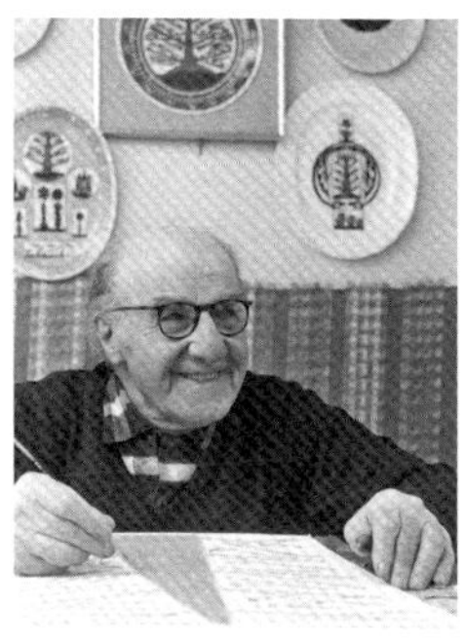

Scottie Wilson
(1891–1972)

Scottie Wilson's parents, Julius and Esther, emigrated from Latvia to England around 1880; according to a family member, they were given the name Freeman by an immigration officer. Louis Freeman (his birth certificate states Lewis) was born in Glasgow, Scotland, in 1891. Scottie lived in London from 1922–1932, dealing in second-hand goods. He moved to Canada around 1930 or 1932 and began creating art. He settled in Toronto, Ontario, until he returned to Great Britain in 1945, where he exhibited his work in Glasgow and London.

Scottie's artwork is featured in many books and journals and held in many international collections, including the Collection de L'Art Brut, Lausanne; Tate Modern, London; and the Museum of Modern Art, New York.

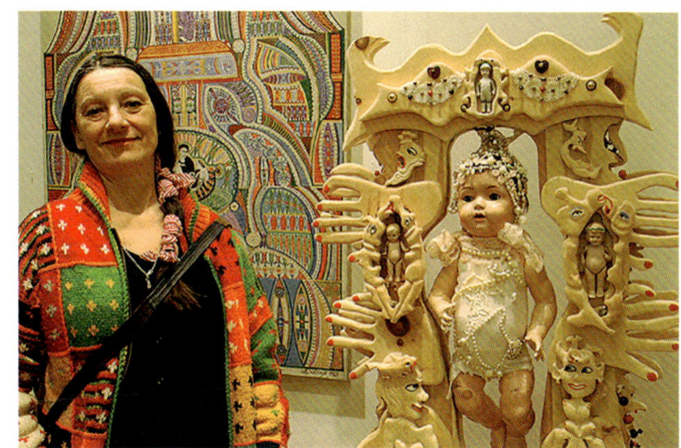

In Memoriam: Martine Birobent

This page is dedicated to Québec artist Martine Birobent (d. 2016), who championed the work of women artists working outside the cultural norm. Birobent believed the creative ventures of self-taught women artists were often dismissed as second careers and not taken seriously. She set out to correct this oversight and championed the work of these singular artists. Birobent and her husband, Jean-Robert Bisaillon, opened La Galerie des Nanas in Québec's Eastern Townships.*
A prolific artist herself, Birobent favoured projects featuring women, particularly those ensnared in the patriarchal system.

* The gallery closed in 2018 after Birobent's death.

With Thanks

Dubuffet declared that art does not go to sleep in the bed made for it; the remarkable artists I met proved the truth of this statement. My sincerest thanks to each and every one of you. I regret that Ian McKay, Floyd Kuptana, and Henriette Valium did not live to see the book in print. I know they would have been delighted to hold a copy.

Canada is a vast and multicultural country, difficult to navigate without guides to lead the way. Discussions with Canadian art experts were essential in uncovering the nuances of outsider art, and I am indebted to those who engaged in a dialogue with me. *Un grand merci* à Robert Poulin, Jean-Robert Bisaillon, Christian Shriqui, Pascale Galipeau, Patrick Cady, et François Bertrand au Québec. In Saskatchewan, Jack Severson, David Thauberger, Timothy Long, Jennifer McRorie, and many others shared their extensive knowledge of local self taught artists and their influence on the broader art community. Their enthusiasm was contagious. Eron Boyd and Guy Bérubé (Ontario) and Vicki DaSilva (Nova Scotia): thank you for responding to my numerous requests. My thanks to Professor Carmen Robertson and David Hannan for generously sharing their expertise on Indigenous art issues. I remain indebted to Professor Donal O'Donoghue for steering my early research in the right direction and for accepting, without question, my need to explore this special genre of art.

I was blessed with the mentorship of international outsider art experts. Marion Harris in New York has been engaged in this project since our first meeting at an outsider art fair many years ago. She never failed to offer support and encouragement with every phone call and visit. The time I spent at Intuit: The Center for Intuitive and Outsider Art in Chicago contributed immensely to my understanding of outsider art. The late Susann Craig inspired me from our first meeting at Intuit and I still feel the loss of her friendship. I came to appreciate the complex issues of outsider art through discussions with experts who always provided insight: Henry Boxer, Anthony Petullo, Eugene Metcalf, Joanne Cubbs, Valerie Rousseau, John MacGregor, Brett Ingram, and Roger McDonald.

This book was many years in the making, which meant that my family and friends were obliged to listen to interminable accounts on its status. Luca Willmer and Cosette Francis— I know my discourses and impassioned speeches on the art establishment and writing woes were tedious. It's definitely time for a new project. (Or is it?) My friend Jacquelyn Wilson Grattan embraced this book as if it were her own. I am grateful for her careful review of multiple drafts, thoughtful comments, and unending patience. Tierney Grattan handled my technology problems with humour and grace. And I will be forever thankful to Robert Paterson and Patrick O'Reilly, who listened, advised, and remained calm on the worst days. Anthony Stevens, my favourite self-taught artist in the UK, saw this book unfold over many years. I enjoyed every one of our virtual visits where I watched, in wonder, as his studio filled with new creations, one stitch at a time.

A million thanks to Editor-in-Chief Aldo Carioli and the team of publishing experts at 5 Continents Editions. And to my editor, Charles Gute: you are amazing. Thank you. I am also grateful for the care taken by Nicolas Véron and Olivier Godefroy in translating and editing the French edition of this book.

And finally, in recognition of my grandfather, Antonio Rainaldi, a self-taught sculptor, who would have said, emphatically: "Certamente, è tutta arte."

Photo Credits

© 2009 Foundation of the Works of C.G. Jung, Zürich. First published by W.W. Norton & Co.: p. 64

© Prinzhorn Collection, University Hospital Heidelberg, Inv. No. 176: p. 22 (Natterer)

Alamy Stock Photo: p. 89 (Pieter Bruegel the Elder, Vienna, Kunsthistorisches Museum)

American Folk Art Museum. Photo: John Parnell: p. 40 (no. 5)

David Barbour: pp. 67, 69

Goran Basaric: pp. 37, 40 (no. 4), 75, 80, 81, 86, 87, 92, 93, 99, 102, 113, 114, 130, 139, 142, 146–147, 150, 152

Heather Bennink: p. 166

Jean Bernier (reproduced from anonymous photo): p. 122

Big Print: pp. 108, 109

René Bouchard. Reproduced with permission of Christian L. Shriqui. All rights reserved: p. 60

Eron Boyd: p. 164

Patrick Cady: p. 137

Canadian Museum of History, 75-2, S93-1661, CD1994-0708-026: p. 40 (no. 3)

Chris Heller/Alamy Stock Photo: p. 11

Collection de l'Art Brut, Lausanne: p. 22 (Zinelli)

Collection of Guy Berube. Photo: Guy Berube: p. 105

Arnaud Conne, Atelier de numérisation – Ville de Lausanne, Collection de l'Art Brut, Lausanne: pp. 28, 29

Courtesy of artist: pp. 58, 59

Courtesy of Iain Baxter and Art Bank Canada Council: p. 19

Courtesy of Anthony Petullo Collection: pp. 79, 103

Courtesy of Art Gallery of Nova Scotia: p. 153

Courtesy of Gardiner Museum, Toronto, Canada: p. 116

Courtesy of Henry Boxer Gallery: pp. 55, 149

Courtesy of La Pulperie de Chicoutimi/ Musée régional du Saguenay – Lac-Saint-Jean: p. 117

Courtesy of the Estate of Henry Darger/Art Resource, NY © ARS, NY: pp. 62–63

Stephen Pitkin/Pitkin Studio, Courtesy Souls Grown Deep Foundation: p. 40 (no. 6)

Courtesy Van Gogh Museum, Amsterdam (Vincent van Gogh Foundation): p. 53

Vicki DaSilva: pp. 156, 157

Dorset Fine Arts: pp. 161, 162

Chris Heller/Alamy Stock Photo: p. 11

Kevin House: pp. 82, 84

Brett Ingram, Collection of Brett Ingram: p. 54

Jeremy Kox: p. 40 (no. 1)

Guy L'Heureux: pp. 126, 129, 130, 131, 132–133, 135, 140, 141

François Lafrance: p. 145

Les Photographes Kedl: p. 148

Paul Litherland: p. 125

Photographer unknown: pp. 88, 89

Brigitte Radecki: p. 91

Marc Reid: p. 123

Reprinted in Anthony Petullo and Katherine Murrell, *Scottie Wilson: Peddler Turned Painter* (Milwaukee, Wisconsin: Petullo Publishing, 2004), 39. Photo permission of Anthony Petullo Collection: p. 78 (poster)

Reproduced with permission of Christian L. Shriqui. All Rights Reserved: p. 61

Gary Robins: pp. 97, 100, 101

Bjorn Smith: pp. 119, 120

The Picture Art Collection, Alamy Stock Photo: p. 26

Trinity Mirror, Mirrorpix, Alamy Stock Photo: pp. 40 (no. 2), 78

Ursula von Engelhardt: p. 90

Walter Willems: pp. 110, 111

ARTIST BIOGRAPHIES PHOTO CREDITS

Page 175 (from left to right)
William Anhang, photo: George Anhang
A. J. AuCoin, photo: Vicki DaSilva
Claude Bolduc, photo: Michel Tremblay
J. P. Danys: photographer unknown

Page 176 (from left to right)
John Devlin, photo: Ken Kam
Daniel Erban, photographer unknown
Levine Flexhaug, photo: Goran Basaric
Karl Goertzen, photo: Jennifer Frost

Page 177 (from left to right)
Luc Guérard, photo: Pascale Galipeau
Patrick Henley (Henriette Valium), photo: © Claude Michaud, 2016
Kevin House, photo: Jeffrey Pratt Gordon
Roger Ing, photo: Gary Robins

Page 178 (from left to right)
Édouard Jasmin, photo: Marc Cramer
Menno Krant, photo: Goran Basaric
Floyd Kuptana, photo: © Pietdesnapp
Karen Labrie, photo: Étienne Ranger/Le Droit

Page 179 (from left to right)
Anik Langelier, photo: Guy L'Heureux
Lessard brothers, photo: Jean-Robert Bisaillon
Maud Lewis, photo: Cora Greenaway, 1961
Jordan MacLachlan, photo: Art Gallery of Burlington

Page 180 (from left to right)
Jahan Maka, photo courtesy of Anthony Petullo Collection
Laurie Marshall, photo: Goran Basaric
Sylvain Martel, photo: Patrick Cady
William McCargar, photo: Gary Robins

Page 181 (from left to right)
Ian McKay, photographer unknown
David Ogilvie, photo: Goran Basaric
Nancy Ogilvie, photo: Guy L'Heureux
Sorgente Palmerino, anonymous photo, reproduced by Jean Bernier

Page 182 (from left to right)
Pandora, photo: John Mackie
Frits Ruhland: family photo
Alma Rumball, family photo
Frank Travis, photo dated 1950, courtesy of Collection de l'Art Brut, Lausanne, photographer unknown

Page 183 (from left to right)
Arthur Villeneuve, photo: courtesy of Micheline Villeneuve
Serge von Engelhardt, photo: Ursula von Engelhardt
Roland Claude Wilkie, photo: © Christian Shriqui, 1996. Reproduced with permission
Scottie Wilson: Trinity Mirror, Mirrorpix, Alamy Stock Photo

Page 185
Martine Birobent, photo: Jean-Robert Bisaillon

5 CONTINENTS EDITIONS

Editor-in-Chief
Aldo Carioli

Design and Art Direction
Stefano Montagnana

Editor
Lucia Moretti

English Editing and Proofreading
Charles Gute

Pre-press
Maurizio Brivio, Milan, Italy

5 Continents Editions
Piazza Caiazzo 1
20124 Milano

www.fivecontinentseditions.com

ISBN: 979-12-5460-037-5

Distributed in Italy and Switzerland by Messaggerie Libri S.p.A. Distributed by ACC Art Books (UK, USA) throughout the world, excluding Italy.

Printed and bound in Italy in October 2023 by Tecnostampa – Pigini Group Printing Division Loreto – Trevi for 5 Continents Editions

Cover
Menno Krant
Untitled, 2005
Acrylic and oil on canvas
30.5 × 30.5 cm